Temple of the Living God

Temple of the Living God

The Influence of Hellenistic Philosophy on Paul's
Figurative Temple Language Applied to the Corinthians

PHILIP N. RICHARDSON

◆PICKWICK *Publications* · Eugene, Oregon

TEMPLE OF THE LIVING GOD
The Influence of Hellenistic Philosophy on Paul's Figurative Temple Language Applied to the Corinthians

Copyright © 2018 Philip N. Richardson. All rights reserved. Except for brief quotations in critical publications or reviews, no part of this book may be reproduced in any manner without prior written permission from the publisher. Write: Permissions, Wipf and Stock Publishers, 199 W. 8th Ave., Suite 3, Eugene, OR 97401.

Pickwick Publications
An Imprint of Wipf and Stock Publishers
199 W. 8th Ave., Suite 3
Eugene, OR 97401

www.wipfandstock.com

PAPERBACK ISBN: 978-1-5326-4167-1
HARDCOVER ISBN: 978-1-5326-4168-8
EBOOK ISBN: 978-1-5326-4169-5

Cataloging-in-Publication data:

Names: Richardson, Philip N.

Title: Temple of the living god : the influence of Hellenistic philosophy on Paul's figurative temple language applied to the Corinthians / by Philip N. Richardson.

Description: Eugene, OR : Pickwick Publications, 2018 | Includes bibliographical references and indexes.

Identifiers: ISBN 978-1-5326-4167-1 (paperback) | ISBN 978-1-5326-4168-8 (hardcover) | ISBN 978-1-5326-4169-5 (ebook)

Subjects: LCSH: Bible. Corinthians—Criticism, interpretation, etc. | Temples. | Hellenism. | Philosophy, Ancient.

Classification: LCC BS2675.52 R44 2018 (print) | LCC BS2675.52 (ebook)

Manufactured in the U.S.A.   12/20/18

Unless indicated otherwise, all Scriptural citations of the Greek NT are taken from Nestle and Aland, *Novum Testamentum Graece*, 27th ed. (Stuttgart: Deutsche Bibelstiftung, 1993).

All Scripture quotations are from *New Revised Standard Version Bible*, copyright © 1989 National Council of the Churches of Christ in the United States of America. Used by permission. All rights reserved worldwide.

Citations from the Septuagint are taken from Alfred Rahlfs, ed., *Septuaginta; Id Est, Vetus Testamentum Graece Iuxta LXX Interpretes* (Stuttgart: Privilegierte Wurttembergische Bibelanstalt, 1935). © 2006 Editio altera by Robert Hanhart. Deutsche Bibelgesellschaft, Stuttgart.

To my father and late mother, Malcolm and Caroline Richardson, whose sacrificial support made this work possible.

Contents

Table | ix
Acknowledgments | xi
Abbreviations | xiii

1 Introduction and History of Research | 1
    1.1 The Focus of the Book | 1
    1.2 A History of Research | 6
    1.3 Figurative Temple Language in Intertestamental Judaism | 26
    1.4 The Object of This Book | 39
    1.5 The Methodology and Plan of the Book | 39

2 Figurative Temple Language in Hellenistic Philosophy | 42
    2.1 Introduction | 42
    2.2 Introduction to Diogenes Laertius | 47
    2.3 Stoicism | 48
    2.4 Middle Platonism | 86
    2.5 Skepticism | 104
    2.6 Neopythagoreanism | 110
    2.7 Epicureanism | 114
    2.8 Miscellaneous | 117
    2.9 Conclusions | 118

3 Figurative Temple Language in Philo of Alexandria | 121
    3.1 Introduction | 121
    3.2 Sacrifice Language | 124
    3.3 Priest Language | 140
    3.4 Temple Language | 146
    3.5 Conclusions | 153

4   Figurative Temple Language in 1 Corinthians | 154
    4.1 Introduction | 154
    4.2 1 Corinthians 3:16 | 159
    4.3 1 Corinthians 6:19 | 169
    4.4 Corresponding Emphases in 1 Corinthians | 183
    4.5 Comparing the Theologies of 1 Corinthians with Hellenistic Philosophy | 192
    4.6 The Contrast between Paul's Understanding and the Philosophers' Understanding | 199
    4.7 Conclusions | 203

5   Figurative Temple Language in 2 Corinthians | 205
    5.1 Introduction | 205
    5.2 2 Corinthians 6:14—7:1 | 210
    5.3 Corresponding Emphases in the Corinthian Correspondence | 219
    5.4 Comparing the Theologies of 2 Corinthians 1–7 with Hellenistic Philosophy | 226
    5.5 Conclusions | 228

6   Conclusions | 230
    6.1 Summary | 230
    6.2 Avenues for Further Study | 234
    6.3 Conclusions | 237

Bibliography | 241
Index of Ancient Documents | 273
Index of Authors | 303

Table

Similarities and Differences between Paul and Philosophy | 238

Acknowledgments

THIS MONOGRAPH IS THE culmination of a number of years of theological study, during the course of which I was privileged to learn from many great teachers. There are too many to name, but in particular I wish to pay tribute to those who first taught me about Paul. At London Bible College (now London School of Theology), I wrestled with Romans with Dr. Eddie Adams (now of King's College, London), had my eyes opened to the theology of Paul with Dr. Steve Motyer and was inspired by Paul's teaching on the Holy Spirit and his letter to the Ephesians by Professor Steve Walton (now of Trinity College, Bristol) and my tutor, Professor Max Turner. In particular, Robert Willoughby was something of a mentor figure to me, and in addition to a stimulating course on 2 Corinthians, he offered patient and wise supervision of an MA dissertation on Romans and 1 Corinthians.

At Asbury Theological Seminary I was privileged to study and teach under many wise tutors. In particular, for this dissertation, I wish to thank Dr. Fredrick J. Long for his incisive comments as my reader, and Dr. Joseph R. Dongell for his wise critique that helped to strengthen my case. Above all, I was privileged to have Dr. Craig S. Keener as my mentor. Dr. Keener is both an exemplary scholar and an exemplary Christian, and I have learnt more than I can express from both his academic and personal example. His coming to Asbury was truly providential for my studies, and his expertise perfectly matched my interests as a returning missionary from Tanzania, who had learnt the vital importance of understanding the historical, social and cultural contexts of his audience.

I could not have survived without the support of friends and family. I enjoyed the mutual support, prayers and camaraderie of my fellow PhD students, especially Tad Blacketer, Jason Myers and Luke Post. Throughout the dissertation process I was kept accountable, cheered on and prayed for by my men's group, Jerry Coleman, Jim Lyons and Robert Ball. I was supported by my church family, Nicholasville United Methodist Church, who both rejoiced with those who rejoiced when I finished at last (!) and mourned with those who mourned, on the passing of my mother in England, mid-way through my studies. In particular, I appreciated my Sunday School group, who endured/enjoyed me leading Bible studies on a number of NT books, including 1 Corinthians, and who prayed for us and encouraged us throughout the PhD process.

Finally, I want to express my deep gratitude to my father, Malcolm Richardson and the memory of my mother, Caroline Richardson, who made great sacrifices to support us financially and were fully supportive of my decision to engage in such a lengthy and expensive course of study, even though it meant living at such a great distance from them once more! Many friends and churches also supported and prayed for us during this long journey. Finally again (in true Pauline fashion!), I cannot say "thank you" enough to my wonderful family: Jasmine and Bethany Richardson, whose father gave a lot of his time to books and writing and not enough time to his children, and to my wonderful wife, Fiona Richardson, who endured "PhD widowhood" for far too long, and who was my greatest supporter, encourager, counselor and prayer warrior throughout this time. It is as much her PhD as mine!

I give thanks and praise to God our Father and the Lord Jesus Christ for his faithfulness to me throughout and for sustaining me to the end. To God be the glory.

Abbreviations

PRIMARY SOURCES

Old Testament/Hebrew Bible

Gen	Genesis
Exod	Exodus
Lev	Leviticus
Num	Numbers
Deut	Deuteronomy
Josh	Joshua
1–2 Sam	1–2 Samuel
1–2 Kgs	1–2 Kings
1 Chr	1 Chronicles
2 Chr	2 Chronicles
Job	Job
Ps/Pss	Psalms
Prov	Proverbs
Isa	Isaiah
Jer	Jeremiah
Ezek	Ezekiel
Dan	Daniel
Joel	Joel
Amos	Amos
Jonah	Jonah
Mic	Micah
Zeph	Zephaniah
Mal	Malachi

Apocrypha

Jdt	Judith
1 Macc	1 Maccabees
Pr Azar	Prayer of Azariah
Sir	Sirach/Ecclesiasticus
Tob	Tobit
Wis	Wisdom of Solomon

Pseudepigrapha

2 Bar.	2 Baruch (Syriac Apocalypse)
1 En.	1 Enoch (Ethiopic Apocalypse)
2 En.	2 Enoch (Slavonic Apocalypse)
4 Ezra	4 Ezra
5 Apoc. Syr. Pss.	Five Apocryphal Syriac Psalms
Jos. Asen.	Joseph and Aseneth
Jub.	Jubilees
L.A.B.	*Liber antiquitatum biblicarum* (Pseudo-Philo)
Let. Aris.	Letter of Aristeas
4 Macc.	4 Maccabees
Pss. Sol.	Psalms of Solomon
Sib. Or.	Sibylline Oracles
T. Levi	Testament of Levi
T. Naph.	Testament of Naphtali
T. Zeb.	Testament of Zebulun

Philo

Agr.	*De agricultura*
Cher.	*De cherubim*
Conf.	*De confusione linguarum*
Congr.	*De congressu eruditionis gratia*
Decal.	*De decalogo*
Det.	*Quod deterius potiori insidari soleat*
Deus	*Quod Deus sit immutabilis*
Ebr.	*De ebrietate*
Fug.	*De fuga et inventione*

Gig.	De gigantibus
Her.	Quis rerum divinarum heres sit
Leg. 1, 2, 3	Legum allegoriae I, II, III
Legat.	Legatio ad Gaium
Migr.	De migratione Abrahami
Mos. 1, 2	De vita Mosis I, II
Mut.	De mutatione nominum
Opif.	De opificio mundi
Plant.	De plantatione
Post.	De posteritate Caini
Praem.	De praemiis et poenis
Prob.	Quod omnis probus liber sit
QE 1, 2	Quaestiones et solutiones in Exodum I, II
QG 1, 2, 3, 4	Quaestiones et solutiones in Genesin I, II, III, IV
Sacr.	De sacrificiis Abelis et Caini
Sobr.	De sobrietate.
Somn. 1, 2	De somniis I, II
Spec. 1, 2, 3, 4	De specialibus legibus I, II, III, IV
Virt.	De virtutibus

Josephus

Ag. Ap.	Against Apion
Ant.	Jewish Antiquities
J.W.	Jewish War

New Testament

Matt	Matthew
Mk	Mark
Luke	Luke
Acts	Acts
Rom	Romans
1 Cor	1 Corinthians
2 Cor	2 Corinthians
Gal	Galatians
Eph	Ephesians
Phil	Philippians

Col	Colossians
1 Thess	1 Thessalonians
1 Tim	1 Timothy
2 Tim	2 Tim
Tit	Titus
Heb	Hebrews
Jas	James
1 Pet	1 Peter
2 Pet	2 Peter
Jude	Jude
Rev	Revelation

Dead Sea Scrolls

1QH	*Hodayot* or *Thanksgiving Hymns*
1QM	*War Scroll*
1QpHab	*Pesher Habakkuk*
1QS	*Rule of the Community*
1QSa	*Rule of the Congregation*
CD	Cairo Genizah copy of the *Damascus Document*
4QFlor	*Florilegium*
4QSD	*Serek Damascus*
4QSapWork B	*Sapiential Work B*
4QShirShabb[a]	*Songs of the Sabbath Sacrifice*[a]
4QpIsa	*Pesher Isaiah*
11Q5 or 11QPs[a]	*Psalms Scroll*[a]
11Q18	*New Jerusalem*

Greco-Roman Writings

Alexander of Aphrodisias

Fat.	*De fato*

Alcinous

Handbook	*Handbook of Platonism*

Apuleius

Metam.   *Metamorphoses*

Arius Didymus

Epitome   *Epitome of Stoic Ethics*

Aulus Gellius

Noct. att.   *Noctes atticae*

Cicero

Amic.	*De amicitia*
Div.	*De divinatione*
Fin.	*De finibus*
Leg.	*De legibus*
lib. inc. fr.	*Fragmenta Librorum de Legibus*
Nat. d.	*De natura deorum*
Parad.	*Paradoxa Stoicorum*
Resp.	*De republica*
Tusc.	*Tusculanae disputationes*

Cleanthes

Hymn to Zeus   *Hymn to Zeus*

Dio Chrysostom

Alex.	*Ad Alexandrinos (Or. 32)*
Borysth.	*Borysthenitica (Or. 36)*
Compot.	*De compotatione (Or. 27)*
Dei cogn.	*De dei cognitione (Or. 12)*
Exil.	*De exilio (Or. 13)*
Fel. sap.	*De quod felix sit sapiens (Or. 23)*
Gen.	*De genio (Or. 25)*

2 Glor.	*De gloria ii (Or. 67)*
Hom.	*De Homero (Or. 53)*
Invid.	*De invidia (Or. 77/78)*
De lege	*De lege (Or. 75)*
Nicaeen	*Ad Nicaeenses (Or. 39)*
Nicom.	*Ad Nicomedienses (Or. 38)*
De philosophia	*De philosophia (Or. 70)*
De philosopho	*De philosopho (Or. 71)*
Rec. mag.	*Recusatio magistratus (Or. 49)*
1 Regn.	*De regno i (Or. 1)*
2 Regn.	*De regno ii (Or. 2)*
3 Regn.	*De regno iii (Or. 3)*
4 Regn.	*De regno iv (Or. 4)*
Rhod.	*Rhodiaca (Or. 31)*
1 Serv. lib.	*De servitute et libertate i (Or. 14)*
1 Tars.	*Tarsica prior (Or. 33)*
Virt. (Or. 69)	*De virtute (Or. 69)*

Diogenes Laertius

Diog. Laert.

Epictetus

Diatr.	Diatribai (Dissertationes)
Ench.	Enchiridion
Frag.	Fragments

Euripides

Tro.	Troades

Homer

Od.	Odyssea

Lucretius

Rerum nat.   *De rerum natura*

Marcus Aurelius

Med.   Meditations

Marcus Cornelius Fronto

Epist. Graecae.   *Epistulae Graecae*

Maximus of Tyre

Or.   Orations

Musonius

frag.   Fragments

Origen

Cels.   *Contra Celsum*

Philostratus

Ep.   *Epistulae*
Vit. Apoll.   *Vita Apollonii*

Pindar

Frag.

Plato

[Ax.]   *Axiochus*
[Epin.]   *Epinomis*

Leg.	*Leges*
Phaedr.	*Phaedrus*
Tim.	*Timaeus*

Plutarch

Adv. Col.	*Adversus Colotem*
Alex. fort.	*De Alexandri magni fortuna aut virtute*
Am. prol.	*De amore prolis*
Amat.	*Amatorius*
An. corp.	*Animine an corporis affectiones sint peiores*
An. procr.	*De animae procreatione in Timaeo*
An seni	*An seni respublica gerenda sit*
Comm. not.	*De communibus notitiis contra stoicos*
Conj. praec.	*Conjugalia Praecepta*
[Cons. Apoll.]	*Consolatio ad Apollonium*
Cons. ux.	*Consolatio ad uxorem*
Cupid. divit.	*De cupiditate divitiarum*
De laude	*De laude ipsius*
Def. orac.	*De defectu oraculorum*
E Delph.	*De E apud Delphos*
Exil.	*De exilio*
Frat. amor.	*De fraterno amore*
Garr.	*De garrulitate*
Gen. Socr.	*De genio Socratis*
Inv. od.	*De invidia et odio*
Is. Os.	*De Iside et Osiride*
Lat. viv.	*De latenter vivendo*
Praec. ger. rei publ.	*Praecepta gerendae rei publicae*
Princ. iner.	*Ad principem ineruditum*
Pyth. orac.	*De Pythiae oraculis*
Quaest. conv.	*Quaestionum convivialium libri IX*
Quaest. plat.	*Quaestiones platonicae*
Sept. sap. conv.	*Septem sapientium convivium*
Sera	*De sera numinis vindicta*
Stoic. rep.	*De Stoicorum repugnantiis*
Suav. viv.	*Non posse suaviter vivi secundum Epicurum*
Superst.	*De superstitione*

Tranq. an.	*De tranquillitate animi*
Virt. mor.	*De virtute morali*
Virt. prof.	*Quomodo quis suos in virtute sentiat profectus*

Seneca

Apol.	*Apocolocyntosis*
Ben.	*De beneficiis*
Brev. vit.	*De Brevitate Vitae*
Clem.	*De clementia*
Const.	*De Constantia*
De otio.	*De otio*
Ep.	*Epistulae morales*
Helv.	*Ad Helviam*
Ira	*De ira*
Marc.	*Ad Marciam de consolatione*
Nat.	*Naturales quaestiones*
Polyb.	*Ad Polybium de consolatione*
Prov.	*De Providentia*
Tranq.	*De tranquillitate animi*
Vit. beat.	*De vita beata*

Sextus Empiricus

Math.	*Adversus mathematicos*

Stobaeus

Anthology	*Anthology*

Valerius Maximus

V. Max.

Virgil

Aen.	*Aeneid*

Early Christian Writings

Eusebius

Praep. ev.   *Praeparatio evangelica*

SECONDARY SOURCES

ANRW	Aufstieg und Niedergang der römischen Welt. Geschichte und Kultur Roms im Spiegel der neueren Forschung. Edited by H. Temporini and W. Haase. Berlin, 1972-.
BDAG	Walter Bauer, Frederick W. Danker, W. F. Arndt, and F. W. Gingrich. *Greek-English Lexicon of the New Testament and Other Early Christian Literature.* 3rd ed. Chicago: University of Chicago Press, 2000.
LCL	Loeb Classical Library
LSJ	Henry George Liddell, Robert Scott, and Henry Stuart Jones. *A Greek-English Lexicon.* 9th ed. Oxford: Clarendon, 1996.
OCD	*Oxford Classical Dictionary.* Edited by S. Hornblower, A. Spawforth and Esther Eidinow. 4th ed. Oxford, 2012.
SVF	*Stoicorum veterum fragmenta.* H. von Arnim. 4 vols. Leipzig, 1903-1924
TDNT	*Theological Dictionary of the New Testament.* 10 vols. Edited by Gerhard Kittel and Gerhard Friedrich. Translated by Geofrey W. Bromiley. Grand Rapids: Eerdmans, 1964-76.

1

Introduction and History of Research

1.1 THE FOCUS OF THE BOOK

IN THREE PLACES IN the Corinthian correspondence the apostle Paul uses figurative temple language to define the identity of his readers. Although when people thought about temples they normally thought about humanly constructed buildings of materials such as stone or wood, Paul and others also used a figurative or symbolic extension of that conventional image.[1] In 1 Cor 3:16 and 6:19 the readers are described as a temple in which God's Spirit dwells and in 2 Cor 6:16 Paul includes *himself* with his readers as "the temple of the living God."[2] While Paul uses cultic language figuratively in a number of his letters,[3] Paul only uses figurative temple

---

1. While it might be possible to use the language of "metaphor" as do Konsmo, *Pauline Metaphors*, and Gupta, *Worship*, instead of a term such as "figurative language," this book will not engage specifically with the study of defining metaphor, which others have done in great detail (such as Gupta). Consequently, I shall exercise caution by confining myself to the term "figurative." I observe that Konsmo, *Pauline Metaphors*, 55, himself notes "the modern English word 'metaphor' distinguishes metaphor from these other forms of figurative language" ("these other forms" being various kinds of speech like metonymy, similes, hyperbole, and proverbs, all of which Aristotle referred to as μεταφορά; documented by Anderson, *Glossary*, 73).

2. Though some manuscripts are closer in content to 1 Cor 3:16–17, substituting the personal pronoun "ὑμεῖς" for "ἡμεῖς." This issue will be addressed in chapter 4 when the passage is explored in detail.

3. E.g., "living sacrifice" in Rom 12:1; the "priestly service of the gospel . . . the

language repeatedly to shape the identity of his audience when writing to the Corinthians.[4] For Paul, a former Pharisee (Phil 3:5; cf. Acts 23:6; 26:5), the image of the temple had primary reference to the temple in Jerusalem: the place where God had promised to dwell, where worshippers longed to meet with God and where his glory had dwelt (1 Kgs 9:3; 2 Chr 5:14; 7:1; Pss 26:8; 43:3) and one day might dwell again (Ezek 43–48).

However, Paul's audience came from a very different context. There are clear indicators that the majority of the readers were Gentiles (1 Cor 6:9–11; 8:7; 12:2), although according to Acts 18:1–11, the church had its origins in the synagogue,[5] so it very likely had a Diaspora Jewish component as well.[6] As residents of a very cosmopolitan and pluralistic city, Corinth, they would have been exposed to a variety of religious, cultural and philosophical influences, such as Roman temples to various gods and the feasts held there on various social and religious occasions, the presence of the Imperial cult, the bi-annual Isthmian games, the customs of Roman law, and the behavior of sophists and their followers, among others.[7] While Paul clearly had no hesitation in using OT traditions and expecting his audience to understand his allusions (e.g., 1 Cor 5:7–8 and 10:1–13), how would such temple language have spoken to them in the context of Corinth itself? Charles H. Talbert, drawing on the work of literary critic Peter J. T. Rabinowitz, enagages with "audience-oriented

---

offering of the Gentiles" in Rom 15:16; "being poured out as a libation over the sacrifice and the offering of your faith" in Phil 2:17; and "a fragrant offering, a sacrifice acceptable and pleasing to God" in Phil 4:18. See Gupta, *Worship*, for a survey of all the possible cultic metaphors in the Pauline corpus. Gupta assigns each potential cultic metaphor one of three categories: "certain," "almost certain," or "probable."

4. Among the disputed Paulines, though, the image also appears in Eph 2:19–22.

5. The historical basis for the account given in Acts 18:1–11 is supported by, among others, Keener, *Acts*, 2681–83, 2694–95, who comments, "The biblical literacy presupposed [in 1 Corinthians] is difficult to explain without a Jewish and/or God-fearing core" (2683) and speaks of "the likelihood that Corinth held Greece's most significant Jewish population, excluding Macedonia" (2694); Johnson, *Acts*, 321–25, writes of Acts 18:1–11, "There is therefore, the stuff of genuine history within Luke's account" (321); cf. also Witherington, *Acts*, 535–37, and Fitzmyer, *Acts*, 619–28.

6. Commentators on 1 Corinthians who accept the historical basis of Acts 18 as background for the letter include Fitzmyer, *First Corinthians*, 37–45, and Thiselton, *First Epistle*, 29–32. For a defense of the use of Acts as a legitimate source for the study of 1 Corinthians, from the perspective of ancient historians and classicists (with examples), see Winter, *After Paul*, xiv.

7. See e.g., Thiselton, *First Epistle*, 1–12; Winter, *After Paul*, 7–25; and more generally, various essays in Friesen et al., *Corinth*.

criticism" in his own studies of Luke-Acts to speak of an "authorial audience" presupposed by the text, stating "To read as authorial audience is to attempt to answer the question: 'If the literary work fell into the hands of an audience that closely matched the author's target audience in terms of knowledge brought to the text, how would they have understood the work?'"[8] Talbert notes that it is important to reconstruct the conceptual world used in the creation and original reception of the text. Material from the milieu can be used as data for reconstructing the reader who might have heard the text in a certain way. Talbert is not claiming that ancient readers would be consciously aware of these actual texts but "Rather these texts help to establish the most likely conceptual world of the readers, the authorial audience."[9]

Of all Paul's letters, only 1 Corinthians contains a lengthy discussion of the temptations posed by idol food, especially the prospect of eating in or around local temples (8:1—11:1, especially 8:10; 10:14). This fact, at the very least, suggests that Paul's figurative temple language would have pointedly contrasted with the reality of Corinth with its many temples.[10] How would this language have compared with the Corinthians' understanding of temples prior to their conversion? What would have been the chief influences on the thinking of the Corinthians when they read Paul's figurative temple language?[11] The evidence of 1 Cor 8:1—11:1 draws our

8. Talbert, *Reading Luke-Acts*, 15.

9. Talbert, *Reading Luke-Acts*, 15–16. Dodson, *Reading Dreams*, 9, elaborates, "The goal of audience criticism is to understand a text in relation to the literary, social, and historical contexts of its readers, and in the case of authorial audience this is the context when the text was first produced." Dodson proposes that when we consider the reception of the text by the original audience, we need to establish an "audience profile," which is a construct based on "a close reading of the text in relation to comparative (literary) material and the larger sociocultural milieu" (9), drawing on data "from the literary and cultural context of the ancient Mediterranean world" (10). See also Tucker and Baker, *T & T Clark Handbook*, 114. These discussions build on the studies of Peter J. T. Rabinowitz in works such as Rabinowitz, "Whirl," 81–100, and "Truth," 121–42. For more on the varieties of Audience-Oriented Criticism, see Suleiman, "Introduction," 3–45. Audience-Oriented Criticism originated in literary criticism and has been applied to the audiences of the gospels in NT scholarship. However, it is also important to consider how the Christian communities, who constituted the first audiences of Paul's letters, would have received his message in their varied contexts.

10. See the many essays that deal with this subject in Schowalter and Friesen, *Urban Religion*, and Winter, *After Paul*, 269–86, and more recently in, e.g., Lanci, *New Temple*, 89–113; Stevenson, *Power*, 37–114; and Liu, *Temple Purity*, 70–105.

11. Cf. Stevenson, who addresses the question of how temple imagery in Revelation would have communicated to a mixed cultural audience in Asia Minor (*Power*, 3)

attention to the religious influences in Corinth and the many opportunities to consume idol food in temple settings. This is clearly an important factor in understanding the social and cultural context of the audience and relates to 1 Cor 3:16; 6:19 and 2 Cor 6:16. However, 1 Cor 8:1—11:1 does not use figurative temple language and because this context to Paul's discussion has been covered so extensively in numerous articles and published monographs, particularly in the last twenty years, it will not be the focus of this book.[12]

It has long been recognized that in order to interpret Paul's letters to the Corinthians, scholars need to understand the behaviors and ideas to which Paul is reacting. These have been conveyed to Paul before the writing of 1 Corinthians by the Corinthians themselves (e.g., 1 Cor 7:1) and in reports which Paul has received from others (e.g., 1 Cor 1:11; 5:1). As Gordon Fee writes, "As former pagans they brought to the Christian faith a Hellenistic worldview and attitude toward ethical behavior."[13] As well as the importance of religion for the worldview of the Corinthians (as evidenced by the discussions in 1 Cor 8:1—11:1),[14] philosophy provided the kind of theological guidance for faith and practice that Paul sought to impart to them.[15]

Some, however, have questioned the relevance of Hellenistic philosophy as an appropriate context for the Corinthian church, such as Dale B. Martin who writes, "ancient philosophers — who represent a tiny fraction of the population — cannot be used to reconstruct views of the broader population."[16] Yet, as one leading scholar of Hellenistic philosophy puts it in his introduction to the field, "In the period covered by this book philosophy became thoroughly institutionalized and practically synonymous with higher education."[17] Although few members of the Corinthian church might have had higher education, those who did

---

and considers Paul's use of temple language in 1-2 Corinthians to provide an analogy to his study of Revelation (*Power*, 19).

12. Published monographs include Willis, *Idol Meat*; Gooch, *Dangerous Food*; Gardner, *Gifts*; Yeo, *Rhetorical Interaction*; Newton, *Deity*; Cheung, *Idol Food*; Smit, *About the Idol Offerings*; Fotopoulos, *Food*; Phua, *Idolatry*; and Shen, *Canaan*.

13. Fee, *First Epistle*, 4.

14. See, e.g., Rives, *Religion*.

15. Ferguson, *Backgrounds*, 320-21, and see also Wilken, "Toward a Social Interpretation," 444.

16. Martin, *Corinthian Body*, 6; cited with approval by May, *Body*, 159.

17. Long, *Hellenistic Philosophy*, 13.

were more influential members socially and may have exerted disproportionate influence on the church (for instance as owners of the homes in which churches met and/or as patrons of the church).

However, the issue is not necessarily whether the Corinthians were especially well-educated, or were philosophers, whether they were capable of reading philosophical works or whether there is evidence of them doing so. Rather, the influence of Hellenistic philosophy was pervasive in the first century. Speakers were to be found in the market-places; gathering disciples. Cynic philosophers were encountered on the street. Orators trained in the other advanced discipline of rhetoric were also trained in philosophy and mediated its ideas; even Hellenistic Jewish writers, such as the author of Wisdom of Solomon, and Philo of Alexandria, drew upon philosophy when writing about wisdom. In various ways then, philosophical ideas trickled down to influence the thought-world of those who may never have read the original works.[18] In this respect, Joseph Fitzmyer, a leading scholar in the study of 1 Corinthians, writes,

> Paul's first letter to the Corinthians seems at times to be coping with secular thinking among the members of the Christian community there, thinking that is at times akin to Epicurean teaching, Stoic tenets, and the rhetoric of the Sophists. That elements of such popular Greek philosophy and secular education were affecting the Christians of Corinth, along with the Roman culture that predominated, is to be expected, because of the heritage of Greek culture and philosophy that would have been there.[19]

Some older studies have, perhaps, tainted this field of research by placing great emphasis on the influences of, say, Stoicism in shaping Paul's *own* theology.[20] However, distancing ourselves from this approach (as I do), should not lead us to neglect the ways in which Paul may have deliberately addressed an audience influenced by these world views. N. T. Wright makes a telling point here, "if Paul did not *derive* the central themes and categories of his proclamation from the themes

---

18. As Long, *Hellenistic Philosophy*, 12, notes, "Epicureans and Stoics were prepared to popularize their teaching. In his *Letter to Herodotus* . . . Epicurus opens by remarking that he has prepared an epitome of his philosophy for those unable to study his technical writings." See also, e.g., Malherbe, *Paul*; Engberg-Pedersen, *Paul and the Stoics*; Barnes, *Reading*.

19. Fitzmyer, *First Corinthians*, 30–31.

20. The study of Wenschkewitz, explored below, being a prime example.

and categories of pagan thought, that doesn't mean he refused to make any use of such things. Indeed, he revels in the fact that he can pick up all kinds of things from his surrounding culture and make them serve his purposes—much as philosophers of his day could quote rival schools in order to upstage or refute them."[21] Some NT scholars have explored the relationship between Hellenistic philosophy and Paul's writings in general.[22] Others have examined the relationship between Hellenistic philosophy (Stoicism in particular) and 1 Corinthians in relation to various topics.[23] Others have set the scene for such a comparison in relation to the subject of this book. Everett Ferguson performed an invaluable service with his 1980 article on "Spiritual Sacrifice in Early Christianity and Its Environment," but since it is so wide ranging, it is necessarily brief and deals only with figurative sacrifice language, not with the language of temples.[24] In any case, Ferguson surveys the use of this language in closed categories (such as "Greek and Roman Poets and Philosophers," "Judaism," "New Testament" etc.); it is not within his purview to attempt a comparison between the NT and other contexts. With these questions in mind, I shall provide an overview of key works from the past century that have addressed Paul's use of temple language. In particular, I shall explore what light these works have shed on the relationship between Paul's language and Hellenistic Philosophy.

1.2 A HISTORY OF RESEARCH

My review of works on Paul's figurative temple language is necessarily limited by constraints of space. With this in mind, my discussion will focus on a sample of what I consider the most significant contributions, which will be supplemented by brief references to other related studies, where appropriate. I shall provide a summary and critique of each work, but my review of each author will be skewed toward their coverage of the possible contexts of the figurative temple language, since that is the

---

21. Wright, *Paul and the Faithfulness*, 201.

22. Notably Malherbe, *Paul*; Malherbe, "Hellenistic Moralists," 267-333; Engberg-Pedersen, *Paul and the Stoics*; and more generally in Sampley, *Paul*. See now the history of research presented in Barnes, *Reading*, 4-28.

23. Such as Deming, *Paul on Marriage*; Lee, *Paul*; Garcilazo, *Corinthian Dissenters*.

24. Ferguson, "Spiritual Sacrifice," 1151-81; see especially 1152-56.

particular interest of my own study.²⁵ I have divided these key studies into three categories that will help us to see more clearly each author's understanding of the possible relationship between Paul, his audience, and the contexts for the metaphor. Firstly, I shall explore the works that focus on the author and emphasize his dependence on a particular milieu. I shall note that this was a trend in earlier studies, many of whose conclusions have since been rejected by contemporary scholarship. Secondly, I shall discuss a number of works that argue that Paul was not dependent on a specific milieu, but rather drew on common tenets of Judaism. Because this is a relatively uncontroversial position, it is unsurprising that both older and more recent works have taken this stance. Finally, I shall note a newer trend. In my third category, I will observe that the majority of more recent interpreters have turned their attention not so much to the influences on Paul himself, but to the way he uses the image of the temple figuratively to address the religious and cultural milieu of his audience.

1.2.1 Author-Focused Approaches: The Dependence of Paul on His Milieu

Hans Wenschkewitz (1932)

The earliest significant modern studies on Paul's temple language concentrated solely on Paul's own context and influences. The first of these was the seminal work of Hans Wenschkewitz,²⁶ which, although now over eighty years old, still forms the starting point for modern discussions of this topic, since it proved so influential in the decades that followed.²⁷ To his credit, Wenschkewitz devoted more space to the relationship between Paul and Hellenistic philosophy than perhaps any other discussion up to the present day,²⁸ but he sought it in the wrong place. Wenschkewitz's

---

25. Most of the works I will consider have already been reviewed from a variety of angles in, e.g., Lanci, *New Temple*, 7–14; Hogeterp, *Paul and God's Temple*, 2–22; Vahrenhorst, *Kultische Sprache*, 10–16; Wardle, *Jerusalem Temple*, 5–8; Gupta, *Worship*, 9–26; Liu, *Temple Purity*, 3–9.

26. Wenschkewitz, *Spiritualisierung*.

27. Discussed by, among others, McKelvey, *New Temple*, 42–43; Schüssler Fiorenza, "Cultic Language," 159–61; Newton, *Concept of Purity*, 8; Lanci, *New Temple*, 9–11; Hogeterp, *Paul and God's Temple*, 2–8; Wardle, *Jerusalem Temple*, 5; Gupta, *Worship*, 9–11; Liu, *Temple Purity*, 3.

28. Wenschkewitz, *Spiritualisierung*, 49–67 deals with Stoic philosophy, and 67–87 with Philo of Alexandria, and discusses some key references to the notion of the divine

thesis is devoted to his concept of *Spiritualisierung* (spiritualization). He contends that the objects of the cult were increasingly spiritualized in an evolutionary process whose origins lie in the OT itself but culminate in the writings of Paul. According to Wenschkewitz, from the Maccabean period onwards, the law began to supplant the temple as the most prominent focus of Judaism, even before the destruction of the temple in 70 CE.[29] Wenschkewitz distinguished between a *naive spiritualization* represented by the OT and subsequent Jewish writings of the Diaspora, and a *reflective spiritualization* exemplified in the doctrine of the individual as the temple of God, which can be found in Stoic teaching and the writings of Philo. It was the genius of Paul to fuse these two distinct notions and combine them in his doctrine of the community as temple.[30] However, the discovery of the Dead Sea Scrolls in 1947, subsequent to Wenschkewitz's study, demonstrated that other communities originating in Palestinian Judaism could use figurative temple language, particularly in relation to their communities. This finding obviated the need for an explanation outside of Judaism (such as Stoic thought), a fact that R. J. McKelvey was one of the first to note.[31] To be fair to Wenschkewitz, he does note that Paul's doctrine of the temple of God as the community, not just the individual, and as the body, not only the soul, is radically different from Hellenistic philosophy and could not have been derived from it.[32]

---

dwelling in the soul/mind of the individual, see, e.g., Wenschkewitz, *Spiritualisierung*, 58.

29. Wenschkewitz, *Spiritualisierung*, 22f.

30. Wenschkewitz, *Spiritualisierung*, 116: "So ergibt sich also, dass die Spiritualisierung des Tempelbegriffes bei Paulus in stoischen Gedankenkreisen ihren Ursprung hat." (So it is clear, therefore, that the spiritualization of the temple concept in Paul has its source in the circles of Stoic thought.)

31. McKelvey, *New Temple*, 42–43, 56, 104, 122; also Newton, *Concept of Purity*, 120; Wardle, *Jerusalem Temple*, 5. Fraeyman, "Spiritualisation," 410–11, had already observed the problems with Wenschkewitz's thesis and postulated that Paul derived his conception of the spiritual temple from Judaism, not Hellenism, though Fraeyman was writing before the publication of the scrolls (also acknowledged by McKelvey, *New Temple*, 56 n. 1). Fraeyman, "Spiritualisation," 398 also notes the contrasts between Paul and Platonic theories of the soul and body, but Fraeyman only relates a Pauline critique of Stoicism to the record of Paul's speech in Acts 17:23–24 (Fraeyman, "Spiritualisation," 411).

32. Wenschkewitz, *Spiritualisierung*, 111–13; e.g., in his comment at 112: "Weder in der Stoa, noch bei Philo treffen wir diesen Gedanken, denn hier war alles auf den Einzelnen, auf das Individuum eingestellt" ("Neither in the Stoics nor in Philo do we meet this idea, because here everything was tailored to the individual, for the individual") and at 165. This point is also recognized in the critiques by Fraeyman,

Nevertheless, Wenschkewitz only thinks in terms of Paul appropriating a Greek concept. He does not explore the possibility that Paul may have intended to challenge or subvert the idea.[33]

Bertil Gärtner (1965)

Bertil Gärtner, writing some thirty years after Wenschkewitz and following the publication of the Dead Sea Scrolls, appreciated the fresh light that the scrolls had cast on the background to aspects of NT doctrine that had previously been attributed to its Hellenistic heritage.[34] Gärtner's studies led him to take an *approach* that was essentially identical to Wenschkewitz, though his *conclusions* were precisely the opposite. Like Wenschkewitz, Gärtner claimed that Paul was dependent on his milieu and strongly emphasized the parallels between Paul and his sources, on which he was dependent.[35] However, for Gärtner, Paul's source was Qumran theology, and Gärtner alludes to Hellenistic Judaism only in order to dismiss it, but makes no reference to the relationship between Paul, his audience, and the temple language in Hellenistic philosophy.[36] Instead, Gärtner's study emphasizes parallels between the language of temple and priesthood in Qumran and the NT (occasionally playing down the role of a literal future temple in the Scrolls, which does not correspond with NT teaching),[37] hypothesizing that former members of Qumran/the Essenes brought these traditions into the church.[38] Like Wenschkewitz, Gärtner does not consider Paul's own unique contribution, preferring to stress similarities between Qumran and traditions across the NT corpus. Gärtner does not consider the possibility that Paul's communities and the Qumran community may occupy similar positions vis-à-vis Judaism

---

"Spiritualisation," 411, and Gupta, *Worship*, 10.

33. Cf. the critique of Gupta, *Worship*, 25, that Wenschkewitz does not consider Paul's unique contribution. Similarly to Wenschkewitz, Klauck, "Kultische Symbolsprache," 109, sees the Hellenistic understanding of the dwelling of God in the soul (citing Philo and a Pythagorean maxim) as the "vorbild" (model) for 1 Cor 3:16.

34. Gärtner, *Temple*, x.
35. Gärtner, *Temple*, x–xi, 47–49, 49–60, 142.
36. Gärtner, *Temple*, 47.
37. E.g., Gärtner, *Temple*, 21.
38. Gärtner, *Temple*, 139.

without one necessarily being dependent upon the other for figurative temple language.[39]

Georg Klinzing (1971)

Georg Klinzing's study is much more focused on the Qumran community than the NT,[40] and presents a very thorough study of cultic language in a variety of texts from Qumran. Klinzing is critical of Wenschkewitz's concept of *Spiritualisierung* and prefers the term *Umdeutung* ("Reinterpretation") to describe how both Qumran and Paul appropriated cultic language in speaking of their respective communities.[41] While Klinzing recognizes that both the Qumran and Christian communities share a belief that they are an eschatological community living in the last days, like Gärtner, Klinzing is certain that the source for Paul's temple language is Qumran, "Wenn die christliche Gemeinde von sich selbst als dem Tempel spricht, kann kein Zweifel darüber bestehen, dass diese Vorstellung aus der Qumrangemeinde stammt."[42] Klinzing's methodical analysis has certainly identified points of similarity between the writings of Qumran and Paul. However, his notion of Pauline dependence is only one way of interpreting the reason for the similarities (such as wider trends within Jewish literature and the similarities between the self-understandings of the two communities in relation to Judaism) and Klinzing plays down some key differences between the two sets of writings which make the "dependency" hypothesis harder to accept.[43] Klinzing follows Gärtner in briefly referring to the Stoic and Philonic background espoused by

---

39. See also the reviews of McKelvey, *New Temple*, 96–97, and Gupta, *Worship*, 14–15.

40. The brevity of the NT section is noted by Gupta, *Worship*, 14.

41. Klinzing, *Umdeutung*, 143–47. See also the critiques of Wenschkewitz's spiritualization thesis in Coppens, "Spiritual Temple," 59, and Strack, *Kultische Terminologie*, 8–9, 375–80, 391, 396.

42. Klinzing, *Umdeutung*, 210 ("If the Christian church speaks of itself as the temple, there can be no doubt about the fact that this idea comes from the Qumran community.") For a more recent work that concurs with this judgment, see Flusser, "Dead Sea Sect," 23–74, especially 71–73.

43. See in particular the insightful questions and critique of Schüssler Fiorenza, "Cultic Language," 164–65, and the analysis of Coppens, "Spiritual Temple," 62–65 in relation to both McKelvey and Gärtner. More recently, the differences between Qumran and Pauline thought are discussed by Strack, *Kultische Terminologie*, 272.

Wenschkewitz, but only in order to dismiss it.⁴⁴ Despite these assertions, in Klinzing's brief discussion of 1 Cor 6:19, he considers it likely that Paul knew the Hellenistic conception of the soul as temple and chose to appropriate it in order to subvert it with his own Judeo-Christian understanding.⁴⁵ Similarly, Joseph Coppens, though critical of both Gärtner and Klinzing, expresses a thought comparable to that of Klinzing, "is it impossible that the ideas about a spiritual worship which were so widely diffused in the world of Hellenism and of hellenistic Judaism also contributed to foster Paul's thought?"⁴⁶ This promising line of thought is not developed by either scholar and, in the case of Klinzing, stands in stark contrast with his conclusions.

Robert J. Daly (1978)

The work of Robert Daly should also be mentioned briefly in regard to the three scholars discussed above. Daly published two works on the origins of the Christian notion of sacrifice in the same year. On the one hand, Daly takes over the evolutionary model of Wenschkewitz to postulate a gradual spiritualizing of the notion of sacrifice, beginning in the OT and finding its fulfillment in Christian writings.⁴⁷ On the other hand, Daly cites with approval Gärtner's conclusions that the resemblance between the Qumran writings and the NT suggests a common background, "but also to indicate that some elements in the Qumran tradition were taken over by the early Church."⁴⁸ Yet, returning to the topic of spiritualizing language, which he notes in Philo and intertestamental literature, he concludes, "Thus, where the same type of spiritualization appears in Qumran and the NT or Early Christian tradition, this is not necessarily an indication of dependence or direct connection"⁴⁹ which appears very much at odds with his earlier comments. The four authors with whom I have engaged each focus on what is influencing Paul, whether Hellenistic thought or Qumran. Where the possibility is raised that Paul may be

---

44. Klinzing, *Umdeutung*, 183–84.
45. Klinzing, *Umdeutung*, 184.
46. Coppens, "Spiritual Temple," 65.
47. Daly, *Origins*, 136–38.
48. Daly, *Christian Sacrifice*, 158, see also 257, 260–61.
49. Daly, *Christian Sacrifice*, 161.

engaging critically with Hellenistic thought in order to address a Gentile audience, this thought is left undeveloped.

1.2.2 Author-Focused Approaches: Paul's Appropriation of Jewish Thought

R. J. McKelvey (1969)

R. J. McKelvey's work, as its titles indicates, engages with the topic of the new temple across the NT corpus, but gives significant coverage to both Jewish and Greco-Roman background to the theme. McKelvey pays careful attention to the exegesis of all the texts he examines, ranging from the OT, to intertestamental texts, relevant Greek and Latin sources, and NT texts by a number of authors. McKelvey finds the new temple theme in a variety of diverse backgrounds, yet while conceding Greek influence on Paul, he also attributes to Paul himself a "Hebraicizing and Christianizing" of the idea.[50] McKelvey's work is relatively uncontroversial because its analysis and conclusions are careful and balanced. For my purposes, I note that McKelvey gives more consideration to Paul's engagement with Hellenistic philosophy than most other writers I will discuss. He recognizes the influence of the Hellenistic milieu on certain Jewish writings,[51] and while acknowledging similarities with Qumran, notes differences and does not posit the dependence of Paul on the scrolls.[52] He surveys a number of key philosophical texts by authors such as Epictetus and Seneca,[53] as well as providing a summary of his main findings from Philo,[54] noting, like Wenschkewitz, the difference between these writings and Paul, with his emphasis on community and body.[55] McKelvey is to be commended for his engagement with a neglected area and his well reasoned conclusions, that stress the positive basis for Paul's spiritualization (McKelvey's term), which differ from the rationale of the Stoics and Philo on the one hand, and Qumran on the other. However, much more could be said, since his main discussion of Hellenistic philosophical writings is

---

50. McKelvey, *New Temple*, 104. See also 42–43, 53, 55–57, 106–7, 179.
51. McKelvey, *New Temple*, 44.
52. McKelvey, *New Temple*, 47–53, 96–97.
53. McKelvey, *New Temple*, 53–54.
54. McKelvey, *New Temple*, 38–40, 54–55.
55. McKelvey, *New Temple*, 55.

only four pages long. In passing, McKelvey refers to Qumran, the Stoics and Philo as Paul's "mentors,"[56] but does not address the possibility that Paul may be, not so much their student, but rather in dialogue with some of these works, perhaps in order to accentuate the differences between his conception and theirs.

Michael Newton (1985)

Like the earlier works of Gärtner, Klinzing and Schüssler Fiorenza (discussed below), Michael Newton's study concentrates on the relationship between Paul and Qumran, while focusing on the concept of purity.[57] Newton's main point is that previous studies by scholars such as Wenschkewitz, Fraeyman and McKelvey were so preoccupied by the question of Paul's "spiritualization" of Jewish thought under the influence of Philo and the Stoics, that they missed the more obvious concern for temple purity that was common to all strands of Judaism and is rooted in the OT itself.[58] For Paul, the temple metaphor is not simply a useful image but a concept that borrows from the temple practice of the OT and applies it to the Christian community.[59] A careful study of purity language at Qumran and its application to the community reveals significant differences between Paul and the scrolls, so that, unlike at Qumran, specific rites are not applied to Paul's churches and their "temple" does not reside in one geographical location.[60] Paul's temple language is not a "spiritualization" fusing Greek and Jewish thought, but rather an outworking of his concern for temple purity, which is applied differently from the OT in the light of the coming of Christ, his death and resurrection.[61] Paul and Qumran shared much in common, but their application of purity language differs too, since one is not dependent on the other; instead both draw on common Jewish thinking which is applied differently in light of a different theological understanding.[62] Because Newton notes

---

56. McKelvey, *New Temple*, 122.
57. Newton, *Concept of Purity*.
58. Newton, *Concept of Purity*, 1, 8.
59. Newton, *Concept of Purity*, 8, 58–59.
60. Newton, *Concept of Purity*, 53; Schüssler Fiorenza, "Cultic Language," 163–64, also makes similar points.
61. Newton, *Concept of Purity*, 77–78, 97, 113–14.
62. Newton, *Concept of Purity*, 115–16.

that Paul's starting point is different from that of Philo and the Stoics, particularly in his focus on community,[63] he dismisses the evidence of these writings and simply does not consider how Paul's language might have sounded to an audience who was aware of temple language used in Hellenistic philosophy.[64]

Nijay Gupta (2010)

Nijay Gupta's published dissertation focuses on the use of non-atonement metaphors in the undisputed Pauline epistles.[65] One chapter is devoted to metaphor theory, in which Gupta elucidates a number of criteria which help him to assess the likelihood of having discovered a cultic metaphor along a continuum from "Certain" to "Probable."[66] Perhaps because Gupta is interested in Paul's rhetorical strategy of using metaphor to reshape the way his audience thinks,[67] he is particularly focused on Paul as author and less on the contexts of Paul's audience. Gupta asks about Paul's reason for innovating by his use of metaphor, the cultic context from which the metaphors originate, and how his own role as apostle shapes the way he uses cultic metaphors.[68] However, perhaps because of the necessary limits of his study, he does not consider how the contexts of Paul's Diaspora audience might have influenced the way that Paul may have chosen to interact with those contexts. There are points in his monograph where Gupta hints at this issue. Gupta, noting the prevalence of cultic metaphors in 1 Corinthians compared to 1 Thessalonians, suggests that, "there were contextual or rhetorical reasons for the extensive employment of

---

63. Newton, *Concept of Purity*, 57. Newton, *Concept of Purity*, 57–58, is also influenced by Kempthorne, "Incest," 568–74, in arguing that the primary referent of 1 Cor 6:19 is corporate, rather than to the individual bodies of the Corinthians. Kempthorne's argument will be reviewed in chapter 4.

64. Lanci, *New Temple*, 11–12, also questions Newton's assumption that Paul would draw exclusively from Jewish cultic purity practices when writing to a majority Gentile audience.

65. Gupta, *Worship*. For another treatment of Pauline metaphors, focused exclusively on those relating to the Holy Spirit, see Konsmo, *Pauline Metaphors*, especially 29–64 on metaphor and 114–23, 191–208 in relation to this passage.

66. Gupta, *Worship*, 46–51. Although this is not noted by Gupta, the criteria are reminiscent of Richard Hays's methodology to identify "echoes of scripture" in Paul; see Hays, *Echoes*.

67. Gupta, *Worship*, 2–4.

68. Gupta, *Worship*, 35.

cultic metaphors in the Corinthian epistle."[69] In his conclusions, Gupta argues that Paul's focus was on what these cultic metaphors *do* in seeking to form the identity of his converts.[70] Agreeing with the work of Francis Watson, Gupta stresses the need to consider Paul as a "social agent" and to take into account Paul's deployment of metaphor in relation to groups, whether they be his converts, their opponents and/or his opponents.[71] I would affirm all these points, but simply note that Gupta does not explore these contextual reasons in relation to Hellenistic philosophy. Not all of the primary sources cited by Gupta are listed in his index of sources, but a perusal of his index suggests that Gupta interacts with very few Greco-Roman sources, though he does interact extensively with Philo. Gupta's conclusions certainly focus on the impact of Paul's metaphors on his target audience, but seldom bring specific Hellenistic literature into the discussion.[72]

1.2.3 Audience-Focused Approaches: Paul's Engagement with the Religious and Cultural Milieu of Corinth

Finally, I turn my attention to works which exhibit perhaps a newer and growing trend: to consider the impact of Paul's temple language on his audience, and therefore to pay much closer attention to the contexts of Paul's audience than the mainly older studies I have so far discussed. This approach was hinted at in some older studies that I will mention in passing, but of the major works I will examine, only one predates the 1990s.

Elizabeth Schüssler Fiorenza (1976)

Elizabeth Schüssler Fiorenza's short article compared cultic language in Qumran and in the NT, while offering a searching analysis of the writings of Wenschkewitz and Klinzing.[73] Schüssler Fiorenza wants to move past

69. Gupta, Worship, 84.
70. Gupta, Worship, 205–9.
71. Gupta, Worship, 218.
72. Space will not allow me to discuss the comprehensive overview of the "biblical theology" of temple found in Beale, Temple. Suffice it to say that Beale focuses squarely on the Jewish context for this canonical theme and is only concerned with the author's perspective. Philo is referenced in various places but other Hellenistic authors are not discussed.
73. Schüssler Fiorenza, "Cultic Language," 159–77.

the language of 'spiritualization', which she sees as too broad to be helpful. Instead, she argues that the term "transference" is more suitable, since it indicates the way that both Jewish as well as Hellenistic cultic concepts were taken up by the respective communities and applied to non-cultic realities.[74] While some scholars have been dazzled by the similarities between the use of cultic language at Qumran and in Paul, Schüssler Fiorenza asks how to account for the *differences*, such that the community of the *War Scroll* does not describe itself as a temple, and the community as temple at Corinth does not adopt a hierarchical priesthood?[75] Instead, Schüssler Fiorenza enquires after "the concrete situation and theological motives that in each community led to the transference of cultic language."[76] Her careful study of some obvious differences between the two indicate that whereas Qumran stressed "sectarian separation," Paul was guided by, "the missionary situation of the early Church."[77] Schüssler Fiorenza makes the tantalizing comment that, "the NT writers evidence affinity not only to the language of Qumran but also to the concepts of religious propaganda in the Greco-Roman world."[78] While she notes that later Christian apologists developed this understanding within their own context to reach those attracted by the philosophical schools of their time,[79] she gives no indication of what she means by this sentence for Paul's social and historical context.[80] Her work raises the question of whether Paul's missionary interest may have included a desire to speak in relevant philosophical language. However, since her focus is on the Qumran and Pauline communities and their relationships with their contexts, her point is left undeveloped and unexplored.[81]

74. Schüssler Fiorenza, "Cultic Language," 161.

75. Schüssler Fiorenza, "Cultic Language," 163–64. Wardle, "Who Is Sacrificing," 99–114, contends that early Christian documents were reticent to appropriate the language of priesthood for the church or its leaders, even figuratively. Wardle's argument depends heavily on a late dating for 1 Peter, on which there is no consensus.

76. Schüssler Fiorenza, "Cultic Language," 161.

77. Schüssler Fiorenza, "Cultic Language," 171, 177.

78. Schüssler Fiorenza, "Cultic Language," 177.

79. Schüssler Fiorenza, "Cultic Language," 171, 177.

80. Cf. Winter, "Carnal Conduct," 191, who is suggestive in the way he relates the Corinthians' worldview to philosophical schools such as Epicureanism. I shall explore this topic in chapters 2, 4, and 5.

81. Cf. Moule, "Sanctuary," 29, 39 who avers that Paul's apologetic interest may have led him to address the objections of both "Jews and pagans" who objected to the absence of temple, priesthood, and sacrifice in Christianity. Strack, *Kultische*

John R. Lanci (1997)

John R. Lanci's published dissertation, in stark contrast to the earlier author-focused works I examined, makes a number of bold claims at the outset, such as, "The goal is to construct a plausible reading of the text, rather than to discover the original intention of its author" and "I will nowhere discuss the original *intention* behind the argument."[82] This assertion seems at odds with Lanci's decision to employ rhetorical analysis, mentioned in the next paragraph,[83] which, though a text-centered method concerned with the "intended effect upon the audience,"[84] tacitly assumes *intent* on the part of an author.[85] In any case, Lanci later defines the role of an interpreter of 1 Cor 3:16-17 as, "to examine the passage closely in terms of its wider purpose in Paul's rhetorical arguments in 1 Corinthians."[86] It is difficult to discern a clear difference between "intention" (which Lanci claims not to discuss) and "purpose" (which he does) and this tension is left unresolved.

Nevertheless, Lanci confronts the question of what Paul's reference to a temple may have evoked when writing to a largely Gentile audience.[87] Lanci is critical of most previous studies which assumed that Paul's referent was the Jerusalem temple; this does not explain for Lanci why Paul would use this concept for a predominantly Gentile audience.[88] Lanci is certainly right to say that the Jerusalem temple might not be the *sole* referent for Paul's audience,[89] and so devotes a chapter to Roman Corinth, which includes some examination of the various temples that would have

---

Terminologie, 380, 392, also suggests that Paul may have used cultic categories in order to communicate the gospel to Gentiles.

82. Lanci, *New Temple*, 3, italics in the original.

83. Lanci, *New Temple*, 3.

84. Aune, *Westminster Dictionary*, 416.

85. Cf. a similar critique made by Gupta, *Worship*, 19.

86. Lanci, *New Temple*, 18. Elsewhere Lanci refers to the passage's "purpose" (123) and Paul's "goal" (134).

87. Lanci, *New Temple*, 3. A topic also pursued more briefly by Böttrich, "Tempel Gottes," 411-25.

88. Lanci, *New Temple*, 9-10. Although I note that Paul is not shy of using OT allusions and citations when writing to the Corinthians in places such as 1 Cor 1:19; 2:9, 16; 3:19-20; 5:7; 6:16; 9:9, 13; 10:1-10, 26; 14:21; 15:26, 32, 45, 54-55; 2 Cor 3:1-18; 4:13; 6:2, 16-18; 8:15; 9:9; 10:17; 11:3 etc., see the observation of Horrell, *Review*, 711, as also noted by Gupta, *Worship*, 19.

89. Lanci, *New Temple*, 9-10.

been found there.⁹⁰ However, Lanci's main interest is in Paul's "construction language," noting the frequent use of words with the root οἰκοδομ- in the letter (e.g., 1 Cor 3:9; 8:1, 10; 10:23; 14:3, 4, 5, 12, 17, 26) and Paul's self characterization as an ἀρχιτέκτων (master builder) in 1 Cor 3:10,⁹¹ as well as Lanci's assumption that the Erastus of Rom 16:23 (probably written from Corinth) is the same aedile as the one referred to in the 'Erastus inscription'.⁹² Lanci's distinctive contribution is to contend that building construction and renovation was a major part of life in first century Corinth,⁹³ and that this explains Paul's use of construction imagery. Lanci ties this in to Margaret Mitchell's argument (which he adopts) that 1 Corinthians is a deliberative letter with 1 Cor 1:10 as its thesis statement and that Paul's overriding intention is to bring about unity by urging his audience to pursue the common good.⁹⁴

Lanci is doubtless correct to detect an emphasis on unity and building up for the common good in 1 Corinthians, and to observe the connection between building imagery in 1 Cor 3:9–10 and the temple metaphor in 1 Cor 3:16–17. However, at times Lanci's thesis threatens to subsume Paul's stated purpose for using figurative temple language under a more general intent related to building imagery. According to Lanci, Paul identifies the Corinthians with a building in 1 Cor 3:9–10 "because of the community-defining role of some temples in Greco-Roman society."⁹⁵ Yet Paul's comment on this image concerns the indwelling presence of God's spirit and the sanctity of this temple and is substantiated with the reason "For God's temple is holy, and you are that temple" (1 Cor 3:17). Again, Lanci avers that "The temple is a secondary image and is not the primary one with which Paul characterizes the community" nor is Paul's purpose "to define the community as a *new* temple" but rather to combat

90. Lanci, *New Temple*, 25–43.

91. Lanci, *New Temple*, 58–60, 77–78.

92. Lanci, *New Temple*, 34. This has been subsequently challenged by Friesen, "Wrong Erastus," 231–56, as also noted by Liu, *Temple Purity*, 7.

93. Lanci, *New Temple*, 33–34, although some of the evidence is rather circumstantial and hypothetical such as Lanci's contention that "there *must have been* many people living there who were associated with construction activity directly or indirectly" (33), despite the fact that we "cannot easily confirm the presence of these people by means of archaeological records (33–34), and yet Lanci suggests that "*one may safely assume* that laborers . . . lived there" (34), which is reiterated in Lanci, *New Temple*, 76; my italics.

94. Lanci, *New Temple*, 45–56, following Mitchell, *Paul and the Rhetoric*.

95. Lanci, *New Temple*, 89.

dissension through construction imagery.[96] Undoubtedly, many different images are used to describe the community in the Corinthian correspondence (such as the body in 1 Cor 12–14), but to view the temple image as non-defining seems strange in view of Paul's repeated use of it when addressing the Corinthians (including 2 Cor 6:14—7:1), and when Lanci concedes that cultic imagery is prevalent throughout 1 Corinthians.[97] Overall, Lanci interacts with an impressive range of primary and secondary sources and identifies one possible context for a major theme in 1 Corinthians, but in doing so he tends to overplay the allusions to building imagery and community formation and downplays Paul's concern for purity and holiness. Paul's own interest in the Jerusalem temple as his context is also neglected.[98]

From the perspective of my topic, Lanci's correct assumption that, "Paul was capable of interacting with the wider culture around him"[99] should include the question of figurative temple language used in Hellenistic philosophy, and Lanci notes the use of this language in the philosophers,[100] but because there are no clear parallels to the use of this image in community contexts, Lanci moves on to discuss the Dead Sea Scrolls. Lanci quite correctly contends that, "when attempting to explain how Paul uses the temple image, we must investigate how people in Corinth understood temples, be they Jewish, Greek, or Roman"[101] but this investigation could be broadened to consider how they were influenced by figurative temple language in philosophical writings.

J. Ayodeji Adewuya (2003, 2007)

J. Ayodeji Adewuya's published dissertation[102] and subsequent article[103] draw attention to the neglected theme of communal holiness in the Corinthian epistles, and helpfully situates 2 Cor 6:14—7:1 within this wider concern of Paul for his readers. Much of Adewuya's analysis and

---

96. Lanci, *New Temple*, 125.
97. Lanci, *New Temple*, 128.
98. See Horrell, Review, and Gupta, *Worship*, 16–19 for similar critiques.
99. Lanci, *New Temple*, 6.
100. Lanci, *New Temple*, 13.
101. Lanci, *New Temple*, 90.
102. Adewuya, *Holiness*.
103. Adewuya, "People," 201–18.

conclusions are relatively uncontroversial, so my review will center on what is most relevant for my topic. Adewuya's monograph raises important questions at the outset like, "What are the differences in Paul's thought world and that of his audience? For example, what is the significance of the temple imagery both to the Jews and Gentiles in Corinth?"[104] He rightly contends, "the question of influences and backgrounds should not always be restricted to the writer. It must include the readers as well"[105] with particular attention paid to "features of the Greco-Roman moral and religious climate in Corinth."[106] A section on religious pluralism observes that Corinth, "maintained many ties with Greek religion, philosophy and the arts. Consequently, the faith of the Corinthians was considerably influenced by a Hellenistic world-view and attitude toward moral behavior."[107] I note that Adewuya specifically cites the influence of philosophy but the section in which these words are found addresses matters of social culture (individualism), socio-economic factors and the role of temples in Corinth (where he summarizes Lanci) but says nothing about the philosophical climate.[108] Adewuya's subsequent article on the general theme of holiness in 2 Corinthians reuses his words cited above, almost word for word, but, similarly, the following section makes no reference to philosophy but addressees religious pluralism, and in addition refers to the influence of the imperial cult in relation to temples.[109] Adewuya is asking the right questions but though his frequent references to Paul's "Hellenistic milieu"[110] allude to Hellenistic philosophy, this topic is nowhere discussed.

Albert L. A. Hogeterp (2006)

Albert L. A. Hogeterp's substantial monograph is a greatly extended version of his PhD dissertation. He focuses on Paul's use of cultic imagery in 1–2 Corinthians in their historical context,[111] and so devotes

---

104. Adewuya, *Holiness*, 6.
105. Adewuya, *Holiness*, 77.
106. Adewuya, *Holiness*, 78.
107. Adewuya, *Holiness*, 85.
108. See Adewuya, *Holiness*, 77–87, and see further 110–15 on temples in Corinth.
109. Adewuya, "People," 202–3.
110. E.g., Adewuya, *Holiness*, 6, 78, 86–87.
111. Hogeterp, *Paul and God's Temple*, 1.

a number of chapters to setting Paul's imagery in various historical and cultural contexts before dealing with each letter in turn. In light of this concern with historical context, it is interesting to note that Hogeterp cites, with approval, Schüssler Fiorenza's contention that Paul "creates" a rhetorical situation which cannot be equated with the historical situation, and, "With this distinction in mind, Paul's cultic imagery cannot be aligned with a presupposed idea of the historical context."[112] Hogeterp has in view the presupposed historical context presented by Wenschkewitz especially, although arguably Wenschkewitz was simply articulating a hypothesis based on his understanding of the literary and historical evidence, just as Hogeterp is trying to do. Hogeterp's "historical interpretation" addresses the question, "What does Paul's cultic imagery signify in view of Paul's gospel mission to the Diaspora?"[113] which would seem to focus on Paul's engagement with the Hellenistic world; whether he is speaking to Jews or Gentiles. Hogeterp repeatedly speaks of the importance of relating Paul's cultic imagery to the original readers' own context, bearing in mind that his converts included both Jews and Greeks (citing 1 Cor 1:22-24).[114] These contexts are often described using the terms "cultic" and "religious."[115] Hogeterp does hint at a philosophical context when noting objections that may have been raised to Paul's gospel message, "that these objections may be of a philosophical, reasoned nature appears to be confirmed by the prominence of the theme of wisdom, σοφία, that is worldly wisdom as opposed to God's wisdom in 1 Cor 1:17–2:13."[116] However, aside from a brief reference to Greek philosophies described by Josephus,[117] Hogeterp does not explore this question any further. In his exegesis of 1 Cor 6:18-20, Hogeterp notes parallels from pagan contexts such as Valerius Maximus 4.7 *ext. 1* and passages from Philo. However, because of the obvious emphasis on the communal and bodily aspect of the image in Paul, Hogeterp dismisses these parallels as relevant background,[118] rather like Gärtner and Newton before him. After perhaps the most extensive discussion available of Paul's cultic

112. Hogeterp, *Paul and God's Temple*, 16, citing Schüssler Fiorenza, *Rhetoric*, 138–140.
113. Hogeterp, *Paul and God's Temple*, 22.
114. E.g., Hogeterp, *Paul and God's Temple*, 297, 300, 301.
115. E.g., Hogeterp, *Paul and God's Temple*, 272, 297.
116. Hogeterp, *Paul and God's Temple*, 310.
117. Hogeterp, *Paul and God's Temple*, 311, citing Josephus, *Ag. Ap.* 2.168.
118. Hogeterp, *Paul and God's Temple*, 342–44.

imagery, Hogeterp's work lacks a strong thesis[119] but concludes that the figurative temple language is used to teach the Corinthians a holy way of life by drawing strict boundaries.[120] Hogeterp's work on Jewish historical background in general and Qumran in particular is thorough, but despite allusions to the philosophical context of the Corinthians, this particular context is neglected.

Martin Vahrenhorst (2008)

Martin Varenhort's published Habilitation thesis takes a broader approach than the works previously discussed, since Varenhorst's interest extends beyond cultic imagery to cultic language more generally. He is concerned with the use of cultic issues with predominantly Gentile addressees and so examines Paul's use of certain purity words in relation to Hellenism.[121] Varenhorst is unconvinced by studies that detect a critique of the temple in Paul's use of cultic language. Rather, Varenhorst contends that Paul uses cultic terminology positively to address his audience's context,[122] though, like Lanci, Varenhorst does not think that Paul has the Jerusalem temple exclusively in mind, since the audience were more familiar with the reality of idol temples in the city in which they lived.[123] Although Varenhorst calls attention to the Greek conception of clean and unclean in both philosophical as well as religious contexts,[124] in practice his study focuses its attention on the use of cultic language on inscriptions on temples and in their vicinity in order to see how the use of the same language would have struck Paul's readers.[125] He does not engage much with the philosophical context, although both Philo and Seneca are briefly discussed in relation to 1 Cor 3:16–17.[126] Ultimately,

---

119. cf. Gupta, *Worship*, 21, for a similar conclusion.

120. Hogeterp, *Paul and God's Temple*, 383–85.

121. Vahrenhorst, *Kultische Sprache*, 1.

122. Vahrenhorst, *Kultische Sprache*, 13, agreeing with Strack, *Kultische Terminologie*, 8–9.

123. Vahrenhorst, *Kultische Sprache*, 13, 15.

124. Vahrenhorst, *Kultische Sprache*, 14.

125. Vahrenhorst, *Kultische Sprache*, 16, though Gupta, *Worship*, 24, questions whether conclusions can be drawn from temple inscriptions that use certain words that were already common in Hellenistic Jewish literature, while, on the other hand, Paul does not use certain cultic terms that were common in non-Jewish literature.

126. Vahrenhorst, *Kultische Sprache*, 151–52.

because Varenhorst limits his detailed study to cultic language in relation to literal practice, the philosophical background is not his focus.

Timothy Wardle (2010)

Timothy Wardle's published dissertation differs from those discussed in this section, in that, while Wardle is focused on the milieu of Paul's audience, his concern is with the Jewish context. Wardle's thesis is a bold one, and envisages a provocative and polemical agenda on the part of Paul, "the decision to proclaim the Christian community as a temple was a bold and calculated move that held particular cultural currency in the first century CE. It was a culturally recognizable way to register dissent. Moreover, the decision to construct an alternative temple *in Jerusalem*, in the shadow of the sanctuary that dominated the skyline of Jerusalem, held potentially explosive socio-religious consequences."[127] In order to establish his thesis, Wardle looks at "patterns of dissent" in Jewish literature, in particular the construction of temples as alternatives to the one in Jerusalem, especially by discussing the Samaritan and Leontoplis temples and the Qumran community's understanding of itself as a rival temple.[128] Wardle's monograph is very well written and researched and certainly establishes his thesis vis-à-vis the temples discussed and may have some relevance to the evidence of certain texts in the gospels.[129]

However, when applied to Paul's writings, Wardle's thesis becomes problematic. He asserts, "if I am correct that the formation of alternative temples was the result of specific instances of conflict with the Jerusalem establishment, then it stands to reason that the early Christian temple ideology was borne of similar convictions."[130] However, it does not "stand to reason" on the basis of the evidence from Paul's letters, nor is there evidence of Paul or his community's, "reaction to the chief priests' involvement in the crucifixion of Jesus and their continued hostility toward the early Christian leadership in Jerusalem."[131] Of course though neither Paul nor the early Christian communities built rival temples, Wardle can point to the example of Qumran, whose understanding of the communi-

---

127. Wardle, *Jerusalem Temple*, 3.
128. Wardle, *Jerusalem Temple*, 4, and see 30–165.
129. For which, see Wardle, *Jerusalem Temple*, 166–91.
130. Wardle, *Jerusalem Temple*, 10.
131. Wardle, *Jerusalem Temple*, 10.

ty as a temple could rival that of the Jerusalem temple.[132] However, since Wardle accepts the evidence of Acts that the early Christians continue to participate in Jerusalem temple worship (e.g., Acts 2:46; 3:1), this would seem to be damaging to his thesis.[133] Comparisons with Qumran might appear to provide the strongest warrant for Wardle's thesis in relation to the Pauline communities. In fact, though, in Wardle's discussion of 1 Cor 3:16–17 and 2 Cor 6:16–18, he explicitly acknowledges that Paul's transference of temple language did not appear to be rooted in a denigration of the Jerusalem cult, nor to involve a concept of the community providing for atonement for sins, unlike at Qumran.[134] When the prevalence of references to figurative temple language is noted across multiple strands of the NT as well as in a variety of contexts for Paul's churches (Wardle deals with Gal 2:9;[135] 1 Cor 3:16–17; 6:19; 2 Cor 6:16–18; Eph 2:19–22; 1 Pet 2:4–10 and Rev 3:12), it becomes difficult to argue that all of them are united in a polemical witness against the Jerusalem priesthood. This is especially problematic when the authors are addressing Christian communities far from Jerusalem whose membership may be predominantly or at least partly Gentiles (such as the readers at Corinth and the recipients of 1 Peter and Ephesians), who, unlike the Qumran community, had little interest in the Jerusalem priesthood and cult.[136] Wardle concedes that, although Paul's primary referent may be the Jerusalem temple, the image may speak to Gentiles converted to Christianity who had been displaced

---

132. Wardle, *Jerusalem Temple*, 139–62, especially p. 159. The question of whether this notion was uniformly held across the relevant scrolls will be discussed below.

133. Wardle, *Jerusalem Temple*, 11. While I shall note below disagreement over the evidence for the Essenes' offering of sacrifices in or around the temple, nobody is arguing that they participated in temple worship to the same degree as everyone else.

134. Wardle, *Jerusalem Temple*, 210–11. Dr. Fredrick J. Long, in personal correspondence, has pointed out the possibility of connecting Paul's critique of the rulers who crucified Jesus in 1 Cor 2:6 (which could include the Jewish Temple establishment) with temple replacement imagery in 1 Cor 3:16. However, Wardle does not make that connection and in fact the first passage that he deals with in the letter is 1 Cor 3:9–15.

135. Ibid., 207–10 argues that "στῦλοι" in Gal 2:9 refers to the role of James, Cephas and John as pillars in the new eschatological temple, consisting of Christians (with, e.g., Bauckham, "Church," 415–80.). However, the connotation is ambiguous, and Paul's audience might equally have taken it to mean something like "pillars of the community," the more common figurative sense, in the absence of explicit temple imagery in context, according to Keener, "Pillars," 51–58.

136. A similar point concerning Wardle's handling of the various texts is made by Snow, Review, 305.

from their own temples.¹³⁷ Wardle does make brief reference to the relevance of Philo's understanding of the divine indwelling of the mind,¹³⁸ but otherwise the philosophical context is not considered because of his very strongly focused thesis in relation to the Jerusalem temple.

Yulin Liu (2013)

Yulin Liu's published PhD dissertation seeks to fill a lacuna, claiming that, "there is no specific work on linking temple and purity in the Corinthian letters."¹³⁹ Liu's objective is to understand Paul's use of temple and purity language in situ by relating Paul's message to the context of both Judaism and the Greco-Roman world.¹⁴⁰ Liu rightly notes that the historical situation of Corinth and the wider Greco-Roman world as well as the implied audience's likely response to Paul's concern for temple purity needs to be taken into account.¹⁴¹ What follows is a very thorough study of both of these contexts, but Liu's distinctive contribution lies in his study of three cults whose temples were found in Corinth (Apollo, Isis and Asklepios)¹⁴² and in his reading of particular passages through the lens of temple purity (especially 1 Cor 5 and 7). Liu does occasionally engage with Hellenistic philosophical literature such as his brief discussion of Philo's figurative temple language.¹⁴³ Liu's reference to *Somn.* 1.149 specifically relates Philo's exhortation to his own soul to become the dwelling place of God to Liu's own discussion of Israel as the temple of God, which does not seem to be the immediate context in Philo,¹⁴⁴ although evidence from Philo is also treated in a number of other places.¹⁴⁵ Liu does directly relate Philo's assertion that the body is the "sacred temple for a reasonable soul" (*Opif.* 137) to 1 Cor 6:19 but merely describes Paul's image as a "similar idea"

---

137. Wardle, *Jerusalem Temple*, 222, citing Stevenson, *Power*, 179.

138. Wardle, *Jerusalem Temple*, 213.

139. Liu, *Temple Purity*, 3, although I note that Michael Newton does address this very issue, while dealing more broadly with the letters of Paul.

140. Liu, *Temple Purity*, 3, 9.

141. Liu, *Temple Purity*, 9–10, 116.

142. Liu, *Temple Purity*, 70–105.

143. Liu, *Temple Purity*, 117.

144. Liu, *Temple Purity*, 117.

145. For instance, Liu, *Temple Purity*, 62–65, devotes more space to the subject of temple purity in Philo, and again in relation to 1 Cor 6:15–20 in *Temple Purity*, 155, and in relation to the priesthood in *Temple Purity*, 166–67.

without noting key differences.[146] Liu also treats the teaching of Epictetus on the indwelling of god, but his discussion summarizes Luke Timothy Johnson's work, including the same citation of a text number that is not found in the Loeb Classical Library edition: *Disc.* 1.14.69.[147] To be fair to Liu, his comprehensive treatment of temple purity demonstrates wide reading in a variety of disciplines and for my purposes exhibits a commendable attention to the Greco-Roman world of Paul's audience, but because the focus is temple purity language, the figurative use of temple language in philosophical texts is only discussed in passing.

It seems then, that in the many works that have appeared over a number of decades, none have sought to review the use of figurative temple language in Hellenistic writers in a comprehensive way and to compare the philosophy of these writers with the temple theology of Paul in 1–2 Corinthians.

1.3 FIGURATIVE TEMPLE LANGUAGE IN INTERTESTAMENTAL JUDAISM

Before proceeding with my study of figurative temple language in Hellenistic philosophical writings, I shall briefly survey the most significant references to such language in two places; firstly, its use in the Dead Sea Scrolls, which has been widely documented, and secondly, its use in the Pseudepigrapha and Apocrypha, which is less frequent and therefore has attracted less attention.

1.3.1 Figurative Temple Language in the Dead Sea Scrolls

The Dead Sea Scrolls exhibit a profound concern for temple purity, and purity language pervades the literature. However, for the sake of brevity, I shall confine my interest to those passages which most obviously speak of priesthood, sacrifice or temple language in a figurative sense.[148] The Rule

---

146. Liu, *Temple Purity*, 155. See also the critique of Son, Review.

147. Liu, *Temple Purity*, 118–19, following Johnson, *Among the Gentiles*, 73. Johnson's citation of the words of Epictetus clearly come from *Disc.* 1.14.6 (there are only seventeen verses in the Loeb text). Liu, *Temple Purity*, 81, also alludes to the concept of the body as a figurative sacred vessel, citing Parker, *Miasma*, 144–45, 213, as evidence.

148. Fragments that simply repeat the same words used in other, longer, extant works will not be listed.

of the Community contains perhaps the single highest concentration of such language. Firstly, atonement is available in the community, yet not through literal sacrifices but by the spirit of God and through the obedience of the worshiper,

> For it is by the spirit of the true counsel of God that are atoned the paths of man, all his iniquities, so that he can look at the light of life. And it is by the holy spirit of the community, in its truth, that he is cleansed of all his iniquities. And by the spirit of uprightness and of humility his sin is atoned. And by the compliance of his soul with all the laws of God his flesh is cleansed by being sprinkled with cleansing waters and being made holy with the waters of repentance.[149]

1QS V, 5-6 and VIII, 3-4, 10 also speak of atonement for the community through lives lived in holiness.[150] Similarly, 1QS IX, 4-5 speaks of atonement through figurative sacrifices, pointedly expressed as, "without the flesh of burnt offerings and without the fats of sacrifice." Instead the sacrifices are right speech/praise and behavior, "the offering of the lips in compliance with the decree will be like the pleasant aroma of justice and the perfectness of behavior will be accepted like a freewill offering."[151] CD XI, 20-21 changes the wording of Prov 15:8 (The sacrifice of the wicked is an abomination to the LORD, but the prayer of the upright *is his delight*) to give it a distinctly cultic flavor, thus depicting prayer as a figurative sacrifice, "the sacrifice of the wicked ones is an abomination, but the prayer of the just ones *is like an agreeable offering*." Similarly 11Q5 XVIII, 9-12 reads, "The person who gives glory to the Most High is accepted like one who brings an offering, like one who offers rams and calfs, like one who makes the altar greasy with many holocausts, like the sweet fragrance from the hand of just ones."[152] 1QS VIII, 1-10 is one of the clearest

---

149. 1QS III, 6-9; cf. also 1QS III, 4, 9-12. All translations are taken from García Martínez and Tigchelaar, *Dead Sea Scrolls*. Knibb, *Qumran Community*, 92-93 understands "spirit" in lines 6, 7 and 8 to refer "to the disposition of the individual," though a variant reading in lines 7b-8a refers to "his spirit of holiness," which would then picture the spirit as God's spirit, which he has given to the community. Regev, "Abominated Temple," 243-78, explores a possible reason for righteous behavior functioning as a means of atonement at Qumran.

150. Though I should note that the scrolls also contain examples of God making atonement for sin, e.g., 1QS II, 8; CD II, 5; as cited by Knibb, *Qumran Community*, 93.

151. 1QS XI, 4-5; see also 1QS X, 6, 8, 14 for "the offering of lips," and cf. 4QSD 7 II, 7-10.

152. A very similar wording is also found in Ps 154:10-11 (11QPs[a] 154) and Ps

passages in the scrolls to speak of the community in terms reminiscent of the temple, "the Community council shall be founded on truth, to be an everlasting plantation, a holy house for Israel and the foundation of the holy of holies for Aaron . . . This the tested rampart, the precious cornerstone . . . the most holy dwelling for Aaron . . . in order to offer a pleasant aroma; and it will be a house of perfection and truth in Israel"[153] and similar language is used in 1 QS IX, 6-7, "the Community shall set apart a holy house for Aaron, in order to form a most holy community, and a house of the Community for Israel" and in 1 QS XI, 8-9, "He unites their assembly to the sons of the heavens in order (to form) the council of the Community and a foundation of the building of holiness to be an everlasting plantation throughout all future ages."[154] The most striking, and disputed passage,[155] is found in 4QFlor I, 6-7, which is rendered by Martínez and Tigchelaar as "And he commanded to build for himself a temple of man, to offer him in it, before him, the works of thanksgiving."

Before moving on, I should note two other types of imagery that may be related to the notion of community figuratively as temple. First, some scrolls speak of the community as a plantation (e.g., 1QS VIII, 5; XI, 8; CD I, 7; 1QH XV, 19; XVI, 5, 6, 9, 10)[156] which is associated with a garden and its streams, sometimes related to Eden itself (cf. 1QH XIV, 15-17; XVI, 5-7, 9-11).[157] Eden was often pictured as the first sanctuary.[158] Second, the reference to "Lebanon" as the council of the community in 1QpHab XII, 3, 4 has been interpreted as signifying the temple.[159] Finally

---

154:10-11 (5 *Apoc. Syr. Ps.* 2) of the Pseudepigrapha.

153. 1QS VIII, 5- 9.

154. The latter passage using field, building, and temple figurative language, rather like 1 Cor 3, which will be examined in chapter 4.

155. See the discussion below.

156. See also Klinzing, *Umdeutung*, 168, the references cited in Newton, *Concept of Purity*, 131-32n9 and the discussion in Brooke, "Miqdash," 291-93.

157. Hogeterp, *Paul and God's Temple*, 112.

158. Beale, *Temple*, 66-79, and throughout the study, expands on this theme in some depth, citing e.g., *Jub.* 18:9: "And he knew that the Garden of Eden is the holy of holies, and the dwelling of the Lord, and Mount Sinai the centre of the desert, and Mount Zion—the centre of the navel of the earth: these three were created as holy places facing each other." Copies of Jubilees were found at Qumran and their ideology may have influenced the community; see Brooke, "Ten Temples," 419-21, 425-26. Brooke, "Miqdash," 289 translates 4QFlor I, 6 as a "sanctuary of Adam," which relates to the garden of Eden; followed by Wassen, "Do You Have to Be Pure," 65-66.

159. In Vermes, "Symbolical Interpretation," 1-12, cited by Best, "Spiritual

I note that figurative priesthood language is not found at Qumran, since the community still functions like the Jewish cult, with distinctions made between laypeople and a priestly order.[160]

I observed earlier that, following Gärtner, comparisons have been made between Paul's use of figurative temple language and the language of Qumran, with Gärtner and others even claiming that Paul is dependent on the theology of the Qumran community. Because this is not the focus of my study, my discussion of this subject will be necessarily brief. However, I cannot move on before observing that the interpretation of certain passages cited by Gärtner from the Dead Sea Scrolls has been disputed in modern Qumran scholarship and the situation is more complex and less clear cut than Gärtner assumed.

Firstly, not every scholar agrees that all of the references cited above use figurative temple language for the community. The most disputed subject is the reference to the מקדש אדם (temple of man/adam) in 4QFlor I, 6–7. Gärtner's asserts that the phrase should be translated "a temple of men," meaning "consisting of men" and disputes Yadin's interpretation "a Sanctuary among men," which, Gärtner claims, would require a preposition (ב).[161] However, Yadin's case has not been as easily dismissed (followed, for instance by Klinzing)[162] and though Gärtner's interpretation is still, perhaps, the most popular view, it has not commanded universal assent. M. O. Wise, writing over twenty five years later, lists four basic lines of interpretation: (1) "A sanctuary made by men, standing among men" (2) "A sanctuary made by God standing among men" (3) "A sanctuary made by men consisting of men" (4) "A sanctuary made by God consisting of men."[163] Wise himself contends that the phrase refers to an eschatological temple, not the community as temple, since CD III, 12–IV, 4 explicitly

---

Sacrifice," 291, and further in Gärtner, *Temple*, 43–44.

160. For just a sampling of the many passages referring to priests in the community, see, e.g., 1QS I, 18–19; II, 1–2, 19–20; V, 2, 9; VI, 3–10, 19–20; VII, 2–3; VIII, 1–4; 1QSa I, 2; II, 2–3; 4QpIsa^{d}1, 2; 4QShirShabb^{a}1 I, 3–8. Other passages speak of those belonging to the "seed of Aaron" e.g., 4QSD 7, II, 3; 4QSapWork B 1, 5. For more on the literal priesthood depicted in the scrolls, see García Martínez, "Priestly Functions," 303–19. Wardle, *Jerusalem Temple*, 143–44, notes the role of priests in the eschatological temple (e.g., (1QM II, 5–6; 2Q24 4 = 11Q18 20).

161. Gärtner, *Temple*, 34–35, citing Yadin, "Midrash," 96.

162. Klinzing, *Umdeutung*, 83–84.

163. Wise, "4QFlorilegium," 107–9, citing at least three major scholars for each view.

links the end time temple with the name of Adam.[164] However, as George Brooke rightly points out, Wise privileges the hermeneutical standpoint of both the *Temple Scroll* (11QT) and the *Damascus Document* (CD) in his interpretation of the disputed phrase, rather than letting the phrase stand in its context.[165] As we shall see below, this is a flawed approach, considering that there may be evidence for historical development in the thinking of the community. Brooke's own approach seems to balance the two perspectives well, arguing that "temple of adam" functions both as a reference to the community but also as the proleptic last-days sanctuary, anticipating a restoration of Eden in an eschatological temple, which will be built by God.[166] A growing number of recent studies also adopt this broad outline,[167] though there is some nuancing of this view, such that Francis Schmidt considers the sanctuary to consist of the priests and laymen who make up the council (not the whole community),[168] and Devorah Dimant interprets the phrase to speak of the congregation of priests only.[169] While some, like Brooke, take the reference to mean "a temple of Adam" and others, like Gärtner, take it to mean "a temple of man", each of these studies agree that the temple is a image for some or all of the community. However, dissenting voices still exist. Daniel R. Schwartz follows Yadin's understanding but translates the phrase as "a man-made temple," referring to the construction of Solomon's temple from a vantage point earlier in Israel's history.[170] Allan J. McNicol also follows Yadin, but his understanding is directly counter to the interpretation of Schwartz, instead seeing it as a reference to the final eschatological temple.[171] Though the most common understanding of "a temple of men/Adam" fits what we find elsewhere in the scrolls, I must acknowledge this is a probable,

---

164. Wise, "4QFlorilegium," 123–27, 131–32.

165. Brooke, "Miqdash," 287–89.

166. Brooke, "Miqdash," 289–91.

167. Such as Schiffman, "Community," 279–80; Schmidt, *How the Temple*, 141, 163–65; Wardle, "Who Is Sacrificing," 157–59; Wassen, "Do You Have to Be Pure," 65–66.

168. Schmidt, *How the Temple*, 141, 164–65.

169. Dimant, "4Q Florilegium," 176–89; cf. also Wassen, "Do You Have to Be Pure," 69 who concludes her study, "The community is not the temple; but, as we have seen, certain aspects of the nature and function of the Temple are transferred to the community and appropriated."

170. Schwartz, "Three Temples," 83–91.

171. McNicol, "Eschatological Temple," 133–141.

rather than certain interpretation. Finally, on this topic, the translation of one of the other references cited above has also been disputed by a minority of scholars. The preposition מִן in 1QS IX, 4-5 often translated as "*without* the flesh of burnt offerings and without the fats of sacrifice" could be translated "*from* the flesh of burnt offerings . . ."[172]

While Gärtner has a tendency to downplay the role of the future eschatological temple,[173] most recognize that the community as temple is seen as only a provisional response to the perceived illegitimacy of the contemporary priesthood in Jerusalem, with the emphasis on the greater glory of the temple to be revealed.[174] Indeed, Brooke argues that the community sees itself as a temple not simply because it understands the Jerusalem temple to be defiled but because its worship was to function as an anticipation of God's intention to establish a new temple.[175] The restoration of the temple is a particularly strong theme in the *War Scroll* (1QM), which does not describe the community as a temple.[176]

On the basis of these and other possible ambiguities, at least one scholar has gone further by questioning whether the Qumran community really saw itself as a temple at all. Jonathan Klawans points to the provisional nature of the community's temple-free existence, the priority given to the future eschatological temple, the ambiguity over some of the references noted above but most importantly for his case, Klawans notes that the term for sanctuary (מִקְדָּשׁ) is never used unambiguously for the community (where the more ambiguous term בַּיִת "house" is used), and asks, in relation to the *Damascus Document*, "If the author(s) of CD wanted to say that the community was truly a temple, why not use the word?"[177] Although Klawans's argument is well made, he seems to un-

---

172. As argued by Carmignac, "L'utilité," 524-32, followed by Schmidt, *How the Temple*, 140-41, and discussed by Klawans, *Purity*, 164. Baumgarten, "Essenes," 67, takes it as a comparative or qualitative judgment, translating the preposition as "more than" meaning 'more important than'. See, however, the counter-arguments of Klinzing, *Umdeutung*, 37-41 and Lichtenberger, "Atonement," 161-63 among others.

173. E.g., Gärtner, *Temple*, 21.

174. E.g., Lichtenberger, "Atonement," 159-71 at 165-67.

175. Brooke, "Miqdash," 297-98.

176. E.g., Hogeterp, *Paul and God's Temple*, 114; Klawans, *Purity*, 164; Schiffman, "Community," 279-80; Schmidt, *How the Temple*, 141.

177. Klawans, *Purity*, 162-166, at 166. Ibid., 166-68 makes further points about the presence of angels with the community rather than an explicit reference to the presence of God, and points to the limited powers of atonement possessed by the community.

derplay the clear point that the community does have its own priests, can make atonement (even if some functions seem inferior to the provisions of the Pentateuch), and that other phrases (such as "house") are also used in the OT when the temple is clearly in view, and in conjunction with words with the קדש root, such as 1 Chr 29:16; 2 Chr 36:14; Ps 5:7 (5:8 MT); Isa 56:7; 64:11 (64:10 MT); 66:20 (and as noted earlier, the majority view is that מִקְדָּשׁ is used in relation to the community in 4QFlor I, 6).

Before concluding my discussion of figurative temple language at Qumran, I should note three further issues that concern the history of the community behind the text that could have a bearing on our interpretation of those texts. Firstly, there is the question of whether the *Damascus Document* presents a different perspective on the sectarians' relationship to the cult than those already considered. Texts like CD XI, 17–20; CD III, 20–IV, 2 and XVI, 13–14 provide regulations for the conduct of sacrifices. Do these suggest that some of the community participated in the sacrificial cult for a time, that they are looking back to an earlier age, or are these regulations for a later age and a future temple?[178] Although we know that there was a definite break with the temple, it is unclear whether the community continued to participate in worship in its early years before attitudes hardened, or whether the reverse is the case. To complicate matters, some believe that the Damascus Document may have a complicated history, with different levels of redaction.[179] It is clear that references to the community as temple are strongest in 1QS, limited in CD, disputed in 4QFlor and not found in 1QH, 1QM and many other writings.[180] McNicol draws attention to the early dating usually given to 1QS and suggests that the writings dated post-63 CE do not portray the community as a temple.[181] Brooke goes so far as to posit a three stage evolutionary approach where a more hierarchical organization gradually gave way to a more egalitarian community.[182]

Secondly, archaeological studies have discovered animal bones at Qumran, raising the question of whether these provide evidence of animal sacrifice. J. Baumgarten discusses this question but, considering the placement of the bones in jars, concludes that these were more likely

---

178. See Klinzing, *Umdeutung*, 75–80; Lichtenberger, "Atonement," 161.
179. Wardle, *Jerusalem Temple*, 148–50.
180. Schüssler Fiorenza, "Cultic Language," 165.
181. McNicol, "Eschatological Temple," 141.
182. Brooke, "Ten Temples," 425–27.

edible remains from communal meals that were preserved in this way as a guard against contamination.[183] There is no corresponding archaeological evidence for a cultic site and Jewish sacrificial regulations contained no requirement for the burying of bones.[184]

Thirdly, there is the question of how to relate seemingly contradictory reports of the Essenes by Josephus and Philo respectively and what credence to give to Josephus's statement about sacrifice and the Essenes. Whereas Philo writes that Essenes show themselves to be "especially devout in the service of God, not by offering sacrifices of animals, but by resolving to sanctify their minds,"[185] Josephus writes, "When they send what they have dedicated to God into the Temple, they do not offer sacrifices, because they profess to have more pure lustrations, therefore they keep themselves from the public precincts of the Temple, but conduct their worship separately."[186] This ambiguous comment is further complicated by conflicting evidence in the Epitome and Latin manuscripts of Josephus that say that the Essenes *do not* perform sacrifices.[187] Klinzing simply evaluated Josephus's evidence as mistaken,[188] but Baumgarten takes Philo's statement not as an absolute denial of sacrifice but as a devaluing of its importance to the life of the community,[189] and therefore thinks it likely that Josephus's language indicates some limited accommodation to participation in the temple by some of the community's members.[190] Others remain agnostic on the issue.[191]

183. Baumgarten, "Essenes," 59–61.

184. Schiffman, "Community," 272; cf. Brooke, *Dead Sea Scrolls*, 429, for references to different archaeological studies. Klawans, *Purity*, 162, follows Schiffman.

185. Philo, *Prob.* 75.

186. Josephus, *Ant.* 18. 1, 5 (Thackeray, LCL). See more generally the evidence of Josephus, *Ant.* 18. 1, 5, 18–22; *J.W.* 2.119–61.

187. Wardle, *Jerusalem Temple*, 145–47; Baumgarten, "Essenes," 62.

188. Klinzing, *Umdeutung*, 48–49.

189. Baumgarten, "Essenes," 67, followed by Wardle, *Jerusalem Temple*, 145–47. If this is Philo's meaning, he could have expressed himself a little more clearly. The translation, "not *by* offering sacrifices of animals, but *by* resolving to sanctify their minds" may be a little misleading on this point. The verb translated "to offer" (καταθύω) could be functioning as a "participle of means" (*by means of* offering sacrifices) but the second verb (κατασκευάζω) is an infinitive. Although this could be functioning as an "infinitive of means," the particular construction is not commonly used this way (see Wallace, *Greek Grammar*, 597–98).

190. Baumgarten, "Essenes," 66–67.

191. See Wardle, *Jerusalem Temple*, 147. This issue is also discussed by Lichtenberger, "Atonement," 160–61; Dimant, "4Q Florilegium," 186–87; Schmidt, *How the*

There are clearly parallels between the use of figurative temple language in Paul and at Qumran. However, the reason for this is harder to come by than some earlier scholars confidently assumed. Both communities knew of the use of figurative sacrifice language in the OT and early Judaism, and the situations and self-understandings of their respective communities may have led them to similar conclusions for different reasons. Certainly, the lack of consistency across the Dead Sea Scrolls and the question of dating should make us cautious about positing a direct influence on Paul. It is also unlikely that the scrolls would have been known to a predominantly Gentile congregation in Corinth and would have influenced their understanding of Paul's words. That said, sources like Philo and Josephus know of the Essenes and speak of them to their Diaspora audiences. Qumran may be a witness to the development of figurative temple language in some segments of early Judaism, a development that is also attested in other ways in the Diaspora Jewish source Philo,[192] to whom I shall turn in chapter 3. The question of how the Corinthian audience might have understood 2 Cor 6:14—7:1, a passage often mined for parallels with Qumran, will be covered in chapter 5.

1.3.2 Figurative Temple Language in the Pseudepigrapha and the Apocrypha

The Pseudepigrapha contain many references to the heavenly temple or to an eschatological temple that God will build or send down from heaven at the end of the age.[193] However, since my focus is on figurative temple language (and not upon a heavenly or eschatological reality, which would be considered to be real and literal), I shall not examine those references here.[194] Since among the Jewish groups of which we are aware, only the Qumran community spoke of themselves as a temple with priests, the

---

Temple, 140.

192. I owe this point to Craig S. Keener.

193. These are found especially in the eschatological books such as *1 En.* 14:1–25; 24–26; 71:5; *4 Ezra* 10:25–28; *2 Bar.* 4:1–7.

194. This would also include the reference to sacrifices in heaven as "a rational and bloodless oblation" in *T. Levi* 3:5–6. For an exploration of some of these themes, see Hayward, *Jewish Temple*, and Rowland, "Temple," 175–98. There is also the strange rejection of animal sacrifice found in *Sib. Or.* 4:27–30, whose referent is disputed. Its target may be idolatry, although a negative assessment of the present Jerusalem cult may also be in view; see Chester, "Sibyl," 62–69.

Pseudepigrapha and the Apocrypha's figurative temple language mainly deals with sacrifice. These ideas appear in occasional verses rather than being developed as a coherent theme as they are in the Dead Sea Scrolls. I shall briefly examine the most obvious references by grouping them by category.

There are several references that emphasize the disposition of the worshiper rather than the sacrifice. While it would be possible to read some of these verses to mean that the sacrifices are negated, it is more likely in each case that the cultic system is maintained, but purity of intention and behavior is understood to give the sacrifices their true value. Judith's hymn of celebration includes the lines, "For every sacrifice as a fragrant offering is a small thing, and the fat of all whole burnt offerings to you is a very little thing; but whoever fears the Lord is great forever."[195] In context, it is hard to read Judith's words (even if originally penned by another author)[196] as a rejection or even a minimizing of the value of the cult, given that Judith's zeal for the law is emphasized throughout the book.[197] Indeed, immediately after the hymn, the narrator couples the exemplary worship of God's people with their sacrificial offerings and the sacrifices of Judith in particular (Jdt 16:18–19). The point of Jdt 16:16 seems to be that sacrifices need to be accompanied by a true reverence for God,[198] a reverence displayed in the account that follows the hymn. The Letter of Aristeas contains a similar sentiment. The narrator recounts the wise answers of each of the putative translators of the Septuagint, and in one case, to the question, "What is the highest form of glory?" the reply is given, "Honoring God. This is not done with gifts or sacrifices, but with purity of heart and of devout disposition" (*Let. Aris.* 234). In context, the point is not so much a disparagement of the cultic system but an apologetic for the law as the highest form of philosophy, a claim not lost on the audience of the dialogue, who respond with admiration (*Let. Aris.* 235).[199] The broader context of the letter bears testimony to the narrator's reverence for the temple and priesthood (*Let. Aris.* 83–99),[200] so the state-

---

195. Jdt 16:16. Unless indicated otherwise, all citations from the Apocrypha are taken from the NRSV and all citations from the Pseudepigrapha come from the translations in the *OTP* edited by James H. Charlesworth.

196. See the discussion in Moore, *Judith*, 252–57; Gera, *Judith*, 464–65.

197. Enslin and Zeitlin, *Book of Judith*, 174.

198. Moore, *Judith*, 251; Gera, *Judith*, 467–68.

199. A theme developed further in 4 Maccabees; see 4 Macc 1:1; 2:22; 5:5, 7, 11, 35; 7:7, 9, 21; 8:15.

200. For which, see Hayward, *Jewish Temple*, 26–37.

ment should be read in that light. Second Enoch ('J' recension) contains another statement similar to that of Aristeas and Judith, "Does the Lord demand bread or lamps or sheep or oxen or any kind of sacrifices at all? That is nothing, but he [God] demands pure hearts, and by means of all those things he tests people's hearts."[201] The assertion comes in the context of the reminder that humanity has been made in God's image (2 En. 44:1) and should act in ways honoring to God and to others (2 En. 44:1–5) and is similar to the kind of prophetic critique found in places such as Ps 40:6; 51:16 and Mic 6:6–8. Later in the book, the sacrificial system is assumed as the right form of worship (e.g., 2 En. 61:4–5; 62:1; 66:2).

The second category concerns passages that view something as an appropriate substitute for sacrifices, such as a right heart or right practices, while not necessarily suggesting that sacrifices per se are discarded. One of the most striking of these is Tobit's refrain that almsgiving is itself a sacrifice (Tob 4:11) which atones from sin (Tob 12:9) and delivers a person from death (Tob 4:10; 12:9). Almsgiving is a particularly important theme for Tobit,[202] and the writer has reinterpreted passages like Prov 10:2; 11:6; 16:7 (LXX) to emphasize this. The Hebrew word צדקה (righteousness), though translated as δικαιοσύνη in each of these verses, came to include the sense of "almsgiving" (ἐλεημοσύνη)[203] which is used here and elsewhere in the book (e.g., Tob 1:3, 16; 2:14; 3:2; 4:7, 8, 16; 13:8; 14:2, 10, 11). The same theme is picked up in Sir 3:30; 35:4 and 40:24. Additionally Ben Sira views obedience to the commandment to honor father and mother as atoning (Sir 3:3), and counts obedience to the commandments generally as a sacrifice (Sir 35:1–2), which is encapsulated in the forsaking of unrighteousness (Sir 35:5). This does not mean, however, that either Tobit or Ben Sira neglect the sacrificial system. Rather, Ben Sira insists that sacrifices are only efficacious if accompanied by a true righteousness (in line with 1 Sam 15:22; Amos 5:21–24 etc.).[204] For Ben Sira, the two must go together, "The offering of the righteous enriches the altar" (Sir 35:8),[205] and the importance of the cult is frequently emphasized in the work (e.g., Sir 7:29–31; 35:1–12; 38:9–11).[206] Similarly,

201. 2 En. 45:3.

202. See Moore, Tobit, 174–77; Fitzmyer, Tobit, 171–72; and on the theme of almsgiving generally, Otzen, Tobit, 35–37.

203. Corley, "Intertextual Study," 179.

204. Skehan and Di Lella, Wisdom, 417–18.

205. Wright, Wisdom, 101.

206. As noted by Wright, "Ben Sira," 242. See also the commentary in Hayward,

Tobit looks forward to a glorious restored temple with right worship (Tob 14:5–6). The writer of Jubilees also views the desires of the people (probably referring to their prayers) as "pleasing fragrance, which is acceptable before him always" (*Jub.* 2:22), but this comes from a work which takes a very strict view of the importance of devotion to the law, embodied in circumcision (*Jub.* 15:24–29), festivals (*Jub.* 6:37; 23:19) and sacrifice (*Jub.* 32:1–15).[207] The Prayer of Azariah 15–17 also envisages "a contrite heart and a humble spirit" as an acceptable substitute for sacrificial offerings. However, the three men found in Daniel are simply unable to make an offering in their situation (Pr Azar 15), a situation mirrored in the lives of most of the readers who live far from the temple.[208] Rather, extenuating circumstances are in view while temple worship is practically impossible for many Jews, whether in time of exile or living in the Diaspora. The Psalms of Solomon compare praise and worship to a first-fruit offering, when it reflects "a devout and righteous heart" (*Pss. Sol.* 15:3), but may go further, in deliberately evoking the sacrifices mandated for unintentional sin in Lev 4:1–2, 27; 5:18 while replacing them with fasting and humbling, "He atones for (sins of) ignorance by fasting and humbling his soul, and the Lord will cleanse every devout person and his house" (*Pss. Sol.* 15:3).[209] Kenneth Atkinson contends that the theological perspective of the Psalms may be similar to that of the Qumran community, in believing the temple to be defiled.[210] Finally in this category, the *Liber antiquitatum biblicarum* has a particular concern with Genesis 22, and in what sense Abraham's offering of Isaac could be considered a sacrifice (*L.A.B.* 18:5; 32:2–4; 40:2). To this end, Pseudo-Philo speaks of Isaac's blood having been shed (*L.A.B.* 18:5) but later, perhaps recognizing that his body was not sacrificed, includes an utterance worthy of Philo himself (as we shall see in chapter 3), "the Lord has made the soul of a man worthy to be a sacrifice" (*L.A.B.* 32:3). Again, within the wider context of the work, there is a deep appreciation of the Temple and worship.[211]

Finally, the death of a martyr came to be seen as atoning for the people of Israel, in the same way that an animal offering could serve for

---

Jewish Temple, 73–84.

207. See also Hayward, *Jewish Temple*, 85–107, and van Ruiten, "Visions," 215–27.
208. Moore, *Daniel*, 59; Horst and Newman, *Early Jewish Prayers*, 210.
209. Atkinson, *Intertextual Study*, 61–63.
210. Atkinson, *Intertextual Study*, 216.
211. Cf. Hayward, *Jewish Temple*, 154–67; though possibly some ambiguity in its appreciation of the temple cult of his day, see Vogel, "Tempel," 251–63.

the nation (e.g., Lev 16). This is particularly prominent in 4 Maccabees when Elezear prays on behalf of himself and those martyred before him, "let our punishment be a satisfaction on their behalf. Make my blood their purification and take my life as a ransom for theirs" (4 Macc 6:28–29). This prayer is seen as fulfilled by the writer later in the book, "they became, as it were, a ransom for the sin of our nation. Through the blood of these righteous ones and through the propitiation of their death the divine providence rescued Israel, which had been shamefully treated" (4 Macc 17:21–22).[212] It is also possible to see the Prayer of Azariah (Pr Azar 15–17), mentioned above, as referring not simply to the prayer itself as an offering, but to the young mens' willingness to die a sacrificial death out of a desire to atone for the people.[213] In summary, writings from the Pseudepigrapha and Apocrypha place a righteous disposition and behaviors above sacrifices, while still expecting that sacrifices should be performed; some works allow for substitutes for sacrifices, such as purity, praise or almsgiving, while not abandoning the belief in the sacrificial system. Some writings consider the death of a martyr to have an atoning efficacy on behalf of the nation.

My findings indicate that figurative temple language is not pervasive in intertestamental literature, save for a number of places in the Dead Sea Scrolls, though the Scrolls are unlikely to have been known to the audience in Corinth.[214]

1.4 THE OBJECT OF THIS BOOK

There is thus something of a lacuna in the literature, with little comprehensive study of the most relevant sources of figurative temple language that could have influenced the Corinthians' thinking; namely philosophical ideas. My aim is not to claim that Hellenistic philosophy is Paul's own background as the author, nor to claim that it provides the sole background for the Corinthians' own thinking on the topic (which might also include their experience of local idol temples as well as Paul's

---

212. For the theology of atonement by martyrs on behalf of the people in 4 Maccabees, see further deSilva, *4 Maccabees*, 137–41.

213. This is the position of Collins, *Daniel*, 201. This may also be how Wis 3:6 reflects on the souls of the righteous as a "sacrificial burnt offering."

214. Certainly, Paul assumes that they recognize the referent of Βελιάρ (2 Cor 6:15), a word that occurs repeatedly in the Dead Sea Scrolls, but the same word is also used in other Jewish literature, especially in the Pseudepigrapha.

own teaching). Rather I aver that Hellenistic philosophy is *one* important context for the audience, which has frequently been neglected, and which Paul may seek to address.[215] The object of this book is to examine the use of figurative temple language in the most relevant Hellenistic philosophical writings in order to understand how they are using this imagery, to what purpose and within what worldview and to compare this with what Paul is doing with such language in 1–2 Corinthians. The benefits of this study are twofold. Firstly, light can be shed on the way that the kinds of philosophical thought known in cities like Corinth may have influenced the Corinthians to think about figurative temple language. Secondly, a better understanding of the way that other philosophies used such language will throw into sharp relief the similarities and differences between Paul's use and theirs and the different worldview that Paul was seeking to communicate to an audience whose thinking and behavior often resembled that of pagans (1 Cor 4:8–21; 5:1; 6:1–6; cf. 1 Cor 3:1).

1.5 THE METHODOLOGY AND PLAN OF THE BOOK

An inductive study will be undertaken of relevant Hellenistic authors in order to discover how figurative temple language was used in Hellenistic philosophy. The parameters for this study cannot be set by searches of relevant words such as ναός, θυσία, or ἱερεύς. Firstly, these words are primarily used for literal sacrifices and appear very commonly in ancient literature. Secondly, writers can speak of the concept of a temple without using these particular words or other technical temple vocabulary.[216] Although Palestinian Jewish works will not be ignored altogether, the focus will be on those writing Hellenistic philosophy in Greek or Latin and, in particular, to those closest to the period in which Paul wrote. Obvious examples of this will include (but not be confined to) those already referenced by Ferguson and McKelvey, such as Epictetus, Plutarch, Seneca, and Apollonius of Tyana, all of whom use figurative temple language.[217]

---

215. This is not to suggest that the Corinthians had read this or that work of philosophy, but rather that philosophical ideas common to Stoicism and other philosophies could trickle down to influence the ordinary person, as discussed at the beginning of this chapter.

216. For instance, the often-cited example from Epictetus, *Diatr.* 2.8.11–13 contains none of these words.

217. While noting that the latter needs to be used with caution, since our source for his writings, Philostratus, probably completed his work in the early third century.

These non-Jewish Hellenistic philosophical writers will be examined in chapter 2. In addition, chapter 3 will survey the corpus of Philo of Alexandria (ca. 20 BCE—50 CE). Although Philo is a Jewish writer, he too is writing to a Diaspora audience and drawing on the philosophical tradition when speaking to a Hellenistic readership about wisdom (cf. Paul's appropriation of wisdom language in 1 Cor 1:18–2:16).[218] Philo's work also contains a considerable number of references to sacrifices, priests and temples used figuratively.[219] For Philo, the contextualization of Judaism in a Hellenistic environment lies at the heart of his work. Peder Borgen summarizes the views of many scholars when he writes, "Philo continues the approach seen especially in the Letter of Aristeas, in Aristobulus, and the Wisdom of Solomon to interpret the Laws of Moses and Jewish existence by means of Greek ideas and religious traditions."[220] Furthermore, Philo drew from the traditions of Stoicism, Middle Platonism and the Pythagoreans,[221] and as such, is one of our best sources for understanding Hellenistic philosophy, given his very sizeable corpus.

The study will thus be a comparative one. The insights gained from studying figurative temple language in the wider literary context of Hellenistic philosophers will be compared to Paul's deliberate use of figurative temple language when writing to an audience influenced by Greek and Roman philosophical and ethical thought in the life of Corinth. This comparison will illuminate Paul's setting of this language in the wider framework of 1–2 Corinthians and the purpose for its use in the argument of the letters. Although I am using a heuristic approach to ancient philosophers by looking for concepts, rather than restricting my survey to certain wording, in chapters 4 and 5 I will limit myself to the places where the language of temple is explicit. Thus, chapter 4 will explore the place of 1 Cor 3:16–17 and 1 Cor 6:19 in relation to philosophy, and in order to provide a focus for the study, one pericope, 2 Cor 6:14—7:1, will

---

Nevertheless, Apollonius lived in the first century and some of Philostratus's material may reflect the earlier thought of Apollonius himself.

218. For scholars who have drawn on Philo and the Jewish wisdom tradition generally when discussing 1 Corinthians, see, e.g., Pearson, *Pneumatikos*, and especially the various essays in Horsley, *Wisdom*.

219. See for instance, the studies of Nikiprowetzky, "Spiritualisation," 97–116; Werman, "God's House," 309–22; Lieber, "Between Motherland," 193–210; and Leonhardt, *Jewish Worship*.

220. Borgen, *Philo*, 43.

221. Borgen, "Philo," 256.

be given special attention in chapter 5.²²² Whereas 1 Cor 3:16 appears in a discussion concerning ministry within the church, and 1 Cor 6:19 relates to the issue of prostitution and the physical body, 2 Cor 6:14—7:1 is set in a cultic context and explicitly challenges the Corinthians over their pagan associations and worldview. Thus, it is a particularly appropriate passage on which to concentrate. Although many scholars have held the pericope to be a non-Pauline interpolation, a growing number of modern studies as well as the two most recent major critical commentaries have defended its place within the original letter.²²³ Finally, chapter 6 will summarize and evaluate my findings and suggest some paths for future research.

---

222. Each of these three references is categorized as a "certain" cultic metaphor according to Gupta, *Worship*, 65–67, 73–75, 96–102.

223. A sample would include: Thrall, *2 Corinthians 1–7*, 25–36; Harris, *Second Epistle*, 15, 21–25; Adewuya, *Holiness*, 25–29; Hogeterp, *Paul and God's Temple*, 365–73; Long, *Ancient Rhetoric*, 168–72.

2

Figurative Temple Language in Hellenistic Philosophy

2.1 INTRODUCTION

IN THIS CHAPTER I shall explore the use of figurative temple language in Hellenistic philosophy. Before I begin, a few preliminary remarks are in order. Firstly, I shall not attempt to document the reporting of descriptions or attitudes toward actual temple worship in these or any other sources (in other words, temple language associated with humanly constructed buildings); my more limited aim is to investigate figurative temple language, just as Paul speaks of temple imagery figuratively in 1 Cor 3:16; 6:19 and 2 Cor 6:16.[1] To do otherwise would broaden the scope of enquiry beyond manageable proportions, and evidence for temple worship in relation to 1–2 Corinthians has been adequately surveyed in other studies.[2] Similarly, the question of the imperial cult (another focus of much attention currently) will not be my interest, though I shall note

---

1. With the respective caveats laid out in chapter 1: that I shall be examining only Paul's *explicit* use of figurative temple language, while here surveying a broader use of figurative temple language *conceptually* in the philosophers. On the question of metaphor itself in relation to cultic imagery, see the methodology laid out in Gupta, *Worship*, 27–51.

2. For instance, more recently in Liu, *Temple Purity*; Wardle, *Jerusalem Temple*, and in earlier studies, such as Willis, *Idol Meat*; and Gooch, *Dangerous Food*.

Figurative Temple Language in Hellenistic Philosophy 43

along the way references to the divinity of particular emperors. Thirdly, as mentioned at the end of the first chapter, the discussion of figurative temple language is not always focused on the use of particular words, since, as we shall see, writers frequently express the concept through common vocabulary that is not specific to temple worship, such as οἶκος or words for indwelling (and in any case, I shall be surveying a number of Latin works, whereas Paul is writing in Greek).³ In this regard, the number of references found that specifically use the language of temple (such as ναός, ἱερόν or οἶκος) are relatively few. However, Hellenistic writers frequently use the imagery of God, the gods, or a δαίμων dwelling in or filling the universe or the individual. Since a number of them do so within the wider context of describing the world or the individual as a temple in their writings (even though not necessarily in the immediate literary context), and since Paul uses the language of indwelling in the references which are the focus of my study (οἰκέω in 1 Cor 3:16; ἐν ὑμῖν in 1 Cor 6:19 and ἐνοικέω in 2 Cor 6:16), I have deemed it legitimate to explore the imagery of the indwelling God/s when explicit temple language is not always in view. Finally, I shall limit my research to the sources more directly relevant to Paul's period, beginning with the schools that marked the start of the Hellenistic era and continued at least into the first century (such as Stoicism and Epicureanism) and ending with works no later than the early third century CE (other than those that report on earlier eras) that show a strong degree of continuity with first century works of the same philosophical tradition.⁴

2.1.1 Philosophy

Firstly, I shall briefly lay out some evidence from the primary sources that demonstrate the central importance that philosophy played in shaping

---

3. A sampling of particularly relevant words can be found, for instance, in Louw and Nida, *Greek-English Lexicon*, citing words relating to sacrifice such as θυσία, σφάγιον, ἱερόθυτος, κορβᾶν, ἀπαρχή, ὁλοκαύτωμα, θυμιάω; θυμίαμα and σπένδω, (53.16–27); words relating to temple such as οἶκος (7.2), ναός, ἱερόν, σκηνή, and ἅγιον (7.15–18); or words relating to priest, such as ἱερουργέω, ἱερατεύω, ἱερατεία, ἱεράτευμα, ἱερωσύνη, and ἱερεύς. (53.85–87).

4. For a survey of Hellenistic philosophy, see e.g., *OCD*, 657–58; Ferguson, *Backgrounds*, 319–95; Long, *Hellenistic Philosophy*; Sharples, *Stoics*; Brunschwig and Sedley, "Hellenistic Philosophy," 151–83; Algra et al., *Cambridge History*.

worldview and behavior in the first century.[5] There could be no greater endeavor than to study and live out philosophy, according to Cicero, since, "philosophy is the richest, the most bounteous, and the most exalted gift of the immortal gods to humanity."[6] Seneca has much to say in praise of philosophy. Philosophers teach people both how to live[7] and how to die and "open to you the path to immortality." Unlike honors and statues, philosophy can never be destroyed and so the wise individual should choose to be a son of the philosophers.[8] Plutarch notes that philosophy is avoided by those sick of soul, but it is their only hope of cure.[9] Philosophy brings revelation and opens up new vistas, leading us to, "but the sight of things most beautiful that have been wrested from darkness and brought into light."[10] This light is for all.[11] By contrast, to remove the Reason that philosophy brings is likened to removing a candle and plunging the room into darkness, or removing the goatherd and scattering the flock.[12] Philosophy "enables us to understand things human and things divine,"[13] which can be summed up simply as "wisdom."[14] Philosophy holds out the promise of equality with God,[15] and is the most appropriate study for a king, who, of all people, most resembles a god, according

---

5. For the relationship between philosophy and religion, see Most, "Philosophy," 300–22. Trapp, "Role," 44, writes of philosophy in this period, "It is a comprehensive discipline, operating at the deepest level of understanding across the whole range of the real, and embracing all the most central human concerns; in our terms, it combines the authority of Science with that of Religion, and other things besides." For a survey of the relationship between certain philosophers and Corinth over time, see Barnes, *Reading*, 126–40.

6. Cicero, *Leg.* 1.22.58 (Keyes, LCL).

7. Seneca, *Ep.* 90.1.

8. Seneca, *Brev. vit.*15.4 (Basore, LCL).

9. Plutarch, *An. corp.* 501A; similarly, Cicero, *Tusc.* 3.3.5–6; 3.6.13.

10. Seneca, *Brev. vit.* 14.1 (Basore, LCL); cf. Plutarch, *Virt. prof.* 81E, who compares the person who gets "inside" philosophy to one who enters a shrine and "has seen a great light"; see also *Is. Os.* 382D, 382F and Cicero, *Tusc.* 1.26.64.

11. Seneca, *Ep.* 44.2.

12. Maximus of Tyre, *Or.* 1.3.

13. Seneca, *Ep.* 31.8 (Gummere, LCL); cf. *Ep.* 90.2–3; Maximus of Tyre, *Or.* 26.1; Diog. Laert. 1.3.63, discussing the views of Plato.

14. Seneca, *Ep.* 89.1–6 (Gummere, LCL); or a striving for wisdom, according to Alcinous, *Handbook*, 3, 152.1.2–5. Sandbach, *Stoics*, 11, sums up the ancients' understanding of philosophy as "love of wisdom."

15. Seneca, *Ep.* 48.12; 73.12. The philosopher should therefore, at the very least, be a follower of the gods (Marcus Aurelius, *Med.* 12.27).

Figurative Temple Language in Hellenistic Philosophy 45

to Dio Chrysostom.[16] According to Plutarch, those who look to states governed by such a ruler can see the light of the knowledge of his image, "which the blessed and the wise copy with the help of philosophy."[17] Musonius Rufus, moreover, asserts that the study of philosophy is commanded by Zeus.[18] Philosophy is equated with the ideal good.[19] Seneca, writing to Lucilius, urges him that whichever philosopher he may follow "we must be philosophers," as if the particular philosophy chosen is less important than the choice to follow philosophy at all.[20] In a similar vein, Seneca speaks with approval of those who learnt directly from the lives of philosophers and cites examples from a variety of schools and eras, such as Socrates, Zeno and Epicurus,[21] Pythagoras, Democritus, Aristotle and Theophrastus.[22] Like their followers, Seneca exhorts his reader to live as they lived.[23] Philosophy has unique authority and demands our complete devotion.[24] Indeed, according to Dio Chrysostom, the pursuit of virtue in character is nothing less than being a philosopher.[25] The road chosen by a philosopher will cause them to stand apart from the majority in their way of life and even in matters such as their food and clothing.[26] Yet it is the road we must take, Marcus Aurelius avers, since philosophy is the only sure guide on our journey through this transient life.[27] The philosopher will be superior to all in regard to truth and knowledge,[28] and philosophy

---

16. Dio Chrysostom, 2 *Regn.* 24, 26. A true philosopher will be like a king, in that they learn to rule well: whether it be to rule themselves or others (*Rec. mag.* 3). Marcus Aurelius, *Med.* 6.12 also notes that philosophy provides rest from the life of the court.

17. Plutarch, *Princ. iner.* 782A.

18. Musonius, *frag.* 16.104.30–32.

19. Musonius, *frag.* 8.64.37–66.1; *frag.* 16.104.36–37.

20. Seneca, *Ep.* 16.5 (Gummere, LCL). However, Dio Chrysostom warns of the dangers of those who wear only the name of philosopher and fail to improve the lives of their pupils or themselves (*Alex.* 8, 18, 20; *De philosopho* 10).

21. Seneca, *Ep.* 6.6.

22. Seneca, *Brev. vit.*14.5; Plutarch, *Alex. fort.* 327E, 328B also mentions Alexander.

23. E.g., Seneca, *Ep.* 5; 6.5–6; 7; 8.1–2, 5.

24. Seneca, *Ep.* 53.8, 9.

25. Dio Chrysostom, *Exil.* 28; Maximus of Tyre, *Or.* 26.1; 35.6–8; Cicero, *Tusc.* 3.17.36; 5.1.1.

26. Dio Chrysostom, *De philosophia* 7, 8; *De philosopho* 6. Thus many, seeing the cost of philosophy, neglect it until the necessity of philosophy cannot be avoided (Dio Chrysostom, *Compot.* 7).

27. Marcus Aurelius, *Med.* 2.17; similarly, Cicero, *Tusc.* 5.2.5.

28. Dio Chrysostom, 2 *Glor.* 1.

is superior to all other study and brought nourishment and wholeness to men such as Socrates and Plato.[29] The philosophers have a noble purpose, since they seek to win "concord and peace and community of interests" for all,[30] and equip people to live the good life, guided by justice and law, which is aided by reason.[31] Philosophy comforts those who are sad and enhances the joy of celebration.[32] Yet the role of philosophy also includes tempering the natural desires, which is compared to a horse-trainer who checks the spirit of the colt with bridle and reins.[33]

I shall survey the evidence for figurative temple language from each Hellenistic Philosopher in whose writings it has been found. This evidence will be presented by school, so far as it is possible to assign the philosopher in question to an individual school, and in approximate chronological order within that school. Separate treatment will be given to those who do not fit into an obvious category or who are summarizing their understanding of these schools from the vantage point of later centuries. In regard to each writer, Sacrifice, Priest and Temple language will be discussed separately where the respective evidence presents itself. I have also appended three additional categories to the discussion of each writer's view. In order to understand the writer's conception of God's indwelling presence, it is important to ask about the writer's understanding of divinity. Thus, where sufficient evidence is available, I consider the character of God and Gods in the writings. This then brings us to the question of how the writer understands the nature of those in whom God dwells, so the writer's doctrine of human nature will briefly be considered. Finally, since Paul's doctrine of the Temple of the Holy Spirit/ Living God had practical consequences for how the Corinthians should live their lives (1 Cor 3:16–18; 6:12–20; 2 Cor 6:14—7:1), it is important to consider what practical consequences each writer saw their doctrine having for their readers, so that we can compare the application of their doctrine with that of Paul's in later chapters.

---

29. Maximus of Tyre, *Or.* 22.6; cf. *Or.* 37.2.
30. Plutarch, *Alex. fort.* 330E (LCL, Babbitt).
31. Plutarch, *Adv. Col.* 1108C; cf. Cicero, *Tusc.* 5.7.20.
32. Maximus of Tyre, *Or.* 1.2.
33. Maximus of Tyre, *Or.* 1.8; 20.6 cf. Jas 3:2–3.

2.2 INTRODUCTION TO DIOGENES LAERTIUS

By something of an historical accident, the loss of so many primary sources for philosophy has left us dependent on the works of Diogenes Laertius, of whom we know little, including the date of his writings (though often dated to the third or fourth centuries CE because of his omission of Neoplatonism and philosophers after the second century).[34] According to the translator of the Loeb edition, R. D. Hicks, "In any given passage he is as useful and reliable as the source he happens to be quoting at that exact moment"[35] but his information is extremely valuable in the absence of so many other extant sources. Diogenes provides a history of the lives and thought of a considerable number of philosophers from the seventh century BCE through to the third century CE. As there are a number of important references in Diogenes to figurative temple language, these will be covered in relation to the individual philosopher to whose writings or conversation he attributes these views. Because I am dealing with much shorter sections than for other writers, a brief summary will be provided for each author rather than using the various categories described above.

2.2.1 Theophrastus according to Diogenes Laertius

Theophrastus (c. 370–286 BCE) was a student of Aristotle and later head of the School from 323 BCE.[36] In bequeathing his property to various friends, he expresses the view that property should not be devoted purely to private use, and so his house and gardens he gives to those desiring to study literature and philosophy, "so that they hold it like a temple (ἱερόν) in joint possession and live, as is right and proper, on terms of familiarity and friendship (οἰκείως καὶ φιλικῶς)."[37] The temple image here speaks of something shared and open to all.

---

34. Laertius, *Lives*, xvi–xix. See also *OCD*, 457. On the question of the scarcity of sources in relation to Hellenistic philosophy, see Mansfeld, "Sources," 3–30.

35. Laertius, *Lives*, xix.

36. Diog. Laert. 5.2.36 and see *OCD*, 1461.

37. Diog. Laert. 5.2.53 (Hicks, LCL).

2.3 STOICISM

2.3.1 Introduction to Stoicism

Zeno of Citium (c. 333–261 BCE) was the founder of the Stoic school in Athens.[38] Stoicism became best known through the writings of the third head of the school, Chrysippus (c. 280–207 BCE)[39] who both restated and developed the positions of his predecessors, distinguishing between logic, physics and ethics, and contending for a strongly materialist, determinist, empiricist and pantheistic view of the world, with a stringent call to live in accordance with nature, seeing virtue as the only good.[40] Stoics aimed to live by a thoroughly comprehensive and all-embracing philosophy in which "cosmic Nature embraces all that there is" so that God and Nature are equated, humans are integrated with that Nature and so must learn the nature of reality in order to live in agreement with it.[41] Stoicism was probably the dominant philosophy of the first century CE.[42]

2.3.2 Zeno according to Diogenes Laertius

Zeno has much to say about the wise man, some of which has a bearing on my topic. He uses divine indwelling language, claiming of them, "They are also, it is declared, godlike; for they have a something divine

---

38. See *OCD*, 1587–88; Sandbach, *Stoics*, 20–27; Long, *Hellenistic Philosophy*, 109–113; Kristeller, *Greek Philosophers*, 22–35; Ferguson, *Backgrounds*, 354–55; Sedley, "School," 8–20.

39. See *OCD*, 316; Long, *Hellenistic Philosophy*, 113–14; Sandbach, *Stoics*, 112–15; Rist, *Stoic Philosophy*, 22–36; Kristeller, *Greek Philosophers*, 60–86; Ferguson, *Backgrounds*, 355; Sedley, "School," 15–20; Diog. Laert. 7.7.179–202.

40. For more on Stoicism, see, e.g., *OCD*, 1403–4; Long, *Hellenistic Philosophy*, 107–209; Sandbach, *Stoics*; Rist, *Stoic Philosophy*; Inwood, *Ethics*; Colish, *Stoic Tradition*, 7–60; Reesor, *Nature of Man*; Long, *Stoic Studies*; Bobzien, *Determinism*; Inwood, *Cambridge Companion*; Ferguson, *Backgrounds*, 354–69; Brunschwig and Sedley, "Hellenistic Philosophy," 163–75; Reydams-Schils, *Roman Stoics*; Thorsteinsson, *Roman Christianity*; Wright, *Paul and the Faithfulness*, 213–18. On living in accordance with nature, see e.g., Kidd, "Stoic Intermediaries," 150–72; Sandbach, *Stoics*, 28–68; Reesor, *Nature of Man*, 83–102; Sharples, *Stoics*, 100–13; Long, *Stoic Studies*, 134–55, 179–223; Brunschwig and Sedley, "Hellenistic Philosophy," 172–75; Schofield, "Stoic Ethics," 239–53. On determinism, see, e.g., Long, "Freedom," 173–99 (arguing for a degree of moral choice within a deterministic framework); Sandbach, *Stoics*, 79–82, 101–8; Hankinson, "Determinism," 513–41.

41. Long, *Hellenistic Philosophy*, 108.

42. Sandbach, *Stoics*, 16.

Figurative Temple Language in Hellenistic Philosophy

within them" (Θείους τ' εἶναι· ἔχειν γὰρ ἐν ἑαυτοῖς οἱονεὶ θεόν).⁴³ There is a reference to priesthood which could be figurative, but perhaps has a more literal meaning, "The wise too are the only priests" (μόνους θ' ἱερέας τοὺς σοφούς).⁴⁴ This could mean that only the wise are truly priests in a figurative sense. However, given that the context speaks of the wise's study of sacrifices, temples and purity, it is more likely to relate to literal priesthood; either that only the wise priests should be recognized as priests or that priests are only appointed from among the wise. As with the Stoic writers considered below in greater detail, Zeno equates God with, "Reason, Fate, and Zeus,"⁴⁵ and the world is "a living being, endowed with soul and reason, and having aether for its ruling principle."⁴⁶ According to Chrysippus, the purer part of this aether is "preeminently God"⁴⁷ and Zeno avers that the world or universe can also be equated with God.⁴⁸ God is the Father of all and known by many names, such as Zeus, Athena, Poseidon and Demeter (so these are different names for God, rather than there being many gods).⁴⁹ Since two of the three temple references in 1–2 Corinthians employ πνεῦμα, it is of interest that for Zeno, the πνεῦμα constituted the world soul, holds the cosmos together and, "accounts for the cohesions of each individual entity."⁵⁰ For the early Stoics, the individual, "is corporeal pneuma, an aggregate of corporeal

43. Diog. Laert. 7.1.119 (Hicks, LCL).

44. Diog. Laert. 7.1.119 (Hicks, LCL).

45. Diog. Laert. 7.1.135.

46. Diog. Laert. 7.1.139 (Hicks, LCL). On the ruling part of the soul in early Stoicism, see Reesor, *Nature of Man*, 137–47.

47. Diog. Laert. 7.1.139.

48. Diog. Laert. 7.1.137. Sandbach, *Stoics*, 79, writes, "Since the world and its events are entirely determined by God, thought of as a plan, he can be identified with Nature, with Fate, and with Providence." For more on this topic, see White, "Stoic Natural Philosophy," 124–52.

49. Diog. Laert. 7.1.147. Algra, "Stoic Theology," 166, argues that Zeno "makes room for a form of polytheism," adding, "This explains why in Stoicism 'god' or 'the gods' are in many contexts interchangeable."

50. Reesor, *Nature of Man*, 4, citing *SVF*, 2.473. See generally, Reesor, *Nature of Man*, 3–4, citing *SVF*, 2.552–53, 634. Algra, "Stoic Theology," 167, speaking of *pneuma*, writes, "even their basically pantheistic conception of a *single* god could take different forms, accordingly as the monistic or the dualistic perspective was predominant." Frede, "Stoic Determinism," 185 adds, "The Stoics were pantheists in the sense that for them the entire world is permeated by the divine *pneuma* . . . (but) the divine *pneuma* is not present everywhere in the same form and does not give consciousness and reason to all things."

qualifications, a single individual quality."[51] As with his followers, Zeno believed that the end of humanity was to live in accordance with nature,[52] whose goal is virtue and to which all others things (such as strength, wealth, pleasure or poverty) are indifferent.[53]

2.3.3 Cicero's Evidence

Although Cicero was primarily a Skeptic (see below for biographical information), a number of his works provide early evidence for the views of Stoic thinkers. Since he is the earliest writer I am considering (reflecting the views of Stoicism from the first century BCE), Cicero's reporting of Stoic positions will be presented here, his reporting of other positions in the appropriate sections and his own views under the Skeptics section of this chapter.[54]

Sacrifice Language

In his work, *De Natura Deorum* (On the Nature of the Gods), Cicero articulates the views of Stoicism through the protagonist Balbus. Balbus repudiates myths about the gods, but recognizes grains of truth in some of the myths in shedding light on, "the personality and the nature of the divinities pervading the substance of the several elements" (referring to the earth and the sea, in his example).[55] Nevertheless, despite his apparent skepticism about these myths, Balbus considers it a duty to worship gods such as Ceres and Neptune "under the names which custom has bestowed upon them." However, Balbus continues, "But the best and

---

51. Reesor, *Nature of Man*, 21. Frede, "Stoic Determinism," 193, writes, "Our inner *pneuma* is indeed independent of the external circumstances and constitutes our personality." Stoic ontology only recognized bodies as "genuinely existent beings" (Brunschwig, "Stoic Metaphysics," 210).

52. Diog. Laert. 7.1.54, 87.

53. Diog. Laert. 7.1.88, 89, 93–117; for more on virtue in Stoic thought, see Long, *Hellenistic Philosophy*, 189–209; Kidd, "Stoic Intermediaries," 150–72. On pleasure in Stoic thought, see Rist, *Stoic Philosophy*, 37–53. For the early Stoic school, see Reesor, *Nature of Man*; Sedley, "School," 7–32.

54. On Cicero in relation to Stoicism, see Colish, *Stoic Tradition*, 61–79, 104–58, and Powell, "Introduction," 23–26. For a synopsis of each of Cicero's philosophical works and their sources, see MacKendrick, *Philosophical Books*.

55. Cicero, *Nat. d.* 2.28.71 (Rackham, LCL).

Figurative Temple Language in Hellenistic Philosophy 51

also the purest, holiest and most pious (castissimus atque sanctissimus plenissimusque pietatis) way of worshipping the gods is ever to venerate them with purity, sincerity and innocence both of thought and of speech."[56] The true way of worship is internal (thought), expressed in the external: speech, without mentioning sacrifices. Balbus distinguishes between religion and superstition (following other philosophers) and seems to identify superstition with sacrifices, while clearly siding with religion.[57]

The Nature of Divinity

Cicero cites Chrysippus (the third head of the Stoic school in the third century BCE, so one of our earlier sources for Stoicism)[58] as believing that, "divine power resides in reason, and in the soul and mind of the universe; he calls the world itself a god, and also the all-pervading world-soul, and again the guiding principle of that soul, which operates in the intellect and reason, and the common and all-embracing nature of things."[59] As we shall see, these beliefs are echoed in later Stoic works; the idea of the world soul, the divine soul which permeates intellect and reason and the identification of the world with divinity, such that all things are connected.[60] For Chrysippus, god is an inference from the superiority of humanity to all other created things, and thus to a creative mind which is superior to it.[61] In the Stoic theology that Balbus expounds, Nature governs and sustains the world[62] and the gods, who exist in community,[63] govern all things by divine providence,[64] exercising great care toward all.[65] We also learn from Cicero that Stoicism understands God to be the one who cares for the safety of all humanity, as indicated by the titles given

56. *Nat. d.* 2.28.71 (Rackham, LCL).
57. *Nat. d.* 2.28.72.
58. See *OCD*, 316.
59. *Nat. d.* 1.15.39 (Rackham, LCL). Sandbach, *Stoics*, 73, says of Stoic theology in relation to this passage, "The mistake lies in supposing that the word 'God' always denotes the same thing.... Stoics could call the whole world 'God'... no less than the immanent force that gave it all its character."
60. See also *Nat. d.* 2.11.30; 2.14.37—2.15.39.
61. *Nat. d.* 2.6.16.
62. *Nat. d.* 2.32.78.
63. *Nat. d.* 2.31.78.
64. *Nat. d.* 2.29.73—2.30.77.
65. *Nat. d.* 2.65.164—2.66.166.

to him, "Most Good and Most Great, of Saviour, Lord of Guests, Rallier of Battles."[66]

Living Out the Philosophy

In the third book of *De Finibus Bonorum et Malorum*, Cicero presents the Stoic view that Virtue or Moral Worth is the only thing of value, to which all else is the means. Other things are indifferent, goodness is absolute and allows of no degrees, and the moral life is thus the only happy life.[67] M. R. Wright details the way that Cicero develops Stoic ethics in *De Finibus* in terms of life stages, with a movement from self-love to a love that potentially reaches out to all of humanity.[68]

2.3.4 Arius Didymus

Little is known of the life of Arius Didymus, but he is presumed to be the author of a work providing a short epitome of Stoic Ethics, and to have lived in the latter half of the first century CE.[69] Because his writing is so brief, I will summarize the main points of interest without employing my usual categories. Arius concurs with later Stoic writers that only the wise man can be a prophet or a priest.[70] In addition to the priest's knowledge of ritual and his experience in the service of the gods, he must also "be inside the divine nature."[71] This tantalizing statement is not expanded upon. Certainly, Arius contrasts the piety of the worthwhile man with the impiety and impurity of the worthless throughout his work.[72] Only the worthwhile man can prophesy and perform service for the gods.[73]

---

66. *Fin.* 3.20.66 (Rackham, LCL); see also Frede, "On the Stoic," 70–74.

67. *Fin.* 3.1.2; 3.3.10–11; 3.6.21; 3.7.25–26; 3.8.28; 3.10.34; 3.14.45–48; 3.15.48–50. For more on Cicero's understanding of this topic see Rist, *Stoic Philosophy*, 97–102 and generally, Frede, "On the Stoic," 71–94.

68. Wright, "Cicero," 171–95.

69. Pomeroy, *Arius*, 1–3; *OCD*, 164. For a more substantial treatment, see Long, *Stoic Studies*, 107–33.

70. Pomeroy, *Arius*, 5b12, 28–29 (25); 5b12, 4–5 (26).

71. Pomeroy, *Arius*, 5b12, 10–11 (26).

72. Pomeroy, *Arius*, 5b, 5–21 (26); 11k, 4–14, 18–20, 26–29 (84).

73. Pomeroy, *Arius*, 11s, 16–19 (98).

2.3.5 Seneca

Lucius Annaeus Seneca (Seneca the Younger) was born somewhere between 4 BCE and 1 CE and died in 65 CE. He was well known in his day as an orator, and had a significant involvement in public life, acting initially as tutor and later as political adviser and minister to the emperor Nero.[74] Seneca produced a very large body of work, but in my survey I shall confine myself to the study of those works that deal specifically with philosophy, that includes his letters. Seneca identifies himself as a Stoic in his writings,[75] and considers the Stoic school to be superior to any other.[76]

Sacrifice Language

Seneca stresses the intent of the worshipper in offering sacrifice; the object itself is considered indifferent, "It is the intention that exalts small gifts, gives lustre to those that are mean, and discredits those that are great and considered of value; the things themselves that men desire have a neutral nature, which is neither good nor evil."[77] This intent is concerned with the piety of the worshipper over the quality of the sacrifice itself in material terms, "the honour that is paid to the gods lies, not in the victims for sacrifice, though they be fat and glitter with gold, but in the upright and holy desire of the worshippers (recta ac pia voluntate venerantium). Good men, therefore, are pleasing to the gods with an offering of meal and gruel; the bad, on the other hand, do not escape impiety although they dye the altars with streams of blood."[78] Seneca internalizes this imagery still further when speaking of worshipping a vision of virtue in a good man's soul. In this discussion, it would appear that material

---

74. *OCD*, 92–95; Sandbach, *Stoics*, 149–62. For a recent biography of Seneca, see Veyne, *Seneca*; the main section of the book (31–155) relates Seneca's life to his Stoicism.

75. E.g., Seneca, *Ben.* 4.2.1; *Nat.* 3.9.1; 3.13.1; 3.22.1; and cf. his references to "our Stoics" (*Nat.* 7.19.1; 7.20.1; 7.21.1); though sometimes disagreeing with them (*Nat.* 7.22.1). Scholars divide the history of Stoicism into Early Stoicism (Zeno-Antipater), Middle Stoicism (Panaetius and Posidonius), and Late Stoicism, and it is the latter on whose writings we almost entirely depend (as represented by Seneca, Epictetus, and others); see Long, *Hellenistic Philosophy*, 115, and especially Gill, "School," 32–58.

76. Seneca, *Clem.* 2.4.2–3. For further studies, see, e.g., Thorsteinsson, *Roman Christianity*, 22–27; Long, "Roman," 203–6; Wright, *Paul and the Faithfulness*, 219–22.

77. Seneca, *Ben.* 1.6.2 (Basore, LCL).

78. *Ben.* 1.6.3 (Basore, LCL).

objects of worship are not involved at all; rather, the sacrifice consists of a pure will, "this worship does not consist in slaughtering fattened bulls, or in hanging up offerings of gold or silver, or in pouring coins into a temple treasury; rather does it consist in a will that is reverent and upright" (pia et recta voluntate).[79] In Seneca's ninety-fifth epistle, although the language of sacrifice is not used, true and sufficient worship is described as imitating the gods (rather than by sacrifice).[80] This worship is explicated as knowing and believing in the gods.[81]

Priest Language

There is scant reference to priestly language in Seneca. The clearest is the brief allusion to "Zeno, Pythagoras, Democritus, and all the other high priests of liberal studies,"[82] which is not directly relevant to my topic.

Temple Language

Seneca explicitly uses figurative temple language on two occasions. In his work *De Beneficiis*, Seneca distinguishes between the whole of creation, which belongs to the gods, and the things of religion which have been expressly consecrated to the gods. Thus, "the whole world (mundus) is the temple of the gods" but sacrilege is committed expressly, "in the nook to which has been assigned the name of a sanctuary"[83] (*fani* from *fanum*), that is, an earthy temple or sanctuary. Similarly, Seneca speaks of "the vast temple of all the gods—the universe (mundus) itself."[84] However, though the *word* for temple may be used rarely in a figurative sense, the

---

79. *Ep.* 115.5 (Gummere, LCL).

80. *Ep.* 95.50.

81. *Ep.* 95.47–48.

82. *Brev. vit.* 14.5 (Basore, LCL). Additionally, the phrase, "Let us, I beseech you, be silent in the presence of this proposition, and with impartial minds and ears give heed" (*Const.* 9.4) is described by translator John W. Basore as "priestly" language in Latin (Faveamus, obsecro vos, huic proposito aequisque et animis et auribus adsimus), commenting, "That the wise man can suffer no wrong is presented as a sort of divine utterance which is to be received in solemn silence" (76 n. a).

83. *Ben.* 7.7.3 (Basore, LCL).

84. *Ep.* 90.29 (Gummere, LCL). The Latin word used is "templum" in both cases. Although Basore translates the first example "world" and Gummere the second example "universe," it is in fact the same word: mundus.

concept of the indwelling God or gods appears frequently (cf. 1 Cor 3:16; 2 Cor 6:16). Firstly, Seneca speaks often of God pervading all things, to the extent that it is difficult to distinguish between God and the universe, "What is god? The mind of the universe. What is god? All that you see, all that you do not see. In short, only if he alone is all things, if he maintains his own work both from within and without, is he given due credit for his magnitude."[85] God is also described as mind and reason in its most complete form.[86] In his *De Vita Beata*, Seneca seems to equate God with the universe, referring to him as "the all-embracing world and the ruler of the universe."[87] In fact, terms such as God (*deus*), Nature (*natura*), Reason (*ratio*), Fate (*fatum*), Fortune (*fortuna*), Providence (*providentia*) and the Universe (*mundus*) can be used interchangeably in Seneca's writings. In one place Seneca asks, "For what else is Nature but God and the Divine Reason that pervades the whole universe and all its parts?"[88] and in addition, "If likewise you should call him Fate, it would be no falsehood."[89] This is because of the pantheistic nature of Stoic doctrine, "In whatever direction you turn . . . there is no Nature without God, nor God without Nature, but both are the same thing, they differ only in their function"[90] and, "So, if you like, speak of Nature, Fate, Fortune, but all these are names of the same God."[91] Earlier in the same work, Seneca speaks of complaints

---

85. *Nat.* Preface.1.13 (Corcoran, LCL).

86. *Nat.* Preface.1.14. Algra, "Stoic Theology," 167 avers that rather than being a Platonizing intrusion, this belongs to a strand "that had been present in orthodox Stoicism all along."

87. *Vit. beat.* 8.4 (Basore, LCL).

88. *Ben.* 4.7.1 (Basore, LCL). Aetius, the first-second century BCE philosopher speaks of the Stoic view of God as "a designing fire," "a breath pervading the whole world," see Aetius 1.7.33 (*SVF* 2.1027, part), translation from Long, *Philosopher*, 1:46A, 276. Alexander of Aphrodisias, a philosopher from c. 200 CE, refers to the Stoic view of God, "They say that god is mixed with matter, pervading all of it and so shaping it, structuring it, and making it into the world" (Alexander, *On mixture* 225, 1–2 (*SVF* 2.3.10, part), translation from Long, *Philosophers*, 1:45H, 273. Similarly, Sextus Empiricus, a third century CE writer, also discusses the Stoic view of God, "it is probable that this is nothing else than some power which pervades it, even as our soul pervades ourselves" (*Math.* 1.75 (Bury, LCL)).

89. *Ben.* 4.7.2 (Basore, LCL).

90. *Ben.* 4.8.2 (Basore, LCL).

91. *Ben.* 4.8.3 (Basore, LCL). Long, *Hellenistic Philosophy*, 168, speaks of "Uncreated and imperishable Nature, God, *pneuma* or universal *logos*." See also Lapidge, "Stoic Cosmology," 1399–1400 on the *spiritus* that permeates and penetrates all things in, e.g., Seneca, *Nat.* 2.6.5; 6.16.1; 3.29.2; *Helv.* 8.3.

against nature and the gods and contrasts them with the gifts of nature and the gods which merit gratitude. In these lines, 'nature' and 'the gods' are spoken of in parallel as if they are synonyms.[92] In the same manner, in *Naturales Quaestiones*, Seneca says of the supreme God, Jupiter, "Any name for him is suitable. You wish to call him Fate? You will not be wrong. It is he on whom all things depend, the cause of causes. You wish to call him Providence? You will still be right"[93] and further, "You wish to call him Nature? You will not be mistaken. It is he from whom all things are naturally born, and we have life from his breath. You wish to call him the Universe? You will not be wrong. He himself is all that you see, infused throughout all his parts, sustaining both himself and his own."[94]

Specifically, Seneca speaks of God or a divine spirit dwelling in a person. In one key epistle, Seneca explicitly contrasts the proximity and intimacy available with God by his indwelling holy spirit with his accessibility in an idol's temple. By claiming that "We do not need ... to beg the keeper of a temple to let us approach his idol's ear, as if in this way our prayers were more likely to be heard,"[95] Seneca, though not speaking of indwelling using the vocabulary of a temple, indicates that God's presence in a person is equal or even superior to what might be available in a temple, "God is near you, he is with you, he is within you ... a holy spirit indwells within us (sacer intra nos spiritus sedet) ... in each good man "A god doth dwell, but what god know we not.""" (Quis deus incertum est, habitat deus)[96] In another epistle, Seneca speaks of an upright soul as "a god dwelling as a guest in a human body."[97] In a further epistle, Seneca writes of reason in much the same way as he has done of God and the soul, "Reason, however, is nothing else than a portion of the divine spirit (pars divini spiritus) set in a human body."[98] Elsewhere he writes, "God comes to men; nay, he comes nearer,—he comes into men. No mind that has not God, is good ... Divine seeds are scattered throughout our mortal bodies" but it is up to the individual to choose whether to receive and

---

92. *Ben.* 2.29.1-6; cf. also *Marc.* 17.6-7; *Nat.* 5.18.5, 13-15 for a similar phenomenon.

93. *Nat.* 2.45.1-2 (Corcoran, LCL).

94. *Nat.* 2.45.2-3 (Corcoran, LCL); and see *Ben.* 6.23.5 for Nature spoken of as creator, and "Fortune" spoken of in the same terms used earlier for "God" in *Prov.* 4.5-12.

95. *Ep.* 41.1 (Gummere, LCL).

96. *Ep.* 41.2 (Gummere, LCL). The final quotation is taken from Virgil, *Aen.* 8.352.

97. *Ep.* 31.2 (Gummere, LCL).

98. *Ep.* 66.12 (Gummere, LCL).

tend the seed, for it is possible to kill off the seed, causing tares to grow where there might have been wheat.[99] While Seneca says that the Stoics appropriated from their ancestors the idea of a Genius in every person,[100] he personally stresses the presence of God in the upright man. Into the perfect soul a part of God is poured out,[101] for a wise man's soul ought to be the proper dwelling place for a God[102] and this being so, he asks, "why should you not believe that something of divinity exists in one who is a part of God? All this universe which encompasses us is one, and it is God; we are associates of God; we are his members."[103] God can come even into the "very midst" of a person's thoughts.[104] Thus it is possible for the mind to commune with the gods,[105] since the mind is "kindred to the gods"[106] and can enjoy "the noblest spectacle of things divine."[107] To take pleasure in the virtues is to take pleasure in the mind of God himself.[108]

The Nature of Divinity

Because of Seneca's pantheism, at times he seems almost agnostic about the character of God, when he refers to, "the great creator of the universe, *whoever he may be* (quisquis formator universi fuit), whether an all-powerful God, or incorporeal Reason contriving vast works, or divine Spirit pervading all things from the smallest to the greatest with uniform energy, or Fate and an unalterable sequence of causes clinging one to the other . . ."[109] However, Seneca may be conceding various possibilities to avoid alienating his audience, since the exact nature of God is not

---

99. *Ep.* 73.16 (Gummere, LCL); cf. Matt 13:24–30. This theme also appears in *Ben.* 4.6.6, where Seneca speaks of the "seeds" of every provision of God: "In us are implanted the seeds of all ages."

100. *Ep.* 110.2.

101. *Ep.* 120.14.

102. *Ep.* 92.3.

103. *Ep.* 92.30 (Gummere, LCL).

104. *Ep.* 83.1 (Gummere, LCL); and a similar phenomenon can occur when theophanies are received in nature, cf. 41.2–4.

105. *Ben.* 6.23.6.

106. *Helv.* 11.7 (Basore, LCL); cf. also *Ep.* 124. 23.

107. *Helv.* 20.2 (Basore, LCL). On Stoic psychology, see Long, "Stoic Psychology," 560–84.

108. *Ben.* 4.8.3.

109. *Helv.* 8.3 (Basore, LCL).

germane to his argument. Certainly, Seneca emphasizes that the ways of God are mysterious, "they both fill and elude our vision. Either their subtlety is greater than the human eye-sight is able to follow or such a great majesty conceals itself in too holy a seclusion" and consequently, "the greatest part of the universe, god, remains hidden."[110] In other places, however, Seneca alludes to the character of the gods.[111] In *De Ira*, Seneca describes the gods as "by nature mild and gentle, as incapable of injuring others as of injuring themselves."[112] In *De Clementia*, he speaks of their kindness by which all, both good and evil, without consideration of their relative merits, are brought forth into the light (presumably a reference to their creation, since it includes those who are evil).[113] Later in the same work, Seneca's guidelines for the model prince assumes that the gods are merciful and forgiving,[114] and in the next paragraph describes them as "merciful and just."[115] In the same vein, the gods send providential blessings like sun, rain, wind and nutrients for the soil upon both the grateful and ungrateful, without thought for the gods' own self-interest.[116] Nevertheless, as we shall see below, a special relationship exists between the gods and the upright, for the gods "are ever best to those who are best."[117] Seneca's sixty fifth epistle cites Plato with approval in affirming God's goodness[118] and adds that while all things are made up of matter and of God, God is more powerful than matter and controls it.[119] Yet, despite this being so, the supreme God submits himself to the same Fate which binds people and gods, "although the great creator and ruler of the universe himself wrote the decrees of Fate, yet he follows them."[120]

110. *Nat.* 7.30.4 (Corcoran, LCL).

111. For the purposes of my study, my attention will not be focused on the imperial cult, but Seneca refers to the divinity of Caesar in, e.g., *Clem.* 1.1.2–6; 1.5.1, 7; 1.14.2; *Polyb.* 12.3, 5; 13.1, 3; 14.1–2; 15.3–4; *Marc.* 14.1–2; *Tranq.* 14.9; *Brev. vit.* 4.2, 5.

112. *Ira* 2.27.1 (Basore, LCL).

113. *Clem.* 1.5.7.

114. *Clem.* 1.7.1.

115. *Clem.* 1.7.2 (Basore, LCL).

116. *Ben.* 4.25.1; 4.26.1–3; 4.28.1, 3; cf. Matt 5:45.

117. *Prov.* 1.5 (Basore, LCL).

118. *Ep.* 65.10. For the integration of Platonism with Middle Stoicism, see Sedley, "School," 20–24.

119. *Ep.* 65.23. See further, Sandbach, *Stoics*, 73–75.

120. *Prov.* 5.9. (Basore, LCL); cf. *Nat.* 3. Preface.12 (Corcoran, LCL), which asserts that "all things happen in accordance with a decree of god." For more on the Stoic conception of divinity, see Algra, "Stoic Theology," 153–78. For Stoic understandings

The Nature of Humanity

Unlike the apostle Paul, Seneca does not consider humanity to be inherently sinful by nature but holds rather "that his natural bent is good,"[121] while recognizing, like Paul, "We have all sinned."[122] Seneca infers the existence of God since, like Paul, he recognizes that a conception of God has been granted to each individual, "there is implanted in everyone an idea concerning deity."[123] Moreover, the human mind itself has the divine not merely as its source, but also as its essence, since it "has been formed from the self-same elements as these divine beings."[124] Like Stoic teaching in general, Seneca has much to say about the soul.[125] The soul is the "peculiar property" of people, where reason is brought to perfection, and this distinguishes them from other creatures.[126] The soul is pre-existent,[127] is preserved by God,[128] and so there are no limits set upon it, "except those which can be shared even by the gods."[129] This same soul comes from above to grant a person a "nearer knowledge of divinity."[130]

Living Out the Philosophy

In common with other Stoic writers, Seneca urges those who recognize the truth of his doctrine to to make it their goal to, "live according to Nature, and to follow the example of the gods."[131] Yet, unlike the gods, who, as we have seen, shower their blessings on both the just and the unjust, the Stoic cannot do good to a bad man.[132] Those who direct their

---

of Providence, see Frede, "Stoic Determinism," 179–205.

121. *Ira* 2.15.3 (Basore, LCL) cf. Rom 3:9; 5:12–21; 6:6, 17, 20; 8:2; Gal 3:22.

122. *Clem.* 1.6.3 (Basore, LCL); cf. Rom 3:23.

123. *Ep.* 117.6 (Gummere, LCL); cf. Rom 1:19–20.

124. *Helv.* 6.8 (Basore, LCL).

125. See, e.g., Long, *Hellenistic Philosophy*, 170–78; cf. Sandbach, *Stoics*, 82–85, on Stoic teaching on the soul.

126. *Ep.* 41.8 (Gummere, LCL).

127. *Ep.* 44.5 (Gummere, LCL).

128. *Ep.* 57.7–9; 58.27–28 (Gummere, LCL).

129. *Ep.* 102.21 (Gummere, LCL).

130. *Ep.* 41.5 (Gummere, LCL).

131. *Ben.* 4.25.1 (Basore, LCL); cf. *De otio.* 5.8; *Vit. beat.* 3.3; 8.1.

132. *Ben.* 5.12.3.

thoughts "on high" are able to commune with the gods,[133] and can be delivered from fear of people, God and death, so as to dedicate themselves to virtue.[134] This is the freedom from (mental disturbance)[135] which is extolled by so many Stoic writers.[136] The good person's response to the gods should be "goodwill" (in gratitude)[137] and virtue, which brings about friendship with the gods.[138] The person of virtue is to be an imitator of God.[139] This virtue is sufficient for happiness regardless of circumstances, and promises "mighty privileges and equal to the divine," to the end that "you may body forth God" (deum effingas).[140] God sends trials and adversities as a way of training the good person in virtue, commenting in a manner strikingly reminiscent of NT teaching, "God hardens, reviews, and disciplines those whom he approves, whom he loves."[141] Therefore, the good person is simply to offer themselves willingly, not begrudgingly, to whatever occurs,[142] and in this way to despise pleasure and overcoming all obstacles, ascend to the highest peak.[143] They do so by means of reason.[144] Yet while fate is unchangeable,[145] in a mysterious way some of fate's actions can come about in response to prayer and sacrifice.[146] The person who grasps these truths and lives them out is the Stoic "wise man" who bears a striking resemblance to the gods in almost every respect, "the wise man is next-door neighbour to the gods and like a god in all save

---

133. *Ben.* 6.23.6; cf. Col 3:1–2.

134. *Ben.* 7.1.7; 7.2.4; cf. also *Ep.* 74.17–18 on freedom from fear of death and gods.

135. *Ben.* 7.2.3; cf. *Ira* 3.6.1; and Seneca's entire treatise, *De tranquillitate animi.*

136. See, e.g., Long, *Hellenistic Philosophy*, 206–7.

137. *Ben.* 7.15.4.

138. *Prov.* 1.5; cf. *Ep.* 31.9.

139. *Vit. beat.* 15.6; *Ep.* 95.50. Virtue needs a guide or director according to *Nat.* 3.30.8.

140. *Vit. beat.* 16.1–2; since all that is not directly related to virtue is neither good nor evil in itself, cf. *Prov.* 5.1. On the Stoic notion that "All sins are equal" see the chapter with that title in Rist, *Stoic Philosophy*, 81–96.

141. *Prov.* 4.7 (cf. Heb 12:5–6) and cf. also *Prov.* 1.5–7; 2.1–9; 3.1, 3.

142. *Prov.* 5.8; cf. *Ep.* 107.12.

143. *Const.* 1.1; 2.1

144. *Ep.* 74.20.

145. *Nat.* 2.36.1.

146. *Nat.* 2.37.2; though Seneca notes the futility of prayer to change the length of a person's life in *Marc.* 21.5–6.

his mortality."[147] The soul who holds its ties to earth and the body loosely enjoys a blessed release and a speedy journey to the gods,[148] finally rewarded by a washing away of all impurity and a serene apprehension of the divine, "There eternal peace awaits it when it has passed from earth's dull motley to the vision of all that is pure and bright."[149] This heavenly journey to its source can be attained when the soul casts off sin and, "in purity and lightness, has leaped up into celestial realms of thought."[150] Therefore, to attain that state the righteous person must be aware of God's judgment of his works,[151] and judge themselves on their own progress in virtue.[152] The wise person, thus, should pray and live openly before God, seeking to hide nothing.[153]

2.3.6 Dio Chrysostom

Dio Chrysostom (c. 40/50–110/120 CE) enjoyed a varied career as an orator, public intellectual and writer.[154] His reference to the Stoics as "our sect" firmly identifies him as one of their own.[155]

Sacrifice Language

Dio Chrysostom has several references to the supremacy of purity over the physical act of sacrifice. As we read through the Discourses, we can

---

147. *Const.* 1.1; 7.2; similar sentiments are expressed in *Ep.* 124.14; cf. *Clem.* 1.19.9 who describes the benevolent ruler (the emperor) as "second only to the gods" and *Tranq.* 2.3; *Ep.* 87.19.

148. *Marc.* 23.1–2; cf. *Polyb.* 9.3, 8; *Helv.* 11.6. See *Ep.* 41.5 for the soul who, though associating with the body, "cleaves to its origin."

149. *Marc.* 24.5; cf. *Helv.* 20.2. The alternate visions, presented in *Ep.* 71.16, of the soul dwelling with deity or being mingled with nature after death, either expresses an agnosticism concerning its fate or the latter pertains to the soul of an unrighteous person.

150. *Ep.* 79.12.

151. *Ep.* 41.2.

152. *Ep.* 26.4–7.

153. *Ep.* 10.4–5. For more on the ethics of Seneca, see Thorsteinsson, *Roman Christianity*, 22–39. For Stoic ethics generally, see Inwood and Donini, "Stoic Ethics," 675–738; and Schofield, "Stoic Ethics," 233–56.

154. *OCD*, 452; Jones, *Chrysostom*.

155. Dio Chrysostom, *Borysth.* 29 (Cohoon, Lamar Crosby, LCL).

see a steadily increasing emphasis on the right spirit of the offerer and a correspondingly decreasing emphasis on literal sacrifices. In his third Discourse on kingship, Dio, speaks of the model king's conception of the gods, who believes that, "the gods also do not delight in the offerings or sacrifices of the unjust, but accept the gifts made by the good alone."[156] As in Seneca and Epictetus, the one presenting their offering must be righteous in the sight of the gods for their offering to be acceptable. However, Dio goes further still to argue that an increase in piety will necessitate a decrease in physical sacrifices, perhaps implying that the reverence of the worshiper will be received as a kind of spiritual sacrifice that will take the place of the sacrifices themselves, "the more god-fearing (from εὐσεβής) and pious (from ὅσιος) you become, the less frankincense and fragrant offerings and garlands there will be among you, and you will offer fewer sacrifices."[157] A Discourse that is later still, raises the possibility not only of lesser sacrifices being acceptable in the case of a righteous person, but of sacrifices being done away with altogether, "And as for the gods, you know, I presume, that whether a person makes a libation to them or merely offers incense or approaches them, so long as his spirit is right, he has done his full duty; for perhaps God requires no such thing as images or sacrifices at all."[158] Finally, in his thirty-third Discourse, Dio reiterates the qualities that make men pleasing to the gods, and these do not include offerings, "it is not river or plain or harbour that makes a city prosperous, nor . . . treasuries of the gods—objects to which deity pays no heed . . . instead it is sobriety and common sense (σωφροσύνη καὶ νοῦς) that save. These make blessed those who employ them; these make men dear to the gods, not frankincense or myrrh, God knows."[159]

Priest Language

There were no figurative priest references found in Dio, other than an exhortation not to shy away from imitating even "priests of purification"

---

156. *3 Regn.* 52 (Cohoon, LCL).
157. *Exil.* 35 (Cohoon, LCL).
158. *Rhod.* 15 (Cohoon, Lamar Crosby, LCL).
159. *1 Tars.* 28 (Cohoon, Lamar Crosby, LCL). There is also an imaginary discourse between Alexander the Great and Diogenes, who tells the king to propitiate his δαίμων. Alexander wrongly imagines he must do so through sacrifices and purifications (*4 Regn.* 76.).

(though the usual word for priest, ἱερεύς, is not used) in the hope of winning souls from wickedness and leading them to virtue.[160]

Temple Language

There are no references in Dio that explicitly make use of temple language. However, in his Fourth Discourse, Dio alludes to the later Stoic understanding of δαίμων that dwells in the soul of each person.[161] In this case, the "genius" or "guardian spirit" will be received when the person has sufficiently matured in their understanding and their relationship with reason, "But come, let us attain a pure harmony ... and extol the good and wise guardian spirit (δαίμονα) or god—us who the kindly Fates decreed should receive Him when we should have gained a sound education and reason."[162] Elsewhere, Dio alludes to the belief that this guiding spirit is divine and expresses his opinion that there is no such thing as a bad δαίμων.[163] Dio also articulates the belief that the universe is the dwelling place of God, or "home of Zeus," but using the metaphor of household and home, rather than temple.[164]

The Nature of Divinity

Dio speaks frequently of God as Zeus. He describes him using a variety of titles to indicate his nature such as "Father," "King," "Protector," "God of Refuge" and "God of Hospitality," "these and his countless other titles signifying goodness and the fount of goodness."[165] He is supremely just and good,[166] peaceful, gentle,[167] beneficent to all and the "common

---

160. *4 Regn.* 89 (Cohoon, LCL). This is Cohoon's translation of τὰ καθάρσια, and is an ironic statement considering, according to Cohoon, (LCL, 209 n. 2) "The kathartai were regarded as charlatans, as we see from Hippocrates and Plutarch."

161. See Rist, *Stoic Philosophy*, 261–71, on the development of this theology in later Stoic thought. For a comparison of Stoic and Epicurean theology, see Mansfeld, "Theology," 452–75.

162. *4 Regn.* 139 (Cohoon, LCL).

163. *Fel. sap.* 10.

164. *Borysth.* 36.

165. *1 Regn.* 39 (Cohoon, LCL); cf. also *Dei cogn.* 22, 74, 75; *Borysth.* 32.

166. *1 Regn.* 16.

167. *Dei cogn.* 74.

protector and father of men and gods."[168] Dio asserts God's governance of the world,[169] and his "watchful care" over humanity, revealing the future, disclosing wisdom to them for their benefit and providing for them all that is for their good.[170] There is a happy "partnership of god with god" (speaking of the stars) in the heavens, where the gods exist as friends, free from strife.[171] Dio prays to multiple gods[172] though the gods have limitations: it is difficult for them to be in many places at once,[173] and the law has such power that even the gods rely on its help.[174] In fact, it is known as "king of men and gods."[175]

The Nature of Humanity

Dio describes both the dark and light side of humanity. Humanity is capable of devoting itself to wanton pleasure[176], a love of glory[177] and captive to "difficult and savage emotions."[178] Those who are depraved flee from the voice of reason[179] that alone could guide them on the right path. The source of evil comes from within, "for it is through man's folly and love of luxury and ambition, that life comes to be vexatious and full of deceit, wickedness, pain, and countless other ills."[180] Yet there has been placed within humanity an innate recognition of God[181] and a desire to worship and honor him.[182] There exists a kinship between God and humanity and the progenitors of humanity have lived in close relationship

168. *2 Regn.* 26 (Cohoon, LCL); cf. *Hom.* 12.
169. *1 Regn.* 42, 56; *3 Regn.* 50.
170. *Alex.* 12-14; cf. *Nicom.* 18.
171. *Borysth.* 22, 23; cf. *Nicom.* 11.
172. *Nicaeen* 8; though in another Discourse dealing with Greek myth, the gods spoken of there are described as a "democratic rabble" (*Invid.* 25).
173. *2 Regn.* 107.
174. *De lege* 5.
175. *De lege* 2.
176. *4 Regn.* 102.
177. *4 Regn.* 118; 126.
178. *4 Regn.* 126 (Cohoon, LCL).
179. *Alex.* 17.
180. *Alex.* 15 (Cohoon, Lamar Crosby, LCL); cf. Matt 15:19; Mk 7:20-23; Rom 1:21, 29-31; Titus 3:3; Jas 3:16.
181. *Dei cogn.* 27.
182. *Dei cogn.* 60; cf. Rom 1:19-21.

to God.[183] Since that intimate fellowship was broken, good people are still loved by the gods[184] but wicked and wanton people hold no pleasure for him.[185]

Living Out the Philosophy

Those who seek to be the kind of people who are loved by the gods can be called "sons of Zeus." Their identity as those of his seed can be discerned by their self-controlled lives.[186] They should seek to imitate the power and goodness of God.[187] The philosopher needs "no ruler other than reason and God."[188] Reason is "the only sure and indissoluble foundation for fellowship and justice."[189] The King should model himself and his rule on Zeus,[190] and his prayers should be appropriate (not asking selfishly or for that which is wicked).[191] The gods do not leave people alone in their quest but send signs and omens to teach them how to live.[192] Consequently, those who heed and obey are wise, and such a wise person is the only one who can be truly free and happy.[193]

2.3.7 Epictetus

Epictetus (c. 55—135/50–120 CE) was a former slave who became a pupil of the Stoic philosopher Musonius Rufus. He established his own school in Nicopolis, and although no writings of his own composition survive, his pupil Arrian published his lecture notes as his *Discourses*, which are summarized in a shorter manual or *Enchiridion*. These writings

---

183. *Dei cogn.* 28.
184. *1 Regn.* 16; *3 Regn.* 51, 53; *1 Tars.* 28; *Rhod.* 58; *Virt. (Or. 69)* 4 and in particular, the king tries to make the gods his friends (*3 Regn.* 115).
185. *1 Regn.* 16; *1 Tars.* 23; *Virt. (Or. 69)* 4.
186. *4 Regn.* 23.
187. *3 Regn.* 82.
188. *Rec. mag.* 3; cf. also *Rec. mag.* 6, 7, 12, 14.
189. *Borysth.* 31.
190. *Hom.* 11–12.
191. *2 Regn.* 62–63.
192. *Nicom.* 18.
193. *1 Serv. lib.* 17; *Gen.* 1. Dio's work *De quod felix sit sapiens* is translated by Loeb as "The Wise Man is Happy."

propounded Stoicism and are said to have greatly influenced the emperor Marcus Aurelius.[194]

Sacrifice Language

There are no obvious examples of figurative sacrifice language in Epictetus, but twice he speaks of the necessity of the offerer approaching sacrifices with the right intent, "with his mind predisposed to the idea that he will be approaching holy rites"[195] and again, "to give of the firstfruits after the manner of our fathers, and to do all this with purity, and not in a slovenly or careless fashion."[196] For Epictetus, right sacrifice has to involve more than correct performance. A pure motivation and a reverent disposition must govern the action of the worshiper.

Priest Language

There is a brief reference to the Cynic philosopher as a ὑπηρέτης of Zeus,[197] a word that can be used as an assistant to a priest.[198] This seems the closest I could find to a figurative priest reference in Epictetus.

Temple Language

Epictetus has much to say about the indwelling presence of God. He stresses the unique status of humanity within the created order. All other created things, such as animals or vegetation are born to serve humanity; they are not "portions of Divinity" (μέρη τοῦ θεῶν).[199] This contrasts with the way a person should see themselves, so Epictetus urges his audience, "But you are a being of primary importance; you are a fragment

---

194. See, e.g., *OCD*, 512–13; Sandbach, *Stoics*, 164–70; Ferguson, *Backgrounds*, 366–69; Thorsteinsson, *Roman Christianity*, 55–58; Wright, *Paul and the Faithfulness*, 223–27 and especially Long, *Epictetus*; see 7–17 for his setting, 27–96 for more on his philosophy, framework, and method, and 97–104 on his Stoicism.

195. Epictetus, *Diatr.* 3.21.14 (Oldfather, LCL).

196. *Ench.* 31.5 (Oldfather, LCL); emphases we find in a later and very different kind of writer such as Marcus Cornelius Fronto, in his *Epist. Graecae.* 8.3, 7.

197. Epictetus, *Diatr.* 3.22.82.

198. "ὑπηρέτης," BDAG, 1035.

199. *Diatr.* 2.8.11 (Oldfather, LCL).

(ἀπόσπασμα) of God; you have within you a part of Him."²⁰⁰ Epictetus emphasizes this here, "God himself is present within you"²⁰¹ and elsewhere, "you are not alone; nay, God is within, and your own genius (δαίμων) is within."²⁰² This a point of which his audience obviously needs reminding, "Have you not God there, where you are?"²⁰³ since Epictetus seems to assume that God is present within all, speaking as an example of "this fellow" who is ignorant of his presence within him.²⁰⁴ So great is this ignorance for some, that Epictetus uses quite stark and striking imagery to drive home the point, "Whenever you mix in society, whenever you take physical exercise, whenever you converse, do you not know that you are nourishing God, exercising God? You are bearing God about with you, you poor wretch, and know it not?"²⁰⁵ Indeed, they are privileged to be bearing the one who governs the universe within them.²⁰⁶ I shall return to the practical consequences of this doctrine in a later section, but for now we must note that Epictetus goes further to draw out the implications of the deep unity that exists between God and humanity for his Stoic-pantheistic understanding of this union, "if our souls are so bound up with God and joined together with Him, as being parts and portions of His being, does not God perceive their every motion as being a motion of that which is His own and of one body with Himself?"²⁰⁷ and so, "you possess a faculty which is equal to that of Zeus."²⁰⁸ Although in one place

200. *Diatr.* 2.8.11 (Oldfather, LCL).

201. *Diatr.* 2.8.14 (Oldfather, LCL).

202. *Diatr.* 1.14.14 (Oldfather, LCL); and cf. *Diatr.* 1.14.12 on the place of a "particular genius" in each person. Long, *Epictetus*, 165 comments, "Here Epictetus speaks as if the *daimôn* were an alter ego or at least a superego." This *daimôn*, Long, *Epictetus*, 166–67 speaks of as close to "the ideally rational or normative self" (166).

203. *Diatr.* 2.8.17 (Oldfather, LCL).

204. *Diatr.* 2.8.15–16.

205. *Diatr.* 2.8.12 (Oldfather, LCL).

206. *Diatr.* 2.16.33.

207. *Diatr.* 1.14.6 (Oldfather, LCL). Alexander of Aphrodisias, a philosopher from c. 200 CE says, of Stoic belief, that "the world is a unity which includes all existing things in itself and is governed by a living, rational, intelligent nature" and thus, "They say that the very fate, nature and rationale in accordance with which the all is governed is god" (Alexander, *On fate* 191,30–192,28 (*SVF* 2.945)); translation from Long and Sedley, *Hellenistic Philosophers*, 1:55N, 337–38.

208. *Diatr.* 1.14.12 (Oldfather, LCL), and like other Stoics, ascribes the same attributes to both God and Nature.

Epictetus describes the cosmos as if it is identified with God,[209] while not uncharacteristic of Stoicism, it is uncharacteristic of Epictetus,[210] and so it is possible to speak of the distinctive qualities of God and the gods.

The Nature of Divinity

Epictetus speaks frequently of Zeus[211] as the supreme God, and he pictures a serene deity who, "communes with himself, and is at peace with himself."[212] The true nature of good is found in him and he can be described using abstractions such as, "intelligence, knowledge, right reason."[213] He governs the universe,[214] provides for all its needs,[215] and is faithful, beneficent, high-minded and free to act as he chooses.[216] Even the motives and thoughts of a person cannot be hidden from him,[217] who looks down from above upon all that takes place and requires that his creatures should live to please him rather than people.[218] This same one guides their thoughts and gives them promptings and directions.[219] When speaking in general of the gods, Epictetus describes them as "pure (καθαρός) and undefiled (ἀχήρατος)."[220]

---

209. *Frag.* 3.

210. See 443 n. 1, on *Frag.* 3 (LCL), though see also *Diatr.* 1.14.10, and the comment on it in Lapidge, "Stoic Cosmology," 1414–1415.

211. E.g., *Diatr.* 1.1.10, 24; 1.12.25; 1.19.9, 12; 1.22.15–16; 1.25.3, 5; 2.17.22, 25; 2.23.42; 3.7.36; 3.11.5–6; 3.22.56–59; 3.24.16, 19; 4.1.131; 4.4.34. Long, *Epictetus*, 143, notes that Epictetus speaks more frequently of Zeus than any proper name other than Socrates.

212. *Diatr.* 3.13.7 (Oldfather, LCL).

213. *Diatr.* 2.8.2 (Oldfather, LCL). Although *Frag.* 8 suggests that divine beings can change, this may be a reference to the "heroes" or to other divinities, such as the stars.

214. *Diatr.* 2.14.25–26; 2.16.33.

215. *Diatr.* 2.14.11; 3.13.7; 3.26.28.

216. *Diatr.* 2.14.13.

217. *Diatr.* 2.14.11.

218. *Diatr.* 1.30.1; cf. Rom 2:29; Col 3:22–23; Gal 1:10; 1 Thess 2:4; Eph 6:5–6.

219. *Diatr.* 1.25.5–6, 13. See Long, *Epictetus*, 144–47, for more on the nature of God. Long considers how the Stoics held together both a pantheistic and yet theistic or "personalist" conception of God, and contends that Epictetus tends to emphasize theism over pantheism (147–48).

220. *Diatr.* 4.11.3 (Oldfather, LCL). In passing, we should also note that Epictetus refers to the practice of worshiping Caesar as a god in *Diatr.* 4.1.60–61, though his argument seems to undercut this particular premise for worshiping him.

The Nature of Humanity

God is described as the father of men as well as gods,[221] thus humanity are his children and there is a close kinship between humanity and gods.[222] One dominating theme of Epictetus' writings is that the gods have given to us our reasoning faculty,[223] which is a part of God's own being,[224] and with it the power to make "correct use of external impressions."[225] We cannot necessarily change situations in which we find ourselves but we have been given the power of moral choice,[226] so that we desire the things that are good, and cultivate an aversion toward what is evil, counting all other things as indifferent, and this results in virtue.[227] These choices are also made possible because we have an innate concept of what is good and what is evil.[228] Moral choice is in our hands alone and no one, not even Zeus, is able to overcome the moral purpose of a person.[229] This faculty of

---

221. *Diatr.* 1.3.1; 1.9.7.

222. *Diatr.* 1.9.1–7, 22–26; cf. Cleanthes, *Hymn to Zeus* (SVF 1.537), 1, who says of all mortals, "we are your offspring" (translation from Long and Sedley, *Hellenistic Philosophers*, 1:54I, 326).

223. *Diatr.* 1.1.4; Aetius, the first–second century BCE philosopher refers to the "reasoning faculty" that is also the "commanding faculty"; the "soul's highest part"; see Aetius 4.21.1–2 (SVF 2.836, part); translation from Long, *Philosophers*, 1:53H, 315.

224. *Diatr.* 1.17.27. Long, *Epictetus*, 145–46, identifies God as "cosmic rationality" in the thought of Epictetus.

225. *Diatr.* 1.1.7 (Oldfather, LCL); also 1.20.5–7; 1.27.15–19; 1.28.1–28; 2.1.4; 4.10.2, 14–17, 36; *Frag.* 4, 9; see also Aetius of Antioch, 4.21.1–4, cited by Long and Sedley, *Hellenistic Philosophers*, 1:315; Long, *Philosophers*, 2:314. The use of impressions was a key question for Stoicism, see, e.g., Sandbach, "Phantasia," 9–21; Long, *Hellenistic Philosophy*, 123–31, 172–75; Sharples, *Stoics*, 20–23; Reesor, *Nature of Man*, 32–82, 103–17; Frede, "Epistemology," 295–322; Brunschwig and Sedley, "Hellenistic Philosophy," 166–67; Brennan, "Psychology," 257–94; Hankinson, "Epistemology," 59–84.

226 A particular focus of the whole of *Diatr.* 4.1 as well as 1.25.1; 2.6.9; 2.10.1; 4.4.47; 4.9.17; *Ench.* 1.1–5. See further on this topic, Bobzien, *Determinism*, 330–57 and Long, *Epictetus*, 27–34.

227. *Diatr.* 1.4.1, 4; 1.29.2–8, 24; 1.30. 3–4; 2.1.5; 2.2.3, 7, 14; 2.6.1; 2.22.1–3; 2.23.19; 3.2.1–5; 3.10.18; 3.12.1–12; 3.18.1–5; 3.24.24; 4.8.12; *Ench.* 2.2; 13; 19; 34.

228. *Diatr.* 2.11.2–3.

229. *Diatr.* 1.1.23; 1.29.60; 2.13.10; 3.3.10; 4.5.23, 34; 4.12.7. In contrast to Pauline teaching here, it is assumed that the will of a person is not in bondage and captive to sin (cf. Rom 6:15–23; 7:7–25), "For it is within you that both destruction and deliverance lie" (Epictetus, *Diatr.* 4.9.17). The will of the individual and their ability to make choices is a key theme in Epictetus; see Long, *Epictetus*, 207–30.

reason is one which humanity alone possesses of all created things[230] and enables us to have communion with God, "being intertwined with him through the reason."[231] The goal of reason and moral choice is to will each thing to be exactly as it is, not concerning oneself with matters beyond our control,[232] and thus to live in accordance with nature.[233] The result of this life will be a freedom from disturbance, since it is only a person's own judgments that have power to disturb them.[234] It is the way to follow God's path,[235] and in fact to be free from fear as a friend of God.[236] Consequently, in exercising these moral choices Epictetus urges his reader, "you possess the faculty of understanding the divine administration of the world."[237] Yet, the "little soul" of a person is only "carrying around a corpse"[238] that, one day, shall be separated from the spirit.[239]

Living Out the Philosophy

Epictetus urges responses from those who understand that the divine spirit dwells within them and who become aware of their duties to exercise moral choice and indifference toward external matters. Firstly, they should have right opinions about the gods,[240] and then set their minds to obey them and to submit to what happens.[241] They should look to God

---

230. *Diatr.* 1.6.15.
231. *Diatr.* 1.9.4–5 (Oldfather, LCL).
232. *Diatr.* 1.4.19; 1.11.33, 37; 1.12.16; 1.25.1; 2.5.8; 2.17.22; *Ench.* 8.
233. *Diatr.* 1.4.18; 1.6.20–21; 1.15.5; 1.26.1–2.
234. *Diatr.* 1.19.7–8; 2.2.3; 2.6.8.
235. *Diatr.* 1.20.15; 1.30.5.
236. *Diatr.* 2.17.29; 4.5.35; 4.7.9; *Frag.* 4.
237. *Diatr.* 2.10.3 (Oldfather, LCL).
238. *Frag.* 26 (Oldfather, LCL).
239. *Diatr.* 2.1.17. See Long, *Epictetus*, 156–62 for the tendency of Epictetus to denigrate the body as an obstacle to kinship with God and even to God's work itself, in a way that Long sees as going beyond traditional Stoicism.
240. *Ench.* 31.1. See Long, *Epictetus*, 180–89 on how much of his moral philosophy stems from right understanding of God/s.
241. *Diatr.* 1.14.16–18; 3.24.95–102; 4.12.12; *Ench.* 31.1.

as guide,[242] and honor the one within.[243] Since they are bearing God in their bodies, his audience must attend to their inner life (so as not to defile God by impure thoughts) and to their outer life (so as not to defile him with "filthy actions,"[244] that may include the reference to intercourse with women).[245] The person must live to imitate God,[246] and offer themselves completely to him.[247] Since, whatever happens is what God wants, submitting to whatever happens (see above) is the same as wanting what God wants.[248] In desiring to become pure in the presence of God,[249] they wish to be of of one mind (ὁμογνωμονέω) with God,[250] showing themselves to be those who have set their heart upon changing into a god.[251] Such a person can live as a friend of God, without fear,[252] since God has set them free from the slavery of bondage to others' esteem or rules.[253] In order to live in this state, the hearers of Epictetus should exercise right judgments in regard to sense impressions (as discussed above) and in that way, their soul will be pure.[254] Thus there is the need to purify their judgments,[255] destroy desire,[256] love their fellow,[257] and so, seek the common good.[258] That is, philosophy should bear real fruit in the lives of its

242. *Diatr.* 2.7.11. So, for example, since Epictetus has within him the true diviner who can reveal to him the true nature of good and evil, divination is rendered unnecessary (*Diatr.* 2.7.3).

243. *Diatr.* 2.8.18–22.

244. *Diatr.* 2.8.12–13.

245. *Diatr.* 2.8.12; cf. 1 Cor 6:15–20.

246. *Diatr.* 2.14.13.

247. *Diatr.* 2.16.42; cf. the command in 4.1.172–73.

248. *Diatr.* 2.17.22; *Ench.* 53.

249. *Diatr.* 2.18.19.

250. *Diatr.* 2.19.26.

251. *Diatr.* 2.19.27. Long, *Epictetus*, 146–47 contends that in the thought of Epictetus, assimilation to the divine "gives persons a potential status that virtually eliminates the qualitative difference between the ideal human and the divine" (147). See also Long, *Epictetus*, 168–72 on becoming a person of virtue and like God.

252. *Diatr.* 2.17.29; 3.24.60; 4.3.9.

253. *Diatr.* 4.7.9, 17.

254. *Diatr.* 4.11.3, 5.

255. A command in *Diatr.* 4.1.112.

256. *Diatr.* 4.1.175.

257. Implied by *Diatr.* 4.4.27.

258. *Diatr.* 4.10.12.

adherents.[259] The fruit of the right use of external impressions is, "freedom, serenity, cheerfulness, steadfastness; it is also justice, and law, and self-control, and the sum and substance of virtue,"[260] the ability to choose and to live by a certain standard of character and values.[261] This is to say that the true philosopher must be devoted to the mind, and specifically to the philosophic principles.[262] There is the need to count the cost of such a life in a thoughtful and considered manner,[263] remembering that both people and things are only mortal.[264] Thus, the philosophic life may involve a difficult road. At times, God sends ordeals and difficulties of various kinds in order to test the person, so that they may become a victor in the moral life, like an Olympic champion.[265]

2.3.8 Marcus Aurelius

Marcus Aurelius (121–180 CE) reigned as emperor from 161–180 CE, having been previously adopted into Hadrian's family and married to his cousin. Marcus studied with a number of famous teachers, including the orator Fronto, and was greatly drawn to philosophy. He was heavily influenced by Epictetus and is most associated with Stoicism.[266]

---

259. *Diatr.* 4.8.20, 32, 36.

260. *Frag.* 4 (Oldfather, LCL) (cf. Gal 5:22–23). See also Long, *Epictetus*, 189–206 on external impressions and 244–54 on feelings in the philosophy of Epictetus.

261. *Ench.* 33.1ff.

262. *Ench.* 41; 46; 48; 52.

263. *Diatr.* 3.6; 3.15.1–7, 11–12.

264. *Diatr.* 3.24.84–89. See Long, *Epictetus*, 154–56 for the balance in Epictetus between his awareness of our mortality and transience, while also highlighting the way that individuals are "parts" of God himself by their minds, citing *Diatr.* 1.12.26; 2.5.13; 4.7.6–7 and 2.8.10–11.

265. *Diatr.* 1.24.1; cf. 1 Cor 9:24–27; 2 Tim 2:5; Jas 1:12. For more on the ethics of Epictetus, see Thorsteinsson, *Roman Christianity*, 58–70.

266. *OCD*, 210; Sandbach, *Stoics*, 172–77; Ferguson, *Backgrounds*, 367–68; Long, "Roman," 207–8; Wright, *Paul and the Faithfulness*, 227–28. For a comprehensive study, see Rutherford, *Meditations*, especially xv–xviii, 1–89 for background to the work, and Hadot, *Inner Citadel*, especially 1–34.

Priest Language

Marcus describes a man who lives in total integrity, whose thoughts are guided by reason away from all vice and whose character and actions are transparently good, "all that is in thee is simple and kindly and worthy of a living being that is social and has no thought for pleasures."[267] His description of, "one who no longer puts off being reckoned now, if never before, among the best, is in some sort a priest and minister of the Gods"[268] could refer to a kind of figurative priest toward *the divine*, but it is more likely to be a straightforward reference to one who acts as God's priest toward *others*. Just before this section, Marcus contemplates what lies beyond death, whether it be life with the gods or merely a state of non-sensation. In regards to the latter possibility, he makes a passing reference to "that which ministers" to the bodily vessel (presumably the soul),[269] using the verb λατρεύω, which is often used in cultic contexts.[270] It is possible that this too is a cultic image, and pictures the soul acting as a priest to the body.

Temple Language

Marcus speaks frequently of an indwelling divine presence. In one place he refers to "the god that is in thee" (ὁ ἐν σοὶ θεὸς)[271] and elsewhere speaks of "one God immanent in all things" (θεὸς εἷς διὰ πάντων)[272]; a subject to which I shall return below. When Marcus is not speaking of the unity of God with all things, but of a presence dwelling in the life of an individual human being, he does not commonly use the language of θεός. Rather, Marcus typically uses the language of the indwelling δαίμων. Although in one place this is rendered by C. R. Haines as "the very deity enthroned in thee"[273] his translations for Loeb prefers phrases such as "the divine genius" within a person.[274] On one occasion Marcus couples the two names,

---

267. Marcus Aurelius, *Med.* 3.4.2 (Haines, LCL); cf. his injunctions in *Med.* 7.54.
268. *Med.* 3.4.3 (Haines, LCL).
269. *Med.* 3.3.2 (Haines, LCL).
270. See "λατρεύω," BDAG, 587.
271. Marcus Aurelius, *Med.* 3.5.1 (Haines, LCL).
272. *Med.* 7.9 (Haines, LCL).
273. *Med.* 3.6.2 (Haines, LCL).
274. *Med.* 2.13, 17; 3.3.2; 3.12, 16; 5.27 (Haines, LCL).

averring that, "it is in my power to do nothing contrary to the God and the 'genius' within me (ὅτι ἔξεστί μοι μηδὲν πράσσειν παρὰ τὸν ἐμὸν θεὸν καὶ δαίμονα)."[275] Since the two nouns, θεός and δαίμων are governed by the same article, neither is impersonal, neither is plural and neither is a proper name, this seems to be an example of the Granville Sharp rule, where the second noun in the construction refers to the same person denoted by the first noun.[276] Hence θεός and δαίμων refer to one person and not two, demonstrating that Marcus can speak of God and a δαίμων interchangeably. Accordingly, elsewhere Marcus can either refer to "that which in thee is divine" (καὶ τὸ ἐν σοὶ θεῖον),[277] using θεῖος, a cognate of θεός, or remind his audience that "thou hast in thyself something better and more god-like" (κρεῖττόν τι καὶ δαιμονιώτερον ἔχεις ἐν σαυτῷ) employing a cognate to δαίμων. Terms from both the roots θεο- and δαίμ- are apparently used by Marcus without any great differentiation of meaning. Reason is sometimes paired with the divine presence within,[278] or this δαίμων is completely identified with intelligence and reason.[279] Marcus reminds his readers that, "each man's intelligence is God and has emanated from Him" (ὁ ἑκάστου νοῦς θεός καὶ ἐκεῖθεν ἐρρύηκε).[280] As we shall see in my next section, God can be equated with reason and intelligence.[281]

The Nature of Divinity

Marcus's conception of God is strongly pantheistic, in common with Stoic doctrine generally.[282] In the same paragraph, Marcus speaks of

---

275. *Med.* 5.10.2 (Haines, LCL).

276. For further explanation, see Wallace, *Greek Grammar*, 270–72. As 272 n. 42, explains, θεός can be pluralized and hence is not a proper name, thus fitting the rule.

277. Marcus Aurelius, *Med.* 12.1.2 (Haines, LCL).

278. E.g., *Med.* 12.1.2.

279. *Med.* 5.27.

280. *Med.* 12.26.

281. The references to "that which holds the mastery within us" (Τὸ ἔνδον κυριεῦον) in Marcus Aurelius, *Med.* 4.1 (Haines, LCL), and to "that Hidden Thing within us" (ἐκεῖνο τὸ ἔνδον ἐγκεκρυμμένον) in *Med.* 10.38. may also be allusions to this same god/ genius. See further Long, *Epictetus*, 163–67, 177–78.

282. Long, *Hellenistic Philosophy*, 150, avers that "fundamentally, Stoic theology is pantheist." Algra, "Stoic Theology," 165, elaborates that the Stoic conception of God or gods is "at first sight perhaps a surprising mixture of pantheism, theism, and polytheism"; cf. Hadot, *Inner Citadel*, 147–63, who makes the connection between Marcus and Seneca, *Nat.* 2.45.1 (158), quoted above.

providence being "the works of the Gods," the "control of Providence," the co-dependence of "Fortune" and "Nature" and "the Nature of the Whole" which brings about good for every part of Nature.[283] Or again, Marcus avers, "there is both one Universe, made up of all things, and one God immanent in all things, and one Substance, and one Law, one Reason common to all intelligent creatures, and one Truth."[284] It is hard to distinguish between God/s, Fortune, Providence and Nature in Marcus's worldview because all is one.[285] Therefore, he admonishes his readers "to think of the Universe as one living Being, possessed of a single Substance and a single Soul."[286] At the same time, Marcus says that all go back to a single source, that is "sentience,"[287] "the all-embracing intelligence,"[288] "Universe" (addressed in the vocative singular: ὦ κόσμε)[289] or controlling Reason.[290] So interconnected are all things, that what "contributes to

283. *Med.* 2.3 (Haines, LCL). Marcus also speaks of the "Nature of the Whole" as a Creator who felt compelled to create the universe in *Med.* 7.75 (Haines, LCL) and of the "Begetter and Upholder of all things" in *Med.* 10.1 (Haines, LCL).

284. *Med.* 7.9 (Haines, LCL); cf. Cleanthes, *Hymn to Zeus* (SVF 1.537), 54I, 327 who speaks of "the universal law." Long, *Philosophers*, Vol 1.

285. According to the fourth century philosopher, Calcidius, Chrysippus also believed that "everything in accordance with fate is also the product of providence, and likewise everything in accordance with providence is the product of fate," whereas Cleanthes distinguished between the two; see Calcidius 144 (SVF 2.933); translation from Long, *Philosophers*, 1:54U, 331. Aulus Gellius (c. 125—after 180 CE) also discusses Chrysippus's view of Providence in a now lost work, *On Providence*, in Gellius, *Noct. att.* 7.1.1-13; 7.2.3-12. On the philosophy of Cleanthes, see Kristeller, *Greek Philosophers*, 35-40.

286. *Med.* 4.40 (Haines, LCL); see 90 n. 1. The Christian theologian Origen (184/185—253/254 CE) later writes of the "god of the Stoics" who "sometimes has the whole substance as his commanding-faculty; this is whenever the conflagration is in being; at other times, when world-order exists, he comes to be in a part of substance" (from Origen, *Contra Celsum* 4.14 (SVF 2.1052, part); translation from Long and Sedley, *Hellenistic Philosophers*, 1:46H, 276.)

287. *Med.* 4.40 (Haines, LCL). *Med.* 8.23 pairs the gods with "the Source of all things."

288. *Med.* 8.54 (Haines, LCL).

289. *Med.* 4.23 (Haines, LCL); see 380 n. 3. Marcus speaks of "the Nature of the Universe" as creator and sustainer in both *Med.* 8.26 and 9.1 (Haines, LCL).

290. *Med.* 5.1; 6.36.2 (Haines, LCL). This is of the essence of Stoicism, as attested by the very early *Hymn to Zeus* by Cleanthes (c. 330-230 BCE, the second head of the Stoic school; see *OCD*, 329), that speaks of "the universal reason [κοινὸν λόγον] which runs though all things and intermingles with the lights of heaven both great and small" and claims that all things "share in a single everlasting reason," Cleanthes, *Hymn to Zeus*, 2-3 (SVF 1.537); translation from Long and Sedley, *Hellenistic Philosophers*,

the health of the Universe" contributes to the well being of Zeus himself, since "there is one harmony of all things."[291] This is also conceptualized as a "universal Substance" (συμπάσης οὐσίας or Ἡ τῶν ὅλων οὐσία) of which all are a part.[292] We also learn from Marcus that the gods lend aid to all,[293] can give freedom from anything (such as lust or fear),[294] and bear fruit in due season.[295]

The Nature of Humanity

Marcus repeatedly stresses the connection between the human and the divine (as we saw above), emphasizing that even an evil doer shares a kinship with him, "partaker of ... intelligence and a morsel of the Divine" (νοῦ καὶ θείας ἀπομοίρας).[296] Humans are both soul and body, or to put it another way "the Causal and the Material."[297] The soul is the ruling part of the person and "the Soul alone deflects and moves herself," forming her own judgments about all things.[298] Just as Marcus speaks of God as "ruling Reason," he frequently uses the same term (ἡγεμονικός) for the reason within.[299] This is a reason that comes from God and is shared in common with the Gods,[300] though some are at variance with "the Reason that administers the whole Universe."[301] The soul, or reason, is the well-spring from which all attitudes, motivations and designs flow, "for every conviction and impulse and desire and aversion is from within, and

---

1:54I, 326–27.

291. *Med.* 5.8.1–2; cf. 6.37–38 (Haines, LCL). See his discussion of the "Universal Nature" in *Med.* 12.26.

292. *Med.* 5.24; 6.1; 12.30, 32 (Haines, LCL). Sometimes Haines translates this phrase (ὅλη οὐσία) as "Universal Nature," e.g., *Med.* 7.5.

293. *Med.* 9.27.

294. *Med.* 9.40.

295. *Med.* 9.10.

296. *Med.* 2.1 (Haines, LCL).

297. *Med.* 5.13 (Haines, LCL).

298. *Med.* 5.19 (Haines, LCL).

299. *Med.* 4.38; 7.16; 8.43, 61; 9.7; 11.20; 12.1 (Haines, LCL). Frede, "Stoic Determinism," 185, explains that in the Stoic view, "Human beings ... are also ruled by a portion of the pneuma in its purest form, namely reason (*dianoia*)."

300. *Med.* 6.35 (Haines, LCL).

301. *Med.* 4.46 (Haines, LCL).

nothing climbs in thither."[302] Although Marcus ascribes all that happens to the Universal Nature, this does not absolve wrongdoers of responsibility for their evil.[303] Throughout Marcus's writings he is keen to reiterate the frailty and dependence of human beings on other forces and their short mortal lives. In his second book he calls his reader to realize, "as an emanation from what Controller of that Universe thou dost subsist."[304] As one who subsists from that controller as part of a greater whole, their destiny is to return to the source from which they came, "Thou shalt vanish into that which begat thee, or rather thou shalt be taken again into its Seminal Reason by a process of change" (τὸν λόγον αὐτοῦ τὸν σπερματικὸν).[305] In other places, however, Marcus seems uncertain as to whether the end of the soul will be, "extinction or translation,"[306] though death can be welcomed as an emergence of the soul from its captivity (as with Platonism).[307]

Living Out the Philosophy

In light of the deep connection between Nature, the Universe, God/the gods and humans, Marcus reasons that "there is nothing to prevent" him from beginning "at once" in living according to nature.[308] This can also be described as living according to reason,[309] or being in tune with the

---

302. *Med.* 5.28 (Haines, LCL); cf. Matt 15:18; Mk 7:21–23. Thus, impulses must be restrained (*Med.* 9.7).

303. *Med.* 12.26; 9.38.

304. *Med.* 2.4 (Haines, LCL). On the question of Marcus' "pessimism," see Hadot, *Inner Citadel*, 163–79.

305. *Med.* 4.14 (Haines, LCL); similarly, on the eventual dissolution of the soul, *Med.* 4.21.1; 4.23; 7.10, 19; 8.18. For further discussion, see Rutherford, *Meditations*, 206–8.

306. *Med.* 5.33 (Haines, LCL); similarly, *Med.* 6.4, 24; 10.7.2.

307. *Med.* 9.3.1; cf. *Med.* 6.28. Some, though, fear death: *Med.* 8.58. Rutherford, *Meditations*, 244–50 notes the preoccupation with death in Marcus, and see also Hadot, *Inner Citadel*, 275–88.

308. *Med.* 9.5 (Haines, LCL); cf. *Med.* 5.3; 7.55.1; 7.56; 7.70; 8.7; 12.1.2. The corollary Marcus draws from this doctrine of providence is that "nothing befalls anyone that he is not fitted by nature to bear." *Med.* 5.18 (Haines, LCL); cf. 1 Cor 10:13. See generally, Hadot, *Inner Citadel*, 183–208.

309. *Med.* 4.1; or people "following narrowly their own ruling reason" *Med.* 4.38 (Haines, LCL); *Med.* 12.1; cf. the opposite behavior in *Med.* 4.46.

Universe,[310] thinking, "in unison with the all-embracing Intelligence"[311] or even doing "nothing contrary to the God and the 'genius' within me."[312] The philosopher should seek to live as they are: a fellow citizen of Gods and people in a common "World-City."[313] There is great danger in cutting ones' soul off from "the soul of all rational things" which also severs their link to the universe and their comprehension of all the things within it, which includes the life of the community.[314] In order not to be cut off in this way, "That which holds the mastery within us"[315] (most likely a reference to the ruling Reason) will adapt itself to whatever happens to it, so long as it is living in accordance with nature.[316] Accordingly, the wise person should be indifferent to what nature treats as indifferent.[317] In this life according to the nature of the universe, death is "just a function of nature" and no longer something to be feared.[318] Similarly, since the soul is preeminent, the body fulfills a lowly function, of little significance; "To the body indeed all things are indifferent, for it cannot concern itself with them."[319] The mind, on the other hand, is only indifferent toward those matters which are external to its affairs.[320] Yet at the same time, Marcus urges his audience to resist bodily inclinations uncompromisingly.[321]

So, practically speaking, how is this life to be lived? At the heart of it all is our attitude to the divine genius, or reason, or intelligence, living within a person. Marcus instructs his reader to serve the δαίμων

---

310. *Med.* 4.23.

311. *Med.* 8.54 (Haines, LCL).

312. *Med.* 5.10 (Haines, LCL).

313. *Med.* 10.1, 15 (Haines, LCL). For more on this topic, see Obbink, "Stoic Sage," 178–95.

314. *Med.* 4.29 (Haines, LCL).

315. *Med.* 4.1 (Haines, LCL).

316. *Med.* 2.12; cf. thus, a person should keep their ruling Reason sound (*Med.* 8.43).

317. *Med.* 9.1.4; cf. *Med.* 4.39; 11.16.

318. *Med.* 2.12 (Haines, LCL). So, life should be lived with a conscious awareness of our own mortality (*Med.* 4.48).

319. *Med.* 6.32 (Haines, LCL); cf. 1 Cor 6:13. Rutherford, *Meditations*, 243–44 refers to the "revulsion from the physical and condemnation of worldly objects" in Marcus, suggesting a "more transcendent view of deity."

320. *Med.* 6.32.

321. *Med.* 7.55.1–2. For more on Marcus' guiding principles, see Hadot, *Inner Citadel*, 35–53.

by keeping it pure,³²² and this kind of service is elaborated as, "to keep it pure from passion and aimlessness and discontent with anything that proceeds from Gods or men."³²³ In other words, this genius is to be "lord of all pleasures and pains."³²⁴ Marcus repeatedly stresses the need for this genius or god to rule, with injunctions like, "let the god that is in thee be lord of a living creature,"³²⁵ and refers to this "very deity" as "enthroned" in the person by bringing all desires "into subjection to itself."³²⁶ Reason is described as having a kingly, legislative function, "in its royal and law-making capacity."³²⁷ It is to have first place in a person's life.³²⁸ Accordingly, the one devoted to his own intelligence and good genius will lead a life of virtue.³²⁹ The theme of purity and cleanliness often occurs in relation to the divine indwelling. Marcus urges his audience to keep their "divine genius" in its "virgin state" (actually καθαρός);³³⁰ or conversely not to "sully" (φύρω, "with a sense of mixing so as to spoil or defile"³³¹) the divine genius, which, he reminds them, again using ruling language, "is enthroned" in their bosom.³³² The true follower of reason will always be ready to be corrected; a turnabout that Marcus describes as a 'conversion' (from μετάγω).³³³ Marcus's writings are filled with injunctions designed to lead his readers toward this goal, and below I list the most obvious ones, in two categories.

Firstly, Marcus deals with the inner life as it relates to the genius within and to relations with the gods. He urges his readers to "walk with

322. *Med.* 2.17. Asmis, "Stoicism," 2243, comments, "This notion of the intellect as an inner deity may be traced back to Posidonius. . . . Nowhere, however, is the notion as prominent as in Marcus' writings; it forms the basis of his ethics." Rutherford, *Meditations*, 237, speaks of the "notorious" difficulties of pinning down the referent to the δαίμων in later Stoic writers and whether they would even distinguish between God, the best part of a person or their guiding spirit.

323. *Med.* 2.13 (Haines, LCL).

324. *Med.* 2.17 (Haines, LCL).

325. *Med.* 3.5.1 (Haines, LCL).

326. *Med.* 3.6.2 (Haines, LCL).

327. *Med.* 4.12 (Haines, LCL); cf. Jas 2:8. Hadot, *Inner Citadel*, 123–25 identifies the δαίμων with "reason" in Marcus.

328. *Med.* 3.6.1–3; thus, one's ruling reason should be kept "sound" (*Med.* 9.7.).

329. *Med.* 3.7.

330. *Med.* 3.12 (Haines, LCL).

331. "φύρω," *LSJ* 1963.

332. *Med.* 3.16 (Haines, LCL).

333. *Med.* 4.12 (Haines, LCL).

the Gods!" by carrying out the will of that genius, identified with intelligence and reason[334] and by keeping their thoughts on God at all times.[335] This is what it means to "rest in philosophy,"[336] and to return to the inner harmony in order to gain control of it.[337] At the same time, the wise person is to be attentive by looking within to seek out the "special quality or worth" of each thing.[338] The "fountain of Good" is also to be found within.[339] Such a wise person will welcome what "Universal Nature" has designed for it,[340] and live each day at peace with themselves, as if the day were their last.[341] The person who has been schooled in philosophy and who is humble of heart will say to Nature, "Give what you will and take back what you will."[342] They should disdain wrong sense-impressions (like Epictetus, above).[343] They can do all this because they live by axioms (δόγμα), which guide all their impulses and actions. These axioms concern the nature of good and evil, and look to the goal of what makes a person, "just, temperate, manly, free."[344] Though Marcus repeatedly stresses providence and destiny, he also emphasizes the free judgment and action of the individual.[345] The gods can be prayed to since they have power to give freedom from wrong impulses, such as fear or lust.[346] Good people can have "the closest commerce with the Divine" and "the most intimate fellowship with it" by pious behavior and acts of worship.[347]

334. *Med.* 5.27 (Haines, LCL).

335. *Med.* 6.7, and so leave no room for wrong thoughts, cf. *Med.* 7.54.

336. *Med.* 6.12 (Haines, LCL).

337. *Med.* 6.11 (Haines, LCL).

338. *Med.* 6.3 (Haines, LCL).

339. *Med.* 7.59.

340. *Med.* 8.7, 25.

341. *Med.* 7.69.

342. *Med.* 10.14; cf. Job 1:21. See also *Med.* 12.11.

343. *Med.* 8.26; or not go beyond initial impressions (*Med.* 8.19).

344. *Med.* 8.1. See further, Hadot, *Inner Citadel*, 101–27.

345. *Med.* 8.16. Frede, "Stoic Determinism," 186, comments that despite the deterministic nature of Stoic philosophy, "individual entities have a certain autonomy. It is the inner makeup of human reason that determines the way in which a person interacted with his or her environment."

346. *Med.* 9.40. For more on prayer in Marcus, see Rutherford, *Meditations*, 200–205.

347. *Med.* 12.5. *Med.* 1.17.6 also speaks directly of communication with the gods; see Rutherford, *Meditations*, 192–95.

Secondly, Marcus stresses the social dimension of the philosopher and instructs them in how to live with other people. He urges his readers not to look around at the affairs of others and to compare themselves with other people[348] but rather, "run straight for the goal,"[349] and thus live the life of the content person.[350] However, in case Marcus be misunderstood as dismissing the relations between the wise person and their fellows, Marcus reminds them to test every case to see how it may affect the community and to respect its judgment, "if the community be not hurt by this, neither am I hurt; but if the community be hurt, there is no need to be angry with him that hath done the hurt, but to enquire, In what hath he seen amiss?"[351] The wise person should seek the common interest.[352] In their behavior toward others they should neither do nor speak evil to anyone.[353] There is a strong social element in Marcus's injunctions. Each person is to see themselves as, "a limb of the organized body of rational things"[354] and so should love all people,[355] even those who stumble.[356] They should deal righteously with their neighbors.[357] This concern for each person, whatever their relationship to them, is enabled by encouraging a sense of empathy with everyone, "Enter into every man's ruling Reason, and give every one else an opportunity to enter into thine,"[358] since humankind was created for the sake of each another.[359] This perspective on life is even described by Marcus as "salvation" (Σωτηρία), which involves an accurate comprehension of reality and "on our doing what is just and speaking what is true with all our soul."[360]

348. *Med.* 4.17; cf. *Med.* 8.56.
349. *Med.* 4.17 (Haines, LCL); cf. Phil 3:13–14; 1 Cor 9:24; Heb 12:1.
350. *Med.* 4.25; cf *Med.* 7.54; 2 Cor 12:10; Phil 4:11; 1 Tim 6:8; Heb 13:5.
351. *Med.* 5.22 (Haines, LCL).
352. *Med.* 11.12. See Hadot, *Inner Citadel*, 210–31.
353. *Med.* 5.31; also *Med.* 8.26. Cf. Tit 3:2; Jas 4:11; 1 Pet 3:10.
354. *Med.* 7.13 (Haines, LCL); cf. 1 Cor 12:12–26.
355. *Med.* 7.31; 11.1.2.

356. *Med.* 7.22; e.g., by forbearing to be angry with those who do not return thanks for their love, and even to care for them (*Med.* 8.8; cf. Luke 6:35), or seeking to convert them to the right path (*Med.* 9.11.).

357. *Med.* 7.54, for instance by not lying to them or committing injustice (*Med.* 9.1.1–2.).

358. *Med.* 8.61.
359. *Med.* 8.59; cf. *Med.* 9.1.1; 11.18.1.
360. *Med.* 12.29 (Haines, LCL).

2.3.9 Hierocles

Heirocles was a Stoic writer from the second century CE, sometime around the reign of Hadrian (117–38 CE). He left behind some of his *Elements of Ethics*, as well as other fragments and excerpts from his writings.[361]

Temple and Priest Language

There is one fleeting figurative temple reference in Hierocles. In his treatise *On Marriage*, Hierocles considers his parents worthy to be honored as gods, since the filial relationship between child and parent is even closer than that between people and gods.[362] Indeed they can be compared to "domestic gods" and this naturally leads Hierocles to consider how we should serve these gods, "we must consider ourselves as kinds of ministers and priests in our home as in a temple (νομιστέον ἑαυτοὺς καθάπερ ἐν ἱερῷ τῇ οἰκίᾳ ζακόρους τινὰς καὶ ἱερέας), elected and consecrated by nature itself and entrusted with the tendance of our parents." This is expressed through care for their bodies, but more especially, for their souls.[363]

The Nature of Divinity

According to Hierocles, the gods are fixed in their judgements, since "changelessness and firmness" typify their virtues. They do chastise, and sometimes natural disasters such as famines, droughts and floods are caused by them.[364] Hierocles, however, wants to stress that the gods are responsible for good because they themselves are good, since they are filled with all the virtues.[365] Zeus can be described as the first god and parent.[366]

---

361. *OCD*, 682–83; Sandbach, *Stoics*, 170–72.

362. Ramelli, *Hierocles*, 82–83.

363. Ramelli, *Hierocles*, 82–87. This whole section corresponds to *SVF*, 4.79.53 (3:95,30–99, 9 Meineke; cf. Anth. 4.25.53 = 4:640,4–644,15 Wachsmuth and Hense).

364. Ramelli, *Hierocles*, 64–65, from the treatise *How Should One Behave toward the Gods?* This section corresponds to *SVF*, 1.3.53–54 (1:63,6–27–1:64, 1–14 Wachsmuth and Hense).

365. Ramelli, *Hierocles*, 66–69. This section corresponds to *SVF*, 2.9.7 (2:181,8–182, 30 Wachsmuth and Hense).

366. Ramelli, *Hierocles*, 68–69. This section corresponds to *SVF*, 3.39.34 (3:730,17–731,15 Wachsmuth and Hense).

The Nature of Humanity

A human being is a mix of body and soul, which are intermingled, with the soul itself understood as corporeal.[367] Evil in the world comes about as a result of vice, not because of God's judgments, and people choose evil freely. Matter is a second cause of evils, after vice.[368]

2.3.10 Summary of My Findings from Stoicism

Summary of Sacrifice Language

As I have surveyed temple language in Stoicism, a number of themes have stood out. Some, like Seneca, Dio Chryostom and Epictetus have, in places, continued to stress the need for physical sacrifices but have also emphasized the vital role of the motivation and inner purity of the worshiper. Seneca speaks in other places of the holy desire and the upright will of the offerer, almost in place of the victim. For Seneca, knowing, believing and imitating the gods itself is worship. Dio Chrysostom's work appears to show a development, as the emphasis on purity increases, so the focus on literal sacrifices appears to decrease. In fact, for Dio, the more pious the worshiper, the fewer sacrifices are needed. Indeed, a later discourse makes sobriety and common sense a sacrifice in its own right. Cicero's evidence also emphasizes purity of thought and speech instead of a literal sacrifice.

Summary of Priest Language

There were fewer obvious uses of figurative priest language. Zeno and Arius Didymus claim that only the wise and godlike are priests. Marcus Aurelius says that a true priest is a man of integrity, guided by reason, who avoids pleasure. Hierocles compares the offspring of parents as priests to them.

---

367. From the treatise *Elements of Ethics* in Ramelli, *Hierocles*, 11, III.60; IV.5–20.

368. Ramelli, *Hierocles*, 66–69, from the treatise *How Should One Behave toward the Gods?* This section corresponds to Stobaeus, *Anthology* 2.9.7 (2:181,8–182, 30 Wachsmuth and Hense).

Summary of Temple Language and the Nature of Divinity

Since many of the writers fuse their understanding of divine indwelling with their observations of the character of divinity, I shall combine these two sections in this summary. Seneca explicitly speaks of the world as being the temple of the gods. Within that context, God is spoken of as infused through the whole universe. Indeed, God is described by him as the mind of the universe, and sometimes equated with Nature, Reason, Fate and Fortune. Reason elsewhere is described as a portion of the divine spirit. In this, Seneca is following Zeno, who speaks of the world as a living soul and also appears to identify God with Reason and Fate (later followed by Marcus Aurelius). Cicero confirms this evidence, describing the world as God and speaking of the all-pervading soul as Reason. Marcus Aurelius also speaks of God as immanent in all things and the source of reason and intelligence. Epictetus, on the other hand, seems to envisage a more distinct role for God than other Stoics, speaking of him as separate from the universe. Seneca also avers that God or the Holy Spirit dwells in individuals, sometimes specified as in each good person, and assumes that communication with the gods is possible. Dio Chrysostom also speaks of the divine in each person, here meaning each person's δαίμων (sometimes translated as "genius" or "guardian spirit"), but adds that they are received when a person matures. Epictetus similarly puts the emphasis squarely on the individual's relationship to God; having much to say about the God within (even within someone who is ignorant, unlike the view of Dio Chrysostom) who is carried around wherever they go. Marcus Aurelius speaks of the person's δαίμων, god and the "godlike" and "divine" inside a person fairly interchangeably. Hierocles, alone of these writers, uses the temple language for the home and compares parents to "domestic gods." Seneca describes the character of the gods as beneficent; gentle, merciful, forgiving and providing for all, especially the good. Dio Chrysostom uses similar language and portrays a harmonious partnership between the gods. However, for Dio the gods are not entirely self-sufficient, since they rely on the law. Epictetus uses abstractions to describe God, such as intelligence, knowledge and right reason. The gods are pure and undefiled and govern the universe. Marcus Aurelius also sees the gods as benevolent beings that lend to all and bring freedom from fear and evil. Hierocles portrays the gods as good and changeless, and likens Zeus to a parent, though one who can punish his children.

Figurative Temple Language in Hellenistic Philosophy 85

Summary of the Nature of Humanity

Seneca's view of humanity balances an understanding of the natural goodness of humanity with their tendency to sin. The human mind is formed from the divine essence and so, alone of all creatures, humans have a conception of divinity. The soul is pre-existent and preserved by God, who grants to it knowledge of divinity. Dio Chrysostom stresses the evil within each individual but also the ability to recognize, worship and have kinship with the gods. Epictetus sees humanity as God's children. They can understand the divine ways and live as friends of God. They have reasoning powers and the ability to desire the good and make right moral choices. They can live according to nature if they choose, and will all things to be as they are. Humans can follow God's path and be free from fear and inward disturbance about their own judgments. According to Marcus Aurelius, human beings partake of the divine intelligence; they are a morsel of the divine. The soul, or Reason, rules the body and is the source of impulses and aversions. People are frail and Marcus seems ambivalent about the soul's destiny (once speaking of its extinction but another time envisaging its translation to a different sphere).

Summary of Living Out the Philosophy

The Stoics, such as Zeno, Seneca, Epictetus and Marcus Aurelius commonly call their audience to live in accordance with nature; that is to will everything to be as God, Nature, Reason, Fate or the gods have allowed it. Both Seneca and Epictetus elaborate on this as a call to follow the example of the gods by living a life of virtue and thus become like them. Seneca calls his readers to commune with the gods in order to enjoy freedom from disturbance. The one who follows God may find themselves trained by him through various trials, according to both Seneca and Epictetus. Seneca says that their soul should cling loosely to the things of the body, which speeds their return to God. The emphasis of Epictetus is on having right opinions about the gods and our own judgments. They should honor the one within and live in purity both within and without. This will include destroying selfish desires, loving their fellows and seeking good. Marcus also stresses this theme and calls his reader to keep their inner genius pure, allowing the deity within to rule. This rule encompasses both the relationship to the gods by avoiding wrong sense-impressions concerning them, and in relationship to others, by running straight for the goal without being distracted by the opinions of others. At the same time, Marcus urges his readers to seek the common interest and to empathize with the experience of others.

2.4 MIDDLE PLATONISM

The term "Middle Platonism" is usually given to the Platonism of the era roughly between Antiochus of Ascalon (d. c. 68 BCE) and Plotinus (b. 205 CE), whose writings herald the start of Neoplatonism. This development of Platonism was eclectic and drew freely on the thinking of other schools, such as the Stoics, the Peripatetics and the Neopythagoreans. Most Middle Platonist works have been lost, with the notable exception of the large literary corpus of Plutarch and Philo.[369]

2.4.1 Plutarch

Plutarch of Chaeronea (c. 45–120 CE) moved in influential circles as a lecturer, philosopher and biographer and was also a priest at Delphi for the last thirty years of his life. He left behind him a voluminous collection of writings. Despite the reputation and extent of his *Parallel Lives*, these works will not be considered in this section, since they are more biographical than philosophical and, instead, I shall concentrate on his philosophical works that reveal Plutarch as indebted to Middle Platonism.[370]

Sacrifice Language

Plutarch's *Isis and Osiris* (his retelling of the Egyptian myth), offers advice for his readers in order that they may avoid superstition on the one hand, and atheism on the other, in their interpretation of the stories about these divinities. They must believe that, "no sacrifice that you can offer, no deed that you may do will be more likely to find favor with the gods than your

---

369. *OCD*, 1158; Ferguson, *Backgrounds*, 387–89. See especially Dillon, *Middle Platonists*, Preface xiv, 1, 115. Philo will be covered separately in the following chapter.

370. See *OCD*, 1165; Ferguson, *Backgrounds*, 389–90; Beck, *Companion*, 13–42. For Plutarch's life, see Russell, *Plutarch*, and Lamberton, *Plutarch* and, briefly, Dillon, *Middle Platonists*, 185–86; Brenk, "Imperial Heritage," 250–56, and for more on Plutarch's Platonism, Dillon, "Plutarch," 61–72.

Figurative Temple Language in Hellenistic Philosophy 87

belief in their true nature."[371] In this instance, a true understanding and trust in the gods is of greater value than sacrifice; making it a kind of figurative sacrifice. That said, this clause is conjoined to a preceding one, which adds an important condition here, "if you always perform and observe the established rites of worship,"[372] so Plutarch is not dismissing the necessity of literal sacrifices. Earlier in the same work, there are two references that are perhaps a little more ambiguous, but may also point to figurative sacrifice language. The first concerns "a longing for the divine" that focuses itself on the effort to arrive at the truth about their nature. This effort will involve study and investigation of "sacred subjects," and "it is a work more hallowed than any form of holy living or temple service" (ἁγνείας τε πάσης καὶ νεωκορίας ἔργον ὁσιώτερον).[373] Since the word translated by Frank Cole Babbitt "temple service" (νεωκόρος) is associated more with one who is responsible for the maintenance and security of the temple (whether an individual, a city, or a deity)[374] than it is for the service of offering sacrifices in the temple, Plutarch cannot be said to be directly comparing such a work with sacrifice. At the very least, however, he does identify study and seeking after divine truth as the holiest (ὅσιος) form of work. In the same book, Plutarch seeks to explain the etymology of the shrine of Isis, the Iseion, by the Greek word οἶδα (to know) in order to stress that a true worshiper can only understand the divine realities of that which they worship by a pure and holy disposition, "we shall comprehend reality if in a reasonable and devout frame of mind we pass within the portals of her shrines."[375] Like the earlier reference in *Isis and Osiris*, the emphasis lies on motivation, attitude and comprehension rather than the physical act of sacrifice. That said, Plutarch elsewhere speaks in a disparaging manner of those who reject belief in divine providence and the divinity of the planets, who are appropriately worshiped through sacrifice as well as prayer.[376] Again, Plutarch does not seem to be repudiating physical sacrifices.

There are two further references that may bear indirectly on the subject of figurative sacrifices. Firstly, in Plutarch's discourse *On Brotherly*

---

371. Plutarch, *Is. Os.* 355D (Babbit, LCL).
372. *Is. Os.* 355D (Babbit, LCL).
373. *Is. Os.* 351E (Babbit, LCL).
374. See "νεωκόρος," BDAG, 670.
375. Plutarch, *Is. Os.* 352A (Babbit, LCL).
376. *Adv. Col.* 1123A.

Love, he comments on duty to parents in view of the greatest honor that Nature and the Law have assigned to parents after the gods, and avers that, "there is nothing which men do that is more acceptable to gods than with goodwill and zeal to repay to those who bore them and brought them up the favours "long ago lent to them when they were young.""[377] This return of favor is more acceptable (κεχαρισμένον from χαρίζομαι) to the gods than anything else which could be offered, and that, presumably, by implication, would include the offering of sacrifices. Finally, in a discourse against the Epicureans, Plutarch insists that sacrifices and feast days are meaningless and do nothing for a person if the god's presence is not felt, "if the god is not present at the sacrifice as master of rites (so to speak) what is left bears no mark of sanctity or holy day and leaves the spirit untouched by the divine influence."[378] For this to happen, people must bring these thoughts close to God and honor and reverence him.[379] It can even be necessary for the sacrifice itself to, "both in body and in soul, be pure, unblemished, and unmarred."[380]

Temple Language

Plutarch's *On Tranquillity of Mind* is in agreement with Seneca (see Seneca, *Ben.* 7.7.3; *Ep.* 90.29 earlier) in affirming that, "the universe is a most holy temple and most worthy of a god."[381] Human beings enter the world as a spectator of its images, not the kind of images crafted by hand and placed in a temple, but "of those sensible representations of knowable things that the divine mind . . . has revealed."[382] Similarly, in his *Platonic Questions*, also acknowledging his debt to Plato, Plutarch states that the universe "has in it a large portion of vitality and divinity, which god sowed from himself in the matter and mixed with it,"[383] and speaking of the soul of the universe he adds, "The soul, however, when it has partaken of intelligence and reason and concord, is not merely a work but also a

---

377. *Frat. amor.* 479F (Helmbold, LCL).

378. *Suav. viv.* 1102A (Einarson, De Lacy, LCL).

379. *Suav. viv.* 1102B.

380. *Def. orac.* 437B.

381. *Tranq. an.* 477C (Helmbold, LCL).

382. *Tranq. an.* 477C (Helmbold, LCL), alluding to Plato's *Timaeus*, 92C and *Epinomis*, 984A.

383. *Quaest. plat.* 2, 1001B (Cherniss, LCL).

part of god and has come to be not by his agency but both from him as source and out of his substance."[384] The universe, then, is infused with god, deriving its life from him and even identified with divinity.[385] In the next question, Plato deals with the same subject, speaking of the god who stretched the soul through everything in the universe and thus preserved its corporeal state from dissolution (unlike the body of human beings which is "subject to mortality").[386] Plutarch also compares an individual to a temple in *How a Man May Become Aware of His Progress in Virtue*. He speaks of the man making progress in the path of virtue, for whom no sin is too small to overlook, and no vice is condoned. Unlike the sloppy laborer who uses whatever materials come to hand to finish a wall, his life has a "golden foundation."[387] His life is compared to "some holy temple or regal palace" where each action is fitted into the place prepared for it "using reason to guide them."[388]

The Nature of Divinity

God orders all things,[389] and "through noiseless ways advancing, guides by Justice all affairs of mortal men."[390] God is the creator (although the soul of the universe was not brought into being by him, but is self-moved, being regulated and ordered by him).[391] God is the source of the radiant vision of philosophy, "that beauty which is for men unutterable and indescribable,"[392] since he is great and majestic.[393] God is timeless;[394] he

---

384. *Quaest. plat.* 2, 1001C (Cherniss, LCL).

385. See also *Quaest. plat.* 8.

386. *Quaest. plat.* 2, 1002C (Cherniss, LCL). There is also a passing reference in *Amat.* 762E to "a god within," citing the words of Telemachus from Homer, *Od.* 19.40.

387. *Virt. prof.* 86A (Babbitt, LCL) (citing Pindar, *Frag.* 206.1.).

388. *Virt. prof.* 86A (Babbitt, LCL). The reference to "the god in his holy temple" in *Def. orac.* 437A concerns a sacrifice performed in a god's temple in order to discern his will.

389. *Is. Os.* 382B; Dillon, *Middle Platonists*, 199.

390. *Is. Os.* 381B (Babbitt, LCL), citing Euripides, *Tro.* 887–888 (see Plutarch, *Is. Os.* 172 n. a).

391. *An. procr.* 1013ABC, 1014BC, E, 1015E, 1016C, 1027A; cf. *Quaest. conv.* 720C.

392. *Is. Os.* 383A (Babbitt, LCL).

393. *Praec. ger. rei publ.* 822B.

394. *E Delph.* 393A (Babbitt, LCL).

binds together the substance of the world and keeps it from dissolution,[395] and sustains the universe.[396] God's qualities are described in passing as including "justice, benevolence and kindness"[397] and "goodness, magnanimity, kindliness, and solicitude."[398] He is the father of all that is honorable, and so it is his nature to bless and to help. He is ready to help because he is always standing near.[399] Plutarch's treatise, *On the Delays of the Divine Vengeance*, as its name suggests, assumes the premise that God does repay the wrongdoer, but considers the reasons why divine punishment is sometimes delayed. God is the great physician, knowing when it would be beneficial to delay punishment;[400] sometimes because he wants people to learn not to be vengeful in applying punishment themselves,[401] and at other times because he knows which souls will respond with repentance, given a period of grace.[402] In other cases, he will punish preemptively, rooting out the evil in someone predisposed to it before they commit wrong.[403]

There is one Reason and one Providence, which watches over all peoples, though the gods may be known by different names in different places, according to local custom.[404] The gods are their own masters, not subject to anyone's control,[405] and indestructible.[406] They are good governors,[407] and are described as acting with, "moderation, adequacy, excess in nothing, and complete self-sufficiency."[408] In accordance with their own nature, the gods derive, "their only or their chief enjoyment"

---

395. *E Delph.* 393F.

396. *Exil.* 601B; *Adv. Col.* 1124F.

397. *Def. orac.* 423D (Babbitt, LCL).

398. *Superst.* 167F (Babbitt, LCL).

399. *Suav. viv.* 1102D.

400. *Sera* 549F.

401. *Sera* 550 E–551 C.

402. *Sera* 551D.

403. *Sera* 562D. For more on Plutarch's conception of God, see Brenk, "Imperial Heritage," 262–75.

404. *Is. Os.* 377F.

405. *Def. orac.* 426C.

406. *Comm. not.* 1074EF–1075D, against the Stoics' claim that, though Zeus was eternal and indestructible, other gods were eventually consumed (since the planets were considered to be gods).

407. *Adv. Col.* 1124F.

408. *Def. orac.* 413F (Babbitt, LCL).

from "the good deeds and noble actions" of those who engage in public affairs.[409] Indeed, they are the most important friends of people.[410] Plutarch has Heracleon in *On the Obsolescence of Oracles* advance the opinion that Providence acts like "a benign and helpful mother, who does everything for us and watches over us."[411] This provision includes things like sight, hearing and medicinal agents.[412] Like Seneca and Marcus Aurelius, Plutarch can speak of Nature using the same language that he uses to speak about God. But Plutarch distinguishes himself from the Stoics in respect to Nature. Unlike them, he does not understand there to be one good, governing force, such as Reason, which doles out both good and evil as part of its good purposes. Rather, Nature has, "commingled" within itself two opposing principles, one of which guides us in a straight line to the right path, but the other down a different path, "Nature must have in herself the source and origin of evil, just as she contains the source and origin of good."[413] Nature takes the initiative in many matters, even acting above God. Nature, together with the Law, is described as assigning honor to gods.[414] Nature is repeatedly described as the source of life and limbs,[415] called "the most holy and great of sacred things"[416] and is the one who implants emotions in her creatures[417] and introduces people "to a conception of justice and law and to the worship of the gods"[418] (rather than the initiative lying with God).

The Nature of Humanity

Plutarch puts into the mouth of one of his characters the view that, "men are divine and dear to God."[419] Their very birth and their "becoming"

---

409. *An seni* 786B (Fowler, LCL).
410. *Conj. praec.* 140D.
411. *Def. orac.* 413C (Babbitt, LCL); see also the treatment of this topic in *Stoic. rep.*
412. *Def. orac.* 436D.
413. *Is. Os.* 369D (Babbitt, LCL); see also Dillon, *Middle Platonists*, 202–4.
414. *Frat. amor.* 479F.
415. E.g., *Frat. amor.* 478DEF; 479CD; 480B.
416. *Frat. amor.* 479D (Helmbold, LCL).
417. *Am. prol.* 494F.
418. *Am. prol.* 495C (Helmbold, LCL).
419. *Gen. Socr.* 593A (De Lacy, Einarson, LCL).

"are a gift of God to make him known."[420] In particular, the king is in the "image" (εἰκών) of God, and forms himself in the "likeness" (ὁμοίωμα) of God by his virtue,[421] "and thus creates a statue most delightful of all to behold and most worthy of divinity," provided the ruler upholds righteous decisions "in God's likeness" (θεουδής[422]).[423] Some the Gods wish to make divine, whereas others, having been set free from the body, become daemons that watch over people.[424] They are like retired athletes, who cheer on those who are still running the race of life, and encourage them to reach their goal.[425] Vice and depravity come from the soul itself, and become its sickness.[426] Elsewhere, Plutarch, citing Homer, avers that the body is the dwelling of both good and evil.[427] In line with Plato's own thought, souls are wanderers, exiled from their true home, who are imprisoned within their bodies,[428] viewed as, "the encasement of their souls."[429] For this reason, persons should have as little association with the body as is possible in their earthy life.[430] The body is the instrument of the soul, but the soul is granted a far loftier role; it is the instrument of God.[431] After death, the soul will be set free from the body, and travels to the realm of things invisible and pure where God truly rules as their king.[432] The soul is imperishable and thus will never die.[433] The honor

---

420. *Lat. viv.* 1129F (De Lacy, LCL).

421. *Princ. iner.* 780E (Fowler, LCL); cf. also *Princ. iner.* 781A.

422. The definition of θεουδής is "fear of God" according to "θεουδής," LSJ, 792, but adds that it can be taken as θεοειδής, meaning "godlike" in works later than Homer; cf. "θεοειδής," LSJ, 790.

423. *Princ. iner.* 780F (Fowler, LCL).

424. *Gen. Socr.* 593D. Dillon, *Middle Platonists*, 46–47 notes the development of the theory of daemons in Plutarch and subsequent Middle Platonic thinkers.

425. *Gen. Socr.* 593DEF; cf. 1 Cor 9:24–27; 1 Tim 6:12; 2 Tim 2:5; 2 Tim 4:7; Heb 12:1–3; Jude 3. On this notion of daemons and guardian spirits in Plutarch, see Dillon, *Middle Platonists*, 217–21, and Brenk, "Imperial Heritage," 275–94.

426. *An. corp.* 500C; cf. Dillon, *Middle Platonists*, 208.

427. *Virt. prof.* 122E, citing Homer, *Od.* 4.392.

428. *Exil.* 607D.

429. *Is. Os.* 353A (Babbitt, LCL).

430. [*Cons. Apoll.*] 108CD; a common view in Middle Platonism, see Dillon, *Middle Platonists*, 47.

431. *Sept. sap. conv.* 163E. For more on the soul in Plutarch, see Dillon, *Middle Platonists*, 194, 202–8, 211–13.

432. *Is. Os.* 383A; cf. *Suav. viv.* 1105D.

433. *Cons. ux.* 611EF, 612A.

or punishment due to the soul for its life on earth is awarded to it after death,[434] but in one passage in *On the Delays of the Divine Vengeance*, Plutarch envisages these rewards and punishments being meted out to the living descendants of the soul.[435]

Living Out the Philosophy

Because Plutarch's *Moralia* is such a large corpus (nearly eighty works) and since ethics is such a major concern of those works, it is not possible in a brief survey of this nature to provide a comprehensive analysis of the ways in which Plutarch's understanding of God's relationship to humanity should affect how people live. Instead, I shall provide a very brief representative sample of his advice by drawing on some of the works cited in earlier sections. Wise people should ask for good things from the gods and in particular that they may gain a knowledge of the gods themselves; that is, a revelation of true reality.[436] The true worshiper cannot simply rely on the knowledge of religious rites communicated to them; they must use reason to understand the truth.[437] This reasoning must come from Philosophy.[438] This is the most divine possession available to humanity, especially the capacity to reason concerning the gods, and nothing has greater power to bring true happiness.[439] Those who are wise should honor the inanimate and incorporeal objects, which point toward the Divine, recognizing them as instruments of God for that purpose.[440] In particular, Reason directs the passions toward the right course.[441] Reasons provides guidance in matters as diverse as, for example, caring for wives,[442] knowing how to speak succinctly and show restraint in speech,[443]

---

434. *Sera* 560F; cf. *Suav. viv.* 1105C.
435. *Sera* 561A.
436. *Is. Os.* 351D.
437. *Is. Os.* 352C.
438. *Is. Os.* 378A.
439. *Is. Os.* 378CD c.f. *Cupid. divit.* 527F.
440. *Is. Os.* 382AB.
441. See generally, *Virt. mor.*
442. *Frat. amor.* 491DE.
443. E.g., *Garr.* 510DE.

how to handle wealth,[444] avoiding envy and hate,[445] and rage,[446] and how to praise oneself for the right reasons,[447] among many other topics. In each of these areas of life, and many more, the person of virtue should copy and aspire to, "the beauty and the goodness that are his."[448] Above all, the soul should be ready to yield itself to the service of God, "for Him to direct it and turn it in whatsoever course He may desire."[449] This emphasis corresponds to a wider pattern in Middle Platonism. Such philosophers tended to see the *telos* of existence as knowing and imitating God, rather than the Stoic goal of living in accordance with nature.[450]

2.4.2 Alcinous

Alcinous is one of two second century Middle Platonic philosophers with whom I shall deal briefly. Although they are both later than Paul (and even the second century dating of Alcinous is the best reasonable conjecture, rather than an established date),[451] their ideas are congruent with earlier writers influenced by Middle Platonism, such as Plutarch and Philo.[452] In the absence of other extant Middle Platonic works earlier than or contemporaneous with Paul, I shall draw on Alcinous and Maximus of Tyre to support my observations from Plutarch (and, in the next chapter, from Philo).

---

444. E.g., *Cupid. divit.* 526AB.
445. *Inv. od.* generally.
446. *Sera* 550E–551C.
447. *De laude* generally.
448. *Sera* 550E (De Lacy, Einarson, LCL).
449. *Sept. sap. conv.* 163E (Babbitt, LCL).
450. See Dillon, *Middle Platonists*, 43–44, 192–93, 229.
451. See *OCD*, 53; Alcinous, *Handbook*, Preface, and ix–xl.
452. John Dillon's commentary in Alcinous, *Handbook*, 51–211, draws out the way Alcinous' work is directly dependent upon and often cites (or alludes to) the work of Plato. The sections with which I will engage evince a particular dependence on Plato's *Timaeus*.

Temple Language

The main allusion to God's indwelling presence, is the statement that, "by his own will he has filled all things with himself," in reference to a "rousing up" of the soul of the world which gives it its intellect.[453]

The Nature of Divinity

Alcinous surmises that whatever is prior to actualized intellect (as actualized intellect is superior to potential intellect, and potential intellect is to the soul) must be God, the "unmoved mover" of Aristotle.[454] Since nothing finer than God's thoughts can be conceived, God must be eternally thinking about his own thoughts,[455] and his own thoughts are eternal and unchanging.[456] This God is also perfect in every way; in beauty, truth and goodness and the Father of all things.[457] God has no parts, and so, is incorporeal.[458] The world always existed but God endowed it with soul and intellect and brought order to the world soul that has also existed eternally.[459] On the other hand, God created the other divinities (including daemons).[460] Of all species, Alcinous considers humanity to be "most akin to the gods" and so God himself created people, and sent down the appropriate number of souls to earth (equal to the stars) and expounded his revelation of the order of things to them (as opposed to animals, fish and birds, whose creation is attributed to lesser gods).[461]

The Nature of Humanity

The soul who engages in contemplation of the divine and its thoughts achieves a state of wisdom, which is described, by negation, as "no other

---

453. Alcinous, *Handbook*, 165.10.3.1–2 (18). The numbers in parentheses denote the page numbers in Dillon's translation.

454. Alcinous, *Handbook*, 164.10.2.18–26 (17) and see Dillon's commentary on 103.

455. Alcinous, *Handbook*, 164.10.3.27–29 (17–18).

456. Alcinous, *Handbook*, 163.9.30–35 (16).

457. Alcinous, *Handbook*, 164.10.31–41 (18).

458. Alcinous, *Handbook*, 165.34–166.14 (19).

459. Alcinous, *Handbook*, 169.14.3–170.4 (23–24).

460. Alcinous, *Handbook*, 171.15.1.15–2.23 (25).

461. Alcinous, *Handbook*, 171.1.38–172.2.12 (26), drawing on Plato, *Tim.* 41 BCD.

than likeness to the divine."[462] The soul's nature is to rule and it is, "imperishable and indestructible."[463]

Living Out the Philosophy

Despite being described as "ineffable," it is possible for the seeker after him to grasp him by the intellect. Alcinous outlines a number of paths to do so, by meditating on his attributes, by analogy, by contemplating his beauty by a series of steps; from beauty in bodies, to souls, to laws and on to a final "intuition of the Good," that becomes like a light shining on the soul as it ascends on its path toward God.[464] Likeness of God, declares Alcinous, following Plato, consists at least in being just, and preferably in being, "intelligent, and just, and pious."[465] This likeness to God is attained by those who have a "suitable nature" and who, further, train that nature by the right habits and disciplines of philosophy, reason and education. This must be coupled by a distancing of oneself from worldly concerns, and a correspondent intimacy with "intelligible reality."[466] Perhaps surprisingly for a Jewish or Christian reader, however, is that the god whose likeness Alcinous says souls should imitate is not the supreme God, but the "god in the heavens" described in chapter 10.[467] The goal of the souls is to return to their "kindred star" and the key to achieving this goal is to achieve dominance over the sensations that would seek to attach themselves to them from the body.[468]

2.4.3 Maximus of Tyre

Little is known of Maximus of Tyre, other than his second century CE date. We have 41 extant Lectures or *Philosophical Orations* that seems to

---

462. Alcinous, *Handbook*, 153.2.5–8 (4); cf. 177.25.34 (33); 181.28.1.19–20 (37), citing Plato.

463. Alcinous, *Handbook*, 177.25.33–35 (33).

464. Alcinous, *Handbook*, 165.10.4–6 (18–19).

465. Alcinous, *Handbook*, 181.28.22–30 (37), and see the references from Plato cited there and the commentary on (170).

466. Alcinous, *Handbook*, 182.4.3–8 (38).

467. Alcinous, *Handbook*, 181.28.3.44–46 (38).

468. Alcinous, *Handbook*, 172.16.2.10–19 (26), drawing on Plato, *Tim.* 42AB.

have been delivered during the reign of Commodus in Rome. His work clearly draws on Middle Platonic thought.[469]

Sacrifice Language

Although Maximus does not directly use the language of sacrifice, he does speak of the kind of worship that the gods require. In his oration on the images of the Gods, he emphasizes that the gods do not need images, statues or dedications; rather, this is more for the benefit of humanity in its own weakness. Yet, "People whose memories are strong, and who can reach straight out for the heavens with their souls and encounter the divine, may perhaps have no need of images."[470] Those who are advanced in their understanding of their worship, "honour them, but by word of mouth alone, believing that the gods have no need of images and dedications,"[471] that would include sacrifices. Direct encounter with the divine and the prayers and praises of the lips are what is needed, rather than literal sacrifices.

Temple Language

There are two obvious instances of 'indwelling' language in Maximus. The first of these reads, "God has breathed expectation of the Good into the human race like a spark of life"[472] but the second says that Nature "has breathed into him [man] an invisible spark to ensure his survival, a spark which men call intelligence, thanks to which his continued survival is assured."[473] Though Maximus uses the language of 'spark' in both instances, one statement refers to an expectation of "the Good" (used by Maximus for the ideal of virtue, as we shall see below) and the other to intelligence.[474] However, what is of interest is that in the first sentence the subject is God, and in the second it is Nature. I shall also observe below

---

469. See *OCD*, 915 and the introduction to Trapp, *Maximus*.
470. Maximus of Tyre, *Or.* 2.2. All translations are taken from Trapp, *Maximus*.
471. *Or.* 2.1.
472. *Or.* 29.6.
473. *Or.* 31.4.
474. A further reference to a spark, this time to philosophy, that knows and communicates to humanity the way to pray, can be found in *Or.* 5.8.

the way that different functions are attributed to God and to Nature in Maximus's philosophy.

The Nature of Divinity

God is described in a number of places as Father and Creator.[475] He is immortal and free from emotion.[476] He is wiser than man,[477] and the source of all beauty, himself beautiful.[478] God is not divided between soul and body, as humans are, but rather, he is incorporeal, "of a single nature, pure intelligence and knowledge and reason."[479] God is understood as "the most perfect form of intellect . . . which thinks all things for ever at the same time,"[480] prompting the translator, Michael B. Trapp, to compare Maximus to the writer I have just surveyed, Alcinous, "where one sees the same slide from God as supreme Intelligible to God as supreme Intelligence."[481] In one revealing Oration that addresses the topic of prayer, Maximus distinguishes between the jurisdictions of different powers, "Of all the things which men pray to obtain, some are under the control of Providence, some are enforced by Destiny, some are at the mercy of fickle Fortune, and some are regulated by Science. Providence is God's work, Destiny the work of Necessity, Science the work of man, and Fortune the work of blind Chance."[482] Therefore, the object and goal of prayer must be related to the particular power that might determine the answer and in some cases, prayer is unnecessary since ineffectual, "nothing that falls under the heading of Providence is to be requested or prayed for."[483] Although the examples I have examined from Stoic writers sometimes suggest fine distinctions between, for instance, Nature and God, many of them blur the boundaries considerably. Maximus, by contrast, demarcates quite separate roles for Nature, Providence, Necessity

---

475. *Or.* 2.10; 11.5; 11.9, 12; 41.2.
476. *Or.* 9.2.
477. *Or.* 6.1.
478. *Or.* 11.11.
479. *Or.* 27.8.
480. *Or.* 11.8; cf. 11.9.
481. Trapp, *Maximus*, 102–3; comparing this passage with Alcinous, *Handbook*, 164.10 (18) that was cited in the discussion on the "Nature of Divinity" in Alcinous.
482. Maximus of Tyre, *Or.* 5.4.
483. *Or.* 5.4.

and Chance in a way that seems foreign to Stoicism.[484] Fate is impersonal, acting in a regular, impartial manner.[485] God is also described as King;[486] he administers the heavens,[487] and governs skillfully with "beauty and artistry and knowledge"; a knowledge which consists in virtue.[488] His government and direction of the universe is compared to a master musician and conductor, a mechanic who understands perfectly the machines he operates (compared to the human power of reasoning), a helmsman who watches the sea, and a doctor whose knowledge of disease and patients leads to the right diagnosis.[489] Despite what I have noted about the separate dispensations of God, Fate, Providence and Chance, at the same time, Maximus claims that in governing, he is assisted by "Chance and Opportunity" but that they are merely "secondary influences"; God is the "all-controlling agent in human affairs."[490] Having made the claim that God is all-controlling, Maximus is quick to point out that evil does not come from the hand of God, nor through Fate.[491] In this, as Trapp indicates, Maximus distances evil from Fate and Providence in a way quite different to Stoic writers, who speak more of only seeming-evils that turn out for the best.[492] Sometimes these evils arise from God's work but they are ancillary; not caused or intended by God, like the anvil and heat from the furnace that are "necessary consequences" of the work done by the master craftsman (this image again), rather than the direct product of his work.[493]

Gods also exist and lend their aid to humanity.[494] Although the Universe is the shared home of both gods and people, the gods do not dwell

---

484. Alexander of Aphrodisias, a philosopher from c. 200 CE, referring to the Stoic view of freedom, writes, "everything they do is done of necessity" (Alexander, *On fate* 181,13–182,20 (SVF 2.979)); translation from Long and Sedley, *Hellenistic Philosophers Vol 1*, 62G, 389–90. For more on fate and necessity in Stoicism, see Rist, *Stoic Philosophy*, 112–32 and especially Bobzien, *Determinism*.

485. Maximus of Tyre, *Or*. 13.4.

486. *Or*. 11.5.

487. *Or*. 8.8.

488. *Or*. 27.8.

489. *Or*. 13.3–4; cf. also *Or*. 41.4 for the craftsman analogy.

490. *Or*. 13.7, citing Plato, *Leg*. 709bc.

491. *Or*. 13.8.

492. Trapp, *Maximus*, 123 n. 33.

493. Maximus of Tyre, *Or*. 41.4; cf. 41.5.

494. *Or*. 2.1.

in the earth but in heaven.[495] Below the gods are the daemons, which are superior to men, since they relate more closely to God than people do. Daemons share in kinship with both, and form a kind of bridge between God and humanity.[496] These daemons share in God's immortality but are susceptible to emotions in a way that God is not.[497] They are disembodied souls who became daemons and act as watchers or guardian angels; acting on behalf of the good and punishing the wicked.[498]

The Nature of Humanity

Maximus assumes that the soul is very close to God and like him in nature.[499] The soul is a compound of both the mortal and the immortal, that has different functions in relation to its components, including perception, intellect and prudence, and "in virtue of its immortal component it unites with the divine, in that it is capable of thought, reasoning, learning, and knowledge."[500] There is a "sparse," yet real, element of good in human nature that can reap a harvest in the lives of great pupils if they fan into flame the "living, breathing spark that alone knows how to pray" by availing themselves of philosophy.[501] Since the soul comes from "the same stock as Beauty itself," it is able to recollect the true Beauty that is "immortal and ineffable."[502] There are rewards and punishments for people, awarded to them by God (vice to those of a wicked nature and virtue to those of a good nature).[503] This assumes that virtue and vice come from within the souls of people,[504] and, despite Maximus's idea of providence and fate, vice can be freely chosen in such a way that God is blameless for the fault.[505] Despite this, elsewhere, Maximus contends that Virtue

---

495. *Or.* 13.6.

496. *Or.* 8.8.

497. *Or.* 9.2.

498. *Or.* 9.6–7; 13.6.

499. *Or.* 2.3, and thus, unlike the animals, in that humans can know God by virtue of reason (see *Or.* 41.5).

500. *Or.* 6.4; cf. also *Or.* 9.6; 33.7.

501. *Or.* 5.8.

502. *Or.* 21.7–8.

503. *Or.* 8.7.

504. Assumed by *Or.* 34.3.

505. *Or.* 41.5.

Figurative Temple Language in Hellenistic Philosophy 101

is distributed by God, and yet God's assistance is needed in the fight between Virtue and Vice, to enable individuals to be victorious in the struggle.[506] The soul rules over the body,[507] holding it together as if a ship in the stormy sea of life.[508] On earth, the soul is like a captive to the body and life is like dreaming while it is still entrapped in the flesh.[509] The soul and body are intertwined and, "the one is implicated in the discomforts and pleasures of the other."[510] However, the soul has innate knowledge ("self-taught") that can be awakened by Reason, and Reason then allows the soul to at least dimly perceive reality.[511] Reason is described as acting like a midwife to the pregnant soul,[512] but in this analogy the soul is the procreator; it has its own powers of discovery, "which are self-generated, natural and innate."[513] However, the soul longs to be free from the body and feels no regret to shed its skin, like a prisoner set free from confinement or a man who swims free to shore.[514] At this point reality is visible at last to the soul who joins the gods, "as a member of the divine host led and commanded by Zeus."[515] The virtuous soul becomes a "daimon," who watches over its former peers for whom it feels pity.[516]

Living Out the Philosophy

In order for the soul to ascend to God it must focus its attention on him. The intellect will see and hear the things of the Divine, "by bringing to bear an upright, vigorous soul, by fixing its gaze firmly on that pure light ... and entrusting its guidance to true Reason and vigorous Love,"[517] and eventually by stripping off the clothing of the body.[518] On this earth, the

---

506. *Or.* 38.6.
507. *Or.* 7.2; 9.6.
508. *Or.* 9.6; 40.5.
509. *Or.* 10.3–5.
510. *Or.* 28.2.
511. *Or.* 10.3, 9.
512. *Or.* 10.4.
513. *Or.* 10.5.
514. *Or.* 7.5; 9.6; cf. 10.9.
515. *Or.* 10.9.
516. *Or.* 9.6.
517. *Or.* 11.10.
518. *Or.* 11.11.

good person should live a life of virtuous action,[519] doing no wrong.[520] For this, moral education is needed,[521] and people should imitate God (for instance, his "preservative and affectionate and paternal qualities"),[522] and seize hold of "the Good," the highest and greatest of all virtue, which can neither be increased nor decreased.[523] At the same time, the soul must resist vice, restraining its impulses by preserving its recollections of God, like a charioteer who restrains the impulses of the horses driving the chariot.[524]

2.4.4 Summary of Our Findings from Middle Platonism

Summary of Sacrifice Language

Plutarch emphasizes a pure motivation in worship, but also speaks of other things that could count as a sacrifice, such as trusting in and understanding the gods and study and seeking after divine truth. Additionally, the return of favor to parents is compared to a sacrifice in the temple. Maximus of Tyre allows for worshiping God with prayer and contemplation as if this could function as a substitute for a physical sacrifice.

Summary of Temple Language

Plutarch speaks of the universe as a holy temple (as Seneca did also), which has been sowed with divinity and is identified with God. A person can also be a temple, guided by reason in the path of virtue, where each action is fitted in its rightful place, just as with each part of the temple. Alcinous agrees that God fills all things with himself, and Maximus says that God and Nature have breathed into people the expectation of good and the spark of intelligence.

---

519. *Or.* 15.6, 10.
520. *Or.* 12.
521. *Or.* 27.9.
522. *Or.* 35.2; cf. 26.9.
523. *Or.* 39.1, 3; 40.3, 4.
524. *Or.* 41.5.

Summary of the Nature of Divinity

Plutarch speaks of God as the creator and sustainer of the universe and the source of philosophy. He is beneficent, timeless and incorporeal. There is one Reason and Providence, and God sends or delays punishment at the appropriate time. The gods are known by different names in different places and act as good governors. Unlike the Stoics, Plutarch sees Nature as the source of both good and evil. It can take the initiative and act almost independently of God. Alcinous sees God more as pure intellect, a kind of Aristotelean unmoved-mover. God is occupied with thinking about his own perfect thoughts. He endowed the pre-existing world with intellect or soul and brought order to the world soul. He communicates with people and created both divinities and daemons. Maximus speaks of God as father, creator, immortal incorporeal (like Alcinous) and source of all beauty and goodness. Like Alcinous, God is conceived as perfect intelligence. Yet not everything is under his control, and Maximus envisages separate roles for Nature and Providence. Elsewhere he speaks of God governing with the assistance of Chance and Opportunity. Evil is not the direct result of God's work and is distinct from Fate and Providence. The gods help people but they reside in the heavens, not the earth.

Summary of the Nature of Humanity

Plutarch understands humanity as divine, and very dear to God. The king in particular is an image of God and can become like God. Some are made divine by God; others are set free from the body and become daemons after death. Both good and evil reside in the soul. After death, the soul is set free and travels to the divine realm. Honor and punishment are meted out after death, but to living descendants. Alcinous, like Plutarch, sees humanity as most akin to the gods. The soul who contemplates the divine can become like it and is imperishable. Maximus agrees with both writers that the soul is like God, and since it is a compound of both the mortal and immortal, it can unite with the divine. Humans can recollect the beauty of the divine and fan into flame the divine spark within them. Virtue and vice come from within and are appropriately rewarded or punished. God can aid these virtues. The soul rules the body and can be awakened by reason and set free.

Summary of Living Out the Philosophy

Plutarch urges his audience to use reason to seek the revelation of God. A person should honor what points to the divine, and follow Reason's guidance with the passions and live a temperate life by imitating God's beauty and goodness and let themselves be directed by God's design. Alcinous claims that one can grasp God by the intellect and become like him in his virtues, although, unlike the other writers, he concedes that it is not the supreme God whom we can imitate but only the "god in the heavens." This process comes about through discipline, moral education and by distancing oneself from the body and worldly concerns. Maximus calls his readers to be guided by Reason and thus fix their gaze on the divine. They should live a life of virtue and imitate God through moral education; seizing the good and resisting Vice.

2.5 SKEPTICISM

The "Academy" was the name given to the school founded by Plato in the fourth century BCE. The "New Academy" was associated more with Skepticism than Platonism,[525] and under heads such as Carneades (214/3–129/8 BCE),[526] and Philon of Larissa (159/8–84/3 BCE), argued for the impossibility of certain knowledge and therefore the suspension of judgment on all matters, though Philon, following Carneades, argued for a theory of "plausible impressions" that would allow Skeptics to follow the view they deemed most convincing. Cicero was a devoted follower of Philon.[527]

2.5.1 Cicero

Here I shall be considering Cicero's own views, as distinct from his summaries of other schools covered elsewhere in this chapter. Marcus Tulles Cicero (106–43 BCE), came from a wealthy and well-connected family, and rose through the ranks to become consul. He studied both philosophy and rhetoric and wrote widely in both fields, through varying

---

525. *OCD*, 2.
526. *OCD*, 282; Kristeller, *Greek Philosophers*, 87–99.
527. *OCD*, 1133; ibid., 99–103.

Figurative Temple Language in Hellenistic Philosophy 105

political fortunes.[528] In this survey I shall limit my investigations to his philosophical works.

Sacrifice Language

At the start of the second book of *De Legibus*, Cicero uses the metaphor of adoption to speak of the relationship between Rome and its citizens. Although, in common with other Italians, they might be expected to give allegiance to the fatherland in which they were born, Cicero uses a sacrificial image to urge total consecration to Rome, "For her it is our duty to die, to her to give ourselves entirely, to place on her altar, and, as it were, to dedicate to her service, all that we possess" (pro qua mori et cui nos totos dedere et in qua nostra omnia ponere et quasi consecrare debemus).[529]

Later, in Cicero's laws on religion, he requires that the worshiper approach the gods in purity, "bringing piety."[530] Although the requirement of purity is the normal standard for worship of the gods, Cicero then clarifies his instructions with the expansion, "that is, purity of mind, for everything is included in that" and, while still requiring bodily purity in worship, he avers, "we ought to be much more careful about the mind."[531] Further, the rule that piety should be brought "means that uprightness is pleasing to God" as well as open access to his presence for all.[532] While the requirements of literal sacrifice are not waived,[533] Cicero is clear that mental and spiritual purity are even more important.

---

528. *OCD*, 1514-19; Ferguson, *Backgrounds*, 380-82. For overviews of Cicero's philosophical thought, see, e.g., Long, "Roman Philosophy," 198-200; MacKendrick, *Philosophical Books*, 1-28; Powell, "Introduction," 1-35; and Schofield, "Writing Philosophy," 73-87. For biographies of Cicero, see Lacey, *Cicero*; Tempest, *Cicero*; and Corbeill, "Cicero," 9-24; and for a biographical portrait that allows Cicero to speak for himself, see Bailey, *Cicero*.

529. Cicero, *Leg.* 2.2.5 (Keyes, LCL).

530. *Leg.* 2.8.19 (Keyes, LCL).

531. *Leg.* 2.10.24 (Keyes, LCL).

532. *Leg.* 2.10.25 (Keyes, LCL).

533. And see *Leg.* 1.15.43 (Keyes, LCL), where he upholds "rites and pious observances in honour of the gods," and that "the sacred rites and ceremonies" should be retained in order to preserve "the institutions of our forefathers" according to *Div.* 2.72.148 (Falconer, LCL).

Temple Language

Philosophy teaches us to know ourselves, according to Cicero. The one who knows himself, will recognize something essential to his being, "he has a divine element within him, and will think of his own inner nature as a kind of consecrated image of God."[534] He cites, seemingly with approval, the view of Socrates that a divine influence (δαιμόνιον) constrains him and ought to be obeyed.[535] In his work *De divinatione*, Cicero understands that the universe, "is wholly filled with the Eternal Intelligence and the Divine Mind" which influences the human soul who is brought into contact with it, usually in sleep.[536] This same idea that the gods fill the universe is expounded using temple terminology in the second book of *De Legibus*, where Cicero substantiates his argument that shrines to the gods should not be shut up in homes or temples, "seeing that this whole universe is their temple and home" (quorumque hic mundus omnis templum esset et domus),[537] in agreement with Seneca and Plutarch. Cicero then connects the dedication of Roman temples to the deification of intellect, piety, virtue and good faith, and says of these qualities, "the purpose being that those who possess them (and all good men do) should believe that the gods themselves are established within their own souls."[538] Cicero cites, with approval, the words of Thales of Miletus (the pre-Socratic seventh-sixth century BCE philosopher), "that men ought to believe that everything they see is filled with the gods."[539] In particular, though all have immortal souls, the souls of those who are brave and good can be described as "divine."[540] The final book (Book 6) of *De republica* narrates the mystical dream of Scipio (*Somnium Scipionis*), a Roman general from an earlier era. As such, it is difficult to be sure

---

534. *Leg.* 1.22.59 (Keyes, LCL).

535. *Div.* 1.54.122; cf. 1.53.120.

536. *Div.* 1.49.110 (Falconer, LCL); cf. also *Div.* 1.52.118.

537. *Leg.* 2.10.26 (Keyes, LCL). We should also note in passing that Cicero makes mention of Xerxes burning the temples at Athens, for "he thought it sacrilege to keep the gods whose home is the whole universe shut up within walls" (*Resp.* 3.9.14 (Keyes, LCL)). The universe is described as their home (domus) rather than temple, but in the immediate literary context the contrast with the Athenian temples *could* suggest that the universe is a superior temple to the Athenian temples.

538. *Leg.* 2.11.28 (Keyes, LCL).

539. *Leg.* 2.11.26 (Keyes, LCL), which is taken from Aristotle, *De an.* 1. 411 A, according to 403 n. 3.

540. *Leg.* 2.11.27 (Keyes, LCL).

whether the beliefs expressed by Scipio are identical to those of Cicero and some of his ideas may be influenced by Stoicism. Since Cicero does not provide a riposte to the views expressed, they are narrated here rather than in the section on Stoic writings. In the dream, Scipio is visited by his father Paulus, who, in passing, alludes to his conviction that everything which Scipio sees is God's temple.[541] Later in the dream, Africanus claims that Scipio is a god, "if a god is that which lives, feels, remembers, and foresees, and which rules, governs, and moves the body over which it is set, just as the supreme God above us rules this universe," comparing the "immortal spirit" ruling his body to the eternal God ruling the universe.[542] This again is suggestive of the concept of the divine ruling the body (the idea of a genius or *daemon*) which we saw in Stoic literature.

Further, in *Tusculanae disputationes*, Cicero contends for the importance of the view that there are divine elements in souls.[543] Whatever else he knows about the soul, "it is divine" and resembles the soul of God.[544] In a passing comment, Cicero alludes to "the God who is master within us" (dominans ille in nobis deus).[545]

The Nature of Divinity

God is a divine mind and a god "of transcendent power."[546] He knows "to their innermost depths" all that people think and do.[547] God is the one who begets human beings and yet, "Nature, alone and unaided, goes a step farther" by strengthening the reason of people,[548] and sustaining the universe.[549] Law also is pictured as a god-like figure, since it is, "something eternal which rules the whole universe by its wisdom in command

---

541. *Resp.* 6.15.15. The one caveat to this finding is that the translator Clinton W. Keyes, remarks that "Templum originally meant a region of the sky marked off for purposes of divination" (Keyes, LCL, 267 n. 1). If this is relevant to the saying, it makes the reference a less certain one for my purposes. That said, we have seen elsewhere that the universe is frequently considered to be the temple of the gods.

542. *Resp.* 6.24.26 (Keyes, LCL).

543. *Tusc.* 1.24.56.

544. *Tusc.* 1.25.62 (King, LCL); so also *Tusc.* 1.26.65; 1.27.66–67; *Parad.* 1.14.

545. *Tusc.* 1.30.74 (King, LCL).

546. *Leg.* 1.7.23 (Keyes, LCL).

547. *Div.* 1.11.17 (Falconer, LCL).

548. *Leg.* 1.7.26–27.

549. *lib. inc. fr.* 2.

and prohibition." It is nothing less than, "the primal and ultimate mind of God,"[550] equated with reason and contemporary with God, who would not be able to function without it, "it is coeval with that God who guards and rules heaven and earth. For the divine mind cannot exist without reason."[551] Yet, elsewhere God is described as the "author," "promulgator" and "enforcing judge" of this Law.[552] The gods rule over all things but they are benevolent, while also taking account of the good and evil characters of people.[553] Either the gods or Mother Nature appoint the day of death.[554] There is at least one recorded instance of a man (Romulus, the founder of Rome) being added to the number of the gods.[555]

The Nature of Humanity

According to Cicero, humanity has a highly exalted status. The human soul has the divine soul as its source.[556] Human beings are the only creatures who share with God in reason and thought and so can attain to wisdom.[557] This is particularly so of those who practice divination and "seem to approach very near to the divine spirit of the gods."[558] This right reason is expressed in Law and so it follows that humans share Law in common with the gods.[559] Gods and human beings share the universe as one commonwealth.[560] The soul was generated by God, and thus share a kind of "blood relationship." Following this, only humans of all creatures have a knowledge of God.[561] Humans share in his likeness and can exhibit Virtue, which is Nature at its pinnacle,[562] or reason "completely

---

550. *Leg.* 2.4.8 (Keyes, LCL).

551. *Leg.* 2.4.8–10 (Keyes, LCL).

552. *Resp.* 2.22.23.

553. *Leg.* 2.7.15–16. Their existence is believed in by "natural instinct" and their nature "by the exercise of reason" according to *Tusc.* 1.16.36 (King, LCL).

554. *Tusc.* 1.49.118; cf. *Div.* 1.51.117.

555. *Resp.* 2.10.17.

556. *Div.* 1.32.70; 1.49.110; cf. *Amic.* 4.13.

557. *Leg.* 1.7.22–23.

558. *Div.* 1.18.34 (Falconer, LCL).

559. *Leg.* 1.7.23; cf. *Leg.* 1.6.18–19, where the Law is seen as the highest reason, implanted in Nature, an intelligent power that preceded any written law.

560. *Leg.* 1.7.23; *Resp.* 1.13.20.

561. *Leg.* 1.7.24.

562. *Leg.* 1.7.25.

developed."563 The life of the mind that is free from the body can be like that of a god (divina vita est),564 since it is immortal and can see all that there is in nature.565 Cicero records the teaching of the ancients that after death, life continues in a new mode "which often served as a guide to heaven for illustrious men and women," some of whom became as gods.566 Cicero also alludes to the view that humans' ultimate destination is to be gods or to be in company with the gods.567

Living Out the Philosophy

According to *De Legibus*, the person who realizes that they have within themselves this divine spark will examine themselves, grasp the means given to them to attain wisdom, perceive the path to be a good and happy man and, "so he will always act and think in a way worthy of so great a gift of the gods."568 Their mind will always and only meditate on divine and eternal subjects.569 According to the god at Delphi, this will cause it to "feel its union with the divine mind" and its desire for gaining immortality will be kindled.570 Such a person will abandon their bondage to their body and its desires, know virtue, leave behind fear of suffering and death and know itself. This will include recognizing all who are joined to them by Nature, and take up, "the worship of the gods and pure religion." Their mental and spiritual vision will concern itself with choosing the good and rejecting the bad, and recognizing the place of each being in the universe, whether it be divine and eternal or mortal and transient. They shall come to see their place as a "citizen of the whole universe" and give themselves to the "ruler and governor of the universe."571 Virtue is attained by knowing the "principles of right living" but bad habits can breed a corruption which stamps out the sparks of fire kindled within people by Nature.572

---

563. *Leg.* 1.16.45 (Keyes, LCL); cf. *Div.* 1.30.65.
564. *lib. inc. fr.* 2; cf. *Div.* 1.57.129.
565. *Div.* 1.51.115; 1.57.131.
566. *Tusc.* 1.12.27–1.13.29 (King, LCL).
567. *Tusc.* 1.32.76.
568. *Leg.* 1.22.59 (Keyes, LCL).
569. *Resp.* 1.17.28.
570. *Tusc.* 5.25.70 (King, LCL).
571. *Leg.* 1.23.60–62 (Keyes, LCL).
572. *Leg.* 1.11.32–1.12.33.

2.6 NEOPYTHAGOREANISM

Pythagoras (sixth century BCE, c. 582–500 BCE) founded a school of philosophy that became known as Pythagoreanism. This philosophy contained both scientific and religious aspects. The religious tradition emphasized the superiority of the soul over the body, especially in relation to its teaching on the immortality and transmigration of the soul (or metempsychosis), that led to vegetarianism and the forbidding of animal sacrifice (since a soul may take up residence in an animal).[573] During the Hellenistic era, there was a renewed interest in Pythagoreanism, now known as Neopythagoreanism.[574] Much of the writings of the most important Neopythagorean writers (such as as Nigidius Figulus, Nicomachus of Gerasa, Moderatus of Gades or Numenius of Apamea) have either not survived, survived in very fragmentary form or do not contain anything of significance for my enquiry. However, via the work of Philostratus, a late second or early third century writer,[575] we have been left significant traditions concerning both the life and letters of Apollonius of Tyana, to whom I now turn.

2.6.1 Apollonius of Tyana, according to Philostratus

According to his biographer, Philostratus, Apollonius was born in Tyana, in Cappadocia around the beginning of the first century CE and died during the reign of Nerva. Philostratus portrays him as an itinerant ascetic wandering holy man and Neoplatonic philosopher.[576]

Sacrifice Language

As we have seen, Pythagoras, like those who followed after him, disdained animal sacrifices, instructing, "not to let victims be brought for sacrifice to the gods, and to worship only at the altar unstained with blood."[577] Philostratus elaborates on the sacrifices that Pythagoras offered in their place; "he never defiled altars with blood (μὴ γὰρ αἱμάττειν

---

573. *OCD*, 1245–46. See also Seneca, *Ep.* 108. 19–22; Philostratus, *Vit. Apoll.* 3.19.1.
574. *OCD*, 1008; Ferguson, *Backgrounds*, 382–84.
575. *OCD*, 1137.
576. *OCD*, 124; Ferguson, *Backgrounds*, 384–86.
577. Diog. Laert. 8.1.22.

τοὺς βωμούς); instead honey cakes, frankincense, and hymns were this Master's offerings to the gods" (καὶ τὸ ἐφυμνῆσαι, φοιτᾶν ταῦτα τοῖς θεοῖς παρὰ τοῦ ἀνδρὸς τούτου).[578] Here it is clear that Pythagoras offered inanimate physical sacrifices (such as honey cakes and frankincense) but that hymns were also considered a kind of sacrifice. When Apollonius defends the philosophical path he chose, he points to the greatness and "ineffable wisdom" of Pythagoras because, "he approached altars in purity, he kept his stomach undefiled by the flesh of living things."[579] These "humble sacrifices" give greater pleasure to the gods, "than those who spill the blood of bulls for them."[580] In the same vein, Philostratus emphasizes the continuity between Pythagoras and the first century Apollonius, when he reports that during the latter's visit to the tomb of the Achaeans, he made many funeral speeches, "and many heroic sacrifices of a bloodless and pure kind" (πολλὰ δὲ τῶν ἀναίμων τε καὶ καθαρῶν καθαγίσας).[581] It is not specified, however, whether these are physical sacrifices or figurative sacrifices (such as hymns). What truly pleases the gods is not sacrifices, but the acquisition of wisdom and good works toward the deserving.[582] Eusebius, a Roman historian and Christian apologist of the third and fourth centuries also cites a purported fragment of Apollonius, that states that God rejects physical sacrifice in favor of pure speech and a noble mind.[583] In an earlier passage, Apollonius claims to know how the deity chooses to receive worship, as well as the identity of virtue, justice and chastity. These things can only be discerned by the soul, "If it is pure and unblemished when it apprehends them, in my opinion it soars much higher than the Caucasus here."[584] Additionally, one such who prophesies "become divine" (θεῖοί) under its influence, "with no pollution besmirching his soul, and no scars of sin traced on his mind."[585]

---

578. Philostratus, *Vit. Apoll.* 1.1.1 (Jones, LCL, 2005).

579. *Vit. Apoll.* 6.11.3 (Jones, LCL, 2005).

580. *Vit. Apoll.* 6.11.6 (Jones, LCL, 2005).

581. *Vit. Apoll.* 4.11.1 (Jones, LCL, 2005); cf. also his aversion to animal sacrifices recorded in *Vit. Apoll.* 1.10.1–2; 1.24.3; 1.31.1–1.32.2.1; 1.38.1; 8.7.30; *Ep.* 27.

582. *Ep.* 26.

583. Eusebius, *Praep. ev.* 4.13.

584. Philostratus, *Vit. Apoll.* 2.5.3 (Jones, LCL, 2005).

585. *Vit. Apoll.* 3.42.1–2 (Jones, LCL, 2005).

The Nature of Divinity

God is the creator of the universe; everything comes from him.[586] The "eternal god" (θεὸς ἀίδιος) is also the "first substance" who acts and is acted upon and is at one with all.[587] The gods reveal themselves to people, especially those who pursue philosophy, and in contexts like the temple of Asclepius.[588] As we have seen, the deity cares for people and loves to receive worship. They reward the sincere and those who are free from sin with every blessing.[589] This worship does not need to consist of sacrifices.[590] They provide for all but give preference, firstly to "virtuous students of wisdom" and next to "innocent people."[591] Neither God nor people can "absolve" (or purify; ἀπονίπτω) a murderer.[592] Human should not "pry into the intentions of the gods."[593]

The Nature of Humanity

As we have already observed, Apollonius, in common with Pythagoras, understood souls to transmigrate; moving from one body to another.[594] Human beings have a kind of kinship with the gods that they do not share with any other creature.[595] Their soul is immortal.[596] There is no such thing as a true death, but only a passing from one thing to another, as when the whole dissolves into its parts or vice versa.[597] At death a person is both described as becoming a god (ὅταν θεὸς ἐξ ἀνθρώπου γένηται)

---

586. *Vit. Apoll.* 8.7.22.

587. *Ep.* 58.3. Sextus Empiricus, the third century CE philosopher, documents the view of Pythagoras and others that "there is one spirit which pervades, like a soul, the whole Universe" (Sextus Empiricus, *Math.* 1.128 (Bury, LCL)).

588. *Vit. Apoll.* 1.1.1–3, 7; 2.5.3.

589. *Vit. Apoll.* 1.1.11.

590. *Ep.* 26.

591. *Vit. Apoll.* 2.39.3.

592. *Vit. Apoll.* 8.7.23 (Jones, LCL, 2005).

593. *Vit. Apoll.* 8.23.1 (Conybeare, LCL, 1912), which seems more accurate than Jones' more recent 2005 translation, which renders θεῶν βουλάς as "decisions of heaven" rather than those of God.

594. *Vit. Apoll.* 3.19.1.

595. *Vit. Apoll.* 8.7.20.

596. *Vit. Apoll.* 8.31.3.

597. *Ep.* 58.1–2.

Figurative Temple Language in Hellenistic Philosophy 113

and going to God.[598] A later second century CE writer, Atticus Gellius, claimed that Pythagoreans located evil impulses within people, who harm themselves "by their own purpose and determination."[599]

Living Out the Philosophy

Pythagoras himself is of course the model for Apollonius's teaching and practice, and he was familiar with the gods, who revealed their identities to him.[600] Apollonius was said to exhibit a wisdom that was even more inspired than that of Pythagoras, "by which he came close to being thought possessed and inspired" (ὑφ' ὧν ἔψαυσε τοῦ δαιμόνιός τε καὶ θεῖος νομισθῆναι).[601] Apollonius was led by his guardian spirit or δαίμων.[602] The consequence of choosing this path is to be self-controlled, just and envious of no one and to cause tyrants to fear them rather than the other way around. Revelation is given to such a one so that they will be able to recognize gods and distinguish them from "insubstantial ghosts."[603] Those who follow the gods should be led by wisdom and their guardian spirit (δαίμων).[604] Those who love prophecy can "become divine under its influence" and even "act for the salvation of mankind" (θεῖοί τε ὑπ' αὐτῆς γίγνονται καὶ πρὸς σωτηρίαν ἀνθρώπων πράττουσι). Such a one must be utterly pure of soul and free from sin.[605] Those who take hold of the virtues that come from God "are close to the gods and holy." Further, "men who are good have some part in God" (καὶ φημὶ τοὺς ἀγαθοὺς τῶν ἀνθρώπων θεοῦ τι ἔχειν).[606] A man who truly resembles God can divert others from the passions and in fact the description of such a man seems to be set in apposition to a reference to God, as if this man is a god (ἀλλὰ δεῖ ἀνδρὸς

---

598. *Ep.* 58.4.
599. Aulus Gellius, *Noct. att.* 7.2.12–13 (Rolfe, LCL).
600. *Vit. Apoll.* 1.1.1–2.
601. *Vit. Apoll.* 1.2.3 (Jones, LCL). This is quite a different translation from the original Loeb one by F. C. Conybeare in 1912 which speaks of "the habits and temper of wisdom by means of which he succeeded in being considered a supernatural and divine being."
602. *Vit. Apoll.* 1.18.1; cf. also *Vit. Apoll.* 2.39.3.
603. *Vit. Apoll.* 6.11.3 (Jones, LCL).
604. *Vit. Apoll.* 1.18.1.
605. *Vit. Apoll.* 3.42.1–2.
606. *Vit. Apoll.* 8.7.21–22.

ὃς ἐπιμελήσεται τοῦ περὶ αὐτὰς κόσμου, θεὸς ὑπὸ σοφίας ἥκων).[607] A true Pythagorean will have true greatness of mind, soul and of manner, piety and knowledge and friendship with both gods and other spirits. They will be frugal, restrained, self-sufficient and at ease in their perceptions.[608]

2.7 EPICUREANISM

Epicureanism, though a major philosophy of the first century, will prove to be the least relevant for my enquiries, which is why it has been treated last. For this reason, and due to constraints of space, I shall offer only a brief summary of the features of Epicureanism that directly relate to my topic, followed by one possible figurative sacrifice reference from an Epicurean writer. This summary should demonstrate that relationship to the gods did not play an important role in the life of an Epicurean, and so we would not expect to find an abundance of figurative temple language. Epicurus of Samos (341–270 BCE) founded a school in Athens in 307/6 BCE, known as "the Garden," where he lived with his followers, both men and women, slaves and free, and avoided public life.[609] According to Epicurus, although nature has imprinted upon the minds of all a conception of the gods, many hold to wrong understandings of their nature.[610] God is an "imperishable and blessed creature."[611] The gods live a peaceful and blissful existence, "far removed and separated from our affairs," they do not need humans for anything and Lucretius, an Epicurean, says of divinity, "it is neither propitiated with services nor touched by wrath."[612] Rather, the world was not designed for the sake of humanity, and Nature orders its path without recourse to the gods.[613] Epicurus

---

607. *Vit. Apoll.* 8.7.23.

608. *Ep.* 52.

609. *OCD*, 513–14; Ferguson, *Backgrounds*, 370–79; Diog. Laert. 10.1–11 speaks of the life and teaching of Epicurus; Lucretius, *Rerum nat.* 1.62–79; 3.1–15; 5.6–12; 6.1–30 sing the praises of Epicurus, whose discoveries about the gods liberated those weighed down by wrong thoughts about them. Seneca, *Const.* 16.1 (Basore, LCL) speaks of Epicurus, "who most of all indulged the flesh."

610. Cicero, *Nat. d.* 1.15.42–17.44.

611. Epicurus, *Letter to Menoeceus* 123–24, cited in Long and Sedley, *Hellenistic Philosophers Vol 1*, 140.

612. Lucretius, *Rerum nat.* 1.44–49 (Smith, LCL); cf. 2.1094–95; 3.18–24; 5.73–90, 146–49; 6.54–67; Diog. Laert. 10.123, 139; Cicero, *Nat. d.* 1.17.45; 1.19.51; cf. Epictetus, *Diatr.* 1.12.1–3. See also Sharples, *Stoics*, 56–58.

613. Lucretius, *Rerum nat.* 2.1–1104; 5.198–99; Diog. Laert. 10.77–78; Cicero, *Nat.*

places great emphasis on sensations and the "perceptions of mental presentations" as the standard by which ideas can be judged.[614] Only two states of feeling exist; pleasure or pain.[615] In order to maximize pleasure (that is the absence of pain) and minimize pain, the wise person should, by the right use of reason, attend to wrong feelings and sense perceptions. These wrong perceptions interfere with the kind of blissed existence lived by the gods that is the model for the Epicurean.[616] Since death is merely the absence of sensation, not the gateway to immortality, it holds no fear for the Epicurean.[617] It is possible for those who follow this teaching to live like a god among men.[618] The wise person is always happy and should live a life unconcerned and uninvolved with anything that might disturb that life, such as responsibility for a wife and family or involvement in politics.[619]

2.7.1 Lucretius, De Rerum Natura

The work of Lucretius (first century BCE) on the nature of things (*De Rerum Natura*) expounds Epicurean philosophy and contains one possible figurative sacrifice reference.[620] He opines that because of humanity's false conception of the gods, they practice a false piety that includes turning toward stones, approaching every altar, and falling prostrate before the shrines of the gods with covered heads.[621] Instead of coming, "to sprinkle altars with the blood of beasts in showers and to link vow to

---

d. 1.20.53.

614. Diog. Laert. 10.31-33; Seneca, *Nat.* 1.3.10.

615. Diog. Laert. 10.34.

616. Diog. Laert. 10.82, 117, 127-31; Cicero, *Nat. d.* 1.20.53. In fact, according to Cicero, "complete absence of pain Epicurus considers to be the limit and highest point of pleasure" (Cicero, *Fin.* 1.11.38 (Rackham, LCL)).

617. Epicurus, *Letter to Menoeceus* 124-27, cited in Long and Sedley, *Hellenistic Philosophers Vol 1*, 144; cf. Lucretius, *Rerum nat.* 3.580-930; Diog. Laert. 10.123-25, 133; see also DeWitt, *Epicurus*; Sharples, *Stoics*, 93-99; and now Warren, *Cambridge Companion*.

618. Epicurus, *Letter to Menoeceus* 135, cited in Long and Sedley, *Hellenistic Philosophers Vol 1*, 144; cf. Lucretius, *Rerum nat.* 3.322.

619. Diog. Laert. 10.118-22 Cicero, *Nat. d.* 1.20.53; 3.16.26; Seneca, *De otio.* 3.2. For further on Epicureanism, see, e.g., Brunschwig and Sedley, "Hellenistic Philosophy," 155-62.

620. Little is known of the life of Lucretius; see *OCD*, 863-65.

621. Lucretius, *Rerum nat.* 5.1194-1200.

vow" (nec aras sanguine multo spargere quadrupedum, nec votis nectere vota) the truly pious person should rather, "be able to survey all things with tranquil mind" (sed mage placata posse omnia mente tueri).[622] Unless the worshiper recognizes that no sacrifice is required and that the gods have no interest in meting out wrath to their followers, "you will not be able to approach their shrines with placid heart, you will not have the strength to receive with tranquil peace of spirit the images which are carried to men's minds from their holy bodies, declaring what the divine shapes are."[623] In this case, Lucretius does not intend the call for a tranquil mind and placid heart to be a figurative sacrifice, since the gods do not require any kind of sacrifice at all.[624]

Further, most rejected the teaching of the Epicureans and it was attacked and ridiculed by many of the leading philosophers of their day. Through the character of Cotta, Cicero voices ridicule of Epicurus's belief in gods as virtuous but not active, and holy while disdaining interest in anyone's affairs but their own.[625] Epicureans themselves are attacked for their self-indulgence and slavery to pleasure.[626] Their philosophy is both expounded, then critiqued, at length by Cicero.[627] Epictetus accuses them of severing the bond between people by their self-centered focus on pleasure and for ignoring sense-perceptions when they should be listening to them.[628] Dio Chrysostom accuses the Epicureans of keeping the gods from being recognized, banishing gods from the universe, leaving the universe with no purpose or direction, and in essence making "pleasure" the only goddess.[629] Seneca ridicules Epicurus's teaching for making the gods both harmless and powerless,[630] and for linking virtue inseparably with

---

622. Lucretius, *Rerum nat.* 5.1200–1203 (Smith, LCL).

623. Lucretius, *Rerum nat.* 6.75–78 (Smith, LCL).

624. See also *Anonymous Epicurean treatise on theology* (Oxyrhynchus Papyrus 215) 1.4–24, cited in Long and Sedley, *Hellenistic Philosophers Vol 1*, 144.

625. Cicero, *Leg.* 1.12.39.

626. Cicero, *Nat. d.* 1.20.53. The reference in Marcus Aurelius, *Med.* 9.1.3 to the impiety of those who seek after pleasure and eschew pain may also be a scarcely veiled reference to the Epicureans.

627. See Cicero, *Fin.* 1.5.13–1.21.72 (exposition); *Fin.* 2.1.1–35.119 (critique); cf. also Cicero, *Tusc.* 5.26.73–74 for further brief critique.

628. Epictetus, *Diatr.* 2.20.6–20.

629. Dio Chrysostom, *Dei cogn.* 36–37.

630. Seneca, *Ben.* 4.19.1; *Ep.* 90.35; *Apol.* 8.

pleasure.[631] Plutarch scorns Epicurus for calling Providence a myth,[632] and for praising his own impassiveness and inactivity.[633] Since their aim is to be rid of anxiety rather than to fear God, they remove both good and evil from their gods and leave themselves no hope of divine favor, no confidence in prosperity, and no refuge in God in adversity.[634] Epicureans, like animals, have no conception of divine justice or reverence for virtue and so only live for pleasure.[635] Yet, in their hypocrisy they still sacrifice to the Gods who need no sacrifice.[636] This sort of ignorance about the gods leads to atheism, in Plutarch's view.[637] Maximus of Tyre simply ridicules Epicurean doctrines as odd, idle, careless, and ignorant of the gods.[638] In conclusion then, Epicureanism does not offer a fruitful field of comparison with Paul's imagery when considering figurative temple language.

2.8 MISCELLANEOUS

Finally, there are two brief references to figurative temples but without the kind of philosophical underpinning found in the other writers explored above. Valerius Maximus, a first century CE writer of a handbook of *Memorable Deeds and Sayings*,[639] compares friendships to temples. He understands friendship as being essential to the fabric of human life. It is due, "almost as much reverence as to the rituals of the immortal gods" since, as public welfare depends on these rituals and traditions, so too the private welfare of individuals depends on networks of friendships. This inspires Valerius to compare the two, "As temples are the sacred domiciles of the one, so the loyal hearts of men are like shrines of the other, filled with a holy spirit" (atque ut illarum aedes sacra domicilia, harum fida hominum pectora quasi quaedam sancto spiritu referta tem-

---

631. Seneca, *Vit. beat.* 7.1; 10.3; *Ep.* 90.35; though he concedes that Epicurus's teaching on pleasure is more austere than his critics admit in *Vit. beat.* 13.1.
632. Plutarch, *Def. orac.* 420B; *Stoic. rep.* 1043B.
633. *Praec. ger. rei publ.* 824B.
634. *Suav. viv.* 1100F–1101C.
635. *Adv. Col.* 1125A.
636. *Stoic. rep.* 1034B.
637. *Superst.* 164EF.
638. Maximus of Tyre, *Or.* 4.8; 4.9.
639. *OCD*, 1534.

pla sunt).⁶⁴⁰ Similarly, in the second century Latin novel *Metamorphoses* (or *The Golden Ass*) by Apuleius, there is a reference to one character entrusting knowledge to "the inner temple" of the "god-fearing heart" of another,⁶⁴¹ but with no explicitly philosophical grounding.

2.9 CONCLUSIONS

2.9.1 Temple Language

Many Stoic writers retained a place for physical sacrifices, while emphasizing a pure motivation but I noted a stronger focus on purity of thought and deed in place of sacrifices. Plutarch, whose affinities lie more with Middle Platonism, also speaks of purity in worship but envisages substitutes for sacrifice like trusting in the gods, searching after divine truth and study of divine things. Maximus conceives of prayer and contemplation as a substitute for sacrifice. Plutarch specifically gives the example of returning what is due to parents as being a figurative sacrifice. Cicero, though a Skeptic, also emphasizes the purity of the worshiper over the purity of the physical sacrifice itself. Apollonius, like his mentor Pythagoras, rejected animal sacrifices and substituted other inanimate offerings or hymns, because of his vegetarianism, stemming from his philosophy of the transmigration of souls. Apollonius may have also spoken of pure thought and speech as a sacrifice. Lucretius contrasted the adoption of a tranquil mind with the offering of sacrifices, though as an Epicurean, this would not constitute a figurative sacrifice, since the gods do not require any kind of sacrifice.

There were few obvious references to figurative priests in Stoic writers and none among the Middle Platonists; some of our Stoic examples were ambiguous and another seemed like a rare analogy with no extant parallels among other Stoic authors. Seneca, significantly, spoke of the universe as being the temple of the gods, as did Plutarch. Among the Stoics, Epictetus seems to make a more ready distinction between God and the world. Many Stoics, such as Dio, Epictetus and Marcus, speak of the divine dwelling within the individual, understood as their δαίμων. Hierocles alone uses the image of the home as a temple, with parents understood as gods to their children. Plutarch also pictured the individual

---

640. V. Max., 4.7. ext. 1 (Bailey, LCL).
641. Apuleius, *Metam.* 3.15.

as a temple, guided by right reason. Alcinous pictures the world as filled with God, and Maximus identifies the roles of God and Nature as breathing things into individuals. Cicero's understanding is remarkably similar to the Stoics, placing the same emphases on the world as the temple of the gods (like Seneca and Plutarch), the filling of the universe with the divine intelligence, and the place of god or a daemon within the individual soul.

2.9.2 The Nature of the Divinity

God is often identified in a pantheistic way with Nature, Fate, Fortune and Reason within Stoicism. Reason is also spoken of using divine language; dwelling within a person. God is immanent in the world and identified with it and there is a close likeness between God and people. Later Stoics like Epictetus and Marcus make a closer identification of God with intelligence. The Middle Platonists, Alcinous and Maximus, seem to take this further and speak of God as simply intelligence. Alcinous emphasizes the abstract nature of God who is preoccupied with his own thoughts. Apollonius also conceives of a God who is at one with the Universe. For the Stoics, the gods are universally viewed as benevolent and governing, though according to Dio, they depend on the law. Cicero goes further and imagines the Law as having god-like characteristics. Maximus and Alcinous stress the perfect qualities of God. For Plutarch, Nature seems to be able to act almost independently of God and appears to be a more dualistic entity, with good and evil flowing from it. Cicero also imagines Nature acting self-sufficiently of God and sustaining the world. Maximus conceives of different roles for Nature and Providence, and God governs with the assistance of Chance. Evils are only the indirect consequence of his government. Like the Stoics, the Middle Platonic thinkers speak positively of the gods in their benevolence and envisage roles for daemons and other divinities (as does Cicero). Apollonius emphasizes the gods' beneficence to those who are virtuous.

2.9.3 The Nature of Humanity

Stoics understand humanity alone as being formed of the divine essence and able to have kinship with the gods. The soul is pre-existent and is able to comprehend the divine, yet evil also comes from within (in this, Cicero concurs). Humans have the ability to live according to Nature (the one things truly are in their unity and comprehensiveness) and can be free of fear and inner disturbance. Soul or Reason is separate from and superior to the body and rules it, responding to both impulses and aversions. Plutarch, Alcinous and Maximus also stresses kinship with God and the capability of the soul to unite with the divine and become like it. Both good and evil come from within. The soul is set free after death and some become daemons. Cicero, though ostensibly a Skeptic, holds remarkably similar views on each of these topics. Apollonius spoke of the soul passing from one creature to another, though ultimately a person will become a god.

2.9.4 Living Out the Philosophy

The Stoics call their readers to live according to Nature and imitate the gods. People are called to exercise right judgments about the gods, themselves and their own judgments (especially in Epictetus). They are to cultivate inner purity by obeying their inner genius/δαίμων and to avoid wrong sense impressions. They are to seek the good, leave the path of self and do good to others. Cicero concurs that the good person should meditate on the divine, choose the good, think rightly of reality and avoid evil, especially that associated with the body. Although the Middle Platonists do not use the vocabulary of "living according to nature" they do speak of avoiding passions, grasping God's nature and imitating his character and ways through contemplation of the divine, reason, discipline and education.[642] Alcinous adds the caveat that it is not the supreme God, but a lesser god that they shall be imitating. Apollonius placed his emphasis on being led by his inner daemon and choosing the path of self-control and virtue.

---

642. Dillon, *Middle Platonists*, 43–44, 122–23, documents the way that Middle Platonist writers like Plutarch, following Eudorus of Alexandria, abandoned the Stoic goal of "living in accordance with nature" in favor of the more Platonic ideal of likeness to, or imitation of, God.

3

Figurative Temple Language in Philo of Alexandria

3.1 INTRODUCTION

I HAVE RESERVED A separate chapter for Philo of Alexandria (ca. 20 BCE—50 CE)[1] for two main reasons. Firstly, unlike those writers surveyed in the last chapter, Philo is clearly Jewish. Philo thus stands in a class of his own in relation to my focus in this study. However, as I noted in my first chapter, Philo is also writing to a Diaspora audience and drawing upon the philosophical tradition when speaking to a Hellenistic readership about wisdom, just as Paul does in his use of wisdom language when writing to a Diaspora audience in 1 Cor 1:18–2:16.[2] Moreover, he is a legitimate source for our understanding of Hellenistic philosophy, because, like the writers surveyed in the previous chapter, he is strongly influenced by Hellenistic thought and his Judaism is mediated through philosophy.[3]

---

1. Helpful introductions to Philo's thought and writings include Goodenough, *Introduction to Philo*; Sandmel, *Philo*; Sandmel, "Philo"; Borgen, "Philo," 233–82; Williamson, *Jews*; Borgen, *Philo*; Schenck, *Brief Guide*; Kamesar, *Cambridge Companion*, especially the first three chapters, that deal with Philo's life and times, his works, and his hermeneutical method. See also now, Seland, *Reading*.

2. See footnote 218 on page 40 in chapter 1 for scholars who interact with Philo and the Jewish wisdom tradition in their discussions of 1 Corinthians.

3. Philo sheds some light on his own philosophical education in *Congr.* 74–76. For recent overviews of this topic, see Nickelsburg, "Philo," 53–72; Koskenniemi,

John M. Dillon's seminal study *The Middle Platonists*, remains, despite its age, the standard work in this field. He describes Philo as a "fully-fledged Middle Platonist,"[4] and devotes a considerable section of his monograph to Philo.[5] Dillon understands Philo's thought, "as essentially adapting contemporary Alexandrian Platonism, which was itself heavily influenced by Stoicism and Pythagoreanism, to his own exegetical purposes"[6] and sees the philosophy of Philo (and Eudorus) as "the true foundation of Middle Platonism."[7] Furthermore, Philo has a lengthy corpus, is one of our best and most extensive sources for Middle Platonism, and by far the greatest number of references to figurative sacrifice, priest and temple language in any ancient writer is found in Philo, as I shall shortly demonstrate.[8] Unlike the last chapter, I shall not devote separate sections to "The Nature of Divinity," "The Nature of Humanity" and "Living out the Philosophy." This has mainly been done in the interests of space. Moreover, these topics were addressed in the last chapter in relation to other Middle Platonic writers, and insofar as Philo supports the evidence of these writers, it is not essential to revisit them. Because Philo is Jewish, he holds some

---

"Philo," 102–28; and Sterling, "Jewish Philosophy," 129–54, as well as older works such as Goodenough, *Introduction to Philo*, 90–111, and Borgen, "Philo," 254–56. For an assessment of Philo's response to the philosophical challenges encountered by Hellenistic Judaism in comparison to other writings, see Winston, "Philo," 124–42.

4. Dillon, *Middle Platonists*, 143.

5. See Dillon, *Middle Platonists*, 139–43, and further Dillon, "Reclaiming," 108–23.

6. Dillon, *Middle Platonists*, 182, cf. 143–44; and similarly Borgen, "Philo," 256. For a brief survey of the influences of Plato and Stoicism on Philo, see Reydams-Schils, "Stoicized Readings," 85–102, who argues that the influences of Plato's *Timaeus* and the Stoics converge in Philo, agreeing with earlier works such as Sandmel, *Philo*, 4, 14–16, 19–21, 25–26, 28. In an earlier thesis, the influential Philo scholar Edwin R. Goodenough argued that Philo's religion was akin to a Greek mystery religion in its thought, in Goodenough, *Light*. However, his pupil and eminent Jewish scholar, Samuel Sandmel opposed this thesis in Sandmel, *Philo*, 140–47. Subsequent Philo scholars have also dissented from Goodenough's position; see, e.g., Borgen, *Philo*, 1–3; Sterling, "Place," 26–27, and in the same work, Cohen, "Mystery Terminology," 173–87; Schenck, *Brief Guide*; Sandelin, "Philo," 20.

7. Dillon, *Middle Platonists*, 183. For a recent reflection of the debate on Philo and Middle Platonism among senior Philo scholars, see the special section of *Studia Philonica* V (1993): Sterling, "Platonizing," 96–111; Runia, "Philo," 112–40; Runia, "Response," 141–46; Tobin, "Philo," 147–50; Dillon, "Response," 151–55. Despite differences of opinion, all agree that Philo is influenced by Middle Platonism and uses its thought in his exegesis.

8. E.g., note the comment of Klawans, *Purity*, 142: "Philo's is the most thorough symbolic exposition of sacrificial ritual known from ancient Jewish times."

Figurative Temple Language in Philo of Alexandria   123

views that are at variance with other Middle Platonists (such as some of his understanding of God) but he also holds some that are peculiar to him (such as his understanding of the *Logos* in relation to God and humanity). Since recording these views does not serve my purposes (to shed light on Middle Platonism and its use of figurative temple language), I have not given special attention to them, although some attention to Philo's distinctive views will appear in passing.

Two more caveats are in order. My main focus will be on figurative temple language in order to illustrate what Philo's approach has in common with other Hellenistic philosophical writers and thus a comprehensive survey of Philo's understanding of the cult will not be attempted.[9] Therefore, my aim is not to propose a thesis that explains all the origins of Philo's figurative temple language, especially vis-à-vis Judaism.[10] Secondly, Philo's expositions concentrate almost exclusively on the Pentateuch (especially Genesis and Exodus); the sacrifices made by Abraham relate to a period before the tabernacle, and the commentary on Exodus describes a period before the temple was built. However, Philo *himself* lived in the second temple era and his writings are indebted to this wider motif of temple figurative language that I have surveyed.[11]

9. For the most extensive discussion of Philo's presentation of Jewish worship in all its dimensions (both literal and figurative) see Leonhardt, *Jewish Worship*.

10. I noted briefly in chapter 1 that the Pseudepigrapha sometimes speak of a heavenly temple or an eschatological temple that God will build or will send down from heaven at the end of the age (especially in eschatological works such as *1 En.* 14:1–25; 24–26; 71:5; *4 Ezra* 10:25–28; *2 Bar.* 4:1–7). I also surveyed the use of figurative sacrifice language in second temple Jewish literature. Additionally, I examined the use of figurative temple language in many parts of the Dead Sea Scrolls. All this evidence indicates that other Jewish literature, which does not appear to have been greatly influenced by Hellenistic philosophy, could use figurative temple language. However, Philo is also greatly influenced by Hellenistic philosophical thought, as argued above.

11. I also note that Philo frequently refers to the subject of philosophy in his works. There are over two hundred references that use the φιλόσοφ- root in Philo. Moses himself was trained in philosophy by teachers from various nations (*Mos.* 1.21–23; cf. *Mos.* 1.48; 2.66), later Philo claims that Moses "had attained the very summit of philosophy" (Philo, *Opif.* 8) and he speaks elsewhere of the law as the philosophy according to Moses (κατὰ Μωυσῆν φιλοσοφοῦσιν) in *Mut.* 223. The creation narrative itself is described as a philosophical account (*Fug.* 68). Philosophy is described as the greatest thing of all for humanity (*Opif.* 53; *Spec.* 1.336; 3.186); even the thing by which man becomes immortal (*Opif.* 77). Philo avers that philosophy leads to virtue (*Leg.* 1.57; cf. *Leg.* 3.72) and is the most perfect of studies (*Ebr.* 51). Indeed, Philo describes his own journey with philosophy (*Congr.* 74–80), which he elucidates as the study of wisdom, itself the knowledge of divine things (*Congr.* 79; cf. *Spec.* 3.1). Philosophy is also said to have come down from heaven (*Spec.* 3.185). Philo represents Moses as speaking of

3.2 SACRIFICE LANGUAGE

3.2.1 Literal Sacrifices Must Be Offered with Reverence and Respect for the Rite

Philo by no means discounts the sacrificial system of the Jerusalem cult. In fact, he affirms the continuing role of the temple as the center of Judaism, the only proper place for sacrifice, and attacks the thought that other altars, whether pagan or otherwise, are legitimate places to offer sacrifice.[12] Although Philo's work is notable for allegorizing the various laws on sacrifice,[13] he is at pains to stress that this should not be at the expense of actual practice: "Why, we shall be ignoring the sanctity of the Temple and a thousand other things, if we are going to pay heed to nothing except what is shewn us by the inner meaning of things."[14] His various commentaries on the scriptures repeatedly emphasize the necessity of a respectful and appropriate approach to the sacrifices. In more than one work, Philo critiques the offering of Cain. In *De agricultura* Philo says of Cain that, "the conditions of his sacrifice had not been holy and perfect" and he was reprimanded for not bringing his offering properly.[15] In *De plantatione*, Philo speaks approvingly of the proper preparations for sacrifice, such as avoiding drunkenness, "in order that both the recollection of their sacrifices and their reverence for the place might lead them to celebrate a festivity in actual truth most holy, sinning neither in word nor deed."[16] Philo speaks in passing of this act as a purification of both body and soul.[17] Thus, Philo by no means discounts literal sacrifices.

---

philosophy as the royal road (ὁδὸς ... βασιλική) that leads to God (*Post.* 101), which he then equates with the word and reason of God (*Post.* 102).

12. E.g., Philo, *Spec.* 1.67–70; see Borgen, *Philo*, 18–21; Schenck, *Brief Guide*, 36–37; Lieber, "Between Motherland," 198–201; Robertson, "Towards an Understanding," 44–58; Sandelin, "Philo," 19–46, at 33–34.

13. For more on Philo's allegorical approach to biblical interpretation, see, e.g., Sandmel, *Philo*, 17–28; Mack, "Philo," 250–62; Williamson, *Jews*, 144–75; Birnbaum, "Allegorical Interpretation," 307–29; Kamesar, "Biblical Interpretation," 65–91.

14. Philo, *Migr.* 92 (see more generally *Migr.* 89–93); cf. Ferguson, "Spiritual Sacrifice," 1160; Williamson, *Jews*, 4. All translations are taken from the Loeb Classical Library, unless otherwise stated.

15. Philo, *Agr.* 127.

16. *Plant.* 162.

17. *Plant.* 162.

3.2.2 Literal Sacrifices Can Only Be Offered with a Pious Life and Spirit

At the same time, these references also betray a deep concern for the state of mind and life of the worshiper. In *De ebrietate*, Philo alludes to the prohibition on wine given to Aaron when entering the tent of meeting in Lev 10:9 and applies it to all those who may find themselves needing to sacrifice, which he refers to as "sacrifices of thanksgiving," and he adds, "these need sober abstinence and a close and ready attention."[18] Philo's claim that Abraham left country and kindred to sacrifice "in a religious spirit"[19] implies that such a spirit is commendable in worship. In his meditation on Exod 12:8, Philo thinks it appropriate that worship should take place at night, so that only the stars bring glory to the humble worshipers who wish, "to repent and purify their souls."[20] The worshiper must prepare both soul and body, by giving up themselves to God and in their body, "by abstaining from uncleanness in holiness and purity."[21] As Philo says elsewhere, "For God does not delight in the fleshiness or fatness of animals, but in the blameless (ἀνυπαίτιος) intention (διάθεσις) of the votary,"[22] or again, "even the least morsel of incense offered by a man of religion is more precious in the sight of God than thousands of cattle sacrificed by men of little worth."[23] Philo is still speaking of literal offerings, but the emphasis is squarely on the personal piety of the worshiper.[24]

Consequently, the Literal Sacrifices Are of No Worth if Offered By an Impious Person

Philo frequently disparages those who offer the prescribed sacrifices but live impure lives, such as drunken men,[25] the arrogant[26] or those in "whose

---

18. *Ebr.* 129.
19. *Spec.* 1.68.
20. *QE* 1.13.
21. *QE* 1.2.
22. *Spec.* 2.35.
23. *Spec.* 1.275.
24. cf. Laporte, "Sacrifice," 34–42; Leonhardt, *Jewish Worship*, 235–53.
25. Philo, *Ebr.* 131.
26. *Spec.* 1.269.

heart is the seat of lurking covetousness and wrongful cravings,"[27] or as thieves[28] or murderers.[29] In such a case, Philo says, "if the worshipper is without kindly feeling or justice, the sacrifices are no sacrifices (ἄθυτοι θυσίαι καὶ ἀνίεροι ἱερουργίαι) . . . it is not a remission but a reminder of past sins which they effect."[30] The sacrifices of the wicked can be called, "the first-fruits of unholiness."[31] Similarly, an insincere repentance can actually worsen the condition of the worshiper (who is compared to the goat of the burnt-offering in Lev 10:16–20).[32] There is no possibility that the righteous judge "would ever accept the ministries of the impious."[33] So solemn is this charge that, "for such a one it were a sacrilege that he should even from a distance behold the sacred fire."[34] When such a sinner enters to sacrifice, their sin "invades and violates the most sacred temples"[35] making the sacrifices unholy. Their white robes and unblemished animals contrast ironically with the wounds of their souls and their mutilated virtues (ἀρετή).[36] The intent of the heart is what counts, and no matter the quantity or quality of the offering made by the sinner, it is the motivation that is judged, "He turns His face away from those who approach with guilty intent, even though they lead to His altar a hundred bullocks every day."[37] To offer sacrifices unwillingly is like making no sacrifice at all, and the worshiper is self-deceived and forgotten (presumably by God).[38] Since the mind is "the most essential victim," it is blemished, and as no blemished thing can approach the altar, a "bad man" cannot

---

27. *Spec.* 1.270.
28. *Plant.* 107.
29. *Ebr.* 66.
30. *Mos.* 2.107; cf. also *Spec.* 1.215.
31. *Spec.* 1.279.
32. *Fug.* 157–60 and see 96 n. a, in the same Loeb volume.
33. *Mos.* 2.279; see also *Mos.* 2.162.
34. *Ebr.* 131. In *Ebr.* 79, Philo implies that had men such as these not followed impious ways, their sacrifices could have been atoning and turned away evil sent by God.
35. *Cher.* 94.
36. *Cher.* 95–97.
37. *Plant.* 108, later adding in the same verse, "He takes no delight in blazing altar fires fed by the unhallowed sacrifices of men to whose hearts sacrifice is unknown. Nay, these sacrifices do but put Him in remembrance of the ignorance and offences of the several offerers."
38. *QE* 2.50.

really perform a sacrifice.³⁹ The mind that is only concerned with human aspirations rather than divine virtue is compared to the scape-goat that is sent into the wilderness.⁴⁰ Therefore, the "soul which sacrifices" should have no room in their head for evil and the passions.⁴¹

A Person Should Take Care to Offer Literal Sacrifices with a Rational and Noble Mind⁴²

For Philo, the unblemished state of the mind of the worshiper is more significant than the unblemished state of the animal being sacrificed. In fact, in *De specialibus legibus*, Book 1, Philo negates the OT stipulations for worship altogether in order to emphasize this point, "So he who intends to sacrifice must consider not whether the victim is unblemished but whether his own mind (διάνοια) stands free from defect (ὁλόκληρος) and imperfection (παντελής)."⁴³ Philo's thought, though focused here on the offering of a literal sacrifice, is beginning to move in the direction of the figurative sacrifices that I shall come to below, "he holds the sacrifice to consist not in the victims but in the offerer's intention (διάνοια) and his zeal (προθυμία) which derives its constancy and permanence from virtue (ἀρετή),"⁴⁴ and likewise, what is precious to God is not how many victims are sacrificed, "but the true purity of a rational spirit in him who makes the sacrifice."⁴⁵ Similarly, Philo avers that God does not rejoice in sacrifices per se, but in the intent and virtue of the offerer, "He rejoices in the will to love Him and in men that practise holiness."⁴⁶ In a highly allegorical interpretation of Genesis 31 in *De somniis*, Book 1, Philo de-

---

39. *Plant.* 164.

40. *Her.* 179; and similarly: *Plant.* 61. The goat used in sacrifice is also understood symbolically in *Her.* 126; *Fug.* 157–60; *Post.* 72; *QG* 3.3.

41. *QE* 2.100. For the passions in Philo, see Lévy, "Philo's Ethics," 154–64.

42. What follows adapts some material from Richardson, "What Are the Spiritual Sacrifices," 10–14. This section of the article was an earlier and much briefer version of my research that was restricted to Philo's figurative uses of θυσία in relation to spiritual sacrifices. The following sections develop and significantly expand that material with many more examples and more specific categories.

43. Philo, *Spec.* 1.283. Younge's translation captures the literal sense here: "but whether his mind is sound, and entire, and perfect" (Philo, *Works*, 561).

44. *Spec.* 1.290.

45. *Spec.* 1.261.

46. *Spec.* 1.271.

scribes what he sees as the author of Genesis's view of Joseph's offering of a sacrifice, "He held no one worthy of offering sacrifices who has not first come to know himself and comprehended human nothingness, inferring from the elements of which he is composed that he is nothing worth."[47] In *De migratione Abrahami*, Philo comments on the descriptions of Moses and Aaron's sacrifices, recorded in Leviticus 8 and 9. The various washings are interpreted allegorically as a cleansing of the soul, "that the better portion of the soul, the rational part (λογικός), that is left, may exercise its truly free and noble impulses toward all things beautiful."[48] In summary, literal sacrifices only have value in so far as the worshiper exhibits the piety of soul seen in one who possesses a rational mind.

3.2.3 The True Sacrifice Is Spiritual and Does Not Have to Be a Literal Sacrifice

In the following section I shall identify the various categories of spiritual sacrifices described by Philo. He notes that the soul and mind can be offered as a spiritual sacrifice. Purity and virtue can be an offering to God and praise itself can be considered a sacrifice.

The Offering of the Soul and Mind

Much of Philo's exegetical writings attempt to contextualize OT laws, presenting allegorical interpretations of them which speak to the new context of his Jewish audience but which also make them palatable to the Greek world.[49] Valentin Nikiprowetzky describes Philo as standing at the crossroads between biblical and Greek philosophical understandings of sacrifice.[50] In many places Philo speaks of sacrifices that are not physical and literal. Frequently he speaks of the offering of the soul (ψυχή).[51] For instance, in *De somniis*, he asserts, "For that which prays, which gives thanks and offers sacrifice truly without blemish, must be as he says a

---

47. *Somn.* 1.212.
48. *Migr.* 67.
49. For more detail on this topic see, e.g., Borgen, *Philo*, 124–57.
50. Nikiprowetzky, "Spiritualisation," 99, and see generally 97–102.
51. For a recent discussion of the concept of ψυχή in Philo see Seland, "Moderate Life," 245–51. For more on Philo's emphasis on the inward and symbolic sacrifice, see, e.g., Seland, "Common Priesthood," 114–16; Lieber, "Between Motherland," 202–9.

"one" only, the soul."[52] In the passage just cited, Philo is giving an allegorical interpretation of the grain offering in Lev 2:1–2, and yet *concentrates on the offering of the soul*. However, in *De vita Mosis*, Book 2, Philo goes further, "if he is pure of heart and just, the sacrifice stands firm, though the flesh is consumed, or rather, *even if no victim at all is brought to the altar*. For the true oblation, what else can it be but the devotion (εὐσέβεια) of a soul which is dear to God? The thank-offering of such a soul receives immortality, and is inscribed in the records of God."[53]

For Philo, the presence or absence of a 'victim' (an animal sacrifice) is irrelevant to determining whether a true sacrifice took place. In this example, it is the piety of the soul being offered which is really important. This piety in life is rooted in the single minded self-offering of the worshiper. In *De specialibus legibus*, Book 1, Philo speaks of the vow of the Nazirite in Numbers 6. According to Philo, the man himself resembles the sacrifice of the entire burnt offering, the sin-offering and the offering for preservation.[54] This is so because, "the penitent is preserved and the person preserved from the maladies of his soul repents, and both of them are pressing forward to that *perfect and wholly sound frame of mind* of which the whole-burnt-offering is a symbol."[55] The word translated perfect (ὁλόκληρος) and its cognate ὁλοκαύτωμα often appear in the LXX in relation to sacrifices (cf. Lev 23:15; Deut 27:6; Josh 8:31; 1 Macc 4:47).[56] All of this is concerned with the offering of the whole person to God. The washing and then the burning of a burnt offering on the altar of Lev 9:14 is allegorized in the same way, "for the wise man consecrates his whole soul as being worthy to be offered to God, owing to its freedom from voluntary or involuntary blemish" (ὅλην γὰρ τὴν ψυχὴν ἀξίαν οὖσαν θεῷ προσάγεσθαι διὰ τὸ μηδένα ἔχειν μήθ' ἑκούσιον μήτ' ἀκούσιον μῶμον ὁ σοφὸς καθαγιάζει).[57] The washing of the belly in Lev 8:21 is interpreted to mean a cleansing away of every kind of desire. When that is effected,

---

52. Philo, *Somn.* 2.72.
53. *Mos.* 2.108.
54. *Spec.* 1.252.
55. *Spec.* 1.253.
56. Cf. Paul's use of the word using sacrificial language in a spiritual sense in 1 Thess 5:23: "Now may the God of peace himself sanctify you completely (ὁλοτελής), and may your *whole* (ὁλόκληρος) spirit and soul and body be kept blameless at the coming of our Lord Jesus Christ."
57. Philo, *Leg.* 3.141.

the worshipper can offer, "the whole burnt offerings of the soul."[58] In *De sacrificiis Abelis et Caini*, Philo recalls that Lev. 2:14 says an offering is to be "new, roasted, sliced, pounded." These four things are understood allegorically, including, "the fire-tested and invincible reason" and "the persistent practice and exercise in what the mind has grasped." When the worshipper acknowledges these things to be what God wills, he "will bring an offering of the first-fruits, even the first and best offspring of the soul."[59]

The image of first-fruits is used elsewhere to describe "the ransom of our souls" that brings liberty,[60] and "the ripe fruits of the soul" are related to, "everything in the soul that tends to peace and friendship and agreement."[61] The first-fruit offering is, "the word of thanksgiving, sent up out of a true and sincere mind."[62] Likewise, Philo explains that the first-fruit offering of Deut 24:6 concerns the reaping of, "the true harvest of the mind," when the, "fruit-bearing of ourselves" is offered to God. This is the product of, "the basket of our reasoning faculties."[63] A similar thought is also found in Philo's meditation on Lev 27:30, 32 concerning the tithe. We are to offer the first-fruits of the "unreasoning creatures" within (the senses), yet, "the first and best thing in us is the reason, and it is only right that from its intelligence, its shrewdness, its apprehension, its prudence and the other qualities which belong to it, we should offer first-fruits to God, who gave to it its fertility of thinking."[64] When Philo considers the propitiation offered in Lev 5:7ff., he considers the "best and most perfect form of purification" to be the offering of speech and mind together, in true speech that originates in pure thoughts.[65] Abel's offering of the firstlings of his flock (Gen 4:4), show that, "the gladness and richness of the soul, all that protects and gives joy, should be set apart for God."[66] In such a case, Philo distinguishes between the parts of the animal related to the body (such as excrement and fat), that should be cast off and the rest that, "show a soul wholly complete in all its parts"

58. *Migr.* 67.
59. *Sacr.* 87.
60. *Sacr.* 117.
61. *Migr.* 202.
62. *Sacr.* 74.
63. *Somn.* 2.272.
64. *Congr.* 98; see generally *Congr.* 96–98.
65. *Mut.* 240; see *Mut.* 245–47, 249–51.
66. *Sacr.* 136.

that "should be given in their entirety as a burnt-offering to God."⁶⁷ These kinds of soul should be completely free from blemish, that is, "innocent and purified."⁶⁸

Philo sometimes compares *specific* sacrifices to the offering of the soul. The libation is one such, that is compared to "the blood of the soul"⁶⁹ or to the mind,⁷⁰ once it abstains from the passions. In *Quis rerum divinarum heres sit*, Philo interprets the division of blood in Exod 24:6 to speak of divine and human wisdom. The divine kind of wisdom, being without mixture, is a reflection of God's own nature, and "therefore is poured as an offering (σπένδω) to God."⁷¹ (the same verse is expounded elsewhere with reference to the unmixed soul that is consecrated to God)⁷² The mind and the soul are spoken of in parallel, as if Philo makes no distinction between them, and when the mind/soul is filled with divine inspiration, free from all mixture and "in its perfect purity" it "is fitly rendered in its entirety as a holy libation (σπονδή) to Him."⁷³ The goal of the offering is that the mind should be purified from all "objects of sense" and become entirely rational.⁷⁴ The blood that is poured in a circle around the altar represents, "a libation of the life-principle." This is explained as concerning the mind "whole and complete" where every word and intention shows that the mind is offered willingly in God's service.⁷⁵ In Philo's commentary on Exodus, "every soul desirous of moral excellence is a libation," which Philo elaborates, "that is if one first pours out and dedicates one's virtue to God."⁷⁶ In *De somniis*, Philo speaks of the person who pours the libation (ὁ σπονδοφόρος), as the great high priest, who offers, "the libation of himself."⁷⁷

---

67. *Sacr.* 139.
68. *Fug.* 80.
69. *Leg.* 2.56.
70. *Ebr.* 152–53.
71. *Her.* 182–83; cf. the figurative use of σπένδω in Phil 2:17; 2 Tim 4:6.
72. See *QE* 2.33.
73. *Her.* 184.
74. *Her.* 185.
75. *Spec.* 1.217.
76. *QE* 2.71. See Laporte, "High Priest," 75, 77, on the libation of the soul.
77. *Somn.* 2.183. Note the emphatic placing of ἑαυτόν at the end of the sentence, in apposition to the preceding noun phrase ὅλον τὸ σπονδεῖον ἀκράτου μεθύσματος ("an entire libation full of unmixed wine," Younge), both in the accusative singular; defining the libation as the person himself.

Philo occasionally speaks of incense as a spiritual sacrifice;[78] the libation just described is also compared to incense,[79] incense is explicated in one place as, "the incense of consecrated virtues,"[80] (καθαγιάζων ἀρετὰς ἐκθυμιᾷ, using the verb ἐκθυμιάω, to burn as incense)[81] incense is likened to the offering of reason (λογισμός),[82] the offering of the whole world that is consumed morning and evening in the censer (and also described as an offering of thanks by the world to its maker),[83] and in one instance he compares incense to the offering of the whole mind to God.[84]

In the first book of *De specialibus legibus*, the shaving of the Nazirite's hair in Num 6:18 is described as the consecration of a portion of himself as representative of the whole, "the votary has vowed to bring himself, . . . that some part of him should be sacrificially offered."[85] In another place, Philo compares different sacrifices (here the offerings of Abraham, described in Gen 15:9) with different parts of a person that align themselves with reason and order (to a soul, "which can easily receive guidance and instruction and ruling," speech that is equipped to defeat sophisms and develop analytical arguments, the sense that relates to the sensible world, and the turtle-dove and pigeon that represent "divine and human reason.")[86] Similarly, in his treatment of the burnt offering in Gen 8:20, *Quaestiones et solutiones in Genesin*, Philo depicts the beasts as the senses and the birds as the mind of the wise man, which come to fruition

---

78. Cf. Ps 141:2 (Ps 140:2 LXX), which could also be a source for Philo's thought here.

79. *QE* 2.71.

80. *Somn.* 2.232.

81. "ἐκθυμιάω," LSJ, 507.

82. Philo, *Ebr.* 87.

83. *Her.* 199–200. Cf. also *Somn.* 1.243 that speaks of the whole world and heaven made a votive offering (ἀνάθημα) to God, which is set in parallel with the offering of "God-beloved souls" (θεοφιλής) who are consecrated to God (cited by Laporte, "High Priest," 71–82 at 75). This is perhaps the only place where a cosmic sacrifice is described (compared to the numerous references to a cosmic/heavenly temple or a cosmic High Priest); noted also by Gupta, "Question," 288.

84. Philo, *Leg.* 2.56. See also *Congr.* 114–15, which speaks of a censer of incense that emits "perfumes exhaled by wisdom and every virtue," and *Spec.* 1.171, which portrays the incenses offerings as a symbol of gratitude for the rational spirit of a person and the blood offerings as a thank offering for the physical nature of the person.

85. *Spec.* 1.254.

86. *Her.* 125–26.

as a thank-offering offered, "as immaculate and unblemished offerings."[87] The willing dispositions are equated with first-fruit offerings.[88] All these parts are indicative of the whole person and their life as it is lived before God, "though the worshippers bring nothing else, in bringing themselves they offer the best of sacrifices, the full and truly perfect oblation of noble living,"[89] since, Philo asks elsewhere, "what votive offering (ἀνάθημα) is more hallowed or more worthy of reverence than a man?"[90]

Both faith and works can be offered as sacrifices. The one who can bear fruit as their virtue because they understand and receive the fruit that comes from God, will offer to him, "the blameless and fairest sacrifice of faith." The Loeb translation might suggest a sacrifice produced by faith or a faithful sacrifice, but the Greek is a neuter accusative noun followed by a feminine accusative noun, with no genitive involved (ἄμωμον καὶ κάλλιστον ἱερεῖον οἴσει θεῷ πίστιν.)[91] This could be described as an "Accusative in Simple Apposition"[92] so Younge's translation might be more appropriate: "will bring to God a faultless and most excellent offering, *namely faith.*" Philo also characterizes good deeds done eagerly and without hesitation as a first-fruits offering.[93]

In several of his works, Philo takes the festival of Passover to depict the life of virtue as a passing over from one state to the next. In one place it is explained as "the passage from the life of the passions to the practice of virtue"[94] and in another, similarly, to the mind passing away from the passions and towards giving thanks to God.[95] The mention of a tenth offered to Melchizedek by Abram in Gen 14:20 speaks of "the soul's passover, the crossing from every passion and all the realm of sense to the tenth, which is the realm of mind and of God," until the radiant soul offers its own progress as "innocent and spotless victims."[96] What Philo

---

87. QG 2.52. In QG 3.3, Philo interprets the different animals offered in Gen 15:9 as different parts of the universe.

88. QE 2.50.

89. Spec. 1.271, also cited below in connection with another topic.

90. Decal. 133. In Spec. 1.66, the stars are compared to votive offerings. This passage is explored in more detail below.

91. Cher. 85.

92. Wallace, *Greek Grammar*, 198–99.

93. Philo, Sacr. 53.

94. Sacr. 63.

95. Migr. 25.

96. Congr. 106.

refers to as "the crossing-festival" (διαβατήρια, speaking of the Passover)[97] represents a crossing, "from the body and the passions,"[98] as does the lamb of the Passover itself that symbolizes the progress of the soul toward a harmony that unites "counsel and justice."[99] Both the mind and the soul have a kind of Passover; the soul from the passions of ignorance, vice, fear, greed and injustice to education, wisdom, confidence, justice and equality, and the mind from the realm of the senses to outward looking thoughts that emulate and love others.[100] Later in the same work, the lamb represents a passing over from the material, passive, bodily and the perceptions of the senses to the active, rational and incorporeal, "more akin to mind and thought" that symbolizes a virtuous soul that desires perfection.[101] This emphasis on a passing over from the corporeal to the incorporeal can also be found in Philo's contention that the, "true sacrifice of God-loving souls" is from visible splendor to an invisible one.[102] To repel the passions that dwell within until they have been completely removed is "to make atonement over them" (ἐξιλάσασθαι ἐπ' αὐτῶν)[103] from ἐξιλάσκομαι, to make expiation, that is to appease God.[104] Once the mind is free from the passions, replaced by good things, it can make its first-fruit offerings to the Lord.[105] Additionally, Ephraim and Manasseh represent two types of groups who offered sacrifices at different times and are compared respectively to "fruitful memory" (those who sacrificed the Passover in the first month and separated themselves immediately from the passions in Egypt) and "recollection" (that is seen as inferior, and thus awarded second place; these are those who looked back to Egypt).[106]

---

97. Cf. *Mos.* 2:224.

98. *Spec.* 2.147.

99. *QE* 1.3.

100. *QE* 1.4.

101. *QE* 1.7–8; cf. also the reference to the Passover lamb in relation to forward motion in *Leg.* 3.165.

102. *QE* 1.13.

103. *Post.* 72.

104. "ἐξιλάσκομαι," BDAG, 350.

105. Philo, *Plant.* 97–99.

106. *Leg.* 3.94.

The Offering of Purity and Virtue

In *De specialibus legibus*, Book 1, this single-minded piety is defined as ἀρετή (virtue), which is viewed as the supreme good. Philo says that the person offering a sacrifice must cleanse their soul before their body, "The mind is cleansed by wisdom and the truths of wisdom's teaching ... and by the sacred company of the other virtues and by the practice of them shewn in noble and highly praiseworthy actions."[107] The goal of this cleansing is "contemplation (θεωρία) of the universe and all that is therein,"[108] the same as in a later section, "the contemplation of things immaterial and conceptual" (πρὸς θεωρίαν τῶν ἀσωμάτων καὶ νοητῶν). This goal is achieved by knowledge (ἐπιστήμη) that guides reason (λογισμός).[109] Here the altar itself is depicted as the soul of the wise person, made up of perfect virtue, upon which the sacred light (wisdom) is kept burning.[110] In the same section, Philo emphasizes the need for both body and soul to be pure before a sacrifice; the soul from "passions (πάθος) and ... every viciousness (κακία) of word and deed"; the body from defilement.[111] Unlike an animal sacrifice, the offering of a person is not consumed since, "the holiness of the sacrifice remains, for sacrifice is not flesh but the pure and unstained life of a holy (person)."[112] The person who cleanses themselves can offer themselves as a sacrifice.[113]

In a different work, Philo's meditation on the head offered with the feet and inner parts in Exod 12:9 leads to the explanation that for a person, "it is fitting for him who is purified to purify his entire soul with his inner desires" and this will lead to words and deeds that accord with this purity.[114] The prohibition against mixing the blood of the sacrifice with leaven in Exod 23:18 is interpreted as a total consecration of the person to God that despises sensual pleasures and conceit.[115] It is "cultivated and fruit-yielding virtue," planted in the soul and bearing fruit free of blemish

---

107. *Spec.* 1.269.
108. *Spec.* 1.269.
109. *Spec.* 1.288.
110. *Spec.* 1.287.
111. *Spec.* 1.257, and generally, *Spec.* 1.257–60.
112. *QE* 2.98.
113. *Spec.* 1.270.
114. *QE* 1.17.
115. *QE* 2.14.

that should be placed on the altar of sacrifice (Gen 2:8).[116] "Righteous conduct, virtues, and virtuous actions" are "first in worth and value" and should be offered as first fruits.[117] The first-fruit offerings are also compared to the "sacred impulses" in a person that accord with virtue and must be dedicated to God. These perfect virtues, unsullied by any taint of evil, are also compared to the undivided sacrifices and burnt offerings that are presented to God.[118] The modesty and chastity of women in marriage, reflecting the beauty of their soul, is also compared to first-fruit offerings.[119]

Philo explains that the young worshipers of Exod 24:5 are the youthful principles of the soul that represent action and complement the elderly principles of the soul that engage in contemplation. Together the two add up to a virtuous life.[120] A thank-offering "of those things which belong to a sound life" combines the "heart of a pious mind" with a soul of "sound and full reason."[121] The blood smeared upon the candidate admitted to the priesthood indicates figuratively that "the fully-consecrated must be pure in words and actions and in his whole life."[122] Philo allegorizes the sacrificial regulations concerning purification and unblemished animals this way, "Mind belongs to a genus wholly superior to sense as man is to woman; unblemished and purged, as perfect virtue (ἀρετή) purges, it is itself the most religious of sacrifices and its whole being is highly pleasing to God."[123] The mind of the worshiper must be sanctified "by exercise in good and profitable thoughts and judgements" and their life must be consistent with these judgements.[124] The same idea is expressed in *De plantatione*, where Philo asserts, "God delights in altars beset by a choir of Virtues (ἀρετή), albeit no fire burn on them."[125] Philo compares favorably those who do not perform a literal sacrifice with those who do, since the former demonstrate the highest quality of a sacrifice: the vir-

---

116. *Leg.* 1.49–50.
117. *Sacr.* 73.
118. *Sacr.* 109–11.
119. *Mos.* 2.137–39.
120. *QE* 2.31.
121. *QE* 2.99.
122. *Mos.* 2.150; see more generally *Mos.* 2.148–51.
123. *Spec.* 1.201.
124. *Spec.* 1.203.
125. *Plant.* 108.

tues; this is in contrast to those who simply go through the motions, but whose lives are full of the opposite of those virtues: impiety. According to Otto Bauerfeind, in his emphasis on virtue (ἀρετή), Philo is drawing on "a leading tool in the language of Greek moral philosophy ... (which) formed an important medium in the dealings of Judaism with the Hellenistic world."[126] According to Samuel Sandmel, Philo sees the true virtues arising from the soul that contemplates a "generic virtue" which exists in the intelligible, rather than the material and sensible world,[127] showing again Philo's debt to Platonic thought. Outward ethical conduct exemplified in obedience to Mosaic law is the counterpart and imitation of the heavenly virtue.[128]

These virtues are linked to other qualities in various places in Philo. In the passage from *De somniis*, Book 2 (cited above), Philo asks, "What then is the offering of an unbodied soul?" What is the fine wheaten flour?" He answers his own rhetorical question this way, "What but the fine flour, the symbol of a will (γνώμη),[129] purified by the councils of instruction (παιδεία)."[130] So the Priest is commanded, "to offer the best of sacrifices, even the whole soul, brimful of truths (δόγμα) of all sincerity (εἰλικρινής) and purity (καθαρός) —a soul, too, rich with fatness, gladdened by light divine and perfumed with the breaths exhaled from justice and the other virtues."[131] In order to exhibit the virtues, the mind and the soul must have been purified by instruction in the right doctrine. Such a soul can offer up truth as its sacrifice, as Philo recounts in his work *Quod deterius potiori insidari soleat* when describing the expectations of God, "who welcomes genuine worship of every kind ... Genuine worship is that of a soul bringing simple reality as its only sacrifice."[132] If a person comes to the shrine full of good (in contrast to the "empty hands" referred to in

126. Bauernfeind, "Ἀρετή," 458.

127. Sandmel, *Philo*, 113–14.

128. Goodenough, *Introduction to Philo*, 118–23. According to Goodenough (122), Philo's concern is both with individual laws as applications of the principle of natural law expressed in the Decalogue, and with how they manifest the primary (Greek) virtues.

129. "That which is purposed or intended, purpose, intention, mind, mind-set" according to "γνώμη," BDAG, 202, and translated "mind" by Younge.

130. Philo, *Somn.* 2.73.

131. *Somn.* 2.74.

132. *Det.* 21.

Exod 23:15) and thus ready to receive spiritual illumination, their soul will be filled with knowledge and wisdom.[133]

The Sacrifice of Praise

In offering up these kind of sacrifices of virtues, the true worshiper is offering a sacrifice of praise,[134] in hymns and songs, "And indeed though the worshippers bring nothing else, in bringing themselves they offer the best of sacrifices, the full and truly perfect oblation of noble living (καλοκἀγαθία), as they honour with hymns and thanksgivings their Benefactor and Saviour, God, sometimes with the organs of speech, sometimes without tongue or lips, when within the soul alone their minds recite the tale or utter the cry of praise."[135] The praise offering of Lev 7:12f. is understood as "hymns and benedictions and prayers and sacrifices."[136] Indeed, the noblest of virtues according to Philo, is gratitude, as he recounts in his work *De plantatione*, "it is not possible genuinely to express our gratitude to God by means of buildings and oblations and sacrifices ... for even the whole world were not a temple adequate to yield the honour due to Him. Nay, it must be expressed by means of hymns of praise."[137] Yet here too Philo has not relapsed into counting the mere singing of hymns a sacrifice, since this would be as great an error as counting physical offerings a sacrifice, so he is at pains to explain that the hymns of which he is speaking, are to be sung, "and these not such as the audible voice shall sing, but strains raised and re-echoed by the mind too pure for eye to discern."[138] Philo's narrative continues with an "old story" concerning the creation of the world, where the only thing wanting in the

---

133. *QE* 2.7.

134. Of course, Philo does also have a precedent for this in the OT in passages such as Ps 51:15–17 (50:17–19 LXX); Jonah 2:9 (2:10 LXX) and possibly, Pss 50:14 (49:14 LXX); 107:22 (106:22 LXX); 116:17 (115:8 LXX).

135. *Spec.* 1.272. Cf. *Spec.* 1.286, "all perfect sacrifices consisted in thanksgiving" (Younge's translation. The Loeb translation understands πρὸς ἔνδειξιν τοῦ τελείας ἐν εὐχαριστίαις εἶναι a little differently).

136. *Spec.* 1.224; cf. *Spec.* 1.193, which says that the practices of worship, such as hymns, prayers, and sacrifices are designed in order to, "make them [the worshiper] enamoured of continence and piety"; cf. also *Spec.* 1.195–96.

137. *Plant.* 126. Leonhardt, *Jewish Worship*, contends that thanksgiving is at the heart of Philo's understanding of worship, and makes this the central theme of her study.

138. *Plant.* 126.

perfection of all that God had made was, according to one of his heavenly ministers, "namely the word to sound their praises."[139] In response to this wise answer, God creates a people who, "should be capable of receiving all learning and of composing hymns of praise."[140] Even here, when speaking of praise, Philo is drawn back to the beauty of the rational mind and the ability to praise is fundamentally tied to the reasoning powers of the worshiper, as he goes on, "the mind that blesses God . . . was himself the fruit that is really "holy and for praise to God," fruit borne not by earth's trees but by those of a rational and virtuous nature."[141] In another instance, a cultivated spirit of thanksgiving purifies the worshiper of wrong and washes away the filthiness that defiles both thought and deed.[142]

Summary of Sacrifice Language

For Philo it is never sufficient merely to perform the right sacrifices in the manner prescribed by the OT. Rather, a sacrifice must be offered with due reverence for the occasion and in accord with the personal piety of the worshiper, as demonstrated in a holy life. The converse of this sentiment is also true; the sacrifices of an impious person count for nothing. Therefore, a person must offer sacrifices with a mind and reason that is pure and noble. Here we see a development that is closer to the Hellenistic thought-world of the Diaspora than it is to the context of Israelite religion. Moreover, Philo agrees with Stoics such as Seneca and Dio Chrysostom and Platonists such as Plutarch and Maximus of Tyre (as well as Cicero) that a true sacrifice can be spiritual rather than literal. This is exemplified in the offering of the whole of one's mind and soul to God as well as the offering of purity and virtue in thought, speech and deed. Praise and thanksgiving can also constitute a sacrifice (as we also find in Maximus of Tyre).

---

139. *Plant.* 128. Young translates this as, "namely for reason, which should be able duly to praise it all."
140. *Plant.* 129 (Younge's translation).
141. *Plant.* 134.
142. *Deus* 7.

3.3 PRIEST LANGUAGE

3.3.1 Priest Represents Divine Direction in the Soul

Philo uses priest language for an internal guide who speaks to the person from God.[143] He characterizes this guide in several different ways, although each of these seem to be a different way of speaking of the same thing, or at least something very similar.

3.3.2 Priest as Reason

In his meditation on Melchizedek the priest (Gen 14:18–20), Philo identifies the wine offered by Melchizedek with the strong drink suitable for souls, "For he is a priest, even Reason (λόγος), having as his portion Him that is, and all his thoughts of God are high and vast and sublime" (ἱερεὺς γάρ ἐστι λόγος κλῆρον ἔχων τὸν ὄντα καὶ ὑψηλῶς περὶ αὐτοῦ καὶ ὑπερόγκως καὶ μεγαλοπρεπῶς λογιζόμενος).[144] A little further on, Philo speaks of the Reasoning faculty (here λογισμός) entering the Holy Place when Aaron himself enters, acting as Priest.[145] Philo speaks of this λογισμός almost synonymously with his reference to Reason (λόγος) a little earlier,[146] and in parallel with the mind (νοῦς) just afterwards.[147] In *De somniis*, Book I, Philo refers to two temples (addressed below). The High Priest of the temple of the universe is, "His First-born, the divine Word" (ὁ πρωτόγονος αὐτοῦ θεῖος λόγος) and that of the "rational soul" (λογικὴ ψυχή) is the "real Man."[148] Unusually for Philo, two High Priests are pictured; one who ministers to the universe and one to the soul, but in both cases words with the λογ- root are used and the emphasis is on word and reason. In an allegorical passage in *De ebrietate*, Philo compares "moderate learning" with a mother and Reason with a Father.[149] Those who adhere closely

---

143. For an excellent and comprehensive analysis of the role of the High Priest in Philo, see Laporte, "High Priest," 71–82. Note also Seland, "Common Priesthood," 87–99.

144. Philo, *Leg.* 3.82.

145. *Leg.* 3.125.

146. *Leg.* 3.123.

147. *Leg.* 3.126.

148. *Somn.* 1.215. The "real man" seems to be a picture of the perfect man, set in contrast with the one who is still progressing toward perfection; see Laporte, "High Priest," 71–82, at 80.

149. E.g., *Ebr.* 68, which places Father (πατήρ) and "right reason" (ὁ ὀρθὸς λόγος) in

to the words of the Father, "right reason" (ὁ ὀρθὸς λόγος) judges worthy of the priesthood, seen as the highest honor.[150] The true Priesthood is for those who obey right reason and resist false arguments and the impulses of the flesh.[151] None can be a true priest who is still at war with the vain opinions contrary to reason.[152] A little further on in the same work, Philo identifies Aaron the Priest directly with the reason, "He is the reason (λογισμός) whose thoughts are lofty and sublime, not with the empty inflated bigness of mere vaunting, but with the greatness of virtue (ἀρετή)."[153] The one who stays away from the path of indiscipline and folly and instead follows the path of "sober abstinence" will gain "the greatest of headships, the priesthood."[154] The High Priest is also identified as Reason in *De migratione Abrahami*, where ἀρχιερεύς is placed in apposition with λογισμός, both in the accusative singular.[155] Thus, the Holy place is discernible by the intellect alone (νοητός),[156] that is, "which only mind can apprehend."[157] Philo stresses that it is the soul (ψυχή) that enters the holy place and the "necessaries" that it requires are "the good things of the mind."[158] Just as Reason (λόγος), sometimes portrayed as divine reason, entered the holy place, now it is the mind/soul that enters.

3.3.3 Priest as Judge of Conscience

Elsewhere in *De fuga et inventione*, Philo explicitly states that, "the High Priest is not a man, but a Divine (θεῖος) Word (λόγος)."[159] In an elaborate

---

apposition, both in the dative case.

150. *Ebr.* 65.

151. See *Ebr.* 68–76.

152. *Ebr.* 76.

153. *Ebr.* 128. I will have more to say about the identification of the Priesthood with virtue below.

154. *Ebr.* 125–29.

155. *Ebr.* 102.

156. *Ebr.* 103. That is "falling within the province of νοῦς," according to "νοητός," LSJ, 1178.

157. Philo, *Ebr.* 104. Despite the translator using the word "mind" instead of "intellect," as he did earlier, both words translate the same Greek adjective νοητός (cf. Young is clearer here, by using "intellect" both times).

158. *Ebr.* 105. Indeed, νοητός is used six times in this short passage (*Ebr.* 102–105).

159. *Fug.* 108, the latter word obviously the same translated "Reason" in other works by Philo. For commentary on *Fug.* 106–112, see Williamson, *Jews*, 138–43.

allegory, the father of the High Priest (who is the Divine Word) is God and his mother is Wisdom. His anointing means that, "his ruling faculty (ἡγεμονικός) is illumined with a brilliant light,"[160] his mind is purified, and he is "betrothed" to a pure virgin, like one wedded to virtue.[161] He is incapable of committing involuntary sin.[162] Philo then advises his reader to pray that this High Priest should dwell in their soul, that is as "Monitor" (ἔλεγχος) "on the seat of justice."[163] In the second book of *De somniis*, Philo refers to a High Priest who is himself the libation (cf. the previous section on sacrifice). This High Priest receives bounties from God and pours them out as himself.[164] He is not only, "able to sow the seed of undefiled and virgin thoughts, but a father also of holy intelligences."[165] The Loeb translator, F. H. Colson explains in two notes how this role symbolizes the relation of the *Logos* to God.[166] This same High Priest is understood as πρύτανις and δημιουργός, translated by Colson as "its president, its chief magistrate."[167] Colson writes of the latter, "The term, used in various Greek states, would be quite familiar to Philo through Thucydides and Demosthenes,"[168] and his image represents "a whole judgement-court, a whole senate,"[169] emphasizing his judicial role in relation to the soul.[170] In *Quod Deus sit immutabilis*, the priest is explicitly identified with "divine reason" (ὁ θεῖος λόγος). Prior to his entry into the soul of a person there is no sense of guilt for shameful thoughts and actions, for there is no understanding of sin.[171] But when the

---

160. Philo, *Fug.* 110.

161. *Fug.* 114-15.

162. *Fug.* 115.

163. *Fug.* 118; ἔλεγχος appears twice in this passage, translated in one place as "conscience" and in another as "judge and convictor" by Younge.

164. *Somn.* 2.183.

165. *Somn.* 2.185.

166. See Philo, *On Flight and Finding*, 524 n. a and 529 n. c. Philo's understanding of *Logos* has generated much discussion, see, e.g., Goodenough, *Introduction to Philo*, 100-110; Dillon, *Middle Platonists*, 154-65; Sandmel, *Philo*, 94-99; Borgen, "Philo," 233-82 at 273-74; Winston, *Logos*; Williamson, *Jews*, 103-43; Barker, "Temple Imagery," 70-102; Laporte, "High Priest," 71-82; Schenck, *Brief Guide*, 58-62; Termini, "Philo's Thought," 97-101; Mackie, "Seeing," 25-47; Radice, "Philo's Theology," 135-40.

167. *Somn.* 2.187.

168. 529 n. a. in the foregoing translation.

169. *Somn.* 2.188.

170. Later in *Somn.* 2.189 and 2.230-32, the High Priest is understood to be transformed into a kind of perfected man, whose thoughts are transfixed on God alone.

171. *Deus* 134.

true priest arrives, twice named as "Conviction" (ἔλεγχος), he exposes the condition of the soul with a pure ray of light, in order that it be healed.[172]

3.3.4 Priest as Purity of the Soul

In his *Legum allegoriae*, Philo notes that Aaron did not wear his robe when he entered into the Holy of Holies (Lev 16:1–4), and compares the idea of the high priest, "laying aside the garment of opinions and impressions of the soul" to that of the soul that loves God disrobing itself of the body and all that is dear to it, in order to gain a foundation in the perfect doctrines of virtue.[173] Similarly, in *Quis rerum divinarum heres sit*, Philo speaks of a man who is divine, not human (οὐκ ἔστιν ἀνθρώπινος, ἀλλὰ θεῖος) when his mind ministers to God in purity.[174] He is like a High Priest whose heart is perfect; that is, one whose soul turns toward God and away from the body, as a stranger sojourning in a foreign land on this earth.[175] Similarly, Philo elsewhere compares the body of a priest with an immortal soul. Philo's interest lies not in the body, but in the need for the soul to be unblemished just as the Priest's body is required to be unblemished by the Levitical laws.[176]

3.3.5 Priest Represents Different Actors

The Priest can represent the Universe acting as a "fellow-ministrant" (συλλειτουργέω) with the High Priest,[177] just as the Priest's garment can transform him, "from a man into the nature of the world."[178] Angels, who are pure intelligent bodiless souls, are described as priests in the temple of the universe.[179] The nation of Israel acts like a priest during the Passover

---

172. *Deus* 135.
173. *Leg.* 2.55–56.
174. *Her.* 84.
175. *Her.* 82–85. Like the work I explored in the previous chapter (such as Plutarch, *Exil.* 607D; *Is. Os.* 353A; Maximus of Tyre, *Or.* 7.5; 9.6; 10.9), we see Platonic influences in references to "the prison-houses of the body" (*Her.* 85).
176. *Spec.* 1.82.
177. *Spec.* 1.95; cf. *Spec.* 1.96.
178. *Mos.* 2.135.
179. *Spec.* 1.66.

(ἱεράομαι) and yet is guiltless,[180] just as they are priest to the whole world.[181] As a microcosm of this image, each household or congregation can act as a pure priest who sacrifices "with one character and one soul."[182]

3.3.6 Garments of the Priest

Garments Are a Symbol of the Soul That Is Pure Inside and Out

The two robes of the Priest are interpreted as symbols of a soul that is pure, both inwardly in its relations to God and outwardly in its relations to the world of the senses and to other people.[183] Philo returns to the garments of Aaron described in Lev 16:4, and claims that the passage speaks in riddles (αἰνίσσομαι), but its symbolic meaning concerns those who worship in purity without deceit (ἄδολος), and reject that which is merely human (ἀνθρώπειος), mortal (θνητός) and false (ψευδής), that is dear to the darkness, and instead aim at immortality (ἀφθαρσία) and live in the light of truth.[184]

Garments Are Associated with Reason

As we have already seen, the High Priest is identified as the Logos, but his garments are also said to owe their source to powers of the mind (νοητός) and the senses (αἰσθητός).[185] The signet/seal and the flowers and bells are also related to the former and latter respectively.[186] In *Quaestiones et solutiones in Exodum* Book II, the garments of the High Priest represent truth,[187] the *Logos*,[188] that described as Reason, restrains the passions.[189]

---

180. *Spec.* 2.145.

181. *Spec.* 2.163.

182. *QE.* 1.10. On the role of macrocosm and microcosm in Philo's use of cultic imagery, see the helpful analysis and chart in Gupta, "Question," 291–95.

183. *Mut.* 44.

184. *Somn.* 1.218.

185. *Migr.* 102.

186. *Migr.* 103.

187. *QE* 2.107, 116.

188. *QE* 2.110, 111, 116, 117, 118, 122, 124.

189. *QE* 2.115; cf. *QE* 2.118. Cf. also *Mos.* 2.124–25, 127–30.

Garments Represent the Virtues

The garments can represent the virtues such as prudence and truth[190] or simply all the virtues.[191] Truth adorns the robe of the high priest in the sacred place where the soul resides. Truth and δήλωσις ("clear showing" in the Loeb translation or "manifestation" in Younge) are placed together and represent the inner and outer qualities or thoughts and actions that are in accord with wisdom.[192]

Garments Represent the World

The garments of the Priest represent the whole world when the Priest enters the sanctuary, since different aspects of the garments correspond to different element of the universe.[193] Their arrangement signifies the rational ordering of the universe in accord with reason,[194] and express to the mind, "the philosophical conceptions which its parts suggest."[195]

3.3.7 Summary of Priest Language

The Priest is often pictured by Philo as an internal guide that provides direction to the soul. It is most often described as Reason, who can act as a judge or arbiter of the conscience and enacts purity within the soul. In other places the Priest is compared to the universe, angels, the nation of Israel and even the household itself. Philo also concentrates attention on the garments of the priest that can symbolize the purity of a soul in relation to God and to the world. The garments are sometimes associated with Reason and can represent the virtues as well as representing the cosmos itself. I found very little evidence of figurative Priest language in other Hellenistic writers with which to compare this, but Philo's emphasis on Reason, virtue and inward purity accords generally with what we find in Hellenistic philosophy.

---

190. *Ebr.* 361–63.
191. *QE* 2.112.
192. *Spec.* 4.69.
193. *Mos.* 2.133, 135; *Fug.* 110; *QE* 2.109, 112–114, 120.
194. *Spec.* 1.88–89, 93.
195. *Spec.* 1.95.

3.4 TEMPLE LANGUAGE

3.4.1 The Soul Is the Dwelling Place of God

In common with other Middle Platonic texts cited in the previous chapter, Philo frequently refers to the soul as the dwelling place of God. However, the soul must be prepared, just as a temple must be set apart as a dwelling place fit for a holy God. Philo urges his readers to make their souls, "as beautiful as we may, to be a lodging fit for God."[196] The word used for "lodging" is ἐνδιαίτημα, which does not have a specific cultic connotation. However, it is used at least once in Philo with reference to the tabernacle,[197] and elsewhere with reference to the temple of the soul[198] and in our present passage, Philo follows this comment by averring that even a temple is not sufficient for God, but "One worthy house there is—the soul that is fitted to receive Him."[199] It is important to build the house of the soul in right order; first, laying the foundations of goodness and teaching, then the virtues and noble actions are built upon these and finally the whole building is ornamented with "the reception of the learning of the schools" (ἡ ἀνάληψις τῶν ἐγκυκλίων προπαιδευμάτων).[200] Philo compares the soul to a dwelling place (ἑστία) into which the divine reason (ὁ θεῖος λόγος) enters.[201] Philo asks rhetorically what house in all creation could be worthier of God's dwelling than a soul that is "perfectly purified" and considers the "only good" to be "moral beauty,"[202] that is, virtue.[203] In *De somniis* Book I, Philo makes reference to Lev 26:12 to assert that a soul must be purged of evil "to the utmost," (ἄκρως)[204] in order that God may dwell within. He speaks as if to himself "Be zealous therefore, O soul, to become a house of God, a holy temple, a most beauteous abiding-place" (σπούδαζε οὖν, ὦ ψυχή, θεοῦ οἶκος γενέσθαι, ἱερὸν

---

196. *Cher.* 98.

197. *Congr.* 116.

198. *Somn.* 1.149, covered below and also in *Spec.* 1.270, addressed earlier, where ἐνδιαίτημα is in apposition to the figurative temple, where a person offers himself as a sacrifice.

199. *Cher.* 100.

200. *Cher.* 101; cf. 1 Cor 3:10–15 that also speaks of building a house with right foundations prior to Paul's temple image in 1 Cor 3:16–17.

201. *Deus* 134.

202. *Sobr.* 62; cf. *Sobr.* 68.

203. Agreeing here with the Stoics; see Dillon, *Middle Platonists*, 148.

204. From ἄκρον; see "ἄκρον," BDAG, 40; "ἄκρον," LSJ, 57.

Figurative Temple Language in Philo of Alexandria 147

ἅγιον, ἐνδιαίτημα κάλλιστον).²⁰⁵ The same Levitical passage is expounded in his second book, where the city in which God will walk is understood to be the soul.²⁰⁶ It is worth noting that Paul seems to allude to this very passage from Leviticus in 2 Cor 6:16 with reference to the Corinthians as the temple of God. Philo also speaks of the "rational soul" (λογικός ψυχή) as a temple of God.²⁰⁷ In an allegorical exposition of Gen 23:9, 11, Philo compares the body and soul to a "double cave." The virtuous man shuts himself off from the outer cave. Reason reigns within his "god-loving soul," "receiving holiness and purity and the possession of a blameless life" and this is compared to the holy of holies within the tabernacle.²⁰⁸ Philo also speaks of a divine inspiration (using θεοληπτέομαι),²⁰⁹ that sometimes possesses his soul.²¹⁰

3.4.2 The Mind Is the Dwelling Place of God

In one place Philo describes the mind (διάνοια) of a wise man as, "a palace and house of God."²¹¹ In another, Philo warns the one who purifies his body and yet enter temples with an impure soul and an unrepentant heart "he shall never escape the eye of Him who sees into the recesses of the mind (διάνοια) and treads its inmost shrine."²¹² The word translated "shrine" in LCL is ἄδυτον, the neuter of ἄδυτος, which is often used substantively for the innermost sanctuary or shrine.²¹³ Younge translates the noun as "secret places," which might cast doubt on its cultic connotations but there are numerous instances in Philo where it is clearly used in the context of a temple,²¹⁴ and the comparison with the literal temple in

205. *Somn.* 1.149.
206. *Somn.* 2.248.
207. *Somn.* 1.215.
208. *QG* 4.80.
209. "θεοληπτέομαι," LSJ, 790; cf. Philostratus, *Vit. Apoll.* 1.2.3.
210. *Cher.* 27.
211. *Praem.* 123.
212. *Deus* 9 (see *Deus* 8–9 more generally).
213. "ἄδυτος," LSJ, 25.
214. See Philo, *Leg.* 1.62; *Cher.* 95; *Post.* 173; *Ebr.* 135; *Her.* 82; *Congr.* 168; *Fug.* 162; *Somn.* 2.232; *Mos.* 2.87, 95, 152, 154, 174, 178; *Spec.* 1.84, 231, 274, 275, 297; *Praem.* 75; *Legat.* 188, 306, 308. It is worth noting that each of these examples is translated by Younge with a cultic sense, such as "innermost shrine" or "holy of holies." The term never appears in the LXX, and in the Pseudepigrapha it appears only in *Sib. Or.*

context makes the referent very likely. In *De vita Mosis* Book 2, Philo uses the same word (ἄδυτον) again to speak of τὰ ἄδυτα τῆς σκηνῆς (the inmost sanctuary of the tabernacle) as symbolically (συμβολικῶς) referring to the mind (νοητός).[215] Indeed, Philo claims that when God was looking to establish his goodness among people, "He found no worthier temple on earth than the reasoning faculty" (νεὼν ἀξιοπρεπέστερον οὐχ εὗρεν ἐπὶ γῆς λογισμοῦ, here using λογισμός).[216]

Similarly, Philo cautions against seeking for Jerusalem and its temple (the "vision of peace") on earth, "for what grander or holier house could we find for God in the whole range of existence than the vision-seeking mind...?"[217] The mind is promised that if it rejects passions and all evils and instead "art worthily initiated and canst be consecrated to God," then it may become "an animate shrine of the Father." A divine vision of holiness is possible for the person who makes their soul "a sanctuary and altogether a shrine of God."[218] Philo views the mind (νοῦς) as "an inseparable portion (ἀπόσπασμα) of that divine and blessed soul"[219] and there are tantalizing references to the head being the temple of the mind,[220] that are not further developed.

3.4.3 People In Their Embodiment Described as Temples

In two places Philo seems to come closer to Paul's understanding of the body as temple than other ancient writers. In his account of the creation of humanity after God's image in Gen 1:26–27, Philo pictures God selecting only the very best materials for "his structure," which in context seems to be a clear reference to the human body, "for a sacred dwelling-place[221] or shrine[222] was being fashioned for the reasonable soul, which

---

8.56, 487; 12.170, each time in a clearly cultic context.

215. *Mos.* 2.82.

216. *Virt.* 188. In his commentary on this verse Wilson, *Virtues*, 389, also cites *SVF* 1.146: "It is not necessary to build temples for the gods, but to have the divine in the mind alone."

217. Philo, *Somn.* 2.250–51.

218. *QE* 2.51.

219. *Det.* 90.

220. *QG* 1.5; *QE* 2.100.

221. Or more literally, "abode" (Younge) translating οἶκος.

222. Actually, two words, "νεὼς ἱερὸς," so better, "sacred temple" (Younge).

man was to carry as a holy image (ἀγαλματοφορέω),²²³ of all images (ἄγαλμα) the most Godlike (θεοειδής)."²²⁴ The reader has already been told that the divine (θεῖος) breath or spirit (πνεῦμα) has been breathed into this being,²²⁵ so the overall image is closer to 1 Cor 3:16; 6:19 than any other Hellenistic writer I have examined.²²⁶ A very similar concept is described in Philo's exposition of the life of Moses, when Moses' audience is astonished at the control of his reason over the impulses of his soul. His mind is pictured as dwelling in his body, "like an image in its shrine" (ἀγαλματοφορέω).²²⁷ In one place the congregation itself is described as a temple. Philo explains that in the time of Moses, there being no temple at that time, "the dwelling together of several good persons in the home was a temple and altar."²²⁸

3.4.4 The Universe as Temple

The World Is a Temple

Philo describes the whole created order as a temple in a number of places.²²⁹ In *De plantatione*, Philo describes the world as, "God's house in the realm of sense-perception," which he explicates as, "a sanctuary" (ἁγίασμα) an outshining of sanctity, so to speak, a copy of the original"²³⁰ that has been prepared "by the "hands" of God."²³¹ Here Philo seems to accept both the Stoic theory of sense-perceptions/impressions²³² and the Platonic

---

223. On this, an example of compound words much loved by Philo (see Runia, *Creation*, 103), consult Runia, *Creation*, 141, 227, 254, 335.

224. *Opif.* 137.

225. *Opif.* 135. See Runia, *Creation*, 326, on the role of πνεῦμα in Philo, Plato, and Stoicism.

226. Similarly, note in agreement the remarks of Runia, *Creation*, 335. However, Seland, "Common Priesthood," 93, notes that Philo is reluctant to speak of a man and his body as a temple, and asserts that the idea is only used of Adam and not of human beings in general, who are only copies of the archetypal man.

227. Philo, *Mos.* 1.27.

228. *QE* 1.10.

229. MacRae, "Heavenly Temple," 184 speaks of the notion of a "Temple-structured Universe" in Philo.

230. A likely reference to the heavenly temple, cf. Philo, *Leg.* 1.78, discussed below.

231. *Plant.* 50; cf. the reference to the temple "not made with [human] hands" (ἀχειροποίητος) in Mk 14:58; cf. also 2 Cor 5:1.

232. Though here using the adjective αἰσθητός rather than the one more commonly

understanding of otherworldly archetypes that form a pattern or model for earthly phenomena.²³³ In one place Philo claims that there are two temples of God; the soul and the world itself,²³⁴ and in another the "whole universe" (ὁ σύμπας κόσμος).²³⁵ When discussing the furnishings of the temple in Exod 26:1, Philo claims that the world existed as a universal temple before the holy temple existed.²³⁶ In a number of places, Philo expresses the view that even the whole world is not a temple sufficient for God's honor.²³⁷ Finally this world is described as "that greatest of houses or cities."²³⁸ Although in the latter citation the metaphor is not that of the temple (and the word used is οἰκία not οἶκος), it does comport with the previous references to the house as a temple and, for our purposes, it is of interest that the metaphor makes reference to the material and construction of the house and of God as its builder or architect (δημιουργός).²³⁹

Heaven Is a Temple

Heaven alone is sometimes pictured as a temple.²⁴⁰ When God created heaven and earth (Gen 1:1), he made heaven first because, "it was destined to be the most holy dwelling-place (pairing οἶκος with ἱερὸς) of manifest and visible gods."²⁴¹ Elsewhere, the stars are described as divine images that God placed in heaven, which are explicitly compared to a temple, "as in the purest temple belonging to corporeal being."²⁴² In a reference just

---

used in Stoic thought; καταληπτικός. See Dillon, *Middle Platonists*, 146.

233. See, e.g., McKelvey, *New Temple*, 38–40; MacRae, "Heavenly Temple," 179–99 at 283–92.

234. Philo, *Somn.* 1.215.

235. *Spec.* 1.66.

236. *QE* 2.85.

237. *Plant.* 33, cf. also *Plant.* 126; *Leg.* 1.44.

238. *Cher.* 127.

239. Cf. the reference in 1 Cor 3:10–17 to God as the master builder of the house that is described as a temple in 1 Cor 3:16–17.

240. For more detail, see, e.g., Werman, "God's House," 309–22. For the OT and ANE context that would also have provided a source for Philo's thought, see Beale, *Temple*, 31–60.

241. Philo, *Opif.* 27, speaking of the stars. See Runia, *Creation*, 160, for this surprising concession to Hellenistic thought.

242. *Opif.* 55; cf. the influence of Plato in passages such as *Tim.* 37c7, also reflected in Seneca, *Ep.* 90.28, cited by Runia, *Creation*, 204.

cited, Philo distinguishes between the universe as a temple (ἱερόν) and its sanctuary, that is heaven (using ναός, which is often specified as the holy of holies).²⁴³

God Fills All Things

As we saw in the previous chapter, Stoic writers referred to God filling the whole universe with his presence.²⁴⁴ Philo expresses similar sentiments in a number of places, and these accord with the idea of the universe being the dwelling place of God. Philo writes that, "God fills and penetrates all things, and has left no spot void or empty of His presence,"²⁴⁵ he "has left nothing empty or destitute of Himself, but has completely filled all things,"²⁴⁶ or to put it another way, he has filled the universe with himself.²⁴⁷

3.4.5 The Dwelling of Wisdom

Wisdom, or prudence (φρόνησις) can be either particular or general. The particular prudence that dwells in an individual is destined to die with them, but universal prudence "has for its abode the wisdom of God (here σοφία) and His dwelling-place" and it is imperishable, because "it abides in an imperishable dwelling-place."²⁴⁸ Within the wider context of second temple Judaism, the reference to an imperishable house, though not specified, is most likely to refer to a temple.²⁴⁹ Wisdom can also be compared to the tabernacle or tent in which the wise man "tabernacles (κατασκηνόω)

---

243. *Spec.* 1.66. Here we see the occasional privileging by Philo of heaven as a temple above the universe as a whole; see, e.g., Gupta, "Question," 282.

244. E.g., Cicero, *Div.* 1.49.110; 1.52.118; *Leg.* 2.11.28; Alcinous, *Handbook*, 165.10.3.1–2 (18).

245. Philo, *Leg.* 3.4; see also *Fug.* 75.

246. *Post.* 6; see also *Conf.* 137–38.

247. *Post.* 14, 30. *Gig.* 27 is another possible reference but it depends on whether the sense is that the Spirit fills all things or that the Spirit is "filled up in all its parts, so as to have no interstices and thus be indivisible," according to Philo, *On the Cherubim*, 459 n. a.

248. *Leg.* 1.78.

249. E.g., 1 Chr 29:16; 2 Chr 36:14; Ps 5:7 (5:8 MT); Isa 56:7; 64:11 (64:10 MT); 66:20; *1 En.* 14:10, 13, 15, 21; 25:5 and throughout the Dead Sea Scrolls, as highlighted in the first chapter.

and dwells (ἐνοικέω)."²⁵⁰ In another work, Reason itself (λόγος) appears to be identified with the "high and heavenly doctrine" and also with a "house" or abode (ἐνδιαίτημα), "which "Thou hast wrought as a Holy Place.""²⁵¹

3.4.6 Tabernacle Language²⁵²

In one place Philo contrasts the tabernacle unfavorably as a symbol of what is earthly, mutable and changeable with the temple that represents heaven, that is unchangeable and consistent.²⁵³ The tabernacle can also be spoken of as the world where God dwells, but without being compared negatively with heaven.²⁵⁴ However, elsewhere the tabernacle figuratively represents human virtue,²⁵⁵ incorporeal virtue,²⁵⁶ wisdom,²⁵⁷ and truth (with its contents "a representation and copy of wisdom,") and the presence of the tabernacle in the midst of uncleanness enables the people to wash away all that defiles them.²⁵⁸

3.4.7 Summary of Temple Language

Philo frequently speaks of the soul or the mind as the dwelling place of God, as do Stoics like Seneca, Epictetus, Dio Chrysostom and Marcus Aurelius and Middle Platonists like Plutarch and Maximus of Tyre. There is also an exceptional reference to a person in their embodiment compared to a temple (though Seland contends that this is only used of the original human, Adam, and not of humanity in general). Philo also

---

250. *Leg.* 3.46

251. *Plant.* 53.

252. MacRae, "Heavenly Temple," 179–99 at 181 argues that we can legitimately speak of temple symbolism when discussing the use of tabernacle imagery in both Philo and Hebrews, "not only because the biblical accounts of the tabernacle are generally thought to reflect temple structure, but because both authors are strongly influenced by contemporary temple symbolism in their exegesis."

253. *QE* 2.83. Just as in *QG* 2.4, Noah's ark is understood as corruptible, compared to the ark of the Temple that symbolizes incorruptibility, stability, and the divine nature.

254. *QE* 2.51.

255. *Det.* 160.

256. *Ebr.* 134.

257. *Congr.* 116–17.

258. *Her.* 112–13.

compares the whole universe to a temple, or contrasts the heaven and the earth as temples, or the heaven as the sanctuary (or holy of holies) of the universe. We hear that God fills all things and Wisdom is said to dwell as in a temple. Tabernacle language is also used for the world and for virtue, wisdom, purity and truth. This cosmic language has analogues with the language and thought of Stoics such as Seneca and Marcus Aurelius and Middle Platonists like Plutarch and Alcinous.

3.5 CONCLUSIONS

My purpose in this chapter has not been to provide a definitive account of Philo's understanding of the cult or even to defend a particular thesis for the origin of his figurative sacrifice, priest and temple language. Nor am I claiming that Philo is influenced purely by Hellenistic philosophy in his use of such figurative language. Clearly, many of Philo's emphases could be seen as a legitimate development of the critique of sacrifices and the emphasis on spiritual sacrifices found in the Apocrypha and Pseudepigrapha, and indeed in the OT itself. Rather, my more limited aim has been to examine the use of figurative temple language in Philo in order to see to what extent his language is consonant with the emphases *already* found in other Hellenistic philosophical writings. Here I have noted similar concepts to those found in Stoic and Middle Platonic writers; namely that the soul and the mind can be a sacrifice, as can purity and virtue in thought, speech and deed; and that the soul can be a temple for reason, or God, just as the universe itself (or one of its components) is a temple for God, who fills all things. Additionally, Philo's almost unique use of figurative Priest language echoes similar themes to those found in Hellenistic writers, emphasizing the place of reason, virtue and purity. My next task will be to compare my findings with the use of these themes in 1–2 Corinthians, to see how Paul's application of figurative temple language might speak to an audience whose familiarity with such language originated in a very different world view.

4

Figurative Temple Language in 1 Corinthians

4.1 INTRODUCTION

I SHALL ADDRESS PAUL's use of figurative temple language in 1 Corinthians in this chapter, by comparing Paul's use of this language to convey a particular message within *his* worldview and context, with the use of figurative temple language in the worldview and context that I examined in the previous two chapters.¹ Paul was using language that would have spoken to an audience familiar with Hellenistic philosophy.² However, this is not

---

1. Given the number of issues discussed in this epistle and the variety of potential contexts proposed for each issue, there is little scholarly agreement on any of them. It is hardly surprising then that the scholarly literature on 1 Corinthians continues to multiply at an extraordinary rate. Fee, *First Epistle*, xvi–xvii, commenting on the twenty-five-year gap between the first edition of his commentary and the second, remarks, "In terms of articles in the scholarly journals alone, the bibliography has in the past twenty-five years multiplied over 300 percent in relationship to all such material in the preceding two centuries!" Therefore, I will be necessarily selective in citing scholarly literature, given that I am commenting not only on the relevant passages (1 Cor 3:16–17; 6:19) but on the letter as a whole.

2. Metzger, *New Testament*, 64, speaks of the Paul presented by Luke in Acts as "one fluent in the popular philosophies of the day and able to turn his knowledge of them to missionary advantage as a point of contact with the audience" (cited by deSilva, "Paul," 549). DeSilva notes that Metzger evaluates the Paul of his letters quite differently, concluding that parallels between Paul and Stoic teaching were limited to

to claim that he borrows from Stoicism or Platonism. Rather, the language and imagery that Paul chose was used for his own purposes to express his own theology but both resonated with and challenged those influenced by the philosophical milieu of the day.[3]

I shall explore Paul's use of figurative temple language in 1 Cor 3:16–17 and 6:19. I will note that in 1 Cor 1:10–4:17 Paul contrasts wisdom of any kind outside of the revelation of the Spirit with the identity of the Corinthians as the temple in which the Spirit dwells (3:16–17). I will seek to demonstrate the corporate dimension of Paul's understanding of this temple there and its exclusiveness to those who belong to Christ and are indwelt by the Spirit, in sharp contrast to the philosophical understanding of indwelling, which is more individual and inclusive. In my discussion of 6:19 and its setting I shall stress Paul's focus on the body and its importance as the place where holiness is expressed. Paul's unashamed use of body language, in which the body is the location of the indwelling Spirit, is very different from the indifference or even disdain shown to the body in philosophy. Additionally, Paul maintains the emphasis on

---

words, not ideas. DeSilva tests out this theory by examining not only verbal parallels but possible conceptual parallels, common *topoi* and figures, and common forms. DeSilva's survey concludes that Paul was familiar with Stoic teaching but deployed the language and forms within a different theological framework.

3. See the similar comments of Lee, *Paul*, 23–24, especially: "Paul did not have to be a Stoic philosopher to use the language of the Stoics to speak to a community familiar with these ideas to convey his own message about Christ and the eschatological community" (24). Brookins, *Corinthian Wisdom*, 104–52, tries to reconstruct the social world of Corinth to question the conclusions of Bruce W. Winter and others that Corinth was thoroughly Roman in this period. Rather, Brookins contends, Greek and Roman influences overlapped and he suggests that some elite members of the Corinthian church could have had access to Greek philosophical training. Brookins, *Corinthian Wisdom*, 153–200, ambitiously attempts to relate every issue in the letter to Stoicism. Barnes, *Reading*, 122–40, provides a helpful summary of the evidence for the philosophical heritage of Corinth, concluding "Corinth... had always been tolerant of the most popular philosophies in the ancient world.... The Isthmian games attracted philosophers ... and Corinth produced many Cynics and Stoics" (165). Dutch, *Educated Elite*, especially 95–167, makes a strong case for the opportunities provided in Corinth for the educated elite to have a Greek gymnasium education. Brookins, *Corinthian Wisdom*, 132–52, agrees with Dutch and seeks to extend his case, especially with relationship to a philosophical education. We might note the caution of Brookins, *Women*, that there might not have been any "elite" in Corinth, strictly speaking. Nevertheless, a more educated minority (1 Cor 1:26) may have had access to this education and could have influenced others. For the coexistence of both Greek and Roman influences in Corinth to support the case of Brookins and Dutch, see, e.g., Friesen et al., *Corinth*, chapters 2, 3, 4, and 5.

the exclusive nature of this temple and its corporate identity, even when discussing individual bodies. Finally, I shall explore some of these themes as they are taken up in the letter as a whole, including Paul's strong opposition to idolatry, that contrasts with the philosophical acceptance of multiple gods. I will conclude the chapter by comparing and contrasting the understanding of God, humanity and what it means to live out their philosophy, in both Paul and the philosophers.

4.1.1 Paul's Introduction to 1 Corinthians

Before I consider the figurative temple references in 1 Corinthians, it is important to set them in their proper context within the epistle. Most commentators recognize at least 1 Cor 1:1–9 as Paul's introduction to his letter,[4] set apart from Paul's address that begins in 1 Cor 1:10;[5] further, others who pay special attention to the epistolary forms used in Greco-Roman letters, have identified 1 Cor 1:1–3 separately as the epistolary prescript.[6] Paul's concern for purity appropriate to a temple is evident from the outset of the letter since it features in this prescript. His address to the church in 1 Cor 1:2 is unique for such a prescript in a Pauline epistle since, in addition to addressing them as κλητοῖς ἁγίοις ("to [the] called holy people/ones"),[7] it combines this with ἡγιασμένοις ἐν Χριστῷ

---

4. I am assuming that 1 Corinthians is a single letter. Although this has been disputed in works such as Schmithals, *Gnosticism*, and Jewett, "Redaction," 398–444, the case for unity has been convincingly argued by, among others, Hurd, *Origin*, 43–47; Mitchell, *Paul and the Rhetoric*, passim; Schrage, *1 Korinther: 1,11—6,11*, 63–71; Thiselton, *First Epistle*, 36–39; and Fee, *First Epistle*, 16.

5. E.g., Robertson and Plummer, *Critical and Exegetical*, xxv; Barrett, *First Epistle*, 28–29; Ciampa and Rosner, *First Letter*, vi–xii; Fitzmyer, *First Corinthians*, viii–ix; Fee, *First Epistle*, vii–xi.

6. Conzelmann, *1 Corinthians*, vi–viii; Lang, *Korinther*, 15; Mitchell, *Paul and the Rhetoric*, x–xi; Schrage, *1 Korinther: 1,11—6,11*, 97; Witherington, *Conflict*, vi–ix; Collins, *First Corinthians*, vii–x; Thiselton, *First Epistle*, v–xiii; Garland, *1 Corinthians*, vii–viii; Keener, *1–2 Corinthians*, 20; Schnabel, *Korinther*, 55; Zeller, *Korinther*, 48; cf. also Aune, *New Testament*, 163, 170; Belleville, "Continuity," 16–18 (noting, "The major concerns and themes of the letter often appear in the modifying phrases of the basic A to B, χάρις . . . formula of the Pauline letter opening" (16), observing that four of the major themes of the letter are introduced in 1 Cor 1:1–3 (16–17)).

7. Author's own translation. 1 Cor 1:2 is usually taken as a verbless clause, with εἰμί supplied in the infinitive, and translated as if κλητός was functioning like a participle form of καλέω: "those called to be saints" (something still to be attained). But the phrase makes sense as it stands in apposition to what precedes (ἡγιασμένοις ἐν Χριστῷ).

Ἰησοῦ ("to those who are sanctified in Christ Jesus").[8] Paul appropriates language used for the people of God in the LXX and applies it to a largely Gentile congregation,[9] while stressing the fact that they have been set apart for God. Other epistles begin by addressing the congregation as those called holy (Rom 1:7; cf. 2 Tim 1:9) or as holy ones (2 Cor 1:1; Phil 1:1; cf. Eph 1:1; Col 1:1) but only here do we find *two* cognate terms sharing the same root as ἅγιος (ἅγιος and ἁγιάζω), denoting that which is set apart or consecrated for cultic purposes and commonly used by the LXX to translate the Hebrew קדש.[10] This unusual opening for Paul is suggestive of a major concern that permeates the letter and relates closely to my topic. As Paul will demonstrate, the Corinthians need reminding that they are the temple of God and are supposed to be *set apart* from all that would defile them (the kinds of issues addressed in subsequent chapters).

Paul's succinct exhortation in 1:10 functions as a thesis statement or the *propositio* or *prothesis* in rhetorical terms[11] and names the immediate problem confronting the Corinthians as σχίσμα (cf. also 11:18; 12:25).[12] For this reason, Margaret M. Mitchell has made a strong and convincing case for unity as a dominant topic throughout the letter; in her view,

---

The Corinthians are the "called saints," the same people who form the Church in Corinth; those sanctified in Christ Jesus. This is recognized in the translation of Collins, *First Corinthians*, 41, and the explanation of 46; cf. also recently Wright, *Paul and the Faithfulness*, 1027; and also recognized in the explanations (even if not necessarily reflected in the translations) of Hays, *First Corinthians*, 15; Keener, *1–2 Corinthians*, 21; Fitzmyer, *First Corinthians*, 126.

8. Taking the perfect participle to emphasize present result.

9. κλητός is often combined with ἅγιος in the LXX to speak of a "holy convocation" in the phrase κλητὴ ἁγία found in, e.g., Exod 12:16; Lev 23:2–37; Num 28:25 (also noted by Conzelmann, *1 Corinthians*, 22 n. 32. God's people are described as holy in Exod 19:5–6 and subsequently in passages such as Deut 7:6; 26:19; Jer 2:3; Dan 7:18–27; *Pss. Sol.* 17:26, as noted by Fee, *First Epistle*, 29, and Ciampa and Rosner, *First Letter*, 56. Paul also uses the phrase κλητοῖς ἁγίοις in addressing the Romans (Rom 1:7).

10. "ἁγιάζω," BDAG, 9–10; "ἅγιος," BDAG, 10–11; Thiselton, *First Epistle*, 76; Zeller, *Korinther*, 73. Schnabel, *Korinther*, 61, links this passage with the identity of Israel as priests to God in Lev 19:6; similarly, Collins, *First Corinthians*, 52, notes its "cultic or political connotations." Fee, *First Epistle*, 28–29, comments, "Believers are set apart for God, just as were the utensils in the Temple."

11. See Mitchell, *Paul and the Rhetoric*, 68–70, 198–200; Witherington, *Conflict*, 98–99; Collins, *First Corinthians*, 69.

12. For further exploration of this topic, see, e.g., Mitchell, *Paul and the Rhetoric*, 71–74 and Schrage, *1 Korinther: 1,11—6,11*, 138–39.

the controlling theme of the epistle.[13] Yet, while her case is well made, the concern for unity in 1:10 is not always the main issue in the letter as a whole[14] (e.g., Paul's forceful case for the resurrection in 1 Cor 15[15]) and even when it clearly has a strong part to play in passages such as 1 Cor 8:1—11:1 (though even here, the central emphases of 1 Cor 9:1—10:22 seem very different) or 1 Cor 11:17—34, Paul sometimes appears to side with the weaker against the stronger party (e.g., 1 Cor 8:9—13; 10:14—22, 28—29).

In relation to this question, Roy E. Ciampa and Brian S. Rosner document something of an emerging consensus among recent commentators on 1 Corinthians: that Paul is addressing a number of problems that appear to stem from the continuing influence of Roman/Corinthian culture and values on the church.[16] I would concur with Ciampa and Rosner that purity, and thus the need to draw careful boundaries, are central to Paul's discourse, and that the rejection of sexual immorality and idolatry (the two intertwined vices singled out in both Jewish and Christian literature as most likely to lead God's people astray from worship and service) are prominent in this letter.[17] I will also aim to show that

---

13. Mitchell, *Paul and the Rhetoric*, passim.

14. Keener, *1–2 Corinthians*, 23, perhaps expresses a note of caution in referring to 1 Cor 1:10 as the thesis, "(at least for the immediate matter)."

15. Note the comment of Keener, *1–2 Corinthians*, 12, "the issues in 1 Cor 15, for example, do not easily reduce to this theme"; and see the concerns of Ciampa and Rosner, *First Letter*, 20–21, 73.

16. Ibid., 4–6, citing the work of Bruce W. Winter, Richard B. Hays, Wolfgang Schrage, Anthony Thiselton, R. B. Terry, and David E. Garland and see the evaluation of Wright, *Resurrection*, 279–80. Martin, *Corinthian Body*, 38–86, posits a division between "high" and "low" status Christians as a comprehensive explanation for the various issues faced (following Theissen, *Social Setting*, 69–119 and others). While 1 Cor 11:22 gives credence to the position that some inevitably had more wealth (such as the ability to take others to court in 1 Cor 6:1; for which see, e.g., Winter, *After Paul*, 58–75; Chow, *Patronage*, 38–112, 123–30; Clarke, *Secular*, 59–71) and status than others (see Theissen, *Social Setting*, 145–74; although 1 Cor 1:26 suggests that the majority did not), Martin's explanation is not the most likely one for *every* issue, although it was undeniably one of the factors in many of the situations Paul addressed (such as 1 Cor 6:1–8; 8:1–11:1; 11:17–34). Barclay, "Thessalonica," 65 n. c, suggests, "It is quite possible that the Corinthians . . . were . . . combining their Hellenistic theological culture with Jewish terms and traditions taught by Paul." Tucker, "Role of Civic Identity," 71–91, has developed Barclay's point about the Corinthians' lack of external opposition, by exploring the transitional nature of civic identity in Corinth that may have influenced the Corinthian Christians.

17. Ciampa and Rosner, *First Letter*, 21–25, with supporting literature. They cite

Figurative Temple Language in 1 Corinthians 159

the temple references in this letter stress both the corporate and bodily nature of God's people and that this agrees with another central concern for Paul.

4.2 1 CORINTHIANS 3:16

4.2.1 1 Corinthians 3:16–17: Literary Context

Our first temple reference, 1 Cor 3:16–17 takes its place within a section that most commentators regard as a distinct unit, 1 Cor 1:10–4:21.[18] Paul counters the obvious divisions in the church (1:11–12)[19] with the message of the cross (1:18), which is contrasted with the wisdom of the world (e.g., 1:20). Between the transitional verse 1 Cor 1:17 (concluding the *narratio* of 1:11–17 and also introducing the section that begins with 1:18),[20] and the end of the section (1 Cor 3:23), there are a high preponderance of words with the σοφ- root. Σοφία (wisdom) appears in 1 Cor 1:17, 19, 21, 22, 24, 30; 2:1, 4, 5, 6, 7, 13; 3:19 (as well as later in 12:8 in a very different context). In each of these verses a wisdom that is described as of this world (κόσμος in 1:20, 21; 3:19) or "human" (ἄνθρωπος in 2:5) is contrasted with the wisdom of God (1:20, 21, 24; 2:7), which is revealed as Christ himself (1:24) who has become wisdom from God for the Corinthians themselves (1:30). Even the wisdom of the wise (τὴν σοφίαν τῶν

---

these two vices as the sins common to NT passages such as Acts 15:20, 29; 21:25; Gal 5:19–21; Eph 5:5; Col 3:5; Rev 22:15.

18. E.g., Barrett, *First Epistle*, 28–29; Mitchell, *Paul and the Rhetoric*, x–xi; Witherington, *Conflict*, vi–ix; Collins, *First Corinthians*, vii–x; Thiselton, *First Epistle*, v–xiii; Garland, *1 Corinthians*, vii–viii; Fitzmyer, *First Corinthians*, viii–x; Fee, *First Epistle*, viii.

19. It falls outside the scope of this chapter to survey the complex debate and the various attempts to identify the different parties, but for a helpful analysis, see, e.g., Thiselton, *First Epistle*, 123–33; cf. also Merklein, *Korinther 1–4*, 134–48; Adams and Horrell, *Corinth*, 13–16, 51–59, 61–70, 79–84, 85–95; Schrage, *1 Korinther: 1,11—6,11*, 142–52. Contributors to this discussion have considered how far Corinthian divisions may have been affected by differences in social stratification, e.g., Theissen, *Social Setting*, 54–67, 69–119; Horrell, *Social Ethos*, 112–17, 131–37. Other studies have considered the influence of "secular" models of leadership on the perceptions of the Corinthians (Clarke, *Secular*, 89–107); the influence of patrons within the congregation (Chow, *Patronage*, passim); and the influence of the sophists, who propagated a competitive spirit and won adherents to them as individual teachers (see Winter, *Philo*, 180–202, and Winter, *After Paul*, 31–43).

20. Agreeing with Keener, *1–2 Corinthians*, 27.

σοφῶν) is judged worthy only of destruction (1:19, citing Isa 29:14). Paul goes so far as to imply that to preach the gospel in a word of wisdom (ἐν σοφίᾳ λόγου) would be to empty it of its power (1:17 cf. 2:5). By contrast, Paul's speech is quite deliberately presented as lacking the kind of wisdom sought by those who value eloquent speech or superiority (ὑπεροχή in 2:1; cf. 1:17; 2:1, 4, 5, 13). In particular, Paul targets the wise person (σοφός; e.g., 1:19, 20, 26, 27; 3:18, 19, 20; cf. 6:5 which uses the word in quite a different context).

A number of recent studies have connected the reference to the σοφός with the place of Greco-Roman rhetoric in the culture and identify Paul's critique with the kind of itinerant orators whose use of rhetorical convention and persuasive strategies contrast with Paul's presentation of the gospel.[21] Bruce W. Winter has further argued that the targets of Paul's argument are the self-serving Sophists of the "Second Sophistic," for which evidence can be found in the mid-first century.[22] Winter's use of evidence has been recently critiqued by Timothy A. Brookins, who contends that some references to σοφός in Winter's sources refer to philosophers not sophists *per se*,[23] and that all of Winter's arguments for a pre-second century date for the sophistic movement rely on late first and early second century sources (at least forty years after Paul's letter was written).[24] At the very least, Paul's comment that *Greeks* (Ἕλλην) seek wisdom (1:22), and his contrast between the wisdom of the world and of this age (αἰών in 2:6) and the wisdom that comes specifically from the Spirit (2:10, 13), granted by revelation alone (2:7, 10, 14), suggests an implicit wider critique of worldly (philosophical) wisdom, not restricted *merely* to the sophists and orators of the day.[25] This critique would naturally ap-

---

21. E.g., Pogoloff, *Logos*, passim; Litfin, *St. Paul's Theology*, especially 137–209; Lamp, *First Corinthians*, 114–15.

22. See Winter, *Philo*, 180–202, applied to 1 Cor 1:10—4:21; followed by Witherington, *Conflict*, 124–26; Thiselton, *First Epistle*, 163.

23. Brookins, *Corinthian Wisdom*, 41–42, 46–47.

24. Brookins, *Corinthian Wisdom*, 49–50.

25. Brookins, *Corinthian Wisdom*, 8–61, provides a critique of the theses of Pogoloff, Litfin, and Winter, arguing from primary sources that "wisdom language was associated in a technical way with philosophy in a way that it apparently was not with rhetoric" (43). van Kooten, *Anthropology*, 262–68, provides strong evidence that philosophical writers like Plato, Plutarch, Epictetus, Dio Chrysostom, and Philostratus disparaged sophism by comparison with philosophy, and compares this to Paul's rhetorical strategy in both 1 and 2 Corinthians. But, could it be that, in fact, Paul is lumping both sophism and philosophy together, as it were, so that his critique covers

ply to Greek philosophy (1:22) in its claim to have discovered wisdom by natural means.[26] Additionally, the *hapax legomenon* συζητητής in 1:20 is related to the verb συζητέω and in the Greek philosophical tradition it could be used in relation to a philosopher, or a seeker after the truth in philosophy.[27] Paul's dismissal of philosophy would have contrasted sharply with the overwhelmingly positive view of philosophy that I highlighted in chapter 2;[28] a view that seemed to hold little regard for *which* philosophy was being discussed.[29] As noted in the same chapter, philosophy was sometimes described specifically as wisdom, or as a search for wisdom.[30] Yet for Paul the only true wisdom is the wisdom of God (2:7), which has been revealed in Christ and his cross (1:23-24, 30; 2:2).

Paul apparently includes the Corinthians with himself as those who have received the Spirit of wisdom and revelation (2:10, 12),[31] he then addresses them as "brothers" (fellow Christians in 3:1a),[32] and ultimately

every wisdom of *this age*?

26. Cf. Keener, *1-2 Corinthians*, 28, "The specific quest for wisdom, however, is attributed especially to Greeks, known for their philosophy (1:22)" and a possible reference to Greek philosophy in general is also alluded to by Lang, *Korinther*, 29, 30; Hays, *First Corinthians*, 30; Fee, *First Epistle*, 74-75, 77-78; Pogoloff, *Logos*, 115-19; Thiselton, *First Epistle*, 170; Schnabel, *Korinther*, 121.

27. See H. Greeven, "ζητέω, ζήτησις, κτλ," TDNT 2:892-96 at 893; Garland, *1 Corinthians*, 69; Fitzmyer, *First Corinthians*, 156; Zeller, *Korinther*, 108.

28. See, e.g., Cicero, *Leg.* 1.22.58; *Tusc.* 1.26.64; 3.3.5-6; 3.6.13; 5.2.5; Seneca, *Ep.* 31.8; 53.8, 9; 90.1-3; *Brev. vit.* 14.1; 15.4; Plutarch, *An. corp.* 501A; *Virt. prof.* 81E; Maximus of Tyre, *Or.* 1.2-3; 22.6; 26.1; 37.2; Marcus Aurelius, *Med.* 2.17; Dio Chrysostom, *2 Glor.* 1.

29. Seneca, *Ep.* 16.5.

30. Seneca, *Ep.* 89.1-6; Alcinous, *Handbook*, 3, 152.1.2-5.

31. Taking the "ἡμῖν" of 2:10 and the "ἡμεῖς" of 2:12 to be inclusive, speaking of the Corinthians as well as Paul and his coworkers; with Robertson and Plummer, *Critical and Exegetical*, 43, 45; Schrage, *1 Korinther: 1,11—6,11*, 256; Witherington, *Conflict*, 126; Collins, *First Corinthians*, 132, 134; Thiselton, *First Epistle*, 255, 261-62; Lindemann, *Der Erste Korintherbrief*, 68; Schnabel, *Korinther*, 145; Fitzmyer, *First Corinthians*, 179; Ciampa and Rosner, *First Letter*, 121 n. 10; Fee, *First Epistle*, 117, 120; against Conzelmann, *1 Corinthians*, 65. As Thiselton, Fee, and others note, the most obvious referent of the personal pronoun in 2:10 is the "those who love him" of 2:9 and the recipients of the δόξα in 2:7. Within the immediate co-text of Paul's description of his ministry and message to the Corinthians (2:1-16 as a whole), it would seem unlikely that they are excluded from this, or that this is merely the self-description of an elite few. Those who receive the things ὑπὸ τοῦ θεοῦ χαρισθέντα (from χαρίζομαι; 2:12) are most likely those μὴ ὑστερεῖσθαι ἐν μηδενὶ χαρίσματι (from χάρισμα; 1:7), which clearly describes all the Corinthians.

32. Fitzmyer, *First Corinthians*, 186.

identifies them as the temple of the same Holy Spirit (3:16-17). It is therefore striking that he also refers to them as those who are "fleshly" (σάρκινος in 3:1 and σαρκικός in 3:3), and behaving in a merely human rather than spiritual way (κατὰ ἄνθρωπον περιπατεῖτε in 3:3). In many ways, Paul's depiction of his audience in 3:1, 3 sounds suspiciously like those described as unspiritual (pertaining to ψυχικός) in 2:14. Yet they are clearly those who are sanctified (1:2) and not lacking any χάρισμα (1:2). Paul's frustration with them was already made clear in 1:10-17 (reiterated at 3:3-4); he should be able to address them as the spiritual person of 2:15; those who are mature (2:6 from τέλειος) but instead he must address them as infants (from νήπιος in 3:1). Paul has repeatedly stressed that the πνεῦμα is at work in believers, given by God himself, who grants them revelation and understanding that is not available from σοφία (2:4, 10, 11, 12, 13, 14; see especially 2:13 where Paul pointedly contrasts the ἀνθρώπινος nature of wisdom with the divine source of the Spirit noted in 2:12, 14).

This sharp contrast between human wisdom and the divine Spirit at work in them prepares the way for Paul's point in 1 Cor 3:16-17: they are failing to live in accordance with their true identity, as one unified temple of the Holy Spirit. In preparation, Paul emphasizes that all share a common work (3:5-9) since the one who assigns them their task is one κύριος (3:5) and θεός (3:6-7).[33] In one pithy phrase, Paul uses three images to summarize his argument and to mark the transition to the next. Paul depicts the apostles as fellow workers (συνεργοί as in 3:5-8) and the Corinthians as the field in which they worked (γεώργιον as in 3:6-8),[34] who he further describes with the metaphor explicated in the new few verses, the building (οἰκοδομή). The building image is elaborated upon in 3:10-15.

---

33. It seems likely that at this juncture κύριος refers to Jesus Christ rather than sharing the same referent as θεός in 3:7; cf. Collins, *First Corinthians*, 145. So far in the epistle, κύριος has either been used unambiguously of Jesus (1:2, 3, 7, 8, 9, 10; 2:8) or seems the likely referent on contextual grounds (in 1:31 referring back to the subject of 1:30); see Robertson and Plummer, *Critical and Exegetical*, 28; Kremer, *Korinther*, 47; Collins, *First Corinthians*, 113; Fitzmyer, *First Corinthians*, 165; Fee, *First Epistle*, 91; and in 2:16a, in parallel to Χριστός in 2:16b; see Jewett, *Paul's Anthropological Terms*, 377; Schrage, *1 Korinther: 1,11—6,11*, 267; Collins, *First Corinthians*, 137; Thiselton, *First Epistle*, 275-76; Ciampa and Rosner, *First Letter*, 137-38; Fee, *First Epistle*, 127; against Fitzmyer, *First Corinthians*, 194.

34. There was sometimes an association between the Temple and the garden in Jewish literature; see Hogeterp, *Paul and God's Temple*, 318; Wassen, "Do You Have to Be Pure," 73, and particularly Beale, *Temple*, 26, 48, 66-78, 123-29, and especially 246-50 on 1 Cor 3.

For the purposes of this discussion I note that Paul describes himself as a master-builder (ἀρχιτέκτων),[35] modified by the adjective σοφός (in context meaning "skilled," yet the implicit comparison with those who have merely human wisdom in 1:19-20 cannot be ignored); that the foundation of the building is Jesus Christ (3:11); and that in view of the testing (δοκιμάζω) of the coming judgment, it is critical to build with the right materials, and that those listed of great value (3:12a) correspond to the ones used in the building of Solomon's temple (cf. 1 Chr 29:2; 22:14-16; 2 Chr 3:6).[36] Additionally, we can note that, though the fire of eschatological judgment (3:13, 15) has clear and numerous parallels in Judaism, it could also have spoken to an audience influenced by Stoicism of the great fiery conflagration to come.[37] This building imagery sets the scene for Paul's figurative temple language in 3:16-17 and underscores the vital importance of living rightly as the temple of God that Paul will develop subsequently. Paul's use of the rhetorical device Οὐκ οἴδατε ὅτι (also in 5:6; 6:2, 3, 9, 15, 16, 19; 9:13, 24) to introduce 3:16-17 expresses strong feelings of dismay at their lack of knowledge of something fundamental.[38]

4.2.2 1 Corinthians 3:16-17: Main Features

For the purposes of my topic I note the following features of 3:16-17 that might have struck an audience influenced by philosophy. Firstly, I observe that Paul's image is corporate.[39] He is at pains to emphasize that the *congregation* is the temple of God/the Spirit, rather than the individual (see my comments below on 6:19). The verb οἶδα appears in the second-person plural, as does the verb εἰμί and the final ὑμῖν. Secondly, Paul uses the word ναός rather than ἱερόν, almost certainly because ναός typically (though not exclusively) indicates the inner sanctuary, whereas ἱερόν

---

35. For more detail, see Shanor, "Paul as Master-Builder," 461-71.

36. deLacey, "οἵτινές ἐστε ὑμεῖς," 391-409 at 404; Collins, *First Corinthians*, 150-51; Ciampa and Rosner, *First Letter*, 150-53 in some detail; Fee, *First Epistle*, 152 n. 396.

37. E.g., Strack, *Kultische Terminologie*, 229; deLacey, "οἵτινές ἐστε ὑμεῖς," 391-409 at 405; Hogeterp, *Paul and God's Temple*, 321 n. 76. For more on Greco-Roman understandings of judgment, see Kuck, *Judgement*, 96-149, who concludes that within Hellenistic philosophy, those influenced by Plato maintained the classical notion of postmortem judgment, but other philosophical schools rejected it (115-20).

38. See especially Fee, *First Epistle*, 158; Lanci, *New Temple*, 119-20.

39. Agreeing with, e.g., Thiselton, *First Epistle*, 316.

is always used for the whole temple, including its precincts and other buildings.[40] The word order suggests that ναός is in an emphatic position; that is, Paul is drawing attention to it.[41] It is also unlikely, according to Daniel B. Wallace's study of "Colwell's Construction," that ναός is to be understood as indefinite (i.e. *a* temple of God).[42] Thirdly, it is the πνεῦμα that constitutes the Corinthians as the ναός τοῦ θεοῦ,[43] and in the preceding discussion the πνεῦμα is only given to certain people, not all. These people are those who have received the πνεῦμα who gives revelation (2:10–14), and a spiritual person (πνευματικός) cannot be evaluated by other people (2:15) for the spiritual person has received the mind of the Lord, that is the mind of Christ. The Spirit, therefore, is tied very specifically to Jesus Christ. This also connotes the strongest possible association between Christ with God and the Spirit.[44] The Spirit that produces the mind of Christ, who is identified as *Lord* (2:15), is the same Spirit whose presence signifies that the temple belongs to God.[45] Fourthly, as well as speaking of God's presence, the temple image speaks of his holiness, and those who are responsible for the temple's destruction will themselves be destroyed (3:17a).[46] This indicates that the temple is sacred and has very

---

40. "ἱερόν," BDAG, 470; "ναός," BDAG, 365–66; O. Michel, "ναός," TDNT 4:880–90; cf. Witherington, *Conflict*, 134; Fee, *First Epistle*, 158–59.

41. See Levinsohn, *Discourse*, 38, citing this example.

42. Wallace, *Greek Grammar*, 256–70, especially at 269–70, draws on Harner, "Qualitative," 75–87, maintaining that anarthrous pre-verbal predicate nouns are rarely indefinite and that this conclusion is even more likely when the construction is a-copulative (lacking a verb altogether), as in the case of 1 Cor 3:16 (however, when Wallace, *Greek Grammar*, 261 cites "Harner's study" of "all pre-verbal predicate nominatives," in context this only means all pre-verbal predicate nominatives in Mark and John, not the NT as a whole. Harner also spends little time on the potential indefiniteness of these nouns).

43. Weiss, *Korintherbrief*, 85, speaks of the καί in 3:16 as explicative, that is, they are the temple of God because the Spirit of God dwells in them.

44. As was noted above in the discussion of references to κύριος in 1 Corinthians.

45. See this theme developed in Fee, *God's Empowering Presence*, 112–18.

46. The verb used here, φθείρω, has a semantic range including "destroy, ruin, corrupt, spoil" ("φθείρω," BDAG, 1054; "φθείρω," LSJ, 1928) but contextually it is more likely that the formula with the repeated verb means, "If anyone destroys the temple, God will destroy them" than, "If anyone corrupts the temple, God will corrupt them." Arguments have been made for the meaning "damage" rather than "destroy" here (see Shanor, "Paul as Master-Builder," 461–71, at 470–71; and Lanci, *New Temple*, 66–68; followed by Collins, *Power of Images*, 161; Liu, *Temple Purity*, 122–23). Liu avers that the verb is used with the sense "to corrupt" in other NT passages, but two of the texts he cites, 2 Pet 2:12 and Jude 10, are usually translated "to destroy," and later Liu, *Temple*

Figurative Temple Language in 1 Corinthians

strict boundaries and that to defile the temple in any way brings very serious consequences. John R. Levison rightly notes how striking it is that the man who has sexual intercourse with his father's wife will only be ostracized temporarily (5:1–8) but, here in 1 Cor 3:17, "dividers of the Church are subject to destruction or severe damage, torn apart as they have torn apart the Church . . . It is inconceivable that the spirit of God should dwell in a portion of the holy of holies without filling the whole of it."[47] The reference to this temple is sandwiched between two discussions that give it its wider context. The foundation of this building (temple) is Christ (3:11). The quality of the work done on the building will be evaluated and revealed for its true worth in a coming judgment (3:12–15). Their labor as the temple has eternal significance. True wisdom does not boast in human terms/matters (3:21a). Rather the Corinthians should recognize that all things belong to them corporately (3:21b–22, so the temple is not to be divided up among them nor claimed by any one person),[48] yet they belong to Christ, who is of God (3:23). Thus, the discussion ends with God himself, again in the closest possible association with Christ, to whom the Corinthians belong. Their identity is centered in God, Christ and the Spirit.

Purity, 134–35, supports a different argument by citing with approval the translation "destroy" for φθείρω when used by Brian Rosner and David Raymond Smith. Cf. the similar formulas of LXX Gen 9:6 and especially Josh 9:5 and the well-rounded arguments for the contextual meaning of "destroy" made by Yinger, *Paul*, 224–25, supported by G. Harder, "φθείρω," TDNT 9:93–106 at 102; and followed by Conzelmann, *1 Corinthians*, 71, 78; Witherington, *Conflict*, 134–35; Thiselton, *First Epistle*, 317–18; Garland, *1 Corinthians*, 120–21; Fee, *First Epistle*, 160–61. Earlier, Robertson and Plummer, *Critical and Exegetical*, 67, argued for the same translation, adding, "All sin is a defiling of the Temple and is destructive of its consecrated state." There is a minor textual variant here, with the second instance of φθείρω read as the present tense φθείρει rather than the future tense φθερεῖ. The external support for the NA[28] reading is strong (p[46] A B C) and the main variant can best be explained as a replication of the present tense of φθείρει immediately before it; cf. Metzger, *Textual Commentary*, 484; Fee, *First Epistle*, 157 n. 417.

47. Levison, "Spirit," 192.

48. The names in εἴτε Παῦλος εἴτε Ἀπολλῶς εἴτε Κηφᾶς (3:22) intentionally pick up on three of the four used in 1 Cor 1:12 and appear in the same order. It is noteworthy that Χριστός is removed from the first list and instead appears at the climax of the discussion in conjunction with the name of θεός to whom he belongs, yet in a different category than any human figure.

4.2.3 Comparing 1 Corinthians 3:16–17 with Hellenistic Philosophy

Philosophy

How would this have compared to the understanding of an audience influenced by philosophy? In the writings of Philo I noted one reference to a *group* of people who were counted as a temple and altar prior to the building of the Jerusalem temple.[49] However this is an isolated incident and peculiar to this particular strand of Hellenistic *Judaism*. Within different strands of philosophy we see two common emphases instead: divine indwelling in an individual or divine indwelling in the cosmos as a whole, so that everything is filled with the divine presence.

Firstly, to summarize the most pertinent of the evidence I have already presented, some writers speak simply of God or a divine spirit dwelling in a person,[50] and specifically of a good[51] or wise person.[52] This presence is sometimes named as a δαιμόνιον,[53] and at other times as Reason, or a divine spirit or element.[54] Many writers make no real distinction between this δαιμόνιον, θεός or λόγος (or its cognates), or intelligence.[55] Some speak of this Reason, δαιμόνιον or genius as residing in each person, regardless of the person's goodness or wisdom.[56] Other writers see such a close fusion between the person and the divinity that dwells within, that there is little to distinguish the two; a person's motions are that of God; their faculty is equal to that of God.[57] Still other writers speak of either

---

49. Philo, *QE* 1.10.

50. Seneca, *Ep.* 41.1; 83.1; 110.2; *Ben.* 6.23.6; Marcus Aurelius, *Med.* 3.5.1; Philo, *Somn.* 1.149, 215; 2.248, 250–51; *Virt.* 188; *Det.* 90. Philo speaks of the temple of the soul: *Somn.* 1.149; *Spec.* 1.270; Epictetus, *Diatr.* 2.8.14; 2.16.33.

51. Seneca, *Ep.* 31.2; 41.1–2; 73.16; 120.14; Cicero, *Leg.* 2.11.26–28; Philo, *Cher.* 98, 100; *Sobr.* 62, 68; *Praem.* 123; *QG* 4.80; *QE* 2.51.

52. Seneca, *Ep.* 92.3; Diog. Laert. 7.1.119; Philo, *Leg.* 3.46.

53. Cicero, *Div.* 1.54.122; Dio, *4 Regn.* 139; Marcus Aurelius, *Med.* 2.17; 5.10; Epictetus, *Diatr.* 1.14.14.

54. Seneca, *Ep.* 66.12; Cicero, *Leg.* 1.22.59; *Tusc.* 1.24.56; 1.25.62; 1.26.65; 1.27.66–67; 1.30.74; *Parad.* 1.14; Marcus Aurelius, *Med.* 3.12, 16; 4.1, 12; 6.35.

55. Cf. Marcus Aurelius, *Med.* 2.13, 17; 3.3.2; 3.6.2; 3.12, 16; 3.5.1; 3.6.2; 4.1; 5.10; 5.27; 10.38; 12.1.2, 26; Philo, *Cher.* 27; Maximus, *Or.* 31.4.

56. Epictetus, *Diatr.* 1.14.12; 2.8.11, 15–17; Marcus Aurelius, *Med.* 2.1 (speaking of an evil doer); 4.38; 7.16; 8.43, 61; 9.7; 11.20; 12.1.

57. See Epictetus, *Diatr.* 1.14.6, 12; *Frag.* 3 (explored further below in relation to the philosophers' conception of divinity).

a loyal heart being a temple,[58] or of a god-fearing one.[59] Paul describes the Corinthians as a temple of the πνεῦμα. Either πνεῦμα[60] or its equivalent in Latin (Spiritus)[61] are described as dwelling within a person in the philosophers.

As I noted earlier, Philo envisages the soul as a building with three layers: the foundations of goodness and teaching; a ground floor of virtues built upon it, and the reception of right teaching as its crowning glory.[62] Similarly, Plutarch compares a person's life to a holy temple whose life has a "golden foundation," and who builds upon it with the right materials. This is the person who makes progress in the path of virtue.[63] This concept has some parallels with Paul's metaphor of the building of the church, whose foundation is Jesus Christ and upon which the right materials must be carefully chosen by the builder, since the Day of judgment will prove the materials by fire (1 Cor 3:10–15).

The second common theme in the philosophers is that God fills all things,[64] or less personally, that the universe is filled with eternal intelligence or the divine mind.[65] The πνεῦμα is said to hold the cosmos together[66] and the world itself is described as the temple of the gods.[67]

Paul

When I compare my findings from the philosophical writers with Paul's words in 1 Cor 3:16–17, a number of points stand out. Firstly, some philosophers speak of the divine presence inhabiting the life of the individual. This is the natural consequence of the doctrine that God's presence fills all things. Paul, by contrast, speaks corporately of the Corinthians, not simply of them as individuals. This is indicated by the second-person

58. V. Max., 4.7. ext. 1.

59. Apuleius, *Metam.* 3.15, though here not in the context of a philosophical writing.

60. *SVF*, 2.473.

61. Seneca, *Ep.* 41.2; 66.12; Cicero, *Resp.* 6.24.26.

62. Philo, *Cher.* 101.

63. Plutarch, *Virt. prof.* 86A (Babbitt, LCL).

64. Marcus Aurelius, *Med.* 7.9; Alcinous, *Handbook*, 165.10.3.1–2 (18); Cicero, *Leg.* 2.11.26; Philo, *Leg.* 3.4; *Fug.* 75; *Post.* 6, 14, 30; *Conf.* 137–38.

65. Cicero, *Div.* 1.49.110; 1.52.118.

66. E.g., citing Zeno in *SVF*, 2.473.

67. Cicero, *Leg.* 2.10.26; *Resp.* 6.15.15; Seneca, *Ben.* 7.7.3; *Ep.* 90.29.

plurals that I observed but also by the context, that pictures the Corinthians as together making up a building (3:10-15). It is noteworthy that, although the philosophers certainly had very distinct schools or groups (such as the Stoics and Epicureans), they do not see membership of those specific groups as the basis for divine indwelling, since none of them refer to the theme in relation to their own group.[68]

Secondly, some writers speak of a divine presence inhabiting all individuals, whereas others stress this presence in the good or the wise. For Paul, the temple of God is those who are sanctified and called holy people (1:2a). We have already had cause to note the critiques of the wisdom of the world Paul makes in 1 Cor 1:18-2:16, and in 3:18-19 (the verses that immediately follow our text) but the Corinthians have the spirit of God dwelling within them, not because many of them were wise (1:26) or good and certainly not because of their impressive growth as spiritual people (3:1-3), but because they have been set apart as God's people (1:2), as those who call upon the name of their Lord Jesus Christ (1:2b) and for whom Jesus Christ is the foundation of the οἰκοδομή (3:9), that is, his temple (3:16). Unlike the philosophers, for whom the πνεῦμα sustains and fills the cosmos, for Paul τὸ πνεῦμα τοῦ κόσμου (2:12a) is to be avoided. Rather, the Spirit of God (2:12b) dwells only in spiritual people who have been taught by the Spirit (2:12-15). They are those in whom the Spirit of God dwells, as the presence of God dwells in a temple (3:16).[69] Finally, it is the temple as God's people (ὑμεῖς in 3:17b) that is holy and distinct. It is not every individual in the world, or particularly good individuals or indeed the world itself without distinction. Rather, these people are a sacred dwelling who belong to Christ as he belongs to God (3:17b, 23) and if anyone is to cause destruction to come upon this temple, God will destroy them (3:17a). This warning is posed to those who threaten the sanctity of the community; quite a different understanding from the Stoic view of the world's conflagration or the Middle Platonic notion of the destruction of the individual's body.[70]

68. I owe this observation to Dr. Craig S. Keener.

69. Wright, *Paul and the Faithfulness*, 1369-1370, and Son, *Corporate Elements*, 139, both note the distinction between the Stoic pantheistic divine indwelling and the select blessing of the Spirit envisaged by Paul. See the excellent essay, Ware, "Moral Progress," 267-83, for a succinct exploration of what this means for Seneca and how it can be distinguished from Paul's theology, despite some surface structural similarities.

70. The reader from a non-Jewish background might also have been struck by the emphasis on *the* temple, rather than the multiplicity of temples found in cities in the Greco-Roman world (with, e.g., McKelvey, *New Temple*, 102), but this is not so

4.3 1 CORINTHIANS 6:19

4.3.1 1 Corinthians 6:19: Literary Context

I now turn to the second figurative temple reference in 1 Corinthians, 1 Cor 6:19. Firstly, we need to examine the wider literary co-text of this verse. The overwhelming majority of commentators recognize 1 Cor 5:1 as the start of a new section. Following Paul's response to the divisions and immaturity of the church in 1 Cor 1:10–4:21, Paul turns to a number of specific issues that have come to his attention through a variety of means. In 5:1-13 he refers to a report of πορνεία among them that has reached his ears (5:1), during which he seems to address a possible misunderstanding of a previous letter (5:9-13). In 6:1 he turns his attention to another topic altogether, involving lawsuits. Paul cites what might be a Corinthian slogan in 6:12 and then deals with another topic that has been brought to his attention,[71] before responding to a matter that seems to have been raised by the Corinthians themselves, signaled by the use of Περὶ δὲ (7:1).[72] Most commentators would class 1 Cor 5:1—6:20 as a unit,[73] with some including 1 Cor 7:1-40 within that same section.[74] Scholars propose quite different reasons for dividing up the material as they do. Anthony C. Thiselton treats 5:1—6:20 as a distinct unit because the topics dealt with "expound what for Paul constitute clear-cut moral and ethical issues" whereas 7:1-11:1 addresses more "grey areas."[75] Gordon Fee takes 5:1—6:20 as sharing a common theme: a "crisis of authority" in which Paul's apostolic authority is challenged in a number

---

relevant to my own study since I am necessarily limited to *figurative* temple references in Hellenistic philosophy.

71. E.g., Collins, *First Corinthians*, 205; Ciampa and Rosner, *First Letter*, 192–94.

72. A view held by Conzelmann, *1 Corinthians*, 115; Ciampa and Rosner, *First Letter*, 272; and Fee, *First Epistle*, 295, as just a few modern examples of a long history of interpretation. The formula is used again in 1 Cor 7:25; 8:1; 12:1; and 16:12, with περί used by itself but in a similar way in 8:4. Mitchell, "Concerning Περὶ δὲ," 229–256, and Mitchell, *Paul and the Rhetoric*, 190–91, has argued convincingly that the formula is a topic marker that Paul uses to introduce his own chosen topics rather than indicating the issues about which the Corinthians wrote, but either way they help to signal a new topic in the letter.

73. E.g., Conzelmann, *1 Corinthians*, vii–viii; Witherington, *Conflict*, vi–ix; Thiselton, *First Epistle*, v–xiii; Garland, *1 Corinthians*, vii–viii; Fee, *First Epistle*, viii.

74. E.g., Mitchell, *Paul and the Rhetoric*, x–xi; Collins, *First Corinthians*, vii–ix; Ciampa and Rosner, *First Letter*, vi–xiii.

75. Thiselton, *First Epistle*, 381.

of different areas.⁷⁶ I would agree with Raymond Collins and Ciampa & Rosner in seeing connections within 5:1—7:40 that speak of the purity of God's holy people.⁷⁷ They note that sexual immorality is a pervasive theme, as is exemplified by the recurrence of words with the πορν- root in this section (5:1 [twice], 9, 10, 11; 6:9, 13, 15, 16, 18 [twice]; 7:2). It should also be noted that at the start of Paul's reply to the issue raised in 1 Cor 7:1, the problem of πορνεία is given as the grounds for Paul's advice in what follows (7:2).⁷⁸ Purity issues and the proper boundaries in relation to purity, the Christian community and those outside of it, are a notable motif (e.g., 5:1, 2, 5, 6–8, 9–13; 6:1–8, 9–11, 12–20; 7:12–16, 34 etc.). This concern is even present in 6:1–11, a passage that is frequently seen as the "odd one out" because its subject matter is the law courts rather than the body and sexual relationships.⁷⁹ There are also frequent references to the σῶμα in this section (e.g., 6:13 [twice], 15, 16, 18 [twice], 19, 20; 7:4 [twice], 34 [twice]), and in general Paul is concerned with the use and abuse of the body in 5:1–13; 6:9–20. The considerable attention that Paul pays to the whole question of marriage and celibacy in 1 Cor 7 speaks of his concern for life in the body, as well as the proper place for sexual relationships and attachments, by contrast with the improper ones described in 5:1–13 and 6:12–20.

From the outset of this section, Paul's stated concern is with an instance of πορνεία (5:1), and the puffed-up attitude of the Corinthians (5:2).⁸⁰ In chapter 1, I noted good indicators that the Corinthians are a majority gentile congregation, so it is striking that Paul should say such

---

76. Fee, *First Epistle*, 212.

77. Ciampa and Rosner, *First Letter*, 21–25; Collins, *First Corinthians*, 203–4.

78. For negative evaluations of πορνεία in both the Jewish and Greco-Roman world, see, e.g., Liu, *Temple Purity*, 146–53.

79. Commentators have struggled to make sense of the place of 6:1–11 (or more properly 6:1–8) within the sequence found in 5:1—6:20. Ciampa and Rosner, *First Letter*, 192–93, are the latest in a line of interpreters to see loose connections between references to judging and legal matters in 5:1–13 and 6:1–11; e.g., Barrett, *First Epistle*, 134–35; Fee, *First Epistle*, 213, 250; Kempthorne, "Incest," 568–69. Deming, "Unity," 289–312, postulates that 1 Cor 5–6 is Paul's response to the failed attempt by some of the Corinthians to take the incestuous man of 1 Cor 5:1–13 to court (hence 1 Cor 6:1–8), that resulted in disunity in the Church. Richardson, "Judgment," 37–58, had previously argued that 6:1–11 addressed a sexual matter which related to 7:1–7 rather than 5:1–13. Richardson's article is very wide-ranging in its attempt to deal with the whole of the letter and multiple possible contexts and is necessarily very speculative.

80. Whether this is over the sin of the "such a one" in 5:1 or over his social status; see Chow, *Patronage*, 130–41 and Clarke, *Secular*, 73–88.

Figurative Temple Language in 1 Corinthians 171

immorality is not even (οὐδέ) among the Gentiles/the nations (ἔθνος), considering that his audience *are* Gentiles. This is a clear indicator that they are to be distinct and set apart from others. Paul elaborates on the implications of the πορνεία by insisting that the offender should be removed (αἴρω, 5:2) from among them. Within the confines of this discussion, I cannot consider the question of what precisely Paul means by, "to hand this man over to Satan for the destruction of the flesh" (5:5),[81] but whatever the exact referent, the Corinthians are to be purified by his removal. The parabolic saying of 5:6-7 confirms this interpretation. According to Thiselton, Paul's illustration of the leaven shows, "the disastrous consequences of letting the church become distorted and misshaped by a tainting element which permeates the whole."[82] At the end of the chapter, Paul adds further confirmation with a command from Deut 17:7 (LXX) to drive out the evil doer from their midst. As Richard B. Hays notes, a command, originally given to Israel, is applied quite unselfconsciously by Paul to this majority Gentile congregation.[83] They are now the saints of God who must not be contaminated by evil. This has implications for how they are to live, meaning that they must exclude the influence of a πόρνος from their midst (5:9-11),[84] and illustrated by a sacrificial metaphor in 5:7-8 that makes clear reference to Passover (πάσχα). This is not a case of the Corinthians making a spiritual sacrifice, since it is Christ who has *already* been sacrificed (θύω) as the Passover lamb (though no reference is made here to a lamb, Χριστός must be understand as the object of sacrifice in apposition to πάσχα and thus, the Passover lamb).[85] Nevertheless, the Corinthians are to *celebrate* this Passover festival and to do so with ἄζυμος (the opposite of which, ζύμη, leaven, from 5:7-8, often stands for that which negatively permeates and influences those around

81. For a thorough survey, see Thiselton, *First Epistle*, 393–400.

82. Thiselton, *First Epistle*, 401; cf. Fee, *First Corinthians*, 236–37; Schrage, *1 Korinther: 1,11—6,11*, 379–85; following Mitton, "New Wine," 339–43, and Howard, "Christ Our Passover," 97–108.

83. Hays, *Echoes*, 96–97, cited by Thiselton, *First Epistle*, 417–18; and see now, in more depth, Hays, *Conversion*, 1–24.

84. Additionally, Rosner, "Temple Prostitution," 336–51, thinks that 1 Cor 3:16–17 provides the "theological framework" for understanding the expulsion of the immoral man in 1 Cor 5:1–13 and traces the progression from purifying the temple in 5:1–6 to celebrating the Passover in 5:7–8. Liu, *Temple Purity*, 127–45, seeks to provide further support for this argument.

85. Thiselton, *First Epistle*, 405; Fitzmyer, *First Corinthians*, 242; Collins, *First Corinthians*, 214; in more detail: Wenthe, "Exegetical Study," 134–40.

them, e.g., Matt 16:6; Luke 12:1; Gal 5:9), which is explicated as ἐν (in/with) εἰλικρίνεια (sincerity or purity of motive) and ἀλήθεια, or in other words, their celebration consists of a pure and truthful life. I have already noted that in Philo, Passover can represent a multitude of different "passings": a passing over from passions to virtue,[86] that might include a crossing away *from* the body,[87] and for the soul from senses to thoughts;[88] a passing over to thankfulness to God[89] or the offering of the soul's own progress as a passover sacrifice.[90] In Philo, the Passover lamb itself can symbolize the progress of the soul toward a harmony of counsel and justice.[91] I shall note shortly that Paul's "passover" does not emphasize the soul at the expense of the body, in contrast to Philo, and other writers influenced by Platonism.

4.3.2 1 Corinthians 6:19: The Context of 1 Corinthians 6:12–20

The very beginning of 1 Cor 6 sets up the contrast that is at the heart of this chapter: between the ἄδικος and the ἅγιος. Although the subject matter of 6:1–8 differs greatly from that of 6:12–20, this distinction between those who belong to Christ and God (3:23) is fundamental to both issues. Between the discussion of the two topics stands 6:9–11 which opens with the familiar phrase οὐκ οἴδατε, drawing attention to their neglect of a fundamental principle (interestingly, six of the ten uses of this phrase occur in this chapter: 6:2, 3, 9, 15, 16, 19). What they should have known is that ἄδικοι θεοῦ βασιλείαν οὐ κληρονομήσουσιν (6:12). At the head of the list of those unrighteous ones are the two types that I highlighted in my introduction, the πόρνοι and the εἰδωλολάτραι (6:9), who are often associated in Jewish thought. 1 Cor 8:1—11:1 deals with the latter, but 1 Cor 6:12–20 focuses on the former.[92] Paul reaffirms their identity as distinct from the unrighteous, reminding them in distinctly cultic language

---

86. Philo, *Sacr.* 63.

87. *Spec.* 2.147.

88. *QE* 1.4 cf. *QE* 1.7–8, where the Passover lamb is spoken of using similar language.

89. *Migr.* 25.

90. *Congr.* 106.

91. *QE* 1.3; cf. also *QE* 1.13; *Post.* 72.

92. Oropeza, "Situational Immorality," 9–10, argues that these vices were actually being practiced in Corinth.

that they have been washed (ἀπολούω),⁹³ set apart (ἁγιάζω) and justified, again carefully connecting God and Jesus. This time it is in the name of the Lord Jesus and "in" or "by" (taking ἐν as a preposition of agency or instrument)⁹⁴ the Spirit of "our" God (6:11). I note the kind of incipient trinitarianism found here⁹⁵ with Jesus, God and the Spirit intertwined and the emphasis on the empowering of the Holy Spirit,⁹⁶ a theme that could be derived from the earlier passage I examined (3:16), and that appears in the passage I will shortly explore (6:19).

One of the immediate challenges an interpreter faces in 6:12-20 is knowing which words reflect the views of Paul and which reflect the views of the Corinthians (or possibly Paul's characterization of their views). This issue must be addressed if we are to rightly contrast the philosophical views that could have influenced the Corinthians with Paul's own position. There is considerable unanimity among scholars that the opening statement Πάντα μοι ἔξεστιν (6:12, "All things are permitted for me")⁹⁷ reflects the position of the Corinthians (cited again in 10:23, which strengthens this case).⁹⁸ However, there is disagreement about the verse that follows. The vast majority of commentators would agree that in 6:12 Paul twice quotes the Corinthian maxim I have just noted, followed

93. See the evidence presented in Gupta, *Worship*, 71-72.

94. E.g., Thiselton, *First Epistle*, 455; Fee, *First Epistle*, 270; Fitzmyer, *First Corinthians*, 258.

95. Witherington, *Conflict*, 167; Fee, *First Epistle*, 271, developed especially in relation to Rom 8:9-11 in Fee, "Christology," 312-31; Ciampa and Rosner, *First Letter*, 244; Fitzmyer, *First Corinthians*, 258.

96. Fee, *First Epistle*, 272-73.

97. Author's own translation. The sense is nicely captured by translations like, "Liberty to do anything" (Thiselton, *First Epistle*, 461) or "I have the right to do anything" (Ciampa and Rosner, *First Letter*, 245).

98. E.g., see Thiselton, *First Epistle*, 461 n. 192, who cites J. C. Hurd's list of twenty-three writers up to 1965, including himself, who held the phrase to be a Corinthian slogan. Thiselton himself agrees with this position and also cites Schrage, *1 Korinther: 6,12—11,16*, 17; Fee, *First Epistle 1987*, 251, and Collins, *First Corinthians*, 243 in agreement. To Thiselton's list, we can also add Conzelmann, *1 Corinthians*, 108; Witherington, *Conflict*, 167; Hays, *First Corinthians*, 102; Keener, *1-2 Corinthians*, 57; Schnabel, *Korinther*, 333; Fitzmyer, *First Corinthians*, 263; Ciampa and Rosner, *First Letter*, 252. Fee, *First Epistle*, 280-81, proposes "a perfect parallelism (with chiasm in the first member of each)" (280). In both Cynic and Stoic circles the wise were free to act as they wish, though often this was circumscribed by the assumption that the wise or the good person understands what is either forbidden by law or is regarded as improper; see for instance Epictetus, *Diatr*. 4.1.1, 4, 14, 18; Dio, *1 Serv. lib.* 17-18; cited by Garland, *1 Corinthians*, 227-28 and the wider discussion at 225-29.

each time by his response, and that 6:13a is another Corinthian slogan. However, most translations' omission of quotation marks around ὁ δὲ θεὸς καὶ ταύτην καὶ ταῦτα καταργήσει ("and God will destroy both one and the other"; 6:13b) suggest that they consider these words to belong to Paul,[99] though most modern scholars attribute the phrase to the Corinthians.[100] The subject becomes even more disputed in regard to later verses in this same passage.

I want to give close attention to 1 Cor 6:18b (πᾶν ἁμάρτημα ὃ ἐὰν ποιήσῃ ἄνθρωπος ἐκτὸς τοῦ σώματός ἐστιν, that is, "Every sin that a person commits is outside the body") because of its relevance to 6:19 and the comparison between temple language used by Paul and its use by philosophers. Might 6:18b reflect the Corinthian position and on what basis can we evaluate these claims? C. F. D. Moule thought it "possibly worth considering" that 6:18b might reflect the Corinthian position.[101] Jerome Murphy O'Connor drew attention to the parallels found in the structure of 6:13–14, the contrast between καταργέω (13) and ἐξεγείρω (14), and the proliferation of the particle δέ in these verses to suggest that Paul takes up the Corinthians' *own words* each time in formulating his response. Thus 6:13b (using καταργέω) is a Corinthian slogan. Murphy O'Connor takes 6:18b as another Corinthian slogan which displays the

---

99. E.g., RSV, NEB, NRSV, ESV, NLT, HCSB, with the NIV 2011 bucking the trend. This is also the position of Fee, *First Epistle*, 281 n. 294; Witherington, *Conflict*, 168, is ambivalent. Lambrecht, "Paul's Reasoning," 481, 485, accepts that this is Paul's position, with the caveat that Paul means that the stomach (κοιλία) will be destroyed; the destiny of the body is different.

100. E.g., Conzelmann, *1 Corinthians*, 110; Gundry, *Sōma*, 54–56; Byrne, "Sinning," 611–612; Schrage, *1 Korinther: 6,12—11,16*, 20; Hays, *First Corinthians*, 102; Collins, *First Corinthians*, 245; Thiselton, *First Epistle*, 462–63, following the earlier Thiselton, "Realized Eschatology," 517; Sandnes, *Belly*, 191–99; Fitzmyer, *First Corinthians*, 264; Burk, "Discerning," 99–121; Murphy-O'Connor, "Corinthian Slogans," 22–25; Ciampa and Rosner, *First Letter*, 252; Brookins, *Corinthian Wisdom*, 84–85; and more generally on the question of method, see Smith, "Slogans," 68–88. Fiore, "Passion," 135–43, speculates that Paul is confronting Epicurean influence in 1 Cor 5–6 and especially here, relying on Plutarch's treatise against the Epicureans. It is possible that this is a factor, but more than this is hard to say, and I would not wish to restrict the influences on the Corinthians to the Epicureans. Tomlin, "Christians," 51–72, explores the possible influence of Epicureanism more comprehensively and makes a convincing case for the contribution that it could have made to the problems discussed in 1 Cor 5–7 (62–64) while recognizing that Corinth was a melting pot for various philosophical and religious influences (70–71).

101. Moule, *Idiom Book*, 196–97.

same lack of concern for the body (found in 6:13), which is "morally irrelevant."[102]

However, scholars such as Gordon Fee follow Brendan Byrne in arguing that the slogan is Paul's,[103] and Fee proposes that the δέ is "exceptive" (suggesting the translation "all *other* sins," where the word *other* is supplied).[104] Yet, Denny Burk draws attention to the authoritative study of J. William Johnston of the NT uses of πᾶς, which concludes that there can be no exceptions implied in 6:18.[105] Further grammatical analysis by Jay E. Smith also provides compelling reasons for doubting the likelihood of this "exceptive" sense.[106] Smith seeks to provide extensive supporting evidence from the Hellenistic-Roman context, especially from Stoicism to demonstrate that "the philosophical 'raw materials' were present for the Corinthians to construct [such] a slogan."[107] Burk also draws atten-

---

102. Murphy-O'Connor, "Corinthian Slogans," 20–31 at 22. This would also explain the need to argue for a physical resurrection against those who dispute it in 1 Cor 15:12 (24). The article was originally published in *CBQ* 40 (1978), 391–96. Murphy O'Connor is followed by UBS Translation Consultant, Omanson, "Acknowledging," 207; Collins, *First Corinthians*, 248; Hays, *First Corinthians*, 105. Smith, "Roots," 65 n. 6, notes the mixed signals found in Thiselton (cf. Thiselton, *First Epistle*, comparing 459 with 471–74). Keener, *1-2 Corinthians*, 58, indicates that he is open to the possibility. Kempthorne, "Incest," 571–72, agrees with Moule and Murphy-O'Connor that 6:18b is a Corinthian slogan but takes σῶμα to mean the body of believers, argued also by E. Schweizer, "σῶμα, σωματικός, σύσσωμος," *TDNT* 7:1070. Mitchell, *Paul and the Rhetoric*, 120 n. 338 assumes that the "body of Christ" metaphor is a "prevailing image" of the letter and that 6:15 refers to this, and to the Corinthians' prior instruction in the matter. This seems unlikely in light of the presence of τὸ ἴδιον in 6:18b and since σῶμα in 6:18a is clearly used of the physical body. Gundry, *Sōma*, 73, asks pointedly, "Did Paul expect the Corinthians to read ch. 12 before ch. 6?" This difficulty is recognized by Fee, *First Epistle*, 283 n. 300, and 289 n. 323.

103. Byrne, "Sinning," 608–16 at 609–10, and followed by May, *Body*, 123–27.

104. Fee, *First Epistle*, 290, agreeing with Gundry, *Sōma*, 73–74, and argued on other grounds by Fisk, "Porneuein," 544 (reflected also by the RSV: "Every other sin ..." and followed by Rosner, *Paul*, 144, and Garland, *1 Corinthians*, 236). Burk, "Discerning," 99–121 at 118 finds no evidence for this usage in any of the major Greek grammars. Lambrecht, "Paul's Reasoning," 484–86, cautiously affirms that 6:18b is Paul's position, based on his structural analysis of 6:12–20.

105. Cited in Burk, "Discerning," 118 n. 61.

106. Smith, "Slogan," 82–83, as well as the difficulties of making sense of 6:18b as a Pauline statement in the context of the letter in 84–87. Smith also tries to propose evidence for seeing ἁμάρτημα as a non-Pauline word (understanding the vocabulary of Rom 3:25 as a pre-Pauline formula, with most commentators) in 87–91.

107. Smith, "Roots," 69, with evidence from Stoicism presented in 69–77, stressing the prime place given to intention over action in Stoic thought, with supporting

tion to the diatribal features of 6:12–20 that strongly suggest the dialogical nature of the passage, with the difference that Paul is interacting with real slogans, not with an imaginary opponent.[108] None of these scholars can establish with certainty that 6:18b are the words (or position) of the Corinthians but they do provide compelling evidence for its likelihood based on a variety of both literary and cultural factors and I shall assume this position here.

Looking at 6:12–20 as a whole, Paul begins by quoting a Corinthian slogan with which many have identified Stoic and Cynic parallels.[109] He counters this focus on individual rights or freedom (ἔξεστιν) with what builds up the community instead.[110] For my purposes I wish to note that the passage has a relentless focus on the physical body. The σῶμα rightly belongs to ὁ κύριος (13), last named as the Lord Jesus Christ (11). Having already identified πόρνοι as the first in a list of offenders who will not inherit the kingdom of God (9), Paul contrasts πορνεία with ὁ κύριος (13). The body is not intended for πορνεία but for the Lord.[111] ὁ θεὸς and ὁ κύριος

---

evidence from Epictetus, Cicero, Marcus Aurelius, Stobaeus, and Sextus Empiricus, and the evidence typically provided for Stoic views in 1 Cor 6:12a from Diogenes Laertius, Dio Chrysostom, and Philo as well as from scholars of Stoicism such as F. H. Sandbach and E. V. Arnold. Smith also sees a possible background in a kind of incipient gnosticism and postulates the possible misunderstanding of the sayings preserved in Mk 7:14–23 (see Smith, "Roots," 77–84 for the former and 84–95 for the latter.) By contrast, Bruce Fisk seeks to demonstrate that the ethos of 6:18b is in agreement with what we find in the Jewish wisdom tradition (Fisk, "Porneuein," 540–558 at 541, with evidence provided in 545–46).

108. Burk, "Discerning," 99–121 at 102–110. Brookins, *Corinthian Wisdom*, 85–86, 188–89 also takes this position.

109. Including *Diog. Laert.* 6.2.72; 7.1.125; see, e.g., Conzelmann, *1 Corinthians*, 108–9; Paige, "Stoicism," 180–93; and Brookins, *Corinthian Wisdom*, 174–75. Winter, *After Paul*, 76–96 locates the setting more in the ethics of the elite.

110. On which see particularly, Mitchell, *Paul and the Rhetoric*, passim; Lanci, *New Temple*, passim.

111. Fee, *First Epistle*, 275–77, is representative of most scholars in understanding Paul to be dealing with a real, rather than hypothetical, scenario. Rosner, "Temple Prostitution," 336–51, and Ciampa and Rosner, *First Letter*, 246–249, lay out the various options and argue for temple prostitution; Kempthorne, "Incest," 568–74, and Deming, "Unity," 289–312, argue that Paul is returning to the problem of incest identified in 1 Cor 5:1; Winter, "Gluttony," 77–90, makes the case that the elite indulged in sexual immorality in Roman banquets. Martin, *Corinthian Body*, 176, asserts that the πόρνη "is not a person in her own right (as if such a thing is imaginable for Paul) but a representative of the cosmos that is estranged and opposed to God and Christ" (see 176–79 generally) but Martin's whole discussion seems scarcely more imaginable than his dismissal of a concrete circumstance (especially in light of references to the specific

continue to be the subject of 6:14, as does the focus on the supremacy of ὁ θεός (he is the one who does the destroying in 6:13 and who raises ὁ κύριος in 6:14; cf. my discussion of 1:23 earlier). Paul hints at a later theme that will be dealt with expansively in 1 Cor 15: God raised the Lord and he will raise *us* through his power (14).[112] This is clearly a reference to the raising of some kind of body, since Paul pointedly addresses the Corinthians directly with the familiar accusatory topic marker οὐκ οἴδατε ὅτι (15) in order to draw attention to the fundamental place that the physical body plays in God's economy. Here the references are plural; it is their bodies that are members of Christ (15a). Thus, Paul's incredulity that they might even make *these* members become members of ἡ πόρνη is signaled by another familiar Pauline phrase of disbelief, and though grammatically a volitive optative (a wish expressed almost like a prayer), it expresses more a note of abhorrence, μὴ γένοιτο (6:15; "May it never be" or "Certainly not!").[113] It would be unthinkable to join (κολλάω) these members of Christ with ἡ πόρνη, signaled by Paul's second use of μὴ γένοιτο, because to do so would create a one body (ἓν σῶμά) relationship with her, or one flesh (6:16; citing Gen 2:24 LXX). Although the "one flesh" relationship (using σάρξ) almost certainly would have been well known from the LXX and from early Christian tradition,[114] Paul's focus in this discourse is on the σῶμα, (eight times in 6:12-20) not the σάρξ. Yet, strikingly, Paul's immediate assertion is that the one joined to the Lord is ἓν πνεῦμά (6:17). Although *one spirit* could mean something like *one in spirit*, referring to the human spirit (as in 2:11a), the immediate context would seem to demand a forward pointing reference to the Holy Spirit, both in 6:19, and then in the discussion that begins with 12:4.[115] Therefore Paul issues a

---

πόρνοις in 5:9-10, using a cognate word).

112. The textual tradition is evenly split between three tenses of the verb ἐξήγειρεν (aorist), ἐξεγείρει (present), and ἐξεγερεῖ (future: the reading of the NA[28]), but the context seems to demand the future reading (Metzger, *Textual Commentary*, 486-87; Fee, *First Epistle*, 274 n. 262) although Comfort, *New Testament*, 495, argues for the present reading as the original, following the "process exhibited in the corrections of p[46]."

113. "γίνομαι," BDAG, 196-99, at 4.a, 97; Burton, *Syntax*, 79 [§177], discussed in Wallace, *Greek Grammar*, 481-82. For its use uniquely in the diatribes of Epictetus and Paul, see Malherbe, *Paul*, 25-33.

114. cf. Matt 19:5; Mk 10:8; and Eph 5:31 (which, of course, *may* have been written by Paul), and the marriage imagery between God and his people is drawn on by Paul in 2 Cor 11:2-3.

115. Fee, *First Epistle 1987*, 260; followed by Thiselton, *First Epistle*, 469. Comfort, *New Testament*, 495-96, however, argues that "spirit" should not be capitalized since

strong warning to flee πορνεία (6:18). As argued earlier, I see good reason for taking 6:18b as the objection (whether actual or or hypothetical) of the Corinthians: that sin as an act has no reference to the body. Paul then uses πορνεύω in participle form as a substantive (the one who engages in sexual immorality) to make a radical claim to an audience influenced by philosophical thought, whether Stoic or Platonic: that such an act would be to sin against their own body (6:18b). Fisk is surely right to note that 6:12–20 is tied together by a "focus on the corporeal" (with the multiple descriptors σῶμα, κοιλία and σάρξ), whether that is *purely* related to the physical body or to the person as a whole "viewed particularly as a physical being."[116]

4.3.3 1 Corinthians 6:19: Main Features

I come now to the next figurative temple reference. For the purposes of my discussion I would note the following points about Paul's words. Firstly, the explicit referent of the temple of the Holy Spirit is the human σῶμα. This goes beyond the sense of 3:16, where the reference to the person could conceivably have been understood by Paul's audience only with respect to the soul. Secondly, although the reference is clearly to the individual body of Christians,[117] Paul chooses not to use the plural of σῶμα here. Instead, he expresses himself very carefully with ὁ σῶμα ὑμῶν, which Moulton and Turner class as a *distributive singular* (something that belongs to each person in a group).[118] This makes clear that the reference is to the body of the individual (who may or may not choose to unite with ἡ πόρνη) but at the same time keeps the corporate dimension of the temple very much in focus, just as in 3:16.[119] Thirdly, the Spirit is specifically defined as ἅγιος. In the earlier discussion, Paul had defined the temple as holy (3:17), and as the place of God's Spirit (3:16). Now he unites the two to provide definition to his characterization of the Spirit. Fourthly, Paul makes even more explicit one inference of 3:16–17: you

---

what is described is a union of the divine Spirit with the human spirit and manuscripts p⁴⁶ and p¹¹ support this, since the scribes did not write πνεῦμα as a nomen sacrum.

116. Fisk, "Porneuein," 548.
117. Garland, *1 Corinthians*, 238.
118. Moulton and Turner, *Grammar*, 23.
119. Agreeing with Gupta, *Worship*, 73–75; Gupta, "Body," 523, and see the article as a whole for a balanced presentation of this subject; also, e.g., McKelvey, *New Temple*, 102; Hogeterp, *Paul and God's Temple*, 340; Wassen, "Do You Have to Be Pure," 74–75.

Figurative Temple Language in 1 Corinthians 179

are not your own; you are like slaves of a different master (6:19b), who have been acquired with a price (and thus possess value).[120] Fifthly, such people are under obligation, consequently, to glorify (δοξάζω) God in the body; again, using the singular form of σῶμα with the possessive plural personal pronoun ὑμῶν (6:20).

4.3.4 Comparing 1 Corinthians 6:19 with Hellenistic Philosophy

Philosophy

I have already observed certain of these emphases in relation to 1 Cor 3:16–17; the most obvious one being that the temple is still a corporate image in 6:19 (though applied to the individual bodies of those within the community). I noted earlier that the indwelling references found in the philosophers related either to the universe as a whole or to the individual. It is not always clear whether these references to the individual could include the body. In Epictetus there is a hint that they may do so. When he admonishes his hearers with the notion that they are nourishing God and exercising God whenever they take physical exercise, or when he speaks of "bearing God about with you"[121] such that God sees the motions of the human soul as corresponding to his own motions so that they are "of one body with Himself,"[122] it is hard not to hear overtones of a physical aspect.[123] I have already drawn attention to places in Philo that refer to the human body as a sacred dwelling-place or shrine for the soul, which is the image of God.[124] However, I noted earlier the caution of Torrey Seland that this corporeal reference only appears in one place in Philo and it is with reference only to Adam, not to human beings in general. Despite each of these references in Epictetus and Philo, it is the norm that philosophers only speak of the divine indwelling in the soul or mind. Philo is the only *Jewish* Hellenistic philosopher that I am considering and so we might imagine that he would have a more positive view of the body

---

120. For the background to this metaphor and its use in a context more explicitly concerned with slavery in Paul's day (1 Cor 7:23), see Thiselton, *First Epistle*, 475–79; 561–65; and specialist studies such as Bartchy, Μᾶλλον, and Martin, *Slavery*, passim.

121. Epictetus, *Diatr.* 2.8.12 (Oldfather, LCL).

122. Epictetus, *Diatr.* 1.14.6 (Oldfather, LCL).

123. Seneca, *Ep.* 31.2 and 66.12 and Cicero, *Resp.* 6.24.26 could also be read in this way.

124. Philo, *Opif.* 137 (see for context; *Opif.* 135).

than pagan Stoic and Middle Platonic thinkers. In fact, for Philo, it is strictly the mind, not the body, that is a temple or dwelling place of God.[125] Philosophy tends to stress that the divine dwells in the soul,[126] or that a δαίμων dwells in the soul of each person.[127]

The special emphasis we find on the soul in philosophy is contrasted with the place of the body. Sometimes the body is spoken of almost with indifference; it is something to which the mind or soul should pay no attention.[128] The soul should have as little association as it is possible to have with the body during its earthly existence.[129] In fact, the body and its inclinations are to be resisted.[130] The body has dwelling within it not only good, but also evil.[131] As in the writings of Plato, later philosophers viewed the body as a prison house for the soul; a time when the soul is in exile.[132] The soul is the instrument of God; the body, merely the instrument of the soul.[133] Therefore, the soul that detaches itself from the things of the body and the earth will enjoy a speedier release from its prison than that of others.[134] The mind's life can be godlike, but only if it is free from the body.[135] In the meantime, Epictetus can even speak of the body as a corpse, in view of its final destiny.[136] Thus the body is like unwanted clothing; only fit to be cast off and thrown away.[137] For the Pythagoreans, this was enshrined in their creeds, since the soul moves (transmigrates)

---

125. Philo, *Praem.* 123; *Deus* 8–9; *Mos.* 2.82; *Virt.* 188; *Somn.* 2.250–51; *Det.* 90.

126. E.g., Seneca, *Ep.* 110.2; 120.14; Cicero, *Leg.* 2.11.27–28; *Tusc.* 1.24.56; 1.25.62; Philo, *Cher.* 98, 100; *Deus* 134; *Sobr.* 62; *Somn.* 1.149; 2.215, 248; *QG* 4.80; see also Hogeterp, *Paul and God's Temple*, 342–44.

127. E.g., Dio, *4 Regn.* 139; Epictetus, *Diatr.* 1.14.12, 14; Marcus, *Med.* 2.13, 17; 3.3.2; 3.12, 16; 5.10.2; 5.27; Cicero, *Div.* 1.54.122.

128. E.g., Marcus, *Med.* 6.32.

129. E.g., Plutarch, [*Cons. Apoll.*] 108CD.

130. E.g., Marcus, *Med.* 7.55.1–2; Alcinous, *Handbook*, 172.16.2.10–19 (26); 182.4.3–8 (38); cf. Plato, *Tim.* 42AB.

131. Plutarch, *Virt. prof.* 122E, cf. Homer, *Od.* 4.392.

132. E.g., Plutarch, *Exil.* 607D; Maximus, *Or.* 7.5; 9.6; 10.3–5; cf. 10.9.

133. E.g., Plutarch, *Sept. sap. conv.* 163E.

134. E.g., Seneca, *Marc.* 23.1–2; *Polyb.* 9.3, 8; *Helv.* 11.6; *Ep.* 41.5

135. Cicero, *lib. inc. fr.* 2; cf. *Div.* 1.57.129.

136. Epictetus, *Frag.* 26; *Diatr.* 2.1.17; cf. Plutarch, *Quaest. plat.* 2, 1002C.

137. E.g., Maximus, *Or.* 11.11.

from one body to another, showing the body to be non-specific to the soul.[138]

In respect to my third point, some philosophers spoke of the spirit as holy. I noted in chapter two that Seneca avers, "a holy spirit indwells within us (sacer intra nos spiritus sedet),"[139] perhaps an extension of the Stoic view that a *spiritus* permeates all there is.[140] I have already noted that for Zeno, the πνεῦμα holds all things together, including individuals.[141]

Timothy A. Brookins sees the phrase οὐκ . . . ἑαυτῶν (1 Cor 6:19b) as a subversion of a Stoic position, citing the use of the expression in Stoic writers but with a different meaning.[142] For the Stoic the body was not their own because it was part of a larger whole, it belonged to the cosmos, or "the self was located not in the body but the soul . . . and especially because the body resided outside the individual's own control, liable as it was to disease, lameness, and most of all the whims of 'tyrants.'"[143] Paul on the contrary attributes great value to the body (6:20a) because it matters to God, who is the master of those who belong to Christ, in whom the Spirit dwells exclusively. The philosophers also speak of a certain obligation to glorify God (cf. 6:20b). For the middle Platonists, the goal was to know and to imitate God and to submit to God's direction in all things,[144] but other writers (including Stoics) also spoke of the need to imitate the example of the gods.[145] The response to the gods should also be a life oriented toward virtue,[146] that includes a life characterized by self-control,[147] with the goal to please God.[148] A person's desire for purity

138. Philostratus, *Vit. Apoll.* 3.19.1.

139. Seneca, *Ep.* 41.2 (Gummere, LCL).

140. Seneca, *Nat.* 2.6.5; 6.16.1; 3.29.2; *Helv.* 8.3.

141. *SVF*, 2.473; cf. *SVF*, 2.552–53, 634.

142. Brookins, *Corinthian Wisdom*, 189, citing Epictetus, *Diatr.* 3.20.1; 3.22.21, 34, 40–41; 4.1.66, 78, 87, 104, 158; 4.7.17, 31–32; *Ench.* 1.1; Seneca, *Ep.* 120.18–19.

143. Brookins, *Corinthian Wisdom*, 189.

144. E.g., Plutarch, *Sept. sap. conv.* 163E.

145. E.g., Alcinous, *Handbook*, 181.28.22–30 (37); 182.4.3–8 (38); Maximus, *Or.* 35.2; cf. 26.9; also in Stoic writers like Seneca, *Ben.* 4.25.1; *Vit. beat.* 15.6; 16:1–2; *Ep.* 95.50; cf. *De otio.* 5.8; *Vit. beat.* 3.3; 8.1; Dio, *3 Regn.* 82; Epictetus, *Diatr.* 2.14.13; 2.16.42.

146. Diog. Laert. 7.1.88, 89, 93–117; Seneca, *Prov.* 1.5; cf. *Ep.* 31.9; Cicero, *Leg.* 1.7.25.

147. Dio, *4 Regn.* 23.

148. Epictetus, *Diatr.* 1.30.1.

before God[149] should lead to an inward purification[150] and the destruction of all thoughts that would tend away from purity.[151] This means being led by and keeping pure your inner δαίμων[152] by honoring him.[153] As I described in the previous two chapters, purity in both thought, word and action could be described as a sacrifice, and thus an offering of worship.[154]

Paul

When I compare these findings with 1 Cor 6:19, there are a number of points to consider. Firstly, whereas the human body is spoken of by philosophers (whether Stoic or Platonic) at best with indifference and at worst with disdain, Paul sees the body itself as the temple of the Holy Spirit, a sacred place where God's presence dwells.[155] Again, I noted the corporate implications of Paul's use of the second-person possessive plural in referring to the body, by contrast to the individual focus of temple references that I have surveyed. Thirdly, the πνεῦμα or *spiritus* inhabits the whole universe in the philosophers, and this includes every individual that dwells within it. By contrast, it is those who have been washed, sanctified and justified in the name of the Lord Jesus and by the spirit of their God who are a temple of the Holy Spirit in Paul (6:11; cf. 1:2; 2:10–13; 3:16–17, 21–23; 12:3). For Paul, the spirit is not the possession of all people irrespective of their relationship to Jesus. Correspondingly, among the philosophers there is no sense that one set of people belong to God in a way that others may not. Finally, the philosophers would concur with Paul that there is an obligation to glorify God (or the gods) by imitating their example, in inward and outward purity. However, Paul adds to the injunction to glorify God ἐν τῷ σώματι ὑμῶν (6:20b). This short phrase encapsulates the heart of the difference between Paul and the phi-

---

149. Epictetus, *Diatr.* 2.18.19; 2.19.26.

150. Epictetus, *Diatr.* 4.1.112.

151. Epictetus, *Diatr.* 2.8.12–13; 4.1.175; Apollonius, *Vit. Apoll.* 3.42.1–2; Marcus Aurelius, *Med.* 7.54

152. Apollonius, *Vit. Apoll.* 1.18.1; 2.39.3; Marcus Aurelius, *Med.* 2.13, 17; 3.5.1; 3.6.2; 3.12; 3.16; 5.27.

153. Epictetus, *Diatr.* 2.8.18–22.

154. E.g., Cicero, *Nat. d.* 2.28.71; Dio, *Exil.* 35; *Leg.* 2.8.19; 2.10.24, 25; Philostratus, *Vit. Apoll.* 6.11.3; Philo, *Spec.* 1.201, 203, 257–60, 269–271, 283, 287; *QE.* 1.17; 2.31, 98–99; *Sacr.* 73; 109–111; *Mos.* 2.137–39, 148–51; *Plant.* 108; *Somn.* 2.73–74.

155. For more on this theme, see, e.g., Fee, *God's Empowering Presence*, 134–37.

losophers: unlike Platonism and Stoicism, he emphasizes a defined group with boundaries set by their relationship to Jesus Christ and stresses the corporeal dimension to identification with and obedience to God.[156]

4.4 CORRESPONDING EMPHASES IN 1 CORINTHIANS

The key emphases I have identified here can also be found elsewhere within the epistle. In this next section I shall comment briefly on a number of other important places in the letter that relate to the issues identified in 1 Cor 3:16-17 and 6:19. I shall be selective and aim to address only those areas that may have been notable for an audience influenced by philosophy, such as the need for holiness to be expressed in the body, idolatry rather than the acceptance of multiple gods, and Paul's positive view of the body and his willingness to use indwelling imagery with material language.

4.4.1 Holiness in the Body

The concern for holiness and for its expression within the body comes to the fore in 1 Cor 7, where Paul gives most of his attention to the question of marriage and whether to marry or remain unmarried. The question, apparently raised by the Corinthians,[157] of whether to touch (ἅπτω) a woman (γυνή)[158] is expressly concerned with sexual relations (7:1),[159]

---

156. May, *Body*, 130, suggests that this phrase connotes the sense that each temple is set apart for the divinity whose image dwells within, "the temple is the property of the resident divinity."

157. The position of most commentators, see Lang, *Korinther*, 89; Schrage, *1 Korinther: 6,12—11,16*, 59; Collins, *First Corinthians*, 252-55, 257; Thiselton, *First Epistle*, 498-500; Schnabel, *Korinther*, 352; Fee, *First Epistle*, 303-8; Ciampa and Rosner, *First Letter*, 272. Barrett, *First Epistle*, 154, and Fitzmyer, *First Corinthians*, 278, cautiously express the view that Paul may be in agreement with the sentiment, but this seems unlikely in the context of the wider discussion and the way that Paul answers Corinthian slogans in other passages.

158. Though this could equally be translated "wife," most adopt the more neutral "woman." See Thiselton, *First Epistle*, 500; Fitzmyer, *First Corinthians*, 278.

159. For evidence for the use of ἅπτεσθαι in the middle voice with the genitive, as a euphemism in Greek literature for sexual intercourse, see Fee, "1 Corinthians 7:1," 307-14; Thiselton, *First Epistle*, 500; Collins, *First Corinthians*, 258; Fee, *First Epistle*, 301-6. Fee, "1 Corinthians 7:1 Revisited," 197-213 restates his case in opposition to the more recent attempt to revive the argument that γυναικὸς μὴ ἅπτεσθαι is a metonymy for marriage, argued by Caragounis, "Fornication," 543-49. More recently,

and thus matters of the body. Paul's foundational principle is that each spouse (ἐξουσιάζω) has authority over the body of the other (7:4).[160] Taking up the language of 1:2, Paul proclaims that an unbelieving spouse in a marriage is sanctified (ἁγιάζω) by the believer, rendering the children holy (ἅγιος) rather than unclean (ἀκάθαρτος) in 7:14.[161] Paul repeats the language of 6:20 (last used in connection with the temple language), in reminding the Corinthians again that they have been bought with a price (ἀγοράζω), that they might not be slaves of people (τιμῆς ἠγοράσθητε in 7:23 and ἠγοράσθητε ... τιμῆς in 6:20b). I also note in passing that in Paul's understanding, the single person's goal is ἵνα ᾖ ἁγία καὶ τῷ σώματι καὶ τῷ πνεύματι (7:34). Holiness must be expressed *in the body* as well as the spirit; Paul is never concerned with matters of the soul alone, but the whole person.[162] Finally in this chapter, Paul places one condition on those who remarry after widowhood, μόνον ἐν κυρίῳ (7:39), which I would understand as meaning that the new spouse must be a member of this community set apart for Jesus Christ.[163]

---

an interesting and persuasive argument has been put forward that the euphemism specifically applied to cases of acting on sexual passions motivated by pleasure or passion, not for procreation; see Ciampa and Rosner, *First Letter*, 272-75, and for fuller details, Ciampa, "Revisiting," 325-38.

160. For the significance of this for Paul's theology of the body and its radical disjunction with contemporary views of the body in marriage see, e.g., Thiselton, *First Epistle*, 504-6; Schrage, *1 Korinther: 6,12—11,16*, 63-66. For a discussion of the possibility that Paul is interacting with a wider Stoic-Cynic debate over marriage, see Balch, "1 Corinthians," 429-39, and Deming, *Paul on Marriage*, passim.

161. Within the confines and narrow focus of this work I do not have space to discuss the interpretation of this contentious verse, for which see Schrage, *1 Korinther: 6,12—11,16*, 104-9; Thiselton, *First Epistle*, 527-33; Fitzmyer, *First Corinthians*, 299-301; Ciampa and Rosner, *First Letter*, 296-302; Fee, *First Epistle*, 330-33.

162. See Conzelmann, *1 Corinthians*, 134 n. 32; Schrage, *1 Korinther: 6,12—11,16*, 180; Fitzmyer, *First Corinthians*, 320; Ciampa and Rosner, *First Letter*, 353-54. Collins, *First Corinthians*, 292, and Barrett, *First Epistle*, 181, speculate that this is a quotation from the Corinthians but there is no evidence for this and it fits comfortably within Paul's argument in the chapter.

163. This is disputed by, e.g., Lightfoot, *Notes*, 235; Barrett, *First Epistle*, 186, but held by most commentators, so Robertson and Plummer, *Critical and Exegetical*, 161; Collins, *First Corinthians*, 303; Thiselton, *First Epistle*, 604; Fitzmyer, *First Corinthians*, 329; Fee, *First Epistle*, 392. Ciampa and Rosner, *First Letter*, 365-66 also understand this as the meaning but are cautious about its universal application.

4.4.2 Idolatry

First Corinthians 8:1–11 is an immensely complex section of the letter and so I can only briefly touch on the areas that relate to the themes of idolatry, purity and temples, while neglecting other important areas of Paul's discussion.[164] Paul introduces the section with the words Περὶ δὲ τῶν εἰδωλοθύτων (8:1).[165] Although many vital topics are discussed along the way, it is essential to always keep in mind that the *subject* of this section is things offered to idols, and more broadly, idolatry. Jerome Murphy O'Connor describes the problem of idol offerings as, "of very limited interest" compared to, "the nature of Christian freedom, the place of the believer in a non-Christian society, and the education of the conscience."[166] For J. C. Brunt, "the specific question of idol meat is transcended by the consideration of love's responsibility."[167] Yet the fact that these topics are introduced *in order* to further Paul's treatment of idolatry is overlooked.[168] Idolatry was a pressing issue for the Corinthians.

Many recent commentators agree that Paul addresses two contexts: meals eaten in or around pagan temples (8:1–10:22) and food sold in the marketplace and eaten at home (10:23–11:1).[169] While it was once common to claim that a distinction could be made between what Bruce Fisk refers to as "harmless social events" at the temple and activities that were "blatantly idolatrous," even Fisk concedes that, "lines . . . were fuzzy, if drawn at all."[170] The study of Peter D. Gooch examined archeological and

---

164. For more detail, see the monographs listed in the first chapter and the relatively recent and comprehensive survey of the literature, found in Fotopoulos, *Food*, 1–48, including the very helpful chart comparing the views of different scholars, found on 41–48.

165. See the discussions of εἰδωλόθυτα in Thiselton, *First Epistle*, 617–20, and dining in Roman Corinth in Witherington, *Conflict*, 191–95.

166. Murphy-O'Connor, "Freedom," 87.

167. Brunt, "Rejected," 121.

168. Note the criticisms of Gooch, *Dangerous Food*, 47–48; Cheung, *Idol Food*, 18–19.

169. E.g., Fee, "Εἰδωλόθυτα," 172–97; Theissen, *Social Setting*, 121–43; Willis, *Idol Meat*, 265–71; Gooch, *Dangerous Food*, 73–97; Witherington, *Conflict*, 186–91; Witherington, "Not So Idle," 237–54; Newton, *Diety*, 389–91; Cheung, *Idol Food*, 82–164 (with some qualifications); Smit, *About the Idol Offerings*, 41; Fotopoulos, *Food*, 38; Fee, *First Epistle*, 394–400.

170. Fisk, "Eating Meat," 63; Willis, *Idol Meat*, 47 expresses a similar sentiment, that "social conviviality and good cheer" was the focus of religious associations meeting in the temple for meals.

literary evidence for the cult of Demeter and Kore and the place of dining rooms at Lerna in relation to the Asklepios and concluded that idol sacrifice went hand in hand with meals of social significance.[171] Gooch's research has been comprehensively updated (and, in places, corrected) by John Fotopoulos, who provides a very thorough discussion of the archeological evidence and concludes that meals in both the temple and its courts would have involved eating idol food with a religious connotation, and that further, many meals were accompanied by sexual encounters[172] (so involving the threat of both idolatry and sexual immorality that I highlighted as a constant concern for Jewish writers, including Paul in this letter). Paul therefore is severe in his warnings against participation in idolatry, focused on alternative temples in Corinth. He does so by drawing on the very heart of Jewish monotheism, the *Shema* (Deut 6:4), for which he provides a "Christological" reinterpretation (8:6),[173] reminiscent of his words in 3:23, in which θεός and κύριος are conjoined once more, and the relationship between the Corinthians and this God and Lord is reaffirmed. Paul draws on his Jewish roots and its universal condemnation of idolatry,[174] but also on both the tradition that idols have no objective reality (8:4a, 5a, c.f. Deut 32:21; Pss 115:4–8; 135:15–18; Isa 40:19–20; 44:9–17) combined with the subjective experience of idols for those who formerly encountered them as pagans, and were influenced by demons through them (8:7, 10, c.f. Deut 18:10–11; 32:17; Ps 106:37; Isa 8:19; 19:3).[175] Some consider it their ἐξουσία ("right" in the context of 8:9) to eat idol food in temple contexts. Whether or not this is a Corinthian term, it certainly encapsulates what is probably a Corinthian catchphrase (Πάντα μοι ἔξεστιν in 6:12 and 10:23). For a Corinthian to eat in an idol temple may "build up" (in an ironic sense: οἰκοδομέω in 8:10; cf. 8:1; 10:23; 14:4, 17) the brother to follow their example. The end result will be destructive (8:11) rather than constructive, and will also constitute a sin

---

171. Gooch, *Dangerous Food*, 1–46; followed by Cheung, *Idol Food*, 27–38; Smit, *About the Idol Offerings*, 49–52.

172. See the evidence provided in Fotopoulos, *Food*, 49–178.

173. The wording of Wright, "Monotheism," 125–29.

174. Cheung, *Idol Food*, 39–81; cf. Tomson, *Paul*, 151–77, although Tomson notes a spectrum of views on the severity of attitudes toward, and interpretations of, idolatry. This work has been supplemented by Phua, *Idolatry*, passim, whose study contends that in the Jewish Diaspora there were various interpretations of what constituted idolatry and so, a variety of responses. See also Paul's vehement attacks on idolatry in other letters such as Rom 1:21–32; 2:22; 2 Cor 6:16; Gal 4:8; 1 Thess 1:9.

175. Cheung, *Idol Food*, 151–52.

against Christ (8:12, emphasizing the unity between believers and believers that is also a vital theme for the letter). Paul's argument in 8:7–13 is not simply about relationships between believers. It is noteworthy that he uses temple language (μολύνω) to describe the polluting effect on a person of weak conscience who is led into eating idol food (8:7).[176]

Paul's discussion of his rights (1 Cor 9) actually constitutes a *de facto* prohibition of the Corinthians' exercise of their rights rather than an affirmation of their freedom.[177] Paul never claims his right to eat idol food just as he never argues that πορνεία (cf. 6:18 with 6:12) would be permissible in different circumstances. The tone and direction of Paul's discussion from 8:7–13 through to the end of 1 Cor 9 is intended to dissuade the Corinthians from such participation.[178] Paul's examples from scripture in 10:1–13[179] warn the Corinthians that their spiritual ancestors had their own kind of "baptism" and "communion" (cf. 10:14–22; 11:17–34) but their dalliance (10:7) came at a terrible cost (10:8–11). The idols are not gods but to participate in idol worship is to enter into κοινωνία with demons (10:19–22).[180] Therefore Paul urges the believers to flee idolatry (φεύγετε ἀπὸ τῆς εἰδωλολατρίας) in 10:14. The other use of the verb φεύγω is in 6:18 in relation to πορνεία, thus demonstrating the twin dangers of idolatry and immorality highlighted by Paul).[181] I would agree with A.

176. Both uses of μολύνω highlighted by "μολύνω," BDAG, 657, relate to purity, defilement, and holiness in connection with temple worship; cf. Thiselton, *First Epistle*, 640. Fitzmyer, *First Corinthians*, 345, comments that the conscience is defiled because in eating εἰδωλόθυτα, "precisely, 'as sacrificed to idols,' that person's conscience is stained by an idolatrous act."

177. *Contra* Murphy-O'Connor, "Freedom," 99. Note the study of Richardson, "Temples," 89–110, who suggests that Paul refused support from the community precisely because other patrons were offering the Corinthian community idol food and Paul wants neither himself nor the community as a holy temple to be tainted by eating.

178. See Cheung, *Idol Food*, 90, 140; Smit, *About the Idol Offerings*, 64, 88, 90, 92–120; Gooch, *Dangerous Food*, 84. Paul does use temple language in 9:13 but this is an illustration of literal temple service, drawn from the LXX (cf. Lev 6:16, 26; 7:6; Num 5:9, 10; 18:8–20; Deut 8:1) rather than *figurative* temple language, so I shall not consider it in my discussion.

179. Drawing on passages such as Exod 13:21–22; 14:22–29; 16:4; 17:6; 32:6; Num 11:4, 34; 14:16, 23, 29–30; 20:11; and others.

180. Winter, "Identifying," 847–68, identifies the δαιμόνιον in 10:20–21 with imperial gods, in line with his understanding of the meals as Roman banquets in imperial temples (see below). Within the limited confines of this study, I will not be able to interact with his proposal.

181. I shall return to consider the words related to idolatry in 1 Cor 8:1—11:1 a little more closely when I examine 2 Cor 6:14—7:1 in the next chapter.

T. Cheung that Paul's very different arguments in 8:1-13 and 10:1-22 are not contradictory nor evidence of partition,[182] but rather evidence of a two stage argument, that presses home the point that Paul prohibits the eating of idol food "with the awareness of their idolatrous origins," especially in idol temples but even in homes.[183] All this means that for those who constitute the temple of the Holy Spirit, there cannot be even the hint of contact with idolatry. As Gordon Fee puts it, "fundamental allegiance is at stake."[184] This perspective would have clashed sharply with the worldview of philosophy that was happy to accommodate many gods; speaking at times of θεός and at other times of θεοὶ, and at home with temples dedicated to different gods, including to the emperor.[185]

Furthermore, the Corinthians' worship is to be distinct and worthy of the Lord, avoiding that which is contrary to nature and imitates Roman cultic practice (11:2-16).[186] Similarly as a Spirit empowered body, they will no longer follow the practice of pagans, who led astray by idols, curse Jesus (or possibly utter a curse in the name of Jesus in 12:3).[187] Incidentally it is notable that Paul refers to them as ἔθνη (12:2) or "nations,

---

182. Contra Yeo, *Rhetorical Interaction*, passim.

183. Cheung, *Idol Food*, 96, 104-9, 116-17, 297; confirmed by rhetorical analysis throughout Smit, *About the Idol Offerings*, passim. This is in contrast to treatments of the passage that stress the "horizontal" emphasis almost to the exclusion of the "vertical." One modern example would be Newton, *Diety*, e.g., 115-276, 290, 305-6, 341, 363, 367, who repeatedly speaks as if "community consciousness" was Paul's only interest; cf. the critique of Smit, *About the Idol Offerings*, 21-23.

184. Fee, *First Epistle*, 524.

185. Cf. Bruce Winter who contends that the problem faced by Paul's converts was the pressure to dine in a temple dedicated to the emperor, caused by the establishing of a federal imperial cult in Corinth itself and the re-siting of the Isthmian Games in Corinth. Both of these events probably happened between Paul leaving Corinth and him writing 1 Corinthians, according to Winter, *After Paul*, 269-86.

186. See the evidence set out in Winter, *After Paul*, 121-41.

187. See Winter, *After Paul*, 164-83, for the latter. Thiselton, *First Epistle*, 918-23, identifies as many as twelve different explanations offered for the use of the phrase Ἀνάθεμα Ἰησοῦς, not counting Winter's position, which is to suggest that we translate "Jesus [Grants] a Curse" (Winter, *After Paul*, 174-76). Winter sees a precedent for this translation in other curse inscriptions that he describes. However, the most natural translation would be to supply εἰμι in either subjunctive ("Jesus be cursed") or indicative mood ("Jesus is cursed" in parallel with "Jesus is Lord") as noted by Thiselton, *First Epistle*, 918; Ciampa and Rosner, *First Letter*, 565 n. 15; see the telling critique of Fitzmyer, *First Corinthians*, 456, that Winter's interpretation depends on inscriptions missing some of the words from the original (unlike Paul, who has simply omitted the verb intentionally).

Gentiles" in the past tense, even though the majority of the congregation are still Gentiles.[188] In the past they, "were being led, being carried away to mute idols"[189] but by implication they have a new identity that precludes any relation to other gods/idols.

4.4.3 Body Language

Next, I shall briefly consider the place of "body" language in 1 Corinthians since this has a bearing on the use of σῶμα in 1 Cor 6:19 and the place of the body in philosophy. Firstly, I note in passing that Paul views the breaking of bread as a κοινωνία in the body (σῶμα) of Christ, and that this participation makes them one σῶμα (10:16–17). Paul revisits this image in 11:27–29 where Paul avers that those who eat the bread and drink the cup in an unworthy manner (ἀναξίως) will be answerable for the body and blood of the Lord. Judgment is pronounced on those who eat and drink μὴ διακρίνων τὸ σῶμα ("without discerning the body," 11:29).[190] In speaking of the Eucharist in both passages, Paul is willing to use a metaphor drawn from the human body to positively describe the relationship between the Corinthian believers and Christ.

This metaphor is elaborated upon at length in 12:1–31, where the believers are explicitly compared to a body with members (τὰ μέλη in 12:12). Just as the Corinthians are the temple of God (3:16a) by virtue of God's spirit (3:16b; 6:19), so too they are members of one body because of the one Spirit (12:13), who energizes all the activities of the body (12:4, 7, 8, 9, 10, 11). There is one body, just as there is one temple.[191] Paul makes evident the fact that that his metaphor is drawn from the human body by his references to specific members: the foot, the hand (12:15), the ear, the eye (12:16), and by implication, the nose (using ὄσφρησις for "sense of smell" in 12:17d).[192] Remarkably, Paul even draws attention to the

---

188. Hays, *Conversion*, 9; Wright, *Paul and the Faithfulness*, 416 n. 225, 541, 1107, 1446; and Ciampa and Rosner, *First Letter*, 563.

189. Author's own translation.

190. For a helpful excursus on this much-debated phrase, see Thiselton, *First Epistle*, 891–94.

191. Collins, "Constructing," 207.

192. Recent scholarship has rightly drawn attention to the *topos* of the body in political rhetoric; see the survey in Thiselton, *First Epistle*, 992–94, drawing upon works such as Mitchell, *Paul and the Rhetoric*, 68–83, 157–64 and Martin, *Corinthian Body*, 38–68, 87–103, citing Plutarch, Epictetus, Dio Chrysostom, and Dionysius of

unpresentable parts (τὰ ἀσχήμονα in 12:23) of the human body and compares them in a positive way to members of the Corinthian church whose status or background might naturally afford them less respect.[193] In fact, God himself gives greater honor in particular to those parts (12:24).

Finally, Paul reserves the longest discussion of a single topic (not counting 8:1–11:1, whose arguments and flow are a little more varied) to his argument for the resurrection in 15:1–58.[194] It is evidently the climax to the variety of topics dealt with in the letter, followed by a brief rounding up of unfinished business in 1 Cor 16. Paul is responding to another issue, either raised by the Corinthians themselves (15:12) or reported back to Paul (cf. 1 Cor 1:11). Paul is at pains to stress that Christ was raised from the dead and appeared to the apostles as proof of this (15:3–9).[195] This is evidence that there will be a future resurrection of the dead ones (15:12). Christ's own resurrection is the ἀπαρχή of the harvest (15:20; cf. 16:15: the household of Stephanas were the first of many converts in the province of Achaia) and the rest of the chapter continues this argument for the future resurrection of those who belong to Christ (15:20–23). Paul's discussion does raise the question of whether the σῶμα πνευματικόν (15:44b) is in some way not physical, since it is contrasted with the σῶμα ψυχικόν (15:44a) and the man who is χοϊκός (earthy), predicated of the ὁ πρῶτος ἄνθρωπος ἐκ γῆς (15:47). This is especially pertinent for my discussion, since when Paul discusses different types of body he gives the example of the heavenly bodies (ἐπουράνιος in 15:40), after which he immediately lists the sun and the stars (15:41)

Halicarnassus among others. I am not denying Paul's use of this common *topos*, nor the political resonances it might have had for his readers. I am merely recognizing that the source of this language was the human body, and although other writers used the analogy of various body parts and internal organs, Paul speaks unashamedly, although obliquely, of its most private members (12:23). For more on the whole relationship between this metaphor in Stoicism and Paul, see Lee, *Paul*, passim.

193. See Martin, *Corinthian Body*, 94–96; "ἀσχήμων," BDAG, 147, which draws attention to the word's application to sexual matters in LXX Deut 24:1 and cf. Dio Chrysostom, *Conc. Apam.* 29, and its use for genitalia here. "ἀσχήμων," LSJ, 266, provides definitions such as "misshapen, ugly," or "unseemly, shameful."

194. Within the constraints of my topic I cannot provide adequate discussion of this lengthy chapter. Schrage, *1 Korinther: 15,1–16*, 24, devotes over four hundred pages to the chapter and Thiselton, *First Epistle*, 1169–1313 provides extensive discussion, excurses, and multiple bibliographies of significant works.

195. See Thiselton, *First Epistle*, 1197–1203 who interacts with the discussion of the relationship between belief in Christ's resurrection and the empty tomb tradition, in 15:3–5.

Figurative Temple Language in 1 Corinthians   191

among his illustrations. In Hellenistic philosophy, it was believed that some became stars (viewed as gods) after their death, sometimes spoken of as "bodies."[196] Dale Martin has in fact revived an older view that a body of πνεῦμα is referring to the kind of ethereal substance of which that body consists, referring to it as, "a stuff of a thinner, higher nature."[197] Paul's point at this juncture though is not to identify the precise material of such a body but to make the more general point that God designs appropriate bodies for the environments to which they are suited. In this instance, the point about the σῶμα πνευματικόν is its appropriateness to the resurrection mode of existence; a mode empowered and sustained by the Spirit.[198] Gordon Fee avers, "the transformed body is not composed of 'spirit'; it is a *body* adapted to the eschatological existence that is under the ultimate domination of the Spirit"[199] or as Anthony Thiselton puts it, "Paul uses the adjective πνευματικός in its regular Pauline sense to denote that which pertains to the Holy Spirit of God"[200] and "the totality of the mode of life of the resurrection body is more than physical but not less."[201] It is evident throughout Paul's discussion that the body itself is critical to

---

196. See the evidence presented in Martin, *Corinthian Body*, 117–20; examples from philosophy would include Seneca, *Marc.* 25.3; *Ep.* 65.17; 102.21, 28.

197. Martin, *Corinthian Body*, 128, and generally 124–29. See the discussion of Thiselton, *First Epistle*, 1276, on precedents to this view. In this, Martin has been followed by Engberg-Pedersen, *Cosmology*, passim, who also wishes to speak of *pneuma* as material, and of what has been typically understood as metaphorical language in Paul (e.g., the *body* of Christ) as literal. Engberg-Pedersen himself admits that not every specialist agrees with his understanding of Stoicism generally, even citing the words of Tad Brennan's analysis of his earlier work on Stoicism: "impressive but, I believe, wholly misguided" (Engberg-Pedersen, *Cosmology*, 249 n. 10). In the same note, Engberg-Pedersen claims that "the doyen of modern Stoic studies," A. A. Long is in far closer agreement with my understanding," citing Long, *Stoic Studies*, 177–78, but Long's comments are not as positive as Engberg-Pedersen's assessment of them might imply. In fact, elsewhere in the same compendium of Long's writings, he accuses Engberg-Pedersen of paying "insufficient regard to the physical and theological underpinning of Stoic ethics" (Long, *Stoic Studies*, 155, and see 154–55 generally). Other scholars of Stoicism have been trenchant in their criticism of Engberg-Pedersen's methodology, assumptions and reliance on Cicero, e.g., Tieleman, Review, 226–32; cf. also the critique in Wright, *Paul and the Faithfulness*, 1392–1406.

198. As Witherington, *Conflict*, 308, puts it, "The resurrection body will be animated and empowered by the Spirit, just as the present physical body (*the Sōma psychikon*) is animated and empowered by a physical life principle or force."

199. Fee, *First Epistle*, 869.

200. Thiselton, *First Epistle*, 1275.

201. Thiselton, *First Epistle*, 1277; see more fully the discussion of 1276–81.

his argument. The word σῶμα is used nine times between 15:35–44, but in any case, references to resurrection, which are repeated throughout the chapter, would have been understood throughout the ancient world as involving a return of a physical body, as has been comprehensively demonstrated by N. T. Wright.[202] Paul embraces and argues passionately for a bodily understanding of life beyond death at the final resurrection. In Paul's articulation of the need for the bonded holiness and the purity of believers in 1 Cor 7 (in addition to the passages I explored earlier in 1 Cor 5–6), his warning to those who would participate in some kind of temple/idol related activities in 1 Cor 8:1—11:1 and his positive emphasis on the physical body in 1 Cor 11, 12 and 15, Paul's message would have challenged those from a background influenced by philosophy. Instead of the easy acceptance of temples and gods in that worldview, Paul demonstrates the threat to the very existence of Christ-centered life that they pose. Instead of the indifferent or even dismissive attitude to the body held within philosophy, Paul positively celebrates it and uses it as a central metaphor for their present existence (as the *body* of Christ) as well as the hope of their future existence (a *body* patterned on the resurrection body of Christ).[203]

4.5 COMPARING THE THEOLOGIES OF 1 CORINTHIANS WITH HELLENISTIC PHILOSOPHY

In the last two chapters I have considered the philosophers' understanding of the nature of divinity, the nature of humanity and how they should live out their philosophy in practice. In the following section I aim to offer the briefest of sketches of what Paul has to say on these topics in 1 Corinthians so that I can compare them with the philosophical positions identified previously.[204]

202. Wright, *Resurrection*, especially 32–84 on the contrast with paganism.

203. Garcilazo, *Corinthian Dissenters*, passim, argues that the denial of the resurrection of the dead stems from the influence of Roman Stoicism on the Corinthians. In my view, Garcilazo's case is weakened by his over-reliance on a small number of texts from Seneca.

204. My aim here is the limited one of simply noting what Paul has to say in one letter. For attempts to address Paul's theology of God, his understanding of humanity (and its predicament), and for Pauline ethics, some modern significant works would include especially Dunn, *Theology*; Schreiner, *Paul*, and, somewhat differently, Wright, *Paul and the Faithfulness*. For a celebrated and more limited attempt to compare the theology of God, humanity, and human relations in Paul with that of one important

4.5.1 Paul's Understanding of God in 1 Corinthians

God has called Paul an apostle in line with his will (1:1) and he has called the Corinthians into the closest possible participation (κοινωνία) with Jesus Christ (1:9). Paul's reference to those who call upon the *name* of the *Lord* evokes allusions to OT examples of this phrase (1:2; cf. Ps 98:6; Joel 3:5 LXX). Yet in Paul's case, the κύριος is the Lord *Jesus Christ*, bringing Jesus into the closest possible connection, or even identity, with God. This "name" of Jesus, identifying him with the one called upon in the NT, appears again in 1:10. God is the *father* to the Corinthians (1:3), and again the fact that he is invoked here in tandem with Jesus suggests their essential unity. God is also described specifically as the *father* of Jesus (1:9). Where the OT might have spoken of the day of the Lord, referring to Yahweh (e.g., Joel 2:31; Isa 2:12; 13:6, 9; Amos 5:18; Zeph 1:17–18) and of God's appearing (cf. Mal 3:2), Paul pairs these two events by making Jesus the subject (1:7–8). God gives grace (χάρις in 1:3–4) so that the Corinthians lack no gift (χάρισμα in 1:7; the verb χαρίζομαι in 2:12); enriching all in speech and knowledge (1:5). He is faithful (1:9) and will sustain/establish (βεβαιόω) those who belong to Christ until his return (1:8). God's wisdom and power is greater than all (1:21, 25; 2:5, 7; 3:18–20) and he manifested it in Christ (1:24; 2:7–8), by choosing those despised by others (1:26–28; 2:6–8) to know wisdom, righteousness, sanctification and redemption from him through Christ (1:30; 2:9–16) and the message of his cross (1:18, 23; 2:2) so that people might only give credit to God (1:29, 31; 2:5). God reveals himself through his Spirit but only to the spiritual person (2:10–16).

God gives the growth in spiritual work; though he has servants who work with him (3:6–9), all the credit belongs to him (3:7) and Corinthian believers belong to him uniquely, described as God's field, God's building (3:9), God's temple (3:16). The foundation of God's work is Jesus Christ (3:11; reminiscent of earlier references that unite the two) and God is a God of judgment (implied by 3:13–15, 17 and stated in 4:4–5). All things belong to God and again the unique place of Christ is stressed (3:22–23). The Lord is the revealer of hearts who will bring everything into the light when he comes (4:5). Everything comes from God (4:7). God's reign comes with power (4:20) and he will be the judge, especially

---

Stoic philosopher, Seneca (who was his near contemporary), see Sevenster, *Paul*, and for a succinct comparison of the writings and worldview of Paul and Seneca, see J. B. Lightfoot's essay "St. Paul and Seneca" in Lightfoot, *Saint Paul's Epistle*, 270–333.

of those outside the church (5:13). God does not give his kingdom to the unrighteous but he has justified, washed and sanctified the Corinthians (6:9–11). The body belongs to the Lord, who does not intend it for πορνεία; he will raise up the Corinthians bodily by his power (6:13–14; cf. 6:19),[205] and he is to be glorified in the body (6:20).

It is God who gives gifts to individuals (χάρισμα in 7:7; cf. 1:7). God calls his people to peace (7:15) and assigns different circumstances to different people (7:17). God has bought his people with a price (7:22; cf. 6:20) and calls his people to be both freed persons in the Lord and slaves of Christ (7:22–23). Anyone who loves God is known by him (8:3). There is only one God and all other seeming-gods are not real (8:4–6). All things exist from God and for him, and through the agency of Jesus Christ (8:6), who, yet again is spoken of in intimate connection with God. Food itself and the eating of it is indifferent to God (8:8). Christ died for the "weak" believer as well as for the "strong" (8:11). Christ is intimately connected with his people, such that to sin against one of them is to sin against him (8:12). In fact, in Paul's retelling of the wilderness wanderings of the Israelites, Christ is viewed as the rock that sustained them (10:4) and the one who must not be put to the test (10:9);[206] both characteristics that would ordinarily be used of God. God is both the one who judges (by overthrowing those who engaged in both idolatry and in immorality; πορνεύω, in 10:5–8), and the one who is faithful to empower the believer to resist temptation (10:12–13). Everything belongs to God (10:26; 11:12b; cf. 3:22–23; 4:7; 8:6, noted earlier).

The head of man is Christ and the head of Christ is God, underlining Christ's intimate connection with God again, his supremacy over people and yet again placing God above Christ in the order of things (11:3; cf. 1:30; 3:22–23; 6:14; 8:6). It is possible to be liable for the body and blood of the Lord by taking the bread or cup of the Lord's supper in an unworthy manner (11:27; cf. 10:21–22). Paul's dire warning in 11:29–32 reminds again of the judgment of the Lord, though here his purpose to discipline (παιδεύω) is stressed (cf. 5:5). In 1 Cor 12:4–6 πνεῦμα, κύριος, and θεός are

---

205. I have already noted and argued for the view that the statement "God will destroy" the stomach/body (6:13b) was made by the Corinthians, not Paul.

206. The textual tradition is split between manuscripts that have Χριστόν and others that have κύριον or θεόν. However, Χριστόν appears to be the reading that best explains the others as it is "attested by the oldest Greek manuscript (p[46]) as well as by a wide diversity of early patristic and versional witnesses" and plausible reasons can be given for changing Χριστόν to one of the other readings (Metzger, *Textual Commentary*, 494; cf. also Comfort, *New Testament*, 506–7).

clearly placed in parallel when speaking of the different workings of the Spirit (12:7), and God is named as the source of these activities (12:6b). Just as the Corinthians are a temple of the Holy Spirit (3:16; 6:19), so too they are a body (of Christ) immersed in the Spirit (12:12-13, 27). God orders the body the way that it is and does not consider one part inferior to the others (12:18, 22, 24). Although 1 Cor 13 does not mention God, if love alone never comes to an end and is the greatest quality that there is (13:8, 13), Paul must be implying that God is a God of love.

In 1 Cor 14, we learn that God can be spoken to (14:2), that God is not a God of disorder (ἀκαταστασία) but of peace (14:33), and that he can cause the secrets of unbelievers' hearts to be exposed so that they confess that, "God is really among you" (14:25, which is obviously seen by Paul as an accurate statement). This is another indicator that the Corinthian believers have become the place where God's presence can be found.[207] In 1 Cor 15 Paul spells out a number of important points about God that have already been stated or implied earlier in the epistle. Christ died for their sins (15:3; implied by 1:13b, 17-18, 23, 30; 2:2, 8; 5:7b; 8:11; 10:16; 11:23-25), he was raised (15:4, presumably a "divine passive," meaning "raised *by God*" as in 15:15b, cf. 6:14). Life comes through Christ (15:22), and at his coming all shall be made alive who belong to him (15:23), yet in another instance of his subordination to "God the Father" (15:24), at the end of Christ's reign, he will destroy all other powers and deliver the kingdom to God at the end (15:24-28) so that God "may be all in all" (cf. 3:23; 11:2). To each of his creatures, God gives the body as he has chosen (15:38) and to his people he gives the victory through their Lord Jesus Christ (15:57).

4.5.2 Paul's Understanding of Humanity in 1 Corinthians

Here we must distinguish between Paul's view of humanity in general and his view of the church in particular. As God's temple in Corinth, the Corinthians have many God-given privileges in Christ (regardless of the behavior of some of them, for which they are chastised frequently in the epistle). They are set apart in Christ (1:2) and called saints (1:2, 24, 26). They are the ones enriched in him in all speech and knowledge (1:5) and they are not lacking any gift as they await the revealing of Christ (1:7), having been called into the fellowship (κοινωνία) of *his* son, who

---

207. Marshall, "Church," 213.

is *their* Lord Jesus Christ (1:9). They are in (ἐν) Christ Jesus, who has become for them their wisdom from God, righteousness, sanctification and redemption (1:30). They have been enabled to understand the things of God because the Spirit interprets those things for them (2:6–16). Jesus Christ is the foundation of their identity (3:11); they are God's field, building (3:9 and temple (3:16–17). All things belong to them and they belong to Christ (3:21–22). People's hearts have hidden motivations that God will judge on the final day (4:4–5). The body is meant for the Lord (6:13) and the bodies of the Corinthians are members of Christ (6:15) and will be raised up at the last day (6:14).[208] The Corinthians belong to God and their bodies are a temple of the Holy Spirit (6:19–20). They have been bought (a redemption image) and belong to the Lord as a slave, while also being a "freedman" of his (6:19b–20; 7:22–23). The body of a husband belongs to his wife and vice versa (7:4); they are bound to one another (7:39), unless a believing partner chooses to separate (7:15) but otherwise the unbelieving members of the family are sanctified by the believing spouse (7:14). By contrast, to unite with a prostitute is to become one body with her (6:15–16). All things are created by God (8:4; 10:26) and exist from and for him and through Jesus Christ (8:6). A person's conscience can be defiled (8:7, 12) and they themselves can be destroyed by idolatrous actions (8:10–11). Christ is the head of every man and the head of woman is man (11:3). Man (as opposed to woman here) is the image and glory of God (11:7). Man and woman are not independent of one another in the Lord (11:11). Overall, Paul teaches that men and women have their place in the divine hierarchy and in relationship to one another (11:2–16). A person is nothing without love (1 Cor 13). The obverse of 15:18 (its implication) is that without Christ, people perish (cf. also 15:19: we are most to be pitied if only hope in Christ for this life).

In one of the richest sections of the letter for our understanding of humanity, we learn that death came through a man; Adam (15:21) and "in Adam," that is, by virtue of their share in his humanity (the man from the dust of earth: 15:47) and the consequences of his actions, all die (15:21–22a). Yet, death and all powers will finally be destroyed (15:20–24) and those who are in Christ will be raised (15:22, 42–55).

Paul paints a very different picture of humanity outside of Christ. They are the ones perishing (τοῖς ἀπολλυμένοις in 1:18), regardless of whether they are considered to be the wise, the discerning, the scribe or

---

208. Although Hooker, "Sanctuary," 349–50, argues that ἐξεγείρω refers to a present reality.

the scholar by the age in which they live (1:19–20). The human standards of the world (κατὰ σάρκα in 1:26) are disregarded by God, and its wisdom is coming to nothing (2:6). Instead, God brings to shame the wisdom and strength of the world, revealing its lack of value (1:26–28). Those of the world are unable to understand the things of God because they lack the Spirit (2:6–16). First Corinthians 5:9–10 implies that there are *at least some* (perhaps *many*) immoral people in world and those who are unrighteous will not inherit the kingdom of God (6:9–10). Paul implies that all need to be saved in 1 Cor 9:19–23. Some have no knowledge of God (15:34) and flesh and blood cannot inherit the kingdom of God (15:50).

4.5.3 Living as the Temple in 1 Corinthians

As so much of 1 Corinthians deals with practical instruction, I shall attempt to deal simply with the most pertinent instructions applicable beyond their immediate context, in summary form. The Corinthians are urged to act as a united body (1:10; cf. 1 Cor 12) and, by implication, to live according to the wisdom of God, the Spirit of God and the word of the cross (1:18—2:16). The language of the Corinthians as God's building in 3:9 imagines each person *still* building upon the foundation of Christ. Each of them is urged to take care when building upon this foundation (3:10–15), to be mindful of what they are (God's building, field, temple), that they may not destroy the temple (3:17) and grow into spiritual maturity (the obverse of 3:1–3). The Corinthians should not make judgments before the coming of the Lord (4:5; 11:32) but imitate Paul (4:16, in the light of Paul's example in 4:1–4, 10–13, 17; cf. 11:1). They should mourn over πορνεία (5:2; cf. the warnings over arrogance and boasting in 1:29; 3:21; 4:8–10, 18–19; 5:2). They are not to associate with the immoral who claim to be one of them (5:4–5), so that they are not polluted by them (5:6–8) but equally they are not to judge those outside the church and be willing to associate with them (5:9–13). They will judge the world (6:2) and so matters for judgment within the church should be settled there, rather than with judges outside the church (6:1–8). They are called to identify as righteous, and (implicitly) not to indulge in the practices enumerated in 6:9–10. They are to flee immorality (6:18) and recognize that their body belongs to God as his temple; thus they should glorify him there (6:13, 19–20).

Husbands and wives should honor one another in marriage (7:3–5) and both married and unmarried should remain in the state to which they have been assigned, if at all possible (7:8–14, 17–40). Ultimately, they should keep the commandments of God (7:19). Love for God (8:3) and for the brother in Christ (implied by 8:7–13) ought to be the hallmark of the body. This love should build others up first and foremost (8:1; 10:23). This ought to involve putting the consciences of others first and doing nothing to put harm in anyone's way rather than the Corinthians claiming their "right/authority" to do something. First Corinthians 9 holds up the example of Paul as an apostle who chose not to make use of his rights for the sake of others and their salvation (cf. also 10:32–33). Therefore, they should not seek their own good but the good of others and their consciences (10:23–30). The Corinthians should run to obtain the prize of their calling by living a life of self-discipline characterized by the athlete (9:24–27). They should be careful not to participate in idolatry (10:7–22; cf. implied in 12:3) and immorality (8:7) and in this, do everything to the glory of God (10:31).

While we have already seen warnings against judging others, they are to make judgments for themselves, especially concerning themselves and their behavior (e.g., 11:13, 31–32). First Corinthians 12:1–31 constitutes an implicit call to unity. They should value members of the body equally, and recognize that all comes from God (12:4–6, 18, 24, 28–30). They are to seek the greater gifts (12:31), especially to prophesy (14:1), which is needed by the church (14:6). Overall, they must do everything for the building up of the church (14:3–5, 12, 17, 26). Everything should be done out of love (1 Cor 13; 14:1) and so they must be eager to excel in gifts that build up the church (14:12). Therefore, they must be mature; not infants in their thinking (14:20) and come to the assembly ready to share the gifts of God; especially the ones that communicate God's revelation to the congregation (14:26).[209] They should stand firm in the gospel by which they are saved and believe in the resurrection of Christ from the dead and the future resurrection (1 Cor 15). Their hope in Christ must

---

209. I leave aside the injunction of Paul toward women in 14:33b–36, partly because it is highly contested but also because I understand it to be highly specific to a particular situation, though authentically Pauline, with, e.g., Witherington, *Conflict*, 287–88; Dunn, *Theology*, 591–92; Thiselton, *First Epistle*, 1146–62; Collins, *First Corinthians*, 516; Garland, *1 Corinthians*, 666, 673; Keener, *1–2 Corinthians*; against, e.g., Conzelmann, *1 Corinthians*, 246; Lang, *Korinther*, 199; Hays, *First Corinthians*, 246–47; Schrage, *1 Korinther: 11,17—14,40*, 481–84; Fee, *First Epistle*, 780–89; Horrell, *Social Ethos*, 184–95; Murphy-O'Connor, *Keys to First Corinthians*, 265–68, 282–84.

not be just for this life (15:19). They should come to themselves and reject wrong teaching about the resurrection (the implication of 15:34) but always be steadfast in the work of the Lord (15:58). In the final chapter of the letter, Paul exhorts them to keep alert, stand firm in their faith, be courageous and strong (16:13) and to let all that they do be done in love (16:14; cf. 1 Cor 13).

4.6 THE CONTRAST BETWEEN PAUL'S UNDERSTANDING AND THE PHILOSOPHERS' UNDERSTANDING

4.6.1 Divinity

I have already noted some features that the Philosophers would share with Paul. The gods are merciful and forgiving (Seneca and Epictetus), pure and undefiled (Epictetus) and perfect in every way (Alcinous, Hierocles). God orders all things, governs the world with care and is referred to with names such as Father, King and Protector (Dio Chrysostom, Epictetus, Plutarch, Alcinous and Maximus of Tyre). He is friends with people and reveals himself to them (especially those who study philosophy). He is benevolent and gentle. There are notable differences too. Many writers identified God with the universe (such as Chrysippus, Marcus Aurelius and Seneca) or identify the universe as divine or infused with divinity (e.g., Plutarch). Writers like Seneca and Marcus Aurelius make little distinction between God, Nature, Reason, Fate and Providence and use these nouns interchangeably. Nature is sometimes given the role that Paul would attribute to God, such as governing and sustaining the world (in the case of the early Stoics, Marcus Aurelius and Cicero). At the same time, gods can seem dependent on a pre-existent law (Cicero and Dio), that governs the universe (Cicero). Plutarch speaks of God binding together the substance of the world and Alcinous holds that God endowed the pre-existent world with wisdom or intellect and bought order to the world soul. Marcus says that Intelligence or Universe or Reason is the source of all that is. For Maximus of Tyre, as for other writers, daemons are the bridge between God and people, since the gods dwell in the heavens and not upon the earth, and people are able to become daemons after death.

Paul's doctrine of God is quite unlike that of the philosophers' at important points. For instance, 1 Cor 8:4–6 stands in contrast to the philosophers' views of many gods. Paul says that all things (πάντα) exist *from* God and *for* him, *through* the agency of Jesus, but he does not say that all things exist *in* him (pantheism). Although philosophical writers will refer to πνεῦμα as what infuses the whole universe,[210] in 1 Corinthians it is those who belong exclusively to Christ who are the temple of the Holy Spirit in whom the Spirit dwells in a unique way and to whom the Spirit reveals the things of God.[211] The role of Christ in close proximity and equality to God (though subordinated to him in the ultimate eschatological plan) is unequalled in what I found in philosophy and there are no obvious analogues in the references I have surveyed.[212] The Corinthians have a distinct identity in relation to God that is different to others in the world by means of their relationship to Christ, described, among other images, as a building laid on his foundation or as his body. They belong to him in a way that others outside the church do not.

---

210. See, e.g., the sources cited in Lee, *Paul*, 49-54.

211. Stowers, "Pauline Christianity," 89-102, identifies seven closely connected areas in which Pauline Christianity resembles a Hellenistic philosophy, including an exclusive adherence to a teacher (such as Epicurus) or a set of doctrines/way of life (like Stoicism), that can almost be classed as a conversion and exclusive adherence to one community. Malherbe, "Conversion," 230-44, also compares some accounts of conversion to philosophy recorded in Lucian of Samosata, Dio Chrysostom, and Musonius Rufus with Paul's accounts of the conversion of Gentiles in his writings. However, my focus has been on ideas common to several traditions and I also note that, in practice, many followers of philosophy were eclectic (as Middle Platonism was itself), and not necessarily strictly attached to one philosophy (e.g., Cicero). Malherbe also notes that Paul's account in 1 Thess 1:9-10 stresses turning from idols to serve one God, which required a change in understanding of the divine and service to God, whereas a conversion to philosophy retained a belief in multiple gods and rarely involved a call to moral transformation that was linked to religion (239-40).

212. As I have already noted, some philosophers equate Fortune, Providence, Nature, etc. with God but this is different from the personal relationship and equality that the person of Jesus Christ enjoys with God. Dr. Fredrick J. Long has drawn my attention to Seneca, *Clem.* 1.5.1, that pictures the young ruler as the soul of the Roman state, which is his body. Since Roman emperors came to be seen as divine, it could be said that this is very similar to the divine filling the world (or at least the Roman world). Dr. Long has also pointed out to me that the emperor most represents/epitomizes the gods on earth, and so is something like a high priest figure in relation to the Roman empire. Since my focus has been on the various philosophies such as Stoicism and Middle Platonism, I am unable to explore this further here.

4.6.2 Humanity

Seneca describes humanity as good on the one hand but on the other he avers that all have sinned. The soul is pre-existent and grants humans a knowledge of divinity not possessed by the rest of creation (Seneca and Alcinous). Although all have immortal souls, only good (Cicero and Apollonius) or wise (Seneca) men are divine, or at least, like gods (Seneca). All humanity are God's children (Epictetus). Human beings are united to the divine by indwelling reason (Epictetus, Marcus and Maximus) that awakens the self-knowledge of the soul so that it can accurately perceive reality (Maximus) by making correct use of sense impressions (Epictetus and Marcus). Philosophers speak of ruling reason that directs them (found in many writers such as Marcus, Alcinous, Maximus and Cicero). Humans have the ability to make right moral choices (Epictetus, Marcus and Cicero) although they need God's help to overcome vice (Maximus). The soul is variously described as in exile or in prison while in the body but after death it is set free from its cage.[213] Different philosophers speculate as to its ultimate destiny; some say that it is made divine by the Gods after death (Cicero; Apollonius); others that it is set free from the body to become a daemon (Plutarch, Maximus); or to travel to the imperishable realm where God is king (Plutarch; Maximus). Some refer to rewards and punishments meted out to the soul after death (Plutarch; Maximus) and Neopythagoreanism taught the transmigration of souls (Apollonius).[214]

By contrast with the philosophers, Paul understands there to be two groups of humanity; those who are in Christ and those who are not. Those who are outside do not possess divinity or a knowledge of the divine that is salvific. The wisdom of the age is to be rejected rather than studied and lived out (as it is in the philosophers). Only those who are part of the temple of the Holy Spirit receive this revelation and knowledge. It is the Spirit, not reason, or the person's daemon, that unites them to God and the foundation of their lives is Jesus Christ, not reason.[215] Paul's

---

213. See also the discussion and references cited by Aune, "Human," 294–97, 305–9.

214. See recently Brookins, *Corinthian Wisdom*, 185–88, 192–96, who compares the body-soul dualism of the Stoics with Paul's teaching here on the resurrection.

215. In this Engberg-Pedersen, *Paul and the Stoics*, 35, is right to say that a commitment to philosophy for the Stoics meant a change in the individual's perception of their identity, that now revolved around reason. Engberg-Pedersen sees an equivalent in Paul, in that, in the place of reason for the Stoic stands "God and Christ" (35) for the Christian. In this he is partly right, except that the Spirit takes the place of reason

focus is very much on the sanctified community, not on the individual and rather than seeking release from the body, that is despised, Christian life is embodied at its very heart and this is confirmed by humanity's final destiny: the resurrection of the body.

4.6.3 Living Out the Philosophy

The goal of Stoic thinkers is to live in accordance with nature (e.g., Zeno, Seneca, Epictetus, Marcus) while that of the Platonists is to know and imitate God (e.g., Plutarch, Maximus), and thus to please Him (Epictetus), though many Stoics also urge their hearers to imitate the example of the gods (Seneca, Epictetus and Alcinous). This means indifference to what nature is indifferent to, which includes the body (Marcus). So, people are urged to resist bodily inclinations (Marcus), have as little to do with the body as possible (Plutarch) and distance themselves from worldly concerns and sensations that would attach to them from the body (Alcinous, Seneca). A person who does these things will enjoy a speedy journey to the gods (Seneca). The goal of life should be virtue (Zeno and Seneca), which is the only thing of value. Devotion to one's own intelligence/genius leads to a life of virtue (Marcus and Apollonius) but a moral education is needed (Maximus), enabling a person to know right principles (Cicero). This will be attained through training in philosophy (Alcinous), that can fan into flame the spark in human nature (Maximus). It is assumed that all humanity possesses this reason.[216] The true philosopher should be ruled by Reason and God (Epictetus, Marcus and Dio) and devoted to the mind (Epictetus) and thus reject the passions (Plutarch). In order to do this, they should honor the one within (Epictetus and Apollonius), keeping pure their inner daemon (Marcus, Apollonius),

---

in communicating God's presence to his people. Yet I would question whether this also transformed the Stoic's self-awareness from "I" to "we" to the same degree as the Pauline communities, who Paul is teaching to see themselves *corporately* as the temple of God. I would not agree with Engberg-Pedersen's claim that Paul looked to Stoic ethics for his model. I concur with Wright, *Paul and the Faithfulness*, 1395–97, that Paul was certainly not "converted" from a self-centered individualistic lifestyle to one opened up to others (*contra* Engberg-Pedersen), in that "his whole pre-conversion identity was ... *corporate*" (1396) and that by comparison the Stoics were nothing like as community orientated as the Pauline churches, a fact that even Engberg-Pedersen himself admits (Wright, *Paul and the Faithfulness*, 1396–97, citing Engberg-Pedersen, *Paul and the Stoics*, 78).

216. See further Lee, *Paul*, 60–83.

purifying their judgments and their outer life (Epictetus), that leads to virtue. The contemplation of God/things on high (Seneca and Alcinous) leads to freedom from disturbance (Seneca and Epictetus) and fear, and freedom from the wrong impulses (Marcus), making a person a friend of God (Epictetus and Marcus) so that they can achieve a kind of likeness to the divine (e.g., Alcinous) or contemplation of God (Maximus and Cicero). Those who seek to be loved by Gods are called sons of God and live self-controlled lives (Dio). The Stoic should will everything to be as it should (Epictetus, Seneca and Marcus). The true student of philosophy should not compare themselves with others but run for the goal while at the same time, seeking the common interest, through avoiding evil and dealing rightly with their neighbor (Marcus). Marcus sees each person as a limb of an organized body of rational things.

Paul, like the philosophers, urges a love for the neighbor, a rejection of evil speaking and thinking, self-control and virtue. However, Paul's foundation is not Reason or the guidance of a daemon, but the empowering of the Holy Spirit, with Jesus Christ and the wisdom of his cross as the foundation. Although Marcus does once use the language of a body, the body consists of all rational things, whereas for Paul the body is limited to the Christian community, joined to Christ. Whereas both Stoics and Platonists treat the body with indifference or disdain and seek to distance themselves from it, Paul urges an active confrontation with sexual immorality and devotes much of his letter to matters involving the physical body, especially in sexual relationships (e.g., 1 Cor 5:1–13; 6:9–20; 7:1–40). He devotes his longest chapter to a celebration of the embodied life of the resurrection in stark contrast to the philosophers' anticipation of a bodiless life. While philosophers seek contemplation of the gods, Paul urges to readers to shun idolatry (10:14).

4.7 CONCLUSIONS

I have observed a number of contrasts between the philosophers' use of figurative temple language, and its implications for their worldview and practice, and the emphases found in 1 Corinthians. In philosophy, the *pneuma* is typically that which infuses the whole universe and within it, each individual, regardless of their beliefs. Reason is the divine guide that enables the life of virtue to be led and it dwells in each individual, although it needs to be cultivated. Wisdom is to be sought from philosophy wherever it is found. The body is spoken of either disparagingly or with indifference and the goal of each individual is to pay the body as little attention as possible in the present life and to escape it in the next. Within philosophy the existence of many gods is accepted and tolerated.

The main features of Paul's figurative temple references in 1 Corinthians also find corresponding emphasis in the letter as a whole and stand in contrast to my findings from Hellenistic philosophy. The temple is corporate, in contrast to the largely individual referents for figurative temple language in the philosophers. It is holy and distinct from the world around it. The temple is sacred and must not be destroyed or defiled. It is constituted by the Spirit, and the Spirit that dwells within it is the Holy Spirit. The Spirit dwells only in those who are this temple, whose foundation is Jesus Christ. The Spirit empowers the life that glorifies God in the body. The wisdom and spirit of the world are foolishness; the true wisdom is found in Christ and his cross. God is distinct from his body and there are clear roles and distinct relationships between God, Jesus Christ and the Holy Spirit. There is only one God; other so-called gods are not real and to worship them is to fall into idolatry and be led astray by (evil) demons. The physical body of all those who constitute the believers at Corinth is a temple. In the letter as a whole I also observed a strong emphasis on the exclusive, bounded nature of the community. Paul frequently stresses the holiness of the body and the importance of keeping it free from defilement, whether that be from immorality or idolatry. Paul uses body language in a number of places, both to describe the nature of the community as it exists now and to contend for the physical nature of believers' existence beyond death.

5

Figurative Temple Language in 2 Corinthians

5.1 INTRODUCTION

To A GREATER EXTENT than any other Pauline epistle, 2 Corinthians has often been treated as a collection of letters rather than a single letter.[1] Although there is no consensus on the topic, perhaps the most commonly recognized division is between 2 Cor 1–9 and 2 Cor 10–13. The largest single grouping of modern commentators recognizes the chapters as having been written in that sequence. Some propose that 2 Cor 10–13 was a separate letter, sent by Paul shortly after the letter now recognized as 2 Cor 1–9.[2] A smaller but growing group of scholars detect a rhetorical and thematic unity to the whole epistle[3] (with some positing a small

---

1. For comprehensive summaries of the scholarly debate and the various advocates of partition theories, see, e.g., Thrall, *2 Corinthians 1–7*, 3–49; Harris, *Second Epistle*, 8–51.

2. E.g., Furnish, *II Corinthians*, 35–41, following the earlier commentaries of Windisch, Bruce, and Barrett, and see recently Oropeza, *Exploring*, 2–15, who brings the discussion up to date.

3. Examples include: Price, "Aspects," 95–106; Young and Ford, *Meaning*, 27–36; Witherington, *Conflict*, 328–39; Barnett, *Second Epistle*, 17–25; Lambrecht, Second Corinthians, 7–9; Hall, *Unity*, 86–112; Long, *Ancient Rhetoric*, 1–14; Keener, *1–2 Corinthians*, 146–51; Harris, *Second Epistle*, 8–51; Seifrid, *Second Letter*, xxix–xxxi; Guthrie, *2 Corinthians*, 23–32.

pause between Paul's writing of 2 Cor 1–9 and 2 Cor 10–13).[4] Since the majority of scholars treat 2 Cor 2:14–7:4 as a discrete unit,[5] and because of constraints of space, unlike the previous chapter, I shall largely confine my remarks to the relationship of 2 Cor 6:14—7:1 to its context in 2 Cor 2:14–7:14 rather than treating the whole canonical epistle. Although I incline to the view that 2 Corinthians is a single letter, my focus on 2 Cor 2:14–7:4 means that a different hypothesis would have little impact on my conclusions. As with the previous chapter, I shall examine Paul's use of explicit temple language in the epistle and then compare it to my earlier findings from Hellenistic philosophy. I shall also seek to demonstrate the way that some of the themes present in 2 Cor 6:14—7:1 are emphasized elsewhere in the Corinthian correspondence and consider how they would have spoken to a reader influenced by philosophy. Finally, I shall also briefly address Paul's theology of God, humanity and Christian living in this section, as it relates to the themes I have discussed.

5.1.1 The Contested Place of 2 Corinthians 6:14—7:1

The place of 2 Corinthians 6:14—7:1 in 2 Corinthians has been such a battleground for interpreters that its relation to Paul and the epistle must be addressed before I can continue. Whilst there is no evidence that the text was ever omitted from manuscripts of 2 Corinthians nor placed anywhere other than its current position,[6] the interpretation of 6:14—7:1 has been dominated by the question of its origins and its placement within the epistle. It is frequently argued that the pericope is an interpolation and therefore Paul is not its author.[7] The effect of this discussion has been

---

4. E.g., Martin, *2 Corinthians*, 68–69.

5. E.g., Thrall, *2 Corinthians 1–7*, xiii; Barnett, *Second Epistle*, 51; Lambrecht, *Second Corinthians*, v; Amador, "Revisiting," 110; Harris, *Second Epistle*, x; Guthrie, *2 Corinthians*, 50, and many specialist studies.

6. See Harris, *Second Epistle*, 22–25; and noted earlier by Plummer, *Critical and Exegetical*, 205; Hughes, *Second Epistle*, 244.

7. In fact, so confident of this was Bultmann, that his commentary contains the sub-heading "6:14—7:1 is an interpolation" and the passage is not discussed. Later he classes the passage as "an insertion" and six sentences are devoted to speculation concerning its origins, but nothing on exegesis; see Bultmann, *Second Letter*, 175, 180. Important works that have argued for this position from a variety of standpoints include, Fitzmyer, "Qumran," 271–80; Gnilka, "2 Cor 6," 48–68; Betz, "2 Cor 6:16—7:1," 88–108; Dahl, "Fragment," 62–69; Duff, "Mind," 160–80; Duff, "2 Corinthians 1–7," 16–21; Walker, "Burden of Proof," 610–18; Walker, "2 Cor 6.14—7.1," 142–44; Heil,

a tendency to neglect the place and theology of the passage within the Corinthian correspondence. It may say something about the lack of attention that the passage has received "in its own right" that while numerous articles have been devoted to the passage, most of them focus on the controversy over its origins and context. Few full-length monographs have been published that deal with the passage's subject matter in the context of 2 Corinthians. It may also say something about the comparative neglect of the passage that the bibliography of William J Webb's 1993 book length study of 2 Cor 6:14—7:1, *Returning Home*, cites no other monographs prior to his that concentrate on the pericope.[8] In the intervening years, there has been only one other published monograph (that of J. Ayodeji Adewuya, published in 2003) and none since.[9]

Since the rise of the historical-critical method in the late eighteenth and early nineteenth centuries, scholars began to contend for the fragmentary nature of 2 Corinthians. In time this led to the proposal that our passage is, at best, dislocated from its original position elsewhere within either 1 or 2 Corinthians, or at worst, a non-Pauline interpolation.[10] The discoveries at Qumran that were made available during the 1950s prompted scholars such as Joseph Fitzmyer and Joachim Gnilka to note numerous parallels between the pericope and the Qumran literature, leading to suggestions of some kind of influence.[11] Between the late 1960s to the early 1980s Margaret Thrall, Gordon Fee and Jan Lambrecht each offered a different theory arguing for the passage's integration within 2

"Absonderung," 717–29, and Hultgren, "2 Cor 6.14—7.1," 39–56, as well as Lang, *Korinther*, 310–11; Klauck, 2. *Korintherbrief*; Leppä, "Believers," 374–90.

8. Webb, *Returning*.

9. Adewuya, *Holiness*.

10. See the helpful survey of Webb, *Returning*, 18–21.

11. Webb, *Returning*, 21–22, and see Gnilka, "2 Cor 6:14," 48–68; and Fitzmyer, "Qumran," 271–80. See also Gärtner, *Temple*, 49–55; Daly, *Christian Sacrifice*, 256–61; Klauck, "Kultische Symbolsprache," 109, for the same kind of argument. Other specialist studies have questioned the idea of direct dependence, e.g., McKelvey, *New Temple*, 96–97; Schüssler Fiorenza, "Cultic Language," 171–72; Newton, *Concept of Purity*, 110–12; and more recently, Son, *Corporate Elements*, 142–44 (following Benoit, "Qumran," 2); Murphy-O'Connor, *Keys to Second Corinthians*, 121–39 (who notes that Paul's language is simply at home within the thought-world of Hellenistic Judaism; e.g., parallels found with the Testament of the Twelve Patriarchs and Philo are even closer than those of Qumran); Tomson, "Christ," 79–131; Brooke, "2 Corinthians 6:14—7:1," 12–16, notes parallels in the thought world and language of Jewish literature in the Graeco-Roman world generally.

Corinthians.[12] Webb claims that the decade prior to the publication of his own research saw a consensual mediating position emerge from the leading commentators of that period, such as Victor Furnish and Ralph Martin. They posit that Paul has taken over a fragment, which has been influenced in some way by Qumran thought.[13] Webb himself sees the passage as Pauline, and explained by, "conceptual threads which tie together the Old Testament traditions."[14]

Recent work by Murray J. Harris and Adewuya has helpfully summarized the various reasons the pericope is often considered un-Pauline (including the claim that 6:14—7:1 disrupts the flow of thought from 6:13 to 7:2 suggested by the verbal links either side of the passage, un-Pauline language, parallels with Qumran literature, an un-Pauline exclusivism, and an abundance of *hapax legomena*) and the proposals made to answer these objections.[15] Margaret Thrall identifies verbal and conceptual links between this pericope and other sections of the letter, notably 2 Cor 4:3-6; 5:11, 18-21.[16] Gordon Fee argues that Paul's "rhetorical flourishes" elsewhere (including in the Corinthian correspondence) tend to include a high proportion of *hapax legomena* (e.g., 1 Cor 4:7-13),[17] and that on closer examination, most of them come from the OT citation, while other terms are related to verbs found elsewhere in the Pauline corpus or are paralleled by Paul's preference for similar $συ\gamma(μ)$ compounds in his letters.[18]

---

12. Webb, *Returning*, 23-26; Thrall, "Problem," 132-48; Fee, "II Corinthians," 140-61; Lambrecht, "Fragment," 531-549.

13. Furnish, *II Corinthians*, 375-83; Martin, *2 Corinthians*, 46-47, 356-60, following, though modifying, Rensberger, "Examination," 25-49. Klinzing, *Umdeutung*, 179-82 earlier posited that Paul used a source, perhaps found in a Qumran baptismal exhortation; see, similarly, Klauck, *2. Korintherbrief*, 60-61 and Wolff, *Korinther*, 146-50.

14. Webb, *Returning*, 28, and see 26-28 generally. Webb also cites Beale, "Old Testament," 550-81, who came to a similar conclusion independently and using different methodology.

15. For a comprehensive survey, see Harris, *Second Epistle*, 15-21, and the summary in Adewuya, *Holiness*, 16-17 and more generally, 13-43.

16. Thrall, "Problem," 132-48 at 144-45.

17. Fee, "II Corinthians," 140-61 at 144.

18. Ibid., 140-61 at 145-47. See the earlier comments of Plummer, *Critical and Exegetical*, 204 on the abundance of uncommon vocabulary in three other Pauline epistles, although two of them are from the disputed Paulines (Ephesians and Colossians).

Adewuya summarized the discussion up to 2003 in his "Current State of Research."[19] In addition to the summaries of Harris and Webb, he notes that the claim by Betz that this is an "Anti-Pauline fragment,"[20] has been rebutted in recent studies and has not gained a following.[21] While there is nothing approaching a consensus, many recent studies and the most significant of recent exegetical commentaries have broadly defended the placement of the pericope in its context in 2 Corinthians by Paul and in most cases, Pauline authorship.[22] In particular, the resurgence of rhetorical-critical approaches has provided credible alternatives to interpolation theories to explain the place of 6:14—7:1 within the epistle.[23]

19. Adewuya, *Holiness*, the name of his second chapter, 13–43.

20. Betz, "Fragment," 88–108.

21. See Adewuya, *Holiness*, 17–18, for examples.

22. Adewuya, *Holiness*, 25–29 and similarly Harris, *Second Epistle*, 15, 21–25, as well as commentaries such as Thrall, *2 Corinthians 1–7*, 25–36; Furnish, *II Corinthians*, 375–83; Lane, "Covenant," 22–25; Bieringer, "2 Korinther 6,14–7," 551–70; Barnett, *Second Epistle*, 15–24; Matera, *II Corinthians*, 29–32; Seifrid, *Second Letter*, 287–89; Martin, *2 Corinthians*, 46–47, 355–60; Guthrie, *2 Corinthians*, 26–27, 346–47. Martin, *2 Corinthians*, 46, rightly states the conundrum for the advocates of interpolation, "It is equally as difficult to understand why the compiler placed the text amidst an apparently irrelevant exhortation as it is to explain why Paul digressed on an ethical homily" (see, similarly, Webb, *Returning*, 162–63). Now see also, e.g., Beale, "Old Testament," 566–75; Scott, *Adoption*, 215–20, and more fully 88–96; deSilva, "Recasting," 3–16 (adapted in deSilva, *Credentials*, 14–29); Amador, "Revisiting," 92–111; Hogeterp, *Paul and God's Temple*, 365–73; Wardle, *Jerusalem Temple*, 212; Gupta, *Worship*, 96; Starling, *Not My People*, 61–101; Aernie, *Paul*, 221–22; Starling, "ἄπιστοι," 45–50; Liu, *Temple Purity*, 196–98; Han, *Swimming*, 107–10; and Nathan, "Fragmented Theology," 211–28, who exhaustively tabulates all known scholars on this issue up to 1994 on 214–15, and provides a synopsis of each scholarly source from 1994 to 2006 (216–22). In *Second Corinthians* (Bieringer et al), many, though not all of the articles, find the concept of one integrated letter the best working hypothesis for their respective studies. The earlier commentaries of Philip E. Hughes, C. K. Barrett, and F. F. Bruce also argued for Pauline authorship and against the interpolation hypothesis. More recently Oropeza, *Exploring*, 424–26, suggests that Paul or his secretary inserted this earlier Pauline piece into a later draft of the letter, consciously disrupting the earlier symmetry/chiasm of 6:11–13 and 7:2–3, which had originally followed in sequence (agreeing on this point with Walker, "2 Cor 6.14—7.1," 142–144).

23. A number of scholars speak of the paragraph as a digression (*egressio*), such as Thrall, "Problem," 132–48 at 144; Danker, *II Corinthians*, 18; Witherington, *Conflict*, 402–6; Amador, "Revisiting," 100–105; Murphy-O'Connor, *Keys to Second Corinthians*, 116–20; others prefer to speak of a climactic argument in relation to a section beginning at 2:1 (e.g., Long, *Ancient Rhetoric*, 169–72). Rhetorical approaches are also highlighted in favor of the unity of the epistle by Young and Ford, *Meaning*, 36–44; Barnett, *Second Epistle*, 17–19; deSilva, *Credentials*, 8–14, 36–43, following on from

The usefulness of these recent studies is that, having made this claim, they are able to consider the reason for Paul's exhortations and promises in their literary context. In an important article, Gordon Fee noted the points of contact between the present passage and 1 Cor 8:1–11:1 and proposed that here Paul is reinforcing his prohibition against participation in temple gatherings and idolatry in general.[24] David DeSilva's exploration of the literary context of 2 Corinthians led him to a different conclusion, arguing that Paul is warning the Corinthians to disassociate from the false preachers/apostles of 2 Cor 2:17 and 5:12 (noting a parallel with Gal 1:6–9 and previous disassociation language in 1 Cor 5:1–13, meaning that 2 Cor 6:14—7:1 need not be a "non-Pauline" oddity).[25] Adewuya's own thesis is that Paul's argument seeks to emphasize communal holiness in the light of the Levitical "holiness code," reflecting God's own holiness, the relationship between God and his people (of which his relationship with Israel was supposed to be the paradigm) and the call to be distinct and separate, found elsewhere in the Corinthian correspondence (e.g., 1 Cor 3:16; 5:1–13; 6:1–20).[26]

5.2 2 CORINTHIANS 6:14—7:1

5.2.1 2 Corinthians 6:14—7:1: Main Features

For the purposes of my topic I note the following features of 6:14—7:1 that might have struck an audience influenced by philosophy. The passage begins emphatically with a prohibition. A present tense imperative (γίνεσθε) carrying general application, but applicable specifically to the problem of idolatry (cf. 1 Cor 8:1–11:1), is combined with a participle

---

deSilva, "Meeting," 5–22 (on the rhetorical unity of 2 Cor 1–7); Thompson, "Paul's Argument," 127–45.

24. Fee, "II Corinthians," 140–61 at 143–44, 148–61; Witherington, *Conflict*, 402–6, agrees with Fee, speaking of the "entangling alliances," including with unbelievers in pagan temples and sees 6:16 as a reference to "spiritual profligacy in the form of attendance at idol feasts in pagan temples" (406). Barnett, *Second Epistle*, 347 identifies unbelievers as unconverted Gentiles "in their characteristic cultic life that involved both idolatry and temple prostitution." Hogeterp, *Paul and God's Temple*, 376–77, also comments, "We should rather understand 2 Cor 6:14—7:1 as serving a more comprehensive purpose of condemning all aspects in relationships with unbelievers which could cause an unbalanced situation by tending to the pagan, idolatrous side."

25. deSilva, "Recasting," 3–16.

26. See the "Summary and Conclusions" in Adewuya, *Holiness*, 193–200.

in a periphrastic construction.²⁷ According to Fredrick J. Long, the use of γίνομαι rather than εἰμί makes the construction more marked and therefore more prominent.²⁸ The use of the periphrastic participle (from ἑτεροζυγέω) draws attention to the verbal action.²⁹ The command warns against being unevenly yoked or mismatched³⁰ with ἄπιστοι. The question of how this is to be understood is answered, to a certain extent, by the conjunction γάρ, which provides the explanatory grounds for what precedes,³¹ with the questions that follow substantiating the implied grounds of the command (i.e. that being yoked, rightly understood, with the ἄπιστοι, is impossible for Paul›s audience). The theme is developed in terms of a strong dualism; such that a partnership between the two groups is ruled out.³² Paul piles up terms for partnership in this section, using *hapax legomena* such as μετοχή (14a), συμφώνησις (15a) and συγκατάθεσις (16a) as well as κοινωνία (14c) and μερίς³³ (15b). People are divided into two groups: unbelievers (presuming an implied group of believers),³⁴ lawless(ness) and righteousness, darkness and light, Christ and Βελιάρ. Paul then returns to the opening theme with πιστός and ἄπιστος used substantively to speak of a believer and an unbeliever (15b), before concluding with the contrast between ναός and εἴδωλα (16α).

It is notable that unbelievers and believers (assuming that the group being addressed in 6:14 are taken to be believers) appear twice; at the start of the series of rhetorical questions and before the concluding question.

27. Long, *2 Corinthians*, 121.

28. Long, *2 Corinthians*, 121.

29. Long, *2 Corinthians*, 21, introducing this feature in relation to 2 Cor 1:9 and citing for support, Porter, *Idioms*, 46.

30. "ἑτεροζυγέω," BDAG, 399.

31. Stephen Levinsohn explains that this feature "constrains the reader to interpret the material it introduces as strengthening an assertion or assumption that has been presented in or implied by the immediate context" (Levinsohn, *Discourse*, 69, cited in relation to 2 Cor 1:8 by Long, *2 Corinthians*, 18).

32. This is not as un-Pauline as is sometimes claimed, as Barrett, *Second Epistle*, 197, exposes the claim by comparing this pericope to Rom 6:19, which contains the same contrast between ἀνομία and δικαιοσύνη as found in 2 Cor 6:14. Thrall, *2 Corinthians 1–7*, 474, notes the contrast between believers as υἱοὶ φωτός and σκότος in 1 Thess 5:5, to which we could also add passages such as Rom 13:12 and Eph 5:8, if Pauline; similarly see, e.g., Adewuya, "People," 210.

33. Although μερίς might appear to be an exception, the sense here is what one party shares with another (see "μερίς," BDAG, 632.2).

34. I shall return below to the question of the referent of ἄπιστος in 2 Cor 6:14–15.

This suggests that Paul's contrasts between images like light and darkness, or concepts like righteousness and lawlessness come down to a contrast between those who believe and those who do not believe. But who or what is the object of their faith? As Long points out, it is probably not accidental that Χριστός and Βελιάρ are placed at the center of the five rhetorical questions beginning with τίς.[35] This observation would suggest that Christ is the one in whom the first group believe, distinguishing them from those who do not believe in him. Βελιάρ is clearly conceived as a being in direct opposition to Christ, just as Βελιάρ, or the variant Βελιάλ, appears as an adversary opposed to God in second temple Jewish literature, especially in the Dead Sea Scrolls.[36] This would suggest that those characterized as aligned with Βελιάρ are more than simply "faithless." The term ἄπιστος appears frequently with a substantive sense in the Corinthian correspondence (cf. 1 Cor 6:6; 7:12, 13, 14, 15; 10:27; 14:22, 23, 24; 2 Cor 4:4; 6:14, 15) and clearly carries the meaning "unbeliever" or "unbelieving" in each of these instances. In its only other use in this letter, the ἄπιστοι are the ones whose eyes ὁ θεὸς τοῦ αἰῶνος τούτου has blinded so that they cannot see the gospel of the glory of Christ (2 Cor 4:4); in other words, they are precisely those who do not believe in Christ; they are non-Christians or "pagans."[37] Therefore, the first thing that might

---

35. Long, *2 Corinthians*, 126.

36. See the summaries in "Βελιάρ," BDAG, 173; Foerster, "Βελιάρ," 1:607; and commentaries including Windisch, *Korintherbrief*, 215; Furnish, *II Corinthians*, 362, 373; Lang, *Korinther*, 309; Wolff, *Korinther*, 150; Thrall, *2 Corinthians 1–7*, 474; Barnett, *Second Epistle*, 347–48; Grässer, *Korinther*, 260; Harris, *Second Epistle*, 503. More recently, Long, "Roman," 138, understands Paul's language for demonic beings here as "the demonization of Rome as 'the dominion of Satan' that arises out of concurrent Jewish apocalyptic thought" (see also Long, *2 Corinthians*, 122; Long, "God," 219–69). In this he is followed and expanded by Tucker, "Reconsidering," 169–85, who argues that Βελιάρ in 2 Cor 6:15 is "a reference to Nero as the representative of the power of Satan in opposition to Christ" (Tucker, "Reconsidering," 171), noting also how Paul can speak of human representatives of Satan in 2 Cor 1:14–15; 12:7 (Tucker, "Reconsidering," 185 n. 66). I would observe the close connection between 2 Cor 6:14–15 and *T. Levi* 19:1, that offers a choice between σκότος and φῶς, ἢ ἔργα Βελιάρ or ἢ νόμον κυρίου (cf. the reference to ἀνομία as the opposite of δικαιοσύνη in 2 Cor 6:14; cf. *T. Naph.* 2:6, that depicts the same contrast). *T. Zeb.* 9:8 provides a tantalizing glimpse of the redemption of humanity from the spirit of Beliar and the consequent appearance of God in human form in the temple. This would provide a neat backdrop for Paul's words in 2 Cor 6:15–16 but the OTP translation signifies that ἐν σχήματι ἀνθρώπου is a restoration of the text and "ἐν ναῷ" is not translated, as it may not be original. The possibility of Christian interpolation in *T. Zeb.* 9:8 also remains.

37. See the thorough survey of Webb, *Returning*, 184–99, who comes to the same

strike our audience is that the ναός signifies those who believe in Christ. Those who do not believe are not the temple. Secondly, the ναός is at the heart of the passage and appears twice (16a and 16b). This ναός is specifically contrasted with εἴδωλα. Idolatry is therefore central to this passage (see further below).[38]

Therefore, to add to what has been said concerning the figurative temple language in 1 Cor 3:16 and 6:19, this temple is contrasted with idolatry; and here the idols are *plural* but the temple is *singular*. Unlike 1 Cor 3:16 and 6:19 that use the *second-person plural*, Paul's address in 2 Cor 6:16 adopts the *first-person plural*, according to the UBS⁵/NA²⁸ text. Both of these claims need to be addressed in light of two significant variants that appear in the manuscripts of 2 Cor 6:16. There is a variant that substitutes ναόι for ναός in only a handful of witnesses. As well as the weak external evidence, this variant does not agree with Paul's singular use in 1 Corinthians,[39] and is probably a correction to bring the noun into line with the plural pronoun and verb.[40] A more important issue is whether to read ἡμεῖς (UBS⁵/NA²⁸) or ὑμεῖς. The variant has reasonable external support from p⁴⁶ ²א C D² F G and Tertullian. The text reading is supported by B D* L and more miniscules than the variant. Although the evidence is fairly evenly split if we only count the *quantity* of manuscripts, ἡμεῖς has stronger support from a wide range of both Alexandrian and Western witnesses,[41] and, on balance, it is more likely that a later scribe made the change to conform the reading to 1 Cor 3:16, as well as guided by the context of verses 14 and 17 (if the alteration was intentional).[42] Assuming the correctness of this text critical decision, Paul's language is inclusive; he includes himself and others in the "*we*" rather than referring to *them* only, as he does in the other figurative temple references. This

---

conclusion.

38. As recognized by, among others, Fee, "II Corinthians," 140–61; Webb, *Returning*, 193–94, 202–4, 209–11, 213–15; Thrall, *2 Corinthians 1–7*, 475–76; Barnett, *Second Epistle*, 341, 347–48, 351, 356; Matera, *II Corinthians*, 162; Harris, *Second Epistle*, 500–501, 504–5, 508.

39. It is rejected by Metzger, *Textual Commentary*, 512; Comfort, *New Testament*, 543, as well as the commentators.

40. Guthrie, *2 Corinthians*, 36; Metzger, *Textual Commentary*, 512.

41. Metzger, *Textual Commentary*, 512.

42. Metzger, *Textual Commentary*, 512; although Comfort, *New Testament*, 543, is more ambivalent, averring that a scribe could have changed the reading to the first-person plural under the influence of 2 Cor 5:1–7. The UBS⁴ upgraded its confidence rating from a C to B (Long, *2 Corinthians*, 122).

same inclusiveness is also emphasized in the quotation καὶ ὑμεῖς ἔσεσθέ μοι εἰς υἱοὺς καὶ θυγατέρας (6:18) by the addition of θυγατέραι to the text alluded to in 2 Sam 7:14.[43] Unlike 1 Cor 3:16 and 6:19, there is no reference to the Holy Spirit; rather God is described as ὁ θεός ζῶν (6:16). Paul elsewhere in 1 Corinthians cites or alludes to the LXX freely, suggesting that, despite his audience being majority Gentile, he assumes that they would recognize these allusions.[44] The phrase "living God" frequently appears in polemical contexts in the LXX, emphasizing the contrast with dead idols and the gods of the other nations,[45] and in this passage it appears in contrast to εἴδωλα (16a). In addition, the reference to them as the temple of the God who is *living* is a reminder of his living presence within them, which in light of the two previous temple references, could indicate that the Spirit dwells within. Three crucial references to "God says/said" underscore the divine authority of this teaching (6:16b, 17a, 18b) and the third, climactic reference, is emphasized by the use of παντοκράτωρ ("Almighty"), again stressing his pre-eminence and superiority over other Gods, as well as recalling the frequent use of this term for God in the LXX as the all-powerful Lord.

The theme of God's presence among the Corinthians is also emphasized by the use of verbs for God dwelling (ἐνοικέω) and walking among them (ἐμπεριπατέω), conflating Lev 26:12 and Ezek 37:27 (16b). In addition to the inclusive first-person plural used in 6:16b, Paul also uses these OT texts to highlight the inclusive relationship that the Corinthians have with their God, καὶ ἔσομαι αὐτῶν θεὸς καὶ αὐτοὶ ἔσονταί μου λαός (6:16c) and then in 6:18 by applying the words of 2 Sam 7:8, 14, combined with the emphasis on θυγατέρας found in texts like Isa 43:6; 49:22 and 60:4, καὶ ἔσομαι ὑμῖν εἰς πατέρα καὶ ὑμεῖς ἔσεσθέ μοι εἰς υἱοὺς καὶ θυγατέρας (6:18), as well as affirming the welcome they will receive (citing Ezek 20:34), κἀγὼ εἰσδέξομαι ὑμᾶς (6:17d). They are treated as sons and daughters of the same father (addressed also as ἀγαπητοί in 7:1), and it is striking that these mainly Gentile former-pagans are addressed using the words reserved in the OT for the people of Israel.

---

43. The reference to θυγατέραι is probably taken from Isa 43:6 or Isa 49:22; 60:4, e.g., Beale, "Old Testament," 572; Harris, *Second Epistle*, 510; Thrall, *2 Corinthians 1-7*, 479.

44. Latterly, there has been fresh interest in allusions to the LXX in 2 Corinthians too. See, e.g., Aernie, *Paul* and Han, *Swimming*, especially 80–110.

45. E.g., Josh 3:10; 1 Sam 17:36; 2 Kgs 19:4, 16; Isa 37:4, 17; Dan 4:22; 5:23; *Jos. Asen.* 8:2, 5; 11:10; 19:8. For development of this theme, see Goodwin, *Paul*, 42–108.

These Gentile Christians are now God's people, so it is ironic and notable that Paul cites words from the OT (Isa 52:11) that once would have been used to urge separation from the nations surrounding Israel (using ἀφορίζω as well as the command to come out, ἐξέλθατε) and applies them to these Corinthians who *are* from the other nations (17), continuing the separation theme of 6:14–16a.[46] These words also take up the language of impurity with the command to touch no unclean thing (καὶ ἀκαθάρτου μὴ ἅπτεσθε).[47] The passage concludes with an exhortation. This hortatory subjunctive is in the first-person plural, like the temple reference of 16b, emphasizing the inclusive calling laid upon both Paul and the Corinthians. As 6:17c used impurity language, so 7:1 appropriates both purity and impurity language with its call *negatively* to cleanse themselves from every defilement of flesh and spirit (καθαρίσωμεν ἑαυτοὺς ἀπὸ παντὸς μολυσμοῦ σαρκὸς καὶ πνεύματος) and *positively* to perfect holiness (ἐπιτελοῦντες ἁγιωσύνην), which, like the implicit call to persuade others in 5:11, has as its motivation the fear of the Lord (ἐν φόβῳ θεοῦ). Although the noun used for the concept of defilement, μολυσμός is a *hapax legomenon*, the cognate verb μολύνω appears in the context of Paul's discussion of the dangers of idolatry in 1 Cor 8:7. The repetition of this defilement terminology used in 1 Corinthians has the effect of confirming the implicit context of idolatry that lies behind 2 Cor 6:14—7:1 (see below), even if the application of Paul's teaching is not limited by this context. Finally, Paul reassures his readers that the promises of 6:16–18 are certain (7:1), as he previously assured them that all God's promises are confirmed in Christ (1:20).[48]

---

46. Oropeza, *Exploring*, 443–4, 452, notes that Paul has "transfigured" (not abandoned) the Jewish idea of cultic purity, such that Gentiles are part of the new temple, and yet "Gentile" behavior is rejected.

47. Which, in its original context, contrasts with τὰ σκεύη κυρίου (Isa 52:11 LXX) so the opposition between priestly purity and idolatry is readily apparent, see Harris, *Second Epistle*, 508; Guthrie, *2 Corinthians*, 356.

48. For a more detailed exploration of the passage with a focus on holiness, see Adewuya, *Holiness*, 89–128.

5.2.2 Comparing 2 Corinthians 6:14—7:1 with Hellenistic Philosophy

Philosophy

If I consider some of these themes as they appear in Hellenistic philosophy,[49] the first comment to make is that, as we saw in the previous chapter, sometimes the emphasis is that the divine presence dwells in the whole world and thus in every individual. However, in other texts certain individuals are said to be those in whom God dwells in a way that, it is assumed, he does not in others, or at least not to the same extent. Since God fills all things in the universe,[50] which itself is the temple of the gods,[51] it logically follows that the divine dwells inside each individual.[52] Indeed, the essence of the human mind is divine,[53] so people are divine.[54] Elsewhere, there is a different emphasis, even within the same writers: the divine dwells especially in a wise[55] or good[56] person. Secondly, the philosophers, rather than speaking of "idols," assume the reality and validity of multiple gods, even if they do not necessarily argue for it. The gods are spoken of in the same language that the philosophers use for the God who pervades the universe, that is, similar qualities are attributed to them. For instance, the gods govern all things,[57] are merciful, forgiving

---

49. Two more recently published dissertations have engaged Hellenistic philosophy in relation to 2 Corinthians. Vegge, *2 Corinthians*, examines the use of Praise and Idealization for rhetorical purposes in the moral philosophers (especially at 54–70) and Nguyen, *Christian Identity*, addresses issues of social identity and social conflict with regard to 2 Corinthians, through the exploration of the idea of *persona* found in Epictetus and Valerius Maximus.

50. E.g., Marcus Aurelius, *Med.* 7.9; Alcinous, *Handbook*, 165.10.3.1–2 (18); Cicero, *Leg.* 2.11.26; Philo, *Leg.* 3.4; *Fug.* 75; *Post.* 6, 14, 30; *Conf.* 137–38; Seneca, *Ben.* 4.7.1; Plutarch, *Quaest. plat.* 2, 1002C; *Quaest. plat.* 8.

51. Cicero, *Leg.* 2.10.26; *Resp.* 6.15.15; Seneca, *Ben.* 7.7.3; *Ep.* 90.29; Plutarch, *Tranq. an.* 477C.

52. E.g., Cicero, *Leg.* 1.22.59; Seneca, *Ep.* 92.30; 110.2 (describing the views of the Stoics); Marcus Aurelius, *Med.* 5.10.2; and see this theme repeated throughout Epictetus, e.g., *Diatr.* 1.14.14; 2.8.11–17; even evildoers, see Marcus Aurelius, *Med.* 2.1.

53. Seneca, *Helv.* 6.8; Cicero, *Div.* 1.32.70; 1.49.110.

54. Plutarch, *Gen. Socr.* 593A; Cicero, *Leg.* 1.7.24.

55. Diog. Laert. 7.1.119; Seneca, *Ep.* 92.3; Philo, *Somn.* 2.248.

56. Seneca, *Ep.* 31:2; 41.2; 73.16; 120.14; Plutarch, *Virt. prof.* 86A; Cicero, *Leg.* 2.11.27; Philo, *Cher.* 98, 100.

57. Cicero, *Nat. d.* 2.29.73–2.30.77; Plutarch, *Adv. Col.* 1124F.; for God governing

and just,[58] send providential blessings upon all people,[59] and lend their aid to humanity,[60] although they look upon the upright with special favor.[61] The gods reveal themselves to people.[62] They are pure and holy.[63] I have already dealt with the theme of God's presence in the individual soul at some length in chapter 2, but I note that Philo uses one of the verbs found in 2 Cor 6:16 (ἐνοικέω) to speak of Wisdom as the tabernacle in which the wise man dwells.[64] In some places God is described as the father of all of humanity (as well as gods)[65] and so there is a special kinship between God and people.[66] As I noted in chapter 3, Philo also refers to Lev 26:12, the same passage that Paul appears to cite in 2 Cor 6:16. Philo makes the connection between God "walking" and purity, writing, "Now the God and governor of the universe does by himself and alone walk about invisibly and noiselessly in the minds (διάνοιαι) of those who are purified in the highest degree."[67] This act of walking fulfills Lev 26:12, which is described by Philo as a prophecy or oracle (θεοπρόπιον). In others, who are yet to fully cleanse themselves, angels or divine words walk. In these souls it is specified that their heavy bodies defile and stain them (κεκηλιδωμένην ἐν σώμασι βαρέσι),[68] and so "troups of evil tenants" must be driven out, in order for them to become a holy temple of God.[69] A

---

the universe, see, e.g., Epictetus, *Diatr.* 2.14.25–26; 2.16.33; Dio Chrysostom, *1 Regn.* 42, 56; *3 Regn.* 50; Marcus Aurelius, *Med.* 10.1. Plutarch, *Quaest. plat.* 2, 1002C; *Is. Os.* 381–82B; *Exil.* 601B; *Adv. Col.* 1124F; Maximus of Tyre, *Or.* 13.7.

58. Seneca, *Clem.* 1.7.1–2; *Ira* 2.27.1; Plutarch, *Def. orac.* 413F; for the same language used for God, see, e.g., Dio Chrysostom, *1 Regn.* 16, 39; *Dei cogn.* 22, 74, 75; *Borysth.* 32. Plutarch, *Is. Os.* 381B; *Def. orac.* 423D; *Superst.* 167F.

59. Cicero, *Nat. d.* 2.65.164–2.66.166; *Leg.* 2.7.15–16; Seneca, *Ben.* 4.25.1; 4.26.1–3; 4.28.1, 3; Marcus Aurelius, *Med.* 2.3; 9.27. The same language is used of a supreme deity in Epictetus, *Diatr.* 2.14.11; 3.13.7; 3.26.28; Dio Chrysostom, *2 Regn.* 26; *Hom.* 12.

60. Maximus of Tyre, *Or.* 2.1.

61. Seneca, *Prov.* 1.5.

62. Philostratus, *Vit. Apoll.* 1.1.1–3, 7; 2.5.3.

63. Epictetus, *Diatr.* 4.11.3.

64. Philo, *Leg.* 3.46.

65. Cleanthes, *Hymn to Zeus* (*SVF* 1.537), 1; Epictetus, *Diatr.* 1.3.1; 1.9.7.

66. Epictetus, *Diatr.* 1.9.1–7, 22–26; Cicero, *Leg.* 1.7.24; Philostratus, *Vit. Apoll.* 8.7.20.

67. Philo, *Somn.* 1.148 (Younge's translation). Lev 26:12 is also cited by Philo, *Somn.* 2.248 speaking of God dwelling in the soul of a wise man.

68. *Somn.* 1.148.

69. *Somn.* 1.149.

soul that is "perfectly purified" can be a house in which God can dwell.[70] Philo also pictures the tabernacle itself as the figurative representation of divine virtue and wisdom sent from heaven in order that people can be purified and washed from everything that defiles their life.[71] Elsewhere in philosophy, true worship of the gods should include purity of speech and thought,[72] judgments,[73] mind[74] and action.[75] Impurity in others is taken to indicate their lack of piety.[76] The philosopher has a duty to keep their inner daemon pure.[77] Philo views wisdom, virtue,[78] instruction[79] and a spirit of thanksgiving[80] as the agents that can cleanse the mind. The unblemished soul is compared to a priest in Philo.[81]

Paul

When I compare these findings with 2 Cor 6:14—7:1, there are a number of points to consider. Firstly, again I note that the temple is corporate: God dwells in his people rather than only in the souls of individuals (as documented at greater length in previous chapters). Instead of many gods and many temples, there is one God and one temple. Whereas the philosophers speak of the gods using the same language as they do for "God" (often ascribing to them the same attributes and qualities of character), Paul, unsurprisingly, sees only *idols* rather than gods (cf. 1 Cor 8:4–7). I noted in a previous chapter that many philosophers will urge their hearers to seek philosophy, almost regardless of which philosophy (and its understanding of divinity) is being discussed. The existence of

---

70. Sobr. 62; see also Epictetus, *Diatr.* 2.18.19; 4.11.3, 5; cf. Philostratus, *Vit. Apoll.* 2.5.3; 3.42.1–2. From a Jewish perspective, Philo recognizes the need for purity of soul in passages such as *Plant.* 162; *QE* 1.13; *Spec.* 1.257–61; *Mos.* 2.108; *Her.* 184; *QE* 2.98; *Sobr.* 62; and cf. the warning of *Deus* 9.

71. *Her.* 112–13.

72. Cicero, *Nat. d.* 2.28.71; see also Philo, *Mut.* 240.

73. Epictetus, *Diatr.* 4.1.112.

74. Cicero, *Leg.* 2.10.24.

75. Epictetus, *Diatr.* 2.8.12–13; Philo, *Mos.* 2.148–51.

76. E.g., Pomeroy, *Arius*, 5b, 5–21 (26); 11k, 4–14, 18–20, 26–29 (84).

77. Marcus Aurelius, *Med.* 2.13, 17; 3.12, 16.

78. Philo, *Spec.* 1.269; *Sobr.* 62.

79. *Somn.* 2.73.

80. *Deus* 7.

81. *Leg.* 2.55–56; *Spec.* 1.82; *Her.* 84.

gods and the worship of them is taken for granted, whether by those who would identify as Stoics, or others more influenced by Middle Platonism.

However, for Paul, partnership with gods rather than the one true God, revealed through Jesus Christ and experienced by the indwelling Spirit, is as different as darkness is from light (2 Cor 6:14c). God is the κύριος παντοκράτωρ (6:18c); the rest are idols. Paul, like the philosophers, speaks of God dwelling in a person and making himself present to them. Yet, for Paul the presence of the "living God" is restricted only to those who are in Christ (6:15a; cf. 1:21; 5:19). For Paul, there is both inclusiveness and separateness. Like the philosophers who speak of God's presence dwelling within each individual, there are no restrictions for Paul: both sons and daughters (6:18b) and Gentiles (not just Jews) can be his temple. Paul does not place himself above his congregations as one who is better or wiser; instead he makes no distinction between groups in the church or between them and him as their apostle; "*we* are the temple of the living God" (6:16b). Unlike the philosophers, being wise or good by others' estimation does not signify that God's presence dwells within. It is those who *believe* in Christ who are his temple. It is not the case that all have divine minds that make them divine. Rather, those who relate to idols rather than being indwelt with the presence of the living God are simply described as *unbelievers*. Purity, and cleansing from defilement, matters both for Paul and for the philosophers in their relationship to God. For the philosophers, a person can cleanse themselves or keep their daemon pure by right thinking and action. However, for Paul, those who are in Christ can do so in the light of all God's promises that find their fulfillment in Christ (1:20) and that guarantee a relationship as intimate as that between "the Father of mercies and the God of all consolation" (1:3) and his sons and daughters (6:18). Believers can be cleansed because God dwells and walks among them (6:16).

5.3 CORRESPONDING EMPHASES IN THE CORINTHIAN CORRESPONDENCE

Some of the key emphases I have identified here can also be found elsewhere within the Corinthian correspondence as a whole. In this next section I shall comment briefly on a number of other important places in the letters that relate to the issues identified in 2 Cor 6:14—7:1. I shall be selective and aim to address only those areas that may have been notable for an audience influenced by philosophy.

5.3.1 Idolatry

Although εἴδωλον is the only idol-related word to appear in 2 Corinthians, such words (beginning with the εἰδωλ- stem) are common in 1 Corinthians. The word εἴδωλον appears in 1 Cor 8:4, 7; 10:19; 12:2; εἰδωλεῖον (idol temple) is used in 1 Cor 8:10; εἰδωλόθυτος (something offered to idols) is the topic of discussion in 1 Cor 8:1—11:1, appearing in 1 Cor 8:1, 4, 7, 10; 10:19; εἰδωλολατρία (idolatry) in 1 Cor 10:14 and εἰδωλολάτρης (idolater) in 1 Cor 5:10, 11; 6:9; 10:7. Eleven occurrences of these cognate terms take place in 1 Cor 8:1—11:1. The prominence of the term εἴδωλον here may suggest that the presenting issue of 1 Cor 8:1—11:1 has not been fully resolved (though this passage need not be limited to that concern).[82] Gordon Fee has presented strong arguments that 1 Cor 8:1—11:1 provides the context for an ongoing dispute between Paul and the Corinthians over idol food and idolatry, represented in the stern warnings of 2 Cor 6:14—7:1.[83] Paul had warned in 1 Cor 8:7 that some eat food as if offered to an idol and their consciences, being weak, are "defiled" and the verb used here, μολύνω, is cognate with the noun μολυσμός (2 Cor 7:1) that Paul urges the Corinthians to cleanse themselves from in our passage.[84]

5.3.2 Separation for the Sake of Purity

Many scholars see Paul's call not to associate with "unbelievers" as problematic given Paul's emphasis on not withdrawing from the immoral of this world (1 Cor 5:10; cf. 5:12).[85] The majority of those who do so understand the use of ἄπιστοι here to refer to "faithless" apostles (presumably

---

82. E.g., Thrall, *2 Corinthians 1-7*, 475; Harris, *Second Epistle*, 500-1; Webb, *Returning*, 202-3; Fee, "II Corinthians," 140-61.

83. Fee, "II Corinthians," 140-61, supported by Goulder, "2 Cor. 6:14—7:1," 50-51.

84. Fee, "II Corinthians," 140-61 at 145 also makes this connection.

85. E.g., Allo, *Saint Paul*, 189; Rensberger, "2 Corinthians 6:14—7:1," 25-49 at 29-31, 37.

the ones spoken of in 2 Cor 10–13, e.g., 11:13)[86] or faithless Christians.[87] The problem with this theory is that it violates the principle of consistency: every other use of ἄπιστος by Paul in the Corinthian correspondence refers unambiguously to non-Christians.[88] Given the contrast between Christ and Beliar in 6:15a, the contrast between ὁ πιστός and ὁ ἄπιστος in 6:15b, that elaborates upon 6:15a, would suggest that one representative person is aligned with Christ and the other with Beliar. In fact, the sole other use of the term ἄπιστος in this letter, in 2 Cor 4:4, is defined in apposition to οἱ ἀπολλύμενοι (4:3), who, elsewhere in the Corinthian correspondence, are depicted as the antithesis of οἱ σῳζόμενοι (1 Cor 1:18; 2 Cor 2:15).[89] The reference to δικαιοσύνη in 6:14 recalls another occurrence of a cognate term in Paul's first letter where he warns them that the ἄδικοι will not inherit the kingdom of God (6:9), in contrast with the present state of the Corinthians who have been justified (δικαιόω). I have already noted the theme of idolatry and the impossibility of believers having a share (μετέχω in 1 Cor 10:21, cognate to μετοχή in 2 Cor 6:14)

86. E.g., Collange, *Enigmes*, 305–6, 316–17; Dahl, "Fragment," 62–69; Rensberger, "2 Corinthians 6:14—7:1," 25–49; Patte, "Structural Exegesis," 45 n. 59; Wolff, *Korinther*, 146–50; deSilva, "Recasting," 3–16; Zeilinger, "Echtheit," 71–80; deSilva, *Credentials*, 17–19, 105–6; Murphy-O'Connor, *Keys to Second Corinthians*, 128–29.

87. Young and Ford, *Meaning*, 33–34; Goulder, "2 Cor 6:14—7:1," 53–54.

88. 1 Cor 6:6; 7:12, 13, 14, 15; 10:27; 14:22, 23, 24; 2 Cor 4:4; see further, e.g., Plummer, *Critical and Exegetical*, 206–8; Windisch, *Korintherbrief*, 218; Barrett, *First Epistle*, 195; Thrall, "Problem," 132–48 at 143; also supported by Webb, *Returning*, 184–99; Fee, "II Corinthians," 140–61; Furnish, *II Corinthians*, 362–63, 371–72, 382; Witherington, *Conflict*, 404; Barnett, *Second Epistle*, 342, 345; Matera, *II Corinthians*, 162; Harris, *Second Epistle*, 499; Aernie, *Paul*, 219; Rabens, "Inclusion," 233–36; Martin, *2 Corinthians*, 361, 365–66; Han, *Swimming*, 85–87; Oropeza, *Exploring*, 431. Rabens, "Inclusion," 229–53 at 243–53, also argues for a *secondary* referent to idolatrous people *inside* the church (including the false apostles of 11:13) as well as *outside* the church (Rabens, "Inclusion," 294–317 is very similar to the preceding article). Similarily, Adewuya, *Holiness*, 101–3 posits an inclusive reference: both to pagans and those who behave like them; Starling, "ἄπιστοι," 45–60, identifies unbelievers as idolatrous pagans but also suggests that *contextually* it is implied that in embracing the false apostles they are becoming "mismatched" with the pagans in their attitudes (59–60). Liu, *Temple Purity*, 202–4 starts from the other end, identifying unbelievers with "false brothers," but concludes that the advice could also apply to pagans. Gupta, *Worship*, 99–100 argues contextually that "unbelievers" is Paul's counter-claim against those who accuse him of being unfaithful to the law (i.e., Jews and perhaps Jewish Christians), following Lambrecht, *Second Corinthians*, 62.

89. Murphy-O'Connor, *Keys to Second Corinthians*, 117. The question is explored in some detail by Webb, *Returning*, 184–99, itself a revision of Webb, "Unequally Yoked Part 1," 27–44.

in the table of demons or being a partner with them (κοινωνός in 1 Cor 10:18, 20, cognate to κοινωνία in 2 Cor 6:14).[90] There is also precedent for the emphasis on separation from that which defiles (2 Cor 6:17; 7:1) in Paul's injunctions in 1 Cor 5:6–13 (especially at 5:7, 13).[91] It is true that in 1 Cor 5, Paul clarifies that he does not oppose the believers mingling/associating with (συναναμίγνυμι) the immoral of this world (5:10) but with the immoral brother (5:11, and thus believer). At the same time, Paul speaks of the unbelieving husband being made holy (ἁγιάζω) by his believing wife, stating that if not for the faith of the wife, both husband and children would be unclean (ἀκάθαρτος in 7:14). The problem of the believer who is already married to an unbeliever is clearly an exceptional case; hence Paul's need to address it (1 Cor 7:12–16). However, if a believer were to enter into a new marriage they should marry μόνον ἐν κυρίῳ (1 Cor 7:39b) since someone outside of the Lord would not be set apart for them. It seems then that Paul must mean something different by speaking of ἑτεροζυγέω in 2 Cor 6:14, rather than συναναμίγνυμι (1 Cor 5:10, 11). Paul is not prohibiting social contact with unbelievers, but instead warning against making "a mismatched covenant" with them.[92] The succession of words that follow emphasize partnership, sharing and fellowship; something stronger than mere association.[93] In light of the explicit contrast between the "living God" and idols, it seems likely that Paul prohibits any kind of activity "which establishes a covenant-like bond with pagans and their literal idols (either through physical or metonymical idolatry)— an action which seriously violates the reader's existing covenant with God."[94]

90. Both points noted by Goulder, "2 Cor 6:14—7:1," 50–51.

91. See Goulder, "2 Cor 6:14—7:1," 47–57 at 51–52. Webb, *Returning*, 190, helpfully contrasts the *purposes* given for the different advice in 1 Cor 5:10 and 2 Cor 6:17; see also Barnett, *Second Epistle*, 341 n. 23.

92. Spicq, *Theological Lexicon*, 2.80–81, speaking of the figurative sense; or "be yoked in unequal partnership" (cf. "ἑτεροζυγέω," LSJ, 701) cf. "ἑτεροζυγέω," BDAG, 399; Rengstorf "ζυγός, ἑτεροζυγέω," *TDNT* 2.896–901. Philo speaks in *Leg.* 3.193 of the person who yoked themselves to the chariot of passions that produced boastfulness and arrogance (using the noun ζυγός) or of pleasure personified who struggles to break free from the yoke (using a cognate verb, ζυγομαχέω), in *Leg.* 3.239. See also, e.g., Plummer, *Critical and Exegetical*, 206; Windisch, *Korintherbrief*, 212–13; Furnish, *II Corinthians*, 361; Harris, *Second Epistle*, 501; Rabens, "Inclusion," 241.

93. See also Webb, *Returning*, 190–92.

94. Webb, *Returning*, 211, and see generally 200–215, itself based on his earlier article, Webb, "Unequally Yoked Part 2," 162–79. Despite Webb's persuasive arguments against a reference to mixed marriages (Webb, *Returning*, 205–9), he hesitantly allows

5.3.3 The Theme of Indwelling in 2 Corinthians

There are a number of passages in the epistle that highlight the theme of divine indwelling. In the context of speaking of the believer's union with Christ[95] (εἰς Χριστὸν in 1:21), Paul speaks of God as the one who has sealed (σφραγίζω) the Corinthians as his own and given them the ἀρραβών (down payment, pledge guaranteeing what is to come),[96] probably best seen as epexegetical, that is, *consisting of* the Spirit[97] ἐν ταῖς καρδίαις ἡμῶν (1:22). The Spirit dwells, not just in their midst, but in their hearts.[98] Similarly, Paul calls the Corinthians an ἐπιστολὴ Χριστοῦ (letter of Christ, 3:3), that has been written πνεύματι θεοῦ ζῶντος, by the Spirit of *the living God* on tablets of fleshly hearts (ἐν πλαξὶν καρδίαις σαρκίναις, 3:4). This is the same living God language that is used in 6:14, and affirms that the Corinthians are a letter of Christ precisely because the life-giving Spirit[99] of God has made them so *within*, in changing them from pagans to bearers of his Spirit.[100] Space does not permit me to properly examine 2 Cor 3:4–18 and the exegetical issues it presents.[101] However, it is clear that the new covenant era, that Paul contrasts with the old, surpasses it in glory and involves a new found ἐλευθερία (3:17).[102] This freedom comes

---

that the passage "lends itself in a secondary sense to a mixed marriage application" (209) and I would agree with Harris, *Second Epistle*, 501 n. 32, that the contracting of a mixed marriage (cf. 1 Cor 7:39) would certainly be included; see also Witherington, *Conflict*, 405–6; Thrall, *2 Corinthians 1–7*, 473; May, *Body*, 228 n. 63; Keener, *1–2 Corinthians*, 193–94; Han, *Swimming*, 87–89.

95. Thrall, *2 Corinthians 1–7*, 155–58; Harris, *Second Epistle*, 205; Martin, *2 Corinthians*, 164.

96. With the NIV: "a deposit, guaranteeing what is to come"; see Harris, *Second Epistle*, 207.

97. With, e.g., Furnish, *II Corinthians*, 137; Fee, *God's Empowering Presence*, 293; Harris, *Second Epistle*, 207; Guthrie, *2 Corinthians*, 115; Long, *2 Corinthians*, 38.

98. Fee, *God's Empowering Presence*, 294.

99. See the translations of Thrall, *2 Corinthians 1–7*, 227; Harris, *Second Epistle*, 264; Keener, *1–2 Corinthians*, 167.

100. Drawing on the promise of new covenant life found in places such as Ezek 11:19; 36:26; Jer 38:33 LXX (31:33 MT), as well as an allusion to God writing on tablets of stone in passages such as Exod 31:18; Deut 4:13; 5:22. See with more detail, Goodwin, *Paul*, 161–89.

101. The section has attracted a great deal of scholarly interest. Among full length monographs, see, e.g., Stockhausen, *Veil*; Belleville, *Reflections*; Hafemann, *Paul*; and see the up-to-date bibliography in Martin, *2 Corinthians*, 197–99.

102. A notion that would appeal to those influenced by Stoicism, as noted by Collange, *Enigmes*, 113–14, and followed by Thrall, *2 Corinthians 1–7*, 276.

from the Lord, the Spirit, who transforms (μεταμορφόω) believers into τὴν αὐτὴν εἰκόνα (3:18), which I take to be the divine image; the image of God found in Christ that is referred to only a few verses later (4:4).[103] Gordon Fee's comment on Paul's use of "the Lord" in the phrase "the Lord (Yahweh) is the Spirit" is apposite for the audience I am considering here, "This usage presupposes the Spirit as the fulfillment of the Presence of God motif in a thoroughgoing way. The Lord to whom Moses turned is the one whose "Presence" tabernacled in the midst of his people Israel . . . the "Lord" to whom God's newly constituted people turn, whose "Presence" is now in their hearts, is none other than the life-giving Spirit of the living God."[104]

In 2 Cor 4, Paul uses a number of indwelling images. Firstly, he speaks of the divine illumination that has entered the hearts of the Corinthians, granting them the knowledge of the glory of God in the face of Jesus Christ (4:6). Then Paul speaks of the frail humanity of his readers[105] as ὀστράκινη σκεύη in which the θησαυρός (probably referring to the gospel in the context of the repeated references to it in 4:3-4 and allusions to it in 4:1, 6)[106] is carried (4:7). This might have reminded some readers of the way that sacred items, manifesting the presence of the deity, were carried in contemporary religious processions.[107] By contrast the Corinthians carry Christ and his gospel within their frail human bodies. Thirdly, after enumerating the ways in which this treasure is displayed in frailty (4:8-9), Paul uses another indwelling image: that they always

---

103. *Pace*, e.g., van Unnik, "Unveiled Face," 153-69; followed by Belleville, *Reflections*, 290, 296; Wright, *Climax*, 175-92, who each speak of transformation into the image of *one another*, but *with* the majority of modern commentators. For those influenced by Middle Platonism, this also would also speak to them of the common notion of being transformed into the image of the deity by contemplating that image; see Thrall, *2 Corinthians 1-7*, 290, 294-95; Keener, *1-2 Corinthians*, 170-71; a recurring theme in Maximus of Tyre and Philo of Alexandria, among our sources influenced by Middle Platonism. See the sources cited by J. Behm, "μεταμορφόω," TDNT 4:755-7; Hagner, "Vision," 81-93; Keener, "Transformation," 13-22; Keener, "Heavenly Mindedness," 175-90; Keener, "We Beheld," 15-25 and Rabens, *Holy Spirit*, 184-86.

104. Fee, *God's Empowering Presence*, 313.

105. Probably including their weak earthly bodies, but perhaps not restricted to this referent; see Plummer, *Critical and Exegetical*, 127; Thrall, *2 Corinthians 1-7*, 323; Harris, *Second Epistle*, 340.

106. Thrall, *2 Corinthians 1-7*, 321; Harris, *Second Epistle*, 339; Savage, *Power*, 164-67.

107. See Duff, "Transformation," 233-37; Duff, "Apostolic Suffering," 160; Long, *2 Corinthians*, 82.

carry around in their bodies the νέκρωσις[108] of Jesus so that the life of Jesus might be manifested in their bodies (4:10). I note here that in addition to further indwelling imagery (both the death/dying and the life of Jesus are to be φανερόω—manifested, same verb in both 4:10, 11), Paul is unashamed about associating this revelation with his physicality. He stresses that the life and death of Jesus are revealed ἐν τῷ σώματι (4:10) and ἐν τῇ θνητῇ σαρκὶ (4:11); clearly placed in parallel. Paul could have simply used σῶμα but the addition and combination of σάρξ with θνητός, according to Murray J. Harris, has the effect, "of emphasizing the transitory, creaturely, and weak nature of the body that, paradoxically, is the very place where Jesus' powerful risen life is on display."[109] Although it is difficult to be sure whether Paul's reference to τὸ αὐτὸ πνεῦμα τῆς πίστεως (4:13) alludes to the disposition of the Psalmist[110] or to the Holy Spirit, a good case can be made for the Holy Spirit, as the one who produces faith, in light of other Pauline usage and to the references to the Spirit in the co-text of 2 Cor 3 and 2 Cor 5:5 (who then arguably produces the faith of 5:7).[111] The picture of the inner self being renewed daily, in its context, also suggests the work of the Spirit bringing about an internal transformation and would have been very suggestive to an audience influenced by Stoic and Platonic thought.[112] This inner transformation is evidenced in the way that Paul endures hardships (6:4–5) and the qualities he displays in the midst of these (6:6–7), including ἁγνότης (purity) generated by the Holy Spirit (6:6).[113]

108. Which may be intended to mean both the *state* of deadness and the *process* of dying, see Fitzgerald, *Cracks*, 178–79; though many commentators understand Paul to be emphasizing the *process* of dying, e.g., Lightfoot, *Epistles of 2 Corinthians*, 52; Plummer, *Critical and Exegetical*, 130; Harris, *Second Epistle*, 345; Guthrie, *2 Corinthians*, 359–60, while Collange, *Enigmes*, 154–55, followed by Thrall, *2 Corinthians 1–7*, 332, thinks the *state* of deadness may be intended, since Paul's only other use of this noun (Rom 4:19) has this nuance.

109. Harris, *Second Epistle*, 349.

110. As argued by, e.g., Thrall, *2 Corinthians 1–7*, 338–39; Guthrie, *2 Corinthians*, 262.

111. See the citations and arguments provided by, e.g., Collange, *Enigmes*, 162–63; Barrett, *Second Epistle*, 142; Furnish, *II Corinthians*, 257–58; Fee, *God's Empowering Presence*, 323–24; and tentatively Keener, *1–2 Corinthians*, 175.

112. See especially Thrall, *2 Corinthians 1–7*, 348–51; also Furnish, *II Corinthians*, 261; Fee, *God's Empowering Presence*, 324 and the philosophical references cited by Keener, *1–2 Corinthians*, 177–78.

113. See Fee, *God's Empowering Presence*, 332–35; Thrall, *2 Corinthians 1–7*, 460. Most English translations also follow the variant reading ἐν ἁγιότητι rather than ἐν

5.4 COMPARING THE THEOLOGIES OF 2 CORINTHIANS 1–7 WITH HELLENISTIC PHILOSOPHY

5.4.1 Paul's Understanding of God in 2 Corinthians 1–7

In this and the following sections, I shall briefly make reference to passages that corroborate my findings from the previous chapter, rather than attempting to provide a comprehensive summary. God is the one who characteristically raises the dead (1:9),[114] and who, like in 1 Corinthians, is intimately associated with Jesus Christ his son (1:3), who is also Lord (1:2–3; 4:5; cf. 1 Cor 8:5–6 on other Lords and 2 Cor 4:4 on the opposing ὁ θεὸς τοῦ αἰῶνος τούτου), through whom all God's promises are fulfilled (1:19–20). God has ownership of, and resides in, his people by his Spirit (1:22). He has written on the hearts of the Corinthians by his Spirit (3:3) to give them life (3:6) and identifies fully with the Spirit as Lord (3:17–18). God's purposes are accomplished through Christ, his image (3:18; 4:6), the agent of revelation (3:14), in whom the Corinthians reveal the knowledge of God to the world (2:14–15; 4:10–11). Like 1 Corinthians, there is a strong emphasis on Jesus as the one who was raised and God as the one who raised him (1:9; 4:14; 5:15), and who will raise the Corinthians with him (4:14; cf. 5:1–10). God urges people to be reconciled with him (5:11–21) since through Christ he has reconciled the world to himself (5:18–21). This grace must be received now (6:1–2) in light of the coming judgment enacted by Christ on God's behalf (5:10). As we observed in the first letter, Paul connects God and his people very closely with bodily resurrection. He dwells through Christ by his Spirit, only in his people who believe and who have been reconciled to him, and not in all people.[115]

5.4.2 Paul's Understanding of Humanity in 2 Corinthians 1–7

Although 2 Cor 6:14—7:1 is well known for its contrasts between believers and unbelievers and what they represent, these same contrasts appear

---

ἁπλότητι found in 1:12. If this is correct, as Windisch, *Korintherbrief*, 54; Comfort, *New Testament*, 534; Thrall, "2 Corinthians 1:12," 366–72; Thrall, *2 Corinthians 1–7*, 130–31, 32–33 and Harris, *Second Epistle*, 183 convincingly argue, this would provide another example of Paul's stress on purity/holiness in behavior in the letter; see also Starling, "ἄπιστοι," 54–55.

114. Noting the present participle with Harris, *Second Epistle*, 157.

115. For a more comprehensive survey, see Young and Ford, *Meaning*, 235–61; Harris, *Second Epistle*, 115–17.

more generally in 2 Cor 2:14—7:4 as a whole. There are some who are being saved and others who are perishing (2:15), and the Gospel is veiled to the latter group (4:3) since the god of this age has blinded their minds so that they cannot see the light of the gospel of the glory of Christ (4:4). All will be judged for what was done in their body (5:10) and the bodies of all will be destroyed (5:1). The world has been reconciled to God through Christ (5:19) but this grace must be received through Christ (5:20; 6:1-2) for people to be transformed into Christ's likeness (3:18; 4:10-18) and finally, to receive the resurrection body (5:1). The goal is not freedom for the soul from the body or absorption into the universe, as in much philosophy, but new creation (5:17).

5.4.3 Living as the Temple in 2 Corinthians 1–7

There are at least two other places in the letter where Paul may be using figurative temple language, but given my focus on explicit temple imagery, I shall briefly discuss them in my final chapter, under *Avenues for further study*.

Some of Paul's remarks confirm those areas of his understanding I discussed in relation to 1 Corinthians that would have struck audiences influenced by philosophy. For instance, Paul expresses his longing that what is θνητός (cf. 4:11) be swallowed up (καταπίνω). This would resonate with those who despised mortal flesh, but in Paul's case, mortality is to be swallowed up by ζωή (5:4), which is defined here as the life of the resurrection body (5:1-5; cf. the use of the same clothing imagery in respect of the resurrection body in 1 Cor 15:53–54).[116] Although many other things could be said about 2 Cor 5:10, for my purposes I note that Paul sees the body as the locus of all activity that merits judgment, whether bad *or good* (rather than the body being associated *only* with all that is evil).

More generally in these early chapters of 2 Corinthians, I note that Paul again addresses believers in Christ as ἅγιοι (1:1). The believers are uniquely owned and established by God and indwelt by the Spirit, who guarantees the consummation of their salvation (1:22), in a way that others are not. The Corinthians are a letter of Christ, written by the Spirit in their hearts (3:3). They stand by faith (1:24) and their character must be

---

116. Harris, *Second Epistle*, 387, notes that the positive reason for Paul's groaning in 5:2, 4, is "not a Hellenistic depreciation of corporeality but an intense longing for investiture with a heavenly body."

tried by obedience (2:9). Paul's recounting of the hardships he has encountered (e.g., 4:7–11; 6:4–10) serve as an example to the Corinthians, that the life of Christ should be revealed through them (4:6, 10–11, 16) in the midst of weakness (4:7–9), dying (4:11) and decay (4:16–5:1) in their bodies (4:10), not merely their souls. They also face opposition from Satan (2:11; 4:4; cf. 11:3, 14; 12:7), so, in following Paul's example (cf. 1 Cor 4:16; 11:1), they should fix their eyes on unseen realities (4:18), make it their aim to please God (5:9), fear him (5:11) and live for Christ (5:15) as his ambassadors (5:20).[117]

5.5 CONCLUSIONS

I have observed a number of contrasts between the philosophers' use of figurative temple language, and its implications for their worldview and practice, and the emphases found in 2 Cor 6:14—7:1. The philosophers often spoke of the divine filling all things and thus indwelling each individual. At the same time, some writings speak of the divine dwelling only in those who are good or wise. The imagery either relates to all without exception (all of creation) or specifically to certain individuals. The acceptance of multiple gods is assumed and affirmed. These gods are held to share identical characteristics with God.

The main features of Paul's figurative temple references in 1 Corinthians also find corresponding emphasis in the letter as a whole and stand in contrast to my findings from Hellenistic philosophy. Paul only speaks of the Spirit indwelling those who believe in Christ, rather than every created person or a category of people, such as those who are especially wise or noble. At the same time, the figurative temple is spoken of corporately—it is a group of people. On the one hand, this is a very restrictive group; only those who believe in Christ have the indwelling Spirit and the rest are aligned with idolatry. On the other hand, the group includes those formerly counted as pagans, who are now spoken of using language previously applied to Israel. Paul's addition of the word for "daughters" from Isa 43:6; 49:22 and 60:4 highlights the inclusive nature of the group; male and female, Jew and Gentile are welcomed and included by God. Whereas, for the philosophers the gods share the same beneficent characteristics as God, for Paul, they are simply idols and he associates them

---

117. For a more comprehensive survey of holiness in the Corinthian correspondence and Paul's emphasis on communal holiness, see Adewuya, *Holiness*, 129–64.

with evil, unbelief, darkness and lawlessness, while the Corinthian believers are associated with Christ, belief, light and righteousness.

6

Conclusions

6.1 SUMMARY

THIS STUDY HAS EXAMINED the use of figurative temple language in Paul's letters to the Corinthians (1 Cor 3:16–17; 6:19; 2 Cor 6:14—7:1) and compared it to the use of such language in Hellenistic philosophy.

In chapter 1, I noted that a number of monographs have considered Paul's own context in Judaism in order to illuminate his use of figurative temple language, particularly focusing on the presence of such imagery in the Dead Sea Scrolls, especially as such language is not pervasive in other Intertestamental literature. However, more recent studies of the scrolls are less confident than earlier ones that we can trace any direct influence on Paul. In any case, the majority of Paul's readers were Gentiles (see, e.g., 1 Cor 6:9–11; 8:7; 12:2) and it is unlikely that the scrolls would have been known to these congregations and would have influenced their understanding of Paul's words. Most scholars writing on the temple language from the 1930s to the 1980s considered the image purely in relation to Paul's own background. A number of recent studies have recognized the significance of the audience's context for the Corinthians' understanding of Paul's language. As Gentiles, they would have been exposed to a variety of religious, cultural and philosophical influences before and after conversion, notably the presence of Roman temples and thus the possibilities of eating idol foods in various contexts (cf. 1 Cor 8:1–11:1).

A steady stream of modern studies have examined Paul's advice on idol offerings in relation to the religious and social context of Corinth, and Paul's temple image has been examined in relation to building projects (John Lanci) and local temples (Yulin Liu).

However, I sought to demonstrate that, for Paul's audience, philosophy provided the worldview and guidance for living that people seek from religion today. I also claimed that the influence of Hellenistic philosophy was pervasive in the first century and its ideas would have trickled down to influence those who had never read philosophy. Although others have compared Paul's theology with Stoicism, or compared spiritual sacrifices in the Greco-Roman world with the NT, I noted a lacuna in the literature, with no available comprehensive study of the most relevant sources of figurative temple language that could have influenced the Corinthians' thinking. While noting that this was not *Paul's* own background, nor the sole background for the Corinthians, it was nevertheless *one* important background for the audience, that has been neglected and that Paul may have sought to address.

In chapter 2, I surveyed relevant non-Jewish Hellenistic writers' use of figurative priest, temple and sacrifice language, beginning with the schools that marked the start of the Hellenistic era and ending with works from the second century CE. Because neither Epicureanism nor Skepticism had a place for the direct involvement of God in human affairs, the vast majority of references were found in writers influenced by Stoicism or Middle Platonism. There were no unambiguous references to figurative priests but plenty of discussion of spiritual sacrifices. Some retained a place for literal sacrifices but placed a greater emphasis on purity of thought and deed as a sacrifice. Substitutes for sacrifices included purity in worship, prayer and contemplation, purity of thought, speech and intention and an attitude that seeks for divine truth or studies divine things. Writers from different traditions spoke of the universe as being the temple of the gods. Some make a fine distinction between God and the world (e.g., Epictetus) but, in speaking of the divine filling all things, others speak of the world in more pantheistic terms. Stoics, in particular, speak of the place of god or a daemon within the individual soul, and there is some ambiguity as to whether this applies to every individual without exception, or solely, or perhaps to a greater degree, in those who are wise and/or good.

In order to place these references within the worldview of their philosophical systems, I also attempted to sketch out the way such writers understood the nature of divinity, humanity and the application of the philosophy to practical living. I noted how God is frequently equated pantheistically with Nature, Fate, Fortune and Reason and in later Stoics, as well as Middle Platonists, he is identified simply as intelligence. Many speak of multiple gods who share the same benevolent and governing characteristics with God. Most philosophers see Soul or Reason as separate from and superior to the body, governing its impulses and aversions. The soul is often understood as pre-existent, of divine essence and capable of comprehending the divine and doing the good. Evil also originates in the soul. Humans have the capacity to live in accordance with Nature and to unite with the divine. At death, the soul is set free from the body and may become a daemon. The Stoics exhort followers to live in accordance with Nature and exercise right judgments about the gods, obeying their inner daemon in order to be pure and to avoid wrong sense impressions. The Middle Platonists speak more in terms of imitating God's character and ways through contemplation of the divine and by choosing the good and avoiding the passions.

Chapter 3 was devoted purely to the writings of Philo of Alexandria (ca. 20 BCE—50 CE). Although Philo is Jewish, his Judaism is mediated through Hellenistic philosophy; he writes to a Diaspora audience and draws upon the philosophical tradition when speaking to a Hellenistic readership about wisdom, just as Paul does. He also provides our largest first century corpus for Middle Platonic thought and there are copious references to figurative priest, temple and sacrifice language in his writings. Although Philo, as a good Jew, affirms literal sacrifices, the offerer must have a pure and noble mind and reason. Yet, he also affirms, with the philosophers that a sacrifice can be spiritual, and like them, emphasizes the offering of the mind and soul. Purity and virtue in thought, speech and word can also be sacrifices. Philo depicts Reason as a priest (rather like the role of the daemon in Stoic or Platonic thought) who acts as internal guide, judge and arbiter of the conscience. The garments of the priest can represent purity of soul, the virtues or the cosmos, and the universe can be compared to a priest (as can the universe, angels, the nation of Israel and a household).

Philo also speaks of both of the mind/soul and of the universe as the dwelling place of God, in agreement with other philosophers. He too speaks of God filling all things and Wisdom dwelling as in a temple. The world, virtue, purity, truth and wisdom are described using tabernacle language. There is a solitary reference to a person in their embodiment as a temple, but this may be restricted to Adam, rather than any individual.

In chapter 4, I compared 1 Cor 3:16–17 and 6:19 with my findings from Hellenistic philosophy. Whereas philosophers speak of the divine presence filling individuals, in 1 Cor 3:16–17 Paul's understanding of the temple is corporate; the Corinthians as a group are the temple. Philosophy speaks of the divine presence inhabiting all individuals or particularly the good or wise, but the Corinthians are the temple by virtue of the Spirit who dwells within them. This Spirit is not given to all, nor to the wise or noble per se, but only to those who belong to Christ—who are set apart and called as holy people (1:2). Christ is the foundation of this building (3:9). The temple is sacred and has very strict boundaries, such that defilement of the temple brings destruction (3:17). This warning of destruction upon any who threaten the sanctity of the community contrasts with the Stoic stress on the world's final destruction or Middle Platonism's teaching on the destruction of the body. Paul's use of figurative temple language in 1 Cor 6:19 has a distinctive emphasis on the physical body, whereas the philosophers, whether Stoic or Platonic, speak of the body with indifference or even disdain. As in the previous passage, the emphasis is still corporate, despite the reference to the bodies of individuals, as Paul makes explicit with his use of the second-person possessive pronoun. In the philosophers, the πνεῦμα or *spiritus* inhabits the whole universe and thus every individual. In Paul, the Spirit inhabits those who have been set apart and cleansed through Jesus. Philosophy emphasizes the obligation to glorify God but in 6:19 the injunction is specifically to glorify God "in your body," an unthinkable notion for the Platonic worldview. The Corinthian temple is a group defined by specific boundaries and relationship to Jesus Christ and is viewed with reference to their corporeal obedience to God. I noted that some of these themes were also emphasized in the wider epistle: holiness in the body, the importance of not defiling the temple (especially through idolatry) and the use of body language to describe believers as well as to speak of their final destiny in terms of the physical resurrection body.

In chapter 5, I noted that Paul's figurative temple language would have challenged any of the Corinthian readers still influenced by the prevailing Hellenistic philosophical worldview. Philosophy spoke of the divine or the gods filling the universe and, with it, every individual, or certain individual souls, and cleansing coming by reason, wisdom or virtue. Paul, however, makes a clear distinction between the true God revealed in Jesus Christ and experienced by the indwelling Spirit and other gods who are merely idols (2 Cor 6:16). The corporate nature of the temple as God's people is always emphasized in the Corinthian figurative temple language, and the Spirit dwells only in those who belong to Jesus Christ, although there are no divisions on the basis of hierarchy, race or gender when it comes to inclusion in this temple (6:18).

6.2 AVENUES FOR FURTHER STUDY

There are a number of potential areas that could be further explored using the data from Hellenistic philosophy that I cited earlier. Firstly, the images used in 2 Cor 2:14-16 clearly draw on the well documented occurrences of Roman triumphal processions. In this passage, Paul uses ὀσμή (2:14b, 16) and εὐωδία (2:15), that are often combined in the Septuagintal formula ὀσμὴ εὐωδίας (e.g., Gen 8:21; Exod 29:18; Lev 4:31; Num 15:5 etc.). However, for some scholars, Paul's avoidance of the *exact* formula, which he does employ elsewhere to speak of sacrifices (in Phil 4:18—and Eph 5:2—if the latter is Pauline), indicates that Paul is still making use of the triumph motif, imagining himself and his colleagues as incense-bearers in the parade.[1] For others, however the use of these commonly associated words signals a shift to the image of OT sacrifice.[2] Given the very close conjunction of two terms very commonly associated with sacrifice in the LXX, the possibility of a sacrificial referent should not be ruled out. The

---

1. See especially Guthrie, *2 Corinthians*, 165–73, and more detail provided in Guthrie, "Paul's Triumphal Procession," 79–91, and previously Plummer, *Critical and Exegetical*, 71; Attridge, "Making Scents," 83–88. Duff, "Metaphor," 79–92, reads the whole image in relation to epiphany processions in the Greco-Roman world, rather than to the triumph in particular (for which see also Duff, "Transformation," 241. Long, "God," 219–69, argues that 2 Cor 2:14—7:2 has been constructed to reflect the triumphal procession, that culminates at the temple (in 6:14—7:1).

2. E.g., Hafemann, *Suffering*, 40–58, who argues that "the technical term ὀσμὴ εὐωδίας as a metonymy for sacrifice seems to have been so well established by the post-exilic period . . . when used in the same context, the terms could also be *separated* and used as *synonyms*," and in Sir 24:15, like 2 Cor 2:14–15, "the *terminus technicus* has been split up, but the two terms have nevertheless retained their sacrificial meaning" (48); supported also by, e.g., Collange, *Enigmes*, 30–31; McDonald, "Paul," 39–42; Thrall, *2 Corinthians 1–7*, 197–98; Harris, *Second Epistle*, 248; Gupta, *Worship*, 87–90; Long, *2 Corinthians*, 57. Aus, *Imagery*, 41, connects the imagery to the triumph but sees one referent as the use of incense in sacrifices of thanksgiving at the end of the procession; Furnish, *II Corinthians*, 176–77 denies the sacrificial referent.

conjunction of the two terms is rare in Hellenistic literature,[3] but εὐωδία or ὀσμή appears in philosophical literature in connection with incense,[4] or a fragrance that indicates the presence of a god in a shrine,[5] or generally in relation to offerings and washings for purification performed at a shrine.[6] For a Corinthian audience influenced by Hellenistic philosophy, Paul's image of himself and his colleagues spreading the fragrance of the knowledge of Christ would certainly have been comprehensible in a sacrificial context.[7]

Secondly, there is a possible temple/tabernacle allusion at 2 Cor 5:1. This verse and the verses that follow comprise one of the most disputed passages in the letter, and space does not permit to consider the timing of the reception of the οἰκοδομή that Paul contrasts with the current ἡ ἐπίγειος ἡμῶν οἰκία τοῦ σκήνους (5:1) nor the relationship between 1 Cor 15 and 2 Cor 5.[8] However, what does seem relatively clear is that while Paul, in common with Hellenistic writings, sees the temporary existence of the earthly body as something from which he longs to be freed (5:1-2),[9] his hope is not in freedom for the soul from the body, but rather for a body from heaven that will be infinitely superior. Paul's use of σκῆνος for "tent" is reminiscent of the way that σκηνή can be used in the LXX for "tabernacle" combined with οἶκος in, e.g., 1 Chr 9:23. Isa 38:12 uses the metaphor of a tent being taken down to depict death and Job 4:19 combines οἰκία with πήλινος (literally made of πηλός, clay) to speak of human bodies (cf. 2 Cor 4:7).[10] Further, ἀχειροποίητος (not made with hands) is used elsewhere in the NT to refer to the earthly temple or taber-

---

3. Plutarch, *Quaest. conv.* 626B is perhaps the only example that does not clearly post-date the New Testament period significantly.

4. E.g., Dio Chrysostom, *2 Regn.* 41 (εὐωδία); Plutarch, *Is. Os.* 383A-C (ὀσμή); *Tranq. an.* 477B (εὐωδία). Plutarch, *Quaest. conv.* 645E speaks of μύρον (perfume) as if it is εὐσέβεια (piety, godliness), so providing an example of a sweet smell used figuratively.

5. Plutarch, *Def. orac.* 437C (εὐωδία).

6. Plutarch, *Pyth. orac.* 402C-D, using the cognate adjective εὐώδης.

7. Renwick, *Paul*, 75-94, thinks the cultic reference is most likely when placing the pericope in the context of cultic images in Second Corinthians.

8. For which, see especially Thrall, *2 Corinthians 1-7*, 357-70; Wright, *Resurrection*, 361-71 and Toney, "Excursus," 250-56.

9. See, for instance, Wis 9:15 (which uses βαρύνω, cognate to βαρέω in 2 Cor 5:4); Plato, *Phaedr.* 81C; [*Ax.*] 365E; 366A; Philo, *Somn.* 1.122; Cicero, *Tusc.* 1.22.51 cited by, e.g., Plummer, *Critical and Exegetical*, 142; Thrall, *2 Corinthians 1-7*, 357-58.

10. Cited by Thrall, *2 Corinthians 1-7*, 357-58.

nacle (Mk 14:58 and similarly, the use of χειροποίητος with verbs negated by οὐ in Acts 7:48; 17:24; Heb 9:11, 24) and given the place of a heavenly temple or future eschatological temple in other Jewish literature,[11] and in the context of church as temple (1 Cor 3:16) and the body as temple (1 Cor 6:19) in the Corinthian correspondence, this reference to the body ἀχειροποίητος is likely to suggest the idea of temple to Paul's readers.[12]

Although recent articles have explored language and imagery that evokes notions of sacrifice[13] or Paul's priestly language in Romans,[14] my research could be applied to other letters to see how Paul's use of figurative temple language there compare to my insights from philosophy. In Romans, Paul speaks of his vocation using two priestly words: his call to be a λειτουργός in priestly service (ἱερουργέω) to make an offering (προσφορά) of the Gentiles (15:16) as well as urging his readers to offer their bodies as θυσίαν ζῶσαν ἁγίαν εὐάρεστον τῷ θεῷ (12:1). In Phil 2:17, Paul paints a picture of himself as a drink offering, using the verb σπένδω in relation to the sacrifice (θυσία) and (cultic) service (λειτουργία) of the Philippians' faith and toward the end of the same letter, in Phil 4:18, Paul calls their gift a fragrant offering, using the same language as 2 Cor 2:14–16 (ὀσμὴν εὐωδίας), as well as an acceptable sacrifice (θυσίαν δεκτήν). Both congregations were majority Gentile, one in Rome and the other a Roman colony (Philippi), so exploring the use of these phrases in their context in the letter and in Roman society and philosophy would be a fruitful exercise. The same verb used in Phil 2:17 (σπένδω, meaning to be poured out as a libation) also appears in 2 Tim 4:6 and could be explored in its context. Ephesians contains a striking parallel to my study in 1–2 Corinthians, with its reference to the people of God growing into "a holy temple in the Lord" (Eph 2:21) with Christ as the center (2:21a) and cornerstone/capstone (2:20), and in whom (2:22a) they are being built into a dwelling place (κατοικητήριον) for God in the Spirit. Given what we know of the religious and philosophical climate in Ephesus (includ-

---

11. McKelvey, *New Temple*, 25–41. Examples include *1 En.* 14:1–25; 24–26; 71:5; *4 Ezra* 10:25–28; *2 Bar.* 4:1–7.

12. With Thrall, *2 Corinthians 1–7*, 359; Harris, *Second Epistle*, 374; Keener, *1–2 Corinthians*, 180. Collange, *Enigmes*, 183, notes that in the LXX, the opposite, χειροποίητος, is frequently used for idols (e.g., Lev 26:1, 30; Isa 2:18, 10:11). It is at least possible for the Corinthian readers that Paul's use of ἀχειροποίητος may suggest to them *that* which comes from God, as opposed to *that* which comes from idolatry. See further, Gupta, *Worship*, 90–96.

13. Adewuya, "Sacrificial-Missiological Function," 88–98.

14. Gibson, "Paul," 51–62.

ing from Acts 18–19), it would be instructive to examine Eph 2:18–22 both in reference to that environment and the wider themes of the letter relating to cosmic unity (1:10; 2:11–22; 3:4–6; 4:6), heavenly and earthly rulers and powers (1:20–22; 2:2; 3:10; 6:10–20) and union with Christ (1:3; 2:1–7; 3:14–21; 4:13; 5:31–32). In the light of these studies, a further study might then be made, comparing the language of figurative sacrifices and temples in the undisputed Paulines (Romans, 1–2 Corinthians, Philippians) with the references found in the disputed Paulines (perhaps including 1 Tim 3:15, if this is a figurative temple reference).

Beyond the study of figurative temple language applied to Christians, while monographs have been written on Jesus as temple in the Gospels,[15] or as a sacrifice in the epistles,[16] a comparison with the figurative temple language in Hellenistic philosophy would illuminate the possible reception of these images among Gentile Christians and others influenced by Hellenism. Similarly, the understanding of Jesus as both Priest and sacrifice and the use of heavenly tabernacle language in Hebrews[17] could be compared with the relevant material.

6.3 CONCLUSIONS

If we compare the three figurative temple passages in Paul with the teaching I have examined in philosophy, we can see a number of points of comparison. Paul concurs with the philosophers that the divine Spirit dwells in people. This is emphasized repeatedly in philosophy and in each of the passages I have explored in Paul. However, all three Pauline references have a corporate dimension (even when Paul is speaking of the individual human body in 1 Cor 6:19), whereas philosophy speaks of the Spirit dwelling in individuals (with a singular exception in Philo). Paul always stresses the holiness or separateness of the temple, as do the philosophers and both speak of the need for this temple to be set apart and cleansed from defilement. For Paul, the temple is holy because its foundation is Jesus Christ (1 Cor 3:11) in whom they believe (2 Cor 6:14–15). The wisdom (1 Cor 1:18–2:13; 3:19) and spirit (1 Cor 2:12) of the world are described negatively. For the philosophers, it is the wise and the good who are indwelt by the Spirit, associated with reason; this Spirit

---

15. E.g., Coloe, *God Dwells*; Perrin, *Jesus*.
16. E.g., Finlan, *Background*; Patterson, *Keeping the Feast*.
17. See, e.g., Son, *Zion Symbolism*.

dwells in all things and Wisdom is to be sought above all. Both Paul and philosophy would agree that the temple is holy because God dwells there.

In sharp contrast to the disparagement of the physical body seen in philosophy (with the exception of a corporeal reference in both Philo and Epictetus, though elsewhere Epictetus is negative about the body), Paul emphasizes that the physical body is included as the place where God dwells in 1 Cor 6:19. For philosophers, only the soul/mind could occupy that role. While philosophers speak of the world without exception being the dwelling place of God, for Paul it is only those people washed, sanctified, and justified in the name of Jesus and the Spirit (1 Cor 6:11), in whom the Spirit dwells. The philosophers would agree with Paul on the necessity of glorifying God, but Paul's addition to this instruction, "in the body" (1 Cor 6:20), stands out from the philosophers' disdain for the corporeal. Philosophy speaks positively of many gods who share the benevolent characteristics of God but Paul sees them only as idols and associates them with unbelief and darkness (2 Cor 6:14–15). Both Paul and the philosophers speak of the temple in inclusive and exclusive terms but with very different frames of reference. Paul stresses that all are welcomed and included; both Jews and Gentiles and sons and daughters, and Paul includes himself in the temple with the congregation, without making distinctions between them. The philosophers often spoke inclusively of the whole world being God's temple. Philosophy sometimes spoke of the temple exclusively too, portraying the wise and the good especially as indwelt by the Spirit. For Paul, by contrast, it is only those who believe in and belong to Christ who are the temple.

These similarities and differences can be represented by the table below:

Paul	Philosophy: Similarities	Philosophy: Differences
1 Cor 3:16–17		
Spirit dwells in people	Spirit/Reason/daemon dwells in people	
Congregation (corporate) is temple		Spirit dwells in individual as temple
Temple is holy; foundation is Jesus Christ (not wisdom)	Temple is holy	Spirit dwells especially in good/wise

Conclusions

Paul	Philosophy: Similarities	Philosophy: Differences
Wisdom of the world (1:18–2:13; 3:19) viewed negatively		Spirit dwells in wise and associated with Reason
Spirit of the world (2:12) viewed negatively		Spirit fills the world
People made holy by God's presence	People made holy by God's presence	
People made holy as God's temple (corporate)	People made holy as God's temple	. . . but as individuals only
1 Cor 6:19–20		
The body is a temple		The soul/mind is a temple. Body treated with indifference/disdain
Corporate dimension (possessive plural personal pronoun with body even though body is singular)		Individual soul or mind; not body
Temple indwelt by Holy Spirit	Temple indwelt by Holy Spirit	
Temple is Holy	Temple is Holy	
Temple is those washed, sanctified and justified in the name of Jesus and the Spirit (6:11)		Temple is world without exception
Glorify God	Glorify God	
. . . in the body		Have as little to do with the body as possible
2 Cor 6:14—7:1		
Only one God; the rest are idols associated with unbelief and darkness		There are multiple gods who share the benevolent characteristics of God
Temple is corporate		Temple is individual
Temple is inclusive: Jews and Gentiles, Sons and daughters; Apostle and congregation	Temple is inclusive: all in the world	

Paul	Philosophy: Similarities	Philosophy: Differences
Temple is exclusive: only those who believe in Christ		Temple is sometimes spoken of exclusively: the wise and the good especially indwelt by the Spirit
Purity vital; cleansing from defilement necessary	Purity vital; cleansing from defilement necessary	

If the Corinthians read Paul's figurative temple language with an awareness of the kinds of emphases I have noted in philosophy, they may have been struck by several points. The human body is a temple, not just the soul/mind and this body must be kept pure and used as a vessel to glorify God. What counts is not the Spirit, wisdom or reason found in the world but the Holy Spirit who grants wisdom to those who belong to Christ. There are no other gods but the God of Jesus Christ; the rest are idols and the temple must avoid idolatry. Most of all, Paul always identifies the temple as a community who are defined by their relationship to Jesus Christ.

Bibliography

PRIMARY SOURCES

Alcinous. *The Handbook of Platonism*. Translated by John Dillon. Clarendon Later Ancient Philosophers. Oxford: Clarendon, 1993.

Apuleius. *Metamorphoses*. Translated by J. Arthur Hanson. 2 vols. Loeb Classical Library. Cambridge: Harvard University Press, 1989-1996.

Aristotle. *On the Soul. Parva Naturalia. On Breath*. Translated by W. S. Hett. Aristotle Vol. VIII. Loeb Classical Library 288. Cambridge: Harvard University Press, 1957.

Arius Didymus. *Epitome of Stoic Ethics*. Society of Biblical Literature Texts and Translations 44. Edited by Arthur J. Pomeroy. Atlanta: Society of Biblical Literature, 1999.

Charlesworth, J. H., ed. *The Old Testament Pseudepigrapha*. 2 vols. Peabody, MA: Hendrickson, 2010.

Cicero. *On Ends*. Translated by H. Rackham. Cicero Vol. XVII. Loeb Classical Library 40. Cambridge: Harvard University Press, 1914.

———. *On the Nature of the Gods. Academics*. Translated by H. Rackham. Cicero Vol. XIX. Loeb Classical Library 268. Cambridge: Harvard University Press, 1933.

———. *On Old Age. On Friendship. On Divination*. Translated by W. A. Falconer. Cicero Vol. XX. Loeb Classical Library 154. Cambridge: Harvard University Press, 1923.

———. *On the Orator: Book 3. On Fate. Stoic Paradoxes. Divisions of Oratory*. Translated by H. Rackham. Cicero Vol. IV. Loeb Classical Library 349. Cambridge: Harvard University Press, 1942.

———. *On the Republic. On the Laws*. Translated by Clinton W. Keyes. Cicero Vol. XVI. Loeb Classical Library 213. Cambridge: Harvard University Press, 1928.

———. *Tusculan Disputations*. Translated by J. E. King. Cicero Vol. XVIII. Loeb Classical Library 141. Cambridge: Harvard University Press, 1927.

Dio Chrysostom. *Discourses 1-11*. Translated by J. W. Cohoon. Dio Chrysostom Vol. I. Loeb Classical Library 257. Cambridge: Harvard University Press, 1932.

———. *Discourses 12-30*. Translated by J. W. Cohoon. Dio Chrysostom Vol. II. Loeb Classical Library 339. Cambridge: Harvard University Press, 1939.

———. *Discourses 31–36.* Translated by J. W. Cohoon, H. Lamar Crosby. Dio Chrysostom Vol. III. Loeb Classical Library 358. Cambridge: Harvard University Press, 1940.

———. *Discourses 37–60.* Translated by H. Lamar Crosby. Dio Chrysostom Vol. IV. Loeb Classical Library 376. Cambridge: Harvard University Press, 1946.

———. *Discourses 61–80. Fragments. Letters.* Translated by H. Lamar Crosby. Dio Chrysostom Vol. V. Loeb Classical Library 385. Cambridge: Harvard University Press, 1951.

Diogenes Laertius. *Lives of Eminent Philosophers.* Vol. 1, *Books 1–5.* Translated by R. D. Hicks. Diogenes Laertius Vol. I. Loeb Classical Library 184. Cambridge: Harvard University Press, 1925.

———. *Lives of Eminent Philosophers.* Vol. 2, *Books 6–10.* Translated by R. D. Hicks. Diogenes Laertius Vol. II. Loeb Classical Library 185. Cambridge: Harvard University Press, 1925.

Epictetus. *Discourses.* Translated by W. A. Oldfather. 2 vols. Loeb Classical Library. Cambridge: Harvard University Press, 1925–28.

Euripides. *Trojan Women. Iphigenia among the Taurians. Ion.* Edited and translated by David Kovacs. Euripides Vol. IV. Loeb Classical Library 10. Cambridge: Harvard University Press, 1999.

Eusebius. *Preparation for the Gospel.* Part 1: Books 1–9. Translated by Edwin Hamilton Gifford. Grand Rapids: Baker Book House, 1981.

Fronto. *Correspondence.* Translated by C. R. Haines. 2 vols. Loeb Classical Library. Cambridge: Harvard University Press, 1919–20.

García Martínez, Florentino, and Eibert J. C. Tigchelaar, eds. *The Dead Sea Scrolls Study Edition.* 2 vols. Grand Rapids: Eerdmans, 1997–1998.

García Martínez, Florentino. *Qumran and Apocalyptic: Studies on the Aramaic Texts from Qumran.* Studies on the Texts of the Desert of Judah 9. Leiden: Brill, 1992.

Gellius. *Attic Nights.* Translated by J. C. Rolfe. 3 vols. Loeb Classical Library. Cambridge: Harvard University Press, 1927.

Homer. *Odyssey.* Vol. 1, *Books 1–12.* Translated by A. T. Murray. Revised by George E. Dimock. Loeb Classical Library 104. Cambridge: Harvard University Press, 1919.

———. *Odyssey.* Vol. 2, *Books 13–24.* Translated by A. T. Murray. Revised by George E. Dimock. Loeb Classical Library 105. Cambridge: Harvard University Press, 1919.

Josephus. *Jewish Antiquities.* Vol. 8, *Books 18–19.* Translated by Louis H. Feldman. Josephus Vol. XII. Loeb Classical Library 433. Cambridge: Harvard University Press, 1965.

———. *The Jewish War.* Vol. 1, *Books 1–2.* Translated by H. St. J. Thackeray. Josephus Vol. II. Loeb Classical Library 203. Cambridge: Harvard University Press, 1927.

———. *The Life. Against Apion.* Translated by H. St. J. Thackeray. Josephus Vol. I. Loeb Classical Library 186. Cambridge: Harvard University Press, 1926.

Long, A. A., and D. N. Sedley. *The Hellenistic Philosophers.* Vol. 1, *Translations of the Principal Sources, with Philosophical Commentary.* Cambridge: Cambridge University Press, 1987.

———. *The Hellenistic Philosophers.* Vol. 2, *Greek and Latin Texts with Notes and Bibliography.* Cambridge: Cambridge University Press, 1987.

Lucretius. *On the Nature of Things.* Translated by W. H. D. Rouse. Revised by Martin F. Smith. Loeb Classical Library. Cambridge: Harvard University Press, 1992.

Bibliography 243

Lutz, Cora E. *Musonius Rufus, "The Roman Socrates."* New Haven: Yale University Press, 1947.

Marcus Aurelius. Translated by C. R. Haines. Loeb Classical Library. Cambridge: Harvard University Press, 1930.

Maximus of Tyre. *The Philosophical Orations.* Translated by M. B. Trapp. Oxford: Clarendon, 1997.

Petronius, Seneca. *Satyricon. Apocolocyntosis.* Translated by Michael Heseltine, W. H. D. Rouse. Revised by E. H. Warmington. Loeb Classical Library 15. Cambridge: Harvard University Press, 1913.

Philo. *Every Good Man Is Free. On the Contemplative Life. On the Eternity of the World. Against Flaccus. Apology for the Jews. On Providence.* Translated by F. H. Colson. Philo Vol. IX. Loeb Classical Library 363. Cambridge: Harvard University Press, 1941.

———. *On Abraham. On Joseph. On Moses.* Translated by F. H. Colson. Philo Vol. VI. Loeb Classical Library 289. Cambridge: Harvard University Press, 1935.

———. *On the Cherubim. The Sacrifices of Abel and Cain. The Worse Attacks the Better. On the Posterity and Exile of Cain. On the Giants.* Translated by F. H. Colson, G. H. Whitaker. Philo Vol. II. Loeb Classical Library 227. Cambridge: Harvard University Press, 1929.

———. *On the Confusion of Tongues. On the Migration of Abraham. Who Is the Heir of Divine Things? On Mating with the Preliminary Studies.* Translated by F. H. Colson, G. H. Whitaker. Philo Vol. IV. Loeb Classical Library 261. Cambridge: Harvard University Press, 1932.

———. *On the Creation. Allegorical Interpretation of Genesis 2 and 3.* Translated by F. H. Colson, G. H. Whitaker. Philo Vol. I. Loeb Classical Library 226. Cambridge: Harvard University Press, 1929.

———. *On the Decalogue. On the Special Laws, Books 1–3.* Translated by F. H. Colson. Philo Vol. VII. Loeb Classical Library 320. Cambridge: Harvard University Press, 1937.

———. *On the Embassy to Gaius. General Indexes.* Translated by F. H. Colson. Index by J. W. Earp. Philo Vol. X. Loeb Classical Library 379. Cambridge: Harvard University Press, 1962.

———. *On Flight and Finding. On the Change of Names. On Dreams.* Translated by F. H. Colson, G. H. Whitaker. Philo Vol. V. Loeb Classical Library 275. Cambridge: Harvard University Press, 1934.

———. *On the Special Laws, Book 4. On the Virtues. On Rewards and Punishments.* Translated by F. H. Colson. Philo Vol. VIII. Loeb Classical Library 341. Cambridge: Harvard University Press, 1939.

———. *On the Unchangeableness of God. On Husbandry. Concerning Noah's Work as a Planter. On Drunkenness. On Sobriety.* Translated by F. H. Colson, G. H. Whitaker. Philo Vol. III. Loeb Classical Library 247. Cambridge: Harvard University Press, 1930.

———. *Questions on Exodus.* Translated by Ralph Marcus. Philo Supplement II. Loeb Classical Library 401. Cambridge: Harvard University Press, 1953.

———. *Questions on Genesis.* Translated by Ralph Marcus. Philo Supplement I. Loeb Classical Library 380. Cambridge: Harvard University Press, 1953.

———. *The Works of Philo: Complete and Unabridged. New Updated Edition.* Translated by C. D. Yonge. Grand Rapids: Hendrickson, 1993.

Philostratus. *Apollonius of Tyana*. Vol. 1, *Life of Apollonius of Tyana, Books 1–4*. Edited and translated by Christopher P. Jones. Philostratus. Apollonius of Tyana Vol I. Loeb Classical Library 16. Cambridge: Harvard University Press, 2005.

———. *Apollonius of Tyana*. Vol. 2, *Life of Apollonius of Tyana, Books 5–8*. Edited and translated by Christopher P. Jones. Philostratus. Apollonius of Tyana Vol II. Loeb Classical Library 17. Cambridge: Harvard University Press, 2005.

———. *Apollonius of Tyana, Volume III: Letters of Apollonius. Ancient Testimonia. Eusebius's Reply to Hierocles*. Edited and translated by Christopher P. Jones. Philostratus. Apollonius of Tyana Vol III. Loeb Classical Library 458. Cambridge: Harvard University Press, 2006.

Pindar. *Nemean Odes. Isthmian Odes. Fragments*. Edited and translated by William H. Race. Pindar Vol. II. Loeb Classical Library 485. Cambridge: Harvard University Press, 1997.

Plato. *Charmides. Alcibiades I and II. Hipparchus. The Lovers. Theages. Minos. Epinomis*. Translated by W. R. M. Lamb. Plato Vol. XII. Loeb Classical Library 201. Cambridge: Harvard University Press, 1927.

———. *Euthyphro. Apology. Crito. Phaedo. Phaedrus*. Translated by Harold North Fowler. Plato Vol. I. Loeb Classical Library 36. Cambridge: Harvard University Press, 1914.

———. *Laws*. Vol. 1, *Books 1–6*. Translated by R. G. Bury. Plato Vol. X. Loeb Classical Library 187. Cambridge: Harvard University Press, 1926.

———. *Timaeus. Critias. Cleitophon. Menexenus. Epistles*. Translated by R. G. Bury. Plato Vol. IX. Loeb Classical Library 234. Cambridge: Harvard University Press, 1929.

Plutarch. *Moralia*. Vol. 1, *The Education of Children. How the Young Man Should Study Poetry. On Listening to Lectures. How to Tell a Flatterer from a Friend. How a Man May Become Aware of His Progress in Virtue*. Translated by Frank Cole Babbitt. Loeb Classical Library 197. Cambridge: Harvard University Press, 1927.

———. *Moralia*. Vol. 2, *How to Profit by One's Enemies. On Having Many Friends. Chance. Virtue and Vice. Letter of Condolence to Apollonius. Advice About Keeping Well. Advice to Bride and Groom. The Dinner of the Seven Wise Men. Superstition*. Translated by Frank Cole Babbitt. Loeb Classical Library 222. Cambridge: Harvard University Press, 1928.

———. *Moralia*. Vol. 4, *Roman Questions. Greek Questions. Greek and Roman Parallel Stories. On the Fortune of the Romans. On the Fortune or the Virtue of Alexander. Were the Athenians More Famous in War or in Wisdom?*. Translated by Frank Cole Babbitt. Loeb Classical Library 305. Cambridge: Harvard University Press, 1936.

———. *Moralia*. Vol. 5, *Isis and Osiris. The E at Delphi. The Oracles at Delphi No Longer Given in Verse. The Obsolescence of Oracles*. Translated by Frank Cole Babbitt. Loeb Classical Library 306. Cambridge: Harvard University Press, 1936.

———. *Moralia*. Vol. 6, *Can Virtue Be Taught? On Moral Virtue. On the Control of Anger. On Tranquility of Mind. On Brotherly Love. On Affection for Offspring. Whether Vice Be Sufficient to Cause Unhappiness. Whether the Affections of the Soul are Worse Than Those of the Body. Concerning Talkativeness. On Being a Busybody*. Translated by W. C. Helmbold. Loeb Classical Library 337. Cambridge: Harvard University Press, 1939.

———. *Moralia*. Vol. 7, *On Love of Wealth. On Compliancy. On Envy and Hate. On Praising Oneself Inoffensively. On the Delays of the Divine Vengeance. On Fate. On *the Sign of Socrates. On Exile. Consolation to His Wife.* Translated by Phillip H. De Lacy and Benedict Einarson. Loeb Classical Library 405. Cambridge: Harvard University Press, 1959.

———. *Moralia.* Vol. 8, *Table-Talk, Books 1–6.* Translated by P. A. Clement, H. B. Hoffleit. Loeb Classical Library 424. Cambridge: Harvard University Press, 1969.

———. *Moralia.* Vol. 9, *Table-Talk, Books 7–9. Dialogue on Love.* Translated by Edwin L. Minar, F. H. Sandbach, W. C. Helmbold. Loeb Classical Library 425. Cambridge: Harvard University Press, 1961.

———. *Moralia.* Vol. 10, *Love Stories. That a Philosopher Ought to Converse Especially With Men in Power. To an Uneducated Ruler. Whether an Old Man Should Engage in Public Affairs. Precepts of Statecraft. On Monarchy, Democracy, and Oligarchy. That We Ought Not to Borrow. Lives of the Ten Orators. Summary of a Comparison Between Aristophanes and Menander.* Translated by Harold North Fowler. Loeb Classical Library 321. Cambridge: Harvard University Press, 1936.

———. *Moralia.* Vol. 13, *Part 1: Platonic Essays.* Translated by Harold Cherniss. Loeb Classical Library 427. Cambridge: Harvard University Press, 1976.

———. *Moralia.* Vol. 13, *Part 2: Stoic Essays.* Translated by Harold Cherniss. Loeb Classical Library 470. Cambridge: Harvard University Press, 1976.

———. *Moralia.* Vol. 14, *That Epicurus Actually Makes a Pleasant Life Impossible. Reply to Colotes in Defence of the Other Philosophers. Is "Live Unknown" a Wise Precept? On Music.* Translated by Benedict Einarson, Phillip H. De Lacy. Loeb Classical Library 428. Cambridge: Harvard University Press, 1967.

Ramelli, Ilaria. *Hierocles the Stoic: Elements of Ethics, Fragments, and Excerpts.* Translated by David Konstan. Society of Biblical Literature Writings from the Greco-Roman World 28. Atlanta: Society of Biblical Literature, 2009.

Seneca. *Epistles.* Vol. 1, *Epistles 1–65.* Translated by Richard M. Gummere. Seneca Vol. IV. Loeb Classical Library 75. Cambridge: Harvard University Press, 1917.

———. *Epistles.* Vol. 2, *Epistles 66–92.* Translated by Richard M. Gummere. Seneca Vol. V. Loeb Classical Library 76. Cambridge: Harvard University Press, 1920.

———. *Epistles.* Vol. 3, *Epistles 93–124.* Translated by Richard M. Gummere. Seneca Vol. VI. Loeb Classical Library 77. Cambridge: Harvard University Press, 1925.

Seneca. *Moral Essays.* Vol. 1, *De Providentia. De Constantia. De Ira. De Clementia.* Translated by John W. Basore. Loeb Classical Library 214. Seneca Vol. I. Cambridge: Harvard University Press, 1928.

———. *Moral Essays.* Vol. 2, *De Consolatione ad Marciam. De Vita Beata. De Otio. De Tranquillitate Animi. De Brevitate Vitae. De Consolatione ad Polybium. De Consolatione ad Helviam.* Translated by John W. Basore. Seneca Vol. II. Loeb Classical Library 254. Cambridge: Harvard University Press, 1932.

———. *Moral Essays.* Vol. 3, *De Beneficiis.* Translated by John W. Basore. Seneca Vol. III. Loeb Classical Library 310. Cambridge: Harvard University Press, 1935.

———. *Natural Questions, Volume I: Books 1–3.* Translated by Thomas H. Corcoran. Seneca Vol. VII. Loeb Classical Library 450. Cambridge: Harvard University Press, 1971.

Sextus Empiricus. *Against Physicists. Against Ethicists.* Translated by R. G. Bury. Sextus Empiricus Vol. III. Loeb Classical Library 311. Cambridge: Harvard University Press, 1936.

Valerius Maximus. *Memorable Doings and Sayings*. Vol. 1, Books 1–5. Edited and translated by D. R. Shackleton Bailey. Valerius Maximus Vol. I. Loeb Classical Library 492. Cambridge: Harvard University Press, 2000.

Virgil. *Eclogues. Georgics. Aeneid: Books 1–6*. Translated by H. Rushton Fairclough. Revised by G. P. Goold. Virgil Vol. I. Loeb Classical Library 63. Cambridge: Harvard University Press, 1916.

SECONDARY SOURCES

Adams, Edward, and David G. Horrell. *Christianity at Corinth: The Quest for the Pauline Church*. Louisville: Westminster John Knox, 2004.

Adewuya, J. Ayodeji. *Holiness and Community in 2 Cor 6:14—7:1: Paul's View of Communal Holiness in the Corinthian Correspondence*. Studies in Biblical Literature 40. New York: Peter Lang, 2001.

———. "The People of God in a Pluralistic Society: Holiness in 2 Corinthians." In *Holiness and Ecclesiology in the New Testament*, edited by Kent E. Brower and Andy Johnson, 201–18. Grand Rapids: Eerdmans, 2007.

———. "The Sacrificial-Missiological Function of Paul's Sufferings in the Context of 2 Corinthians." In *Paul as Missionary: Identity, Activity, Theology, and Practice*, edited by Trevor J. Burke and Brian S. Rosner, 88–98. Library of New Testament Studies 420. London: T&T Clark, 2011.

Aernie, Jeffrey W. *Is Paul Also Among the Prophets?: An Examination of the Relationship between Paul and the Old Testament Prophetic Tradition in 2 Corinthians*. Library of New Testament Studies 467. London: T&T Clark, 2012.

Algra, Keimpe. "Stoic Theology." In *The Cambridge Companion to the Stoics*, edited by Brad Inwood, 153–78. New York: Cambridge University Press, 2003.

———, et al., eds. *The Cambridge History of Hellenistic Philosophy*. Cambridge: Cambridge University Press, 1999.

Allo, E.-B. *Saint Paul: Seconde Épître aux Corinthiens*. Etudes bibliques. 2nd ed. Paris: Gabalda, 1956.

Amador, J. D. H. "Revisiting 2 Corinthians: Rhetoric and the Case for Unity." *New Testament Studies* 46.1 (2000) 92–111.

Anderson, R. Dean. *Glossary of Greek Rhetorical Terms Connected to Methods of Argumentation, Figures and Tropes from Anaximenes to Quintilian*. Contributions to Biblical Exegesis and Theology 24. Leuven: Peeters, 2000.

Asmis, Elizabeth. "The Stoicism of Marcus Aurelius." *ANRW* 36.3:2228–52.

Atkinson, Kenneth. *I Cried to the Lord: A Study of the Psalms of Solomon's Historical Background and Social Setting*. Supplements to the Journal for the Study of Judaism 84. Leiden: Brill, 2004.

———. *An Intertextual Study of the Psalms of Solomon: Pseudepigrapha*. Studies in the Bible and Early Christianity 49. Lewiston, NY: Edwin Mellen, 2001.

Attridge, Harold W. "Making Scents of Paul: The Background and Sense of 2 Cor 2:14–17." In *Early Christianity and Classical Culture: Comparative Studies in Honor of Abraham J. Malherbe*, edited by John T. Fitzgerald et al., 71–88. Supplements to Novum Testamentum 110. Leiden: Brill, 2003.

Aune, David E. "Human Nature and Ethics in Hellenistic Philosophical Traditions and Paul: Some Issues and Problems." In *Paul in His Hellenistic Context*, edited by Troels Engberg-Pedersen, 291–312. Edinburgh: T&T Clark, 1994.

———. *The New Testament in Its Literary Environment*. Library of Early Christianity. Philadelphia: Westminster John Knox, 1987.

———. *The Westminster Dictionary of New Testament and Early Christian Literature and Rhetoric*. Louisville: Westminster John Knox, 2003.

Aus, Roger David. *Imagery of Triumph and Rebellion in 2 Corinthians 2:14–17 and Elsewhere in the Epistle: An Example of the Combination of Greco-Roman and Judaic Traditions in the Apostle Paul*. Lanham, MD: University Press of America, 2005.

Bailey, D. R. Shackleton. *Cicero. Classical Life and Letters*. New York: Scribner, 1971.

Balch, David L. "1 Corinthians 7:32–35 and Stoic Debates about Marriage, Anxiety, and Distraction." *Journal of Biblical Literature* 102.3 (1983) 429–39.

Barclay, John M. G. "Thessalonica and Corinth: Social Contrasts in Pauline Christianity." *Journal for the Study of the New Testament* 47 (1992) 49–74.

Barker, M. "Temple Imagery in Philo: An Indication of the Origin of the Logos?" In *Templum Amicitiae: Essays on the Second Temple Presented to Ernst Bammel*, edited by W. Horbury, 70–102. Journal for the Study of the New Testament: Supplement Series 48. Sheffield: JSOT, 1991.

Barnes, Nathan J. *Reading 1 Corinthians with Philosophically Educated Women*. Eugene, OR: Pickwick, 2014.

Barnett, Paul. *The Second Epistle to the Corinthians*. New International Commentary on the New Testament. Grand Rapids: Eerdmans, 1997.

Barrett, C. K. *The First Epistle to the Corinthians*. Black's New Testament Commentaries. Peabody, MA: Hendrickson, 1968.

———. "Paul's Opponents in II Corinthians." *New Testament Studies* 17 (1971) 233–54.

———. *The Second Epistle to the Corinthians*. Black's New Testament Commentaries. New York: Harper & Row, 1973.

Bartchy, S. Scott. *Μᾶλλον χρῆσαι: First Century Slavery and the Interpretation of 1 Corinthians 7:21*. Society of Biblical Literature Dissertation Series 11. Missoula, MT: Scholars Press, 1973.

Bauckham, Richard. "James and the Jerusalem Church." In *The Book of Acts in Its Palestinian Setting*, 415–80. The Book of Acts in Its First Century Setting 4. Grand Rapids: Eerdmans, 1995.

———. "The Parting of the Ways: What Happened and Why." *Studia theologica* 47 (1993) 135–51.

Bauer, W., F. W. Danker, W. F. Arndt, and F. W. Gingrich. *Greek-English Lexicon of the New Testament and Other Early Christian Literature*. 3rd ed. Chicago: University of Chicago Press, 2001.

Bauernfeind, Otto. "ἀρετή." In Vol. 1 of *Theological Dictionary of the New Testament*, edited by Gerhard Kittel, 457–61. Translated by Geoffrey Bromiley. Grand Rapids: Eerdmans, 1964.

Baumgarten, J. "The Essenes and the Temple—A Reappraisal." In *Studies in Qumran Law*, edited by Joseph M. Baumgarten, 57–74. Studies in Judaism in Late Antiquity 24. Leiden: Brill, 1977.

———. "Sacrifice and Worship among the Jewish Sectarians of the Dead Sea (Qumrân) Scrolls." *Harvard Theological Review* 46 (1953) 141–59.

Bibliography

Beale, Gregory K. "The Old Testament Background of Reconciliation in 2 Corinthians 5–7 and Its Bearing on the Literary Problem of 2 Corinthians 6:14—7:1." *New Testament Studies* 35.4 (1989) 550–81.

———. *The Temple and the Church's Mission: A Biblical Theology of the Dwelling Place of God*. New Studies in Biblical Theology 17. Downers Grove, IL: IVP, 2004.

Beck, Mark, ed. *A Companion to Plutarch*. Malden, MA: Wiley-Blackwell, 2014.

Becker, Jürgen. "Die Gemeinde als Tempel Gottes und die Tora." In *Das Gesetz im frühen Judentum und im Neuen Testament: Festschrift für Christoph Burchard zum 75. Geburtstag*, edited by Dieter Sanger and Matthias Konradt, 9–25. Novum Testamentum et Orbis Antiquus 57. Göttingen: Vandenhoeck & Ruprecht, 2006.

Belleville, Linda L. "Continuity or Discontinuity: A Fresh Look at 1 Corinthians in the Light of First-Century Epistolary Forms and Conventions." *Evangelical Quarterly* 59.1 (1987) 15–37.

———. *Reflections of Glory: Paul's Polemical Use of the Moses-Doxa Tradition in 2 Corinthians 3:1–18*. Journal for the Study of the New Testament: Supplement Series 52. Sheffield: Sheffield Academic, 1991.

Benoit, Pierre. "Qumran and the New Testament." In *Paul and Qumran: Studies in New Testament Exegesis*, edited by Jerome Murphy-O'Connor, 1–30. Chicago: Priory, 1968.

Best, Ernest. "Spiritual Sacrifice: General Priesthood in the New Testament." *Interpretation* 14 (1960) 273–99.

Betz, H. D. "2 Cor 6:16—7:1: An Anti-Pauline Fragment?" *Journal of Biblical Literature* 92 (1973) 88–108.

Bieringer, Reimund. "2 Korinther 6,14—7,1 Im Kontext des 2. Korintherbriefes: Forschungsüberblick und Versuch eines Eigenen Zugangs." In *Studies On 2 Corinthians*, edited by Reimund Bieringer and Jan Lambrecht, 551–70. Bibliotheca ephemeridum theologicarum lovaniensium 112. Leuven: Leuven University Press, 1994.

———, et al. *Second Corinthians in the Perspective of Late Second Temple Judaism*. Compendia Rerum Iudaicarum ad Novum Testamentum 14. Leiden: Brill, 2014.

Birnbaum, Ellen. "Allegorical Interpretation and Jewish Identity Among Alexandrian Jewish Writers." In *Neotestamentica et Philonica: Studies in Honor of Peder Borgen*, edited by David E. Aune et al., 307–29. Supplements to Novum Testamentum 106. Leiden: Brill, 2003.

Bobzien, Susanne. *Determinism and Freedom in Stoic Philosophy*. New York: Oxford University Press, 1998.

Borgen, Peder. "Philo of Alexandria." In *Jewish Writings of the Second Temple Period: Apocrypha, Pseudepigrapha, Qumran Sectarian Writings, Philo, Josephus*, edited by Michael E. Stone, 233–82. Compendia Rerum Iudaicarum ad Novum Testamentum. Philadelphia: Fortress, 1984.

———. *Philo of Alexandria: An Exegete for His Time*. Supplements to Novum Testamentum 86. Leiden: Brill, 1997.

Böttrich, Christfried. ""Ihr Seid der Tempel Gottes": Tempelmetaphorik und Gemeinde bei Paulus." In *Gemeinde ohne Tempel: Zur Substituierung und Transformation des Jerusalemer Tempels und seines Kults im Alten Testament, antiken Judentum und frühen Christentum*, edited by Beate Ego et al., 411–25. Wissenschaftliche Untersuchungen zum Neuen Testament 118. Tübingen: Mohr (Siebeck), 1999.

Brenk, Frederick E. "An Imperial Heritage: The Religious Spirit of Plutarch of Chaironeia." *ANRW* 36.1:248–349.
Brennan, Tad. "Stoic Moral Psychology." In *The Cambridge Companion to the Stoics*, edited by Brad Inwood, 257–94. New York: Cambridge University Press, 2003.
Brooke, George J. "2 Corinthians 6:14—7:1 Again: A Change in Perspective." In *The Dead Sea Scrolls and Pauline Literature*, edited by Jean-Sébastien Rey, 1–16. Studies on the Texts of the Desert of Judah 102. Leiden: Brill, 2014.
———. *The Dead Sea Scrolls and the New Testament*. Minneapolis: Fortress, 2005.
———. "Miqdash Adam, Eden and the Qumran Community." In *Gemeinde ohne Tempel: Zur Substituierung und Transformation des Jerusalemer Tempels und seines Kults im Alten Testament, antiken Judentum und frühen Christentum*, edited by Beate Ego et al., 285–301. Wissenschaftliche Untersuchungen zum Neuen Testament 118. Tübingen: Mohr (Siebeck), 1999.
———. "The Ten Temples in the Dead Sea Scrolls." In *Temple and Worship in Biblical Israel*, edited by John Day, 416–34. London: T&T Clark, 2005.
Brookins, Timothy A. *Corinthian Wisdom, Stoic Philosophy, and the Ancient Economy*. Society for New Testament Studies Monograph Series 159. New York: Cambridge University Press, 2014.
Brower, Kent. *Living as God's Holy People: Holiness and Community in Paul*. Eugene, OR: Wipf & Stock, 2009.
Brunschwig, Jacques. "Stoic Metaphysics." In *The Cambridge Companion to the Stoics*, edited by Brad Inwood, 206–32. New York: Cambridge University Press, 2003.
Brunschwig, Jacques, and David Sedley. "Hellenistic Philosophy." In *The Cambridge Companion to Greek and Roman Philosophy*, edited by David Sedley, 151–83. Cambridge: Cambridge University Press, 2003.
Brunt, J. C. "Rejected, Ignored or Misunderstood? The Fate of Paul's Approach to the Problem of Food Offered to Idols in Early Christianity." *New Testament Studies* 31 (1985) 113–24.
Bultmann, Rudolf. *The Second Letter to the Corinthians*. Translated by Roy A. Harrisville. Minneapolis: Augsburg Fortress, 1985.
Burk, Denny. "Discerning Corinthian Slogans through Paul's Use of the Diatribe in 1 Corinthians 6:12–20." *Bulletin for Biblical Research* 18.1 (2008) 99–121.
Burridge, Richard A. "About People, by People, for People: Gospel Genre and Audiences." In *The Gospels for All Christians: Rethinking the Gospel Audiences*, edited by Richard Bauckham, 113–45. Grand Rapids: Eerdmans, 1998.
Burton, Ernest De Witt. *Syntax of the Moods and Tenses in New Testament Greek*. Chicago: University of Chicago Press, 1900.
Byrne, Brendan. "Sinning against One's Own Body: Paul's Understanding of the Sexual Relationship in 1 Corinthians 6:18." *Catholic Biblical Quarterly* 45.4 (1983) 608–16.
Capes, D. B. *Old Testament Yahweh Texts in Paul's Christology*. WUNT 2:47. Tübingen: Mohr Siehbeck, 1992.
Caragounis, C. "'Fornication' and 'Concession'? Interpreting 1 Cor 7, 1–7." In *The Corinthian Correspondence*, edited by R. Bieringer, 543–60. Bibliotheca ephemeridum theologicarum lovaniensium. Leuven: Leuven University Press, 1996.
Carmignac, J. "L'utilité ou l'inutilité des sacrifices sanglants dans la "Règle de la Communauté" de Qumrân." *Revue biblique* 63 (1956) 524–32.

Chester, Andrew. "The Sibyl and the Temple." In *Templum Amicitiae: Essays on the Second Temple presented to Ernst Bammel*, edited by William Horbury, 37–69. Journal for the Study of the New Testament: Supplement Series 48. Sheffield: Sheffield Academic, 1991.

Cheung, A. T. *Idol Food in Corinth: Jewish Background and Pauline Legacy*. Journal for the Study of the New Testament: Supplement Series 176. Sheffield: Sheffield Academic, 1999.

Chow, John K. *Patronage and Power: A Study of Social Networks in Corinth*. Journal for the Study of the New Testament: Supplement Series 75. Sheffield: Sheffield Academic, 1992.

Ciampa, Roy E. "Revisiting the Euphemism in 1 Corinthians 7.1." *Journal for the Study of the New Testament* 31.3 (2009) 325–338.

Ciampa, Roy E., and Brian S. Rosner. *The First Letter to the Corinthians*. Pillar New Testament Commentary. Grand Rapids: Eerdmans, 2010.

Clarke, Andrew D. *Secular and Christian Leadership in Corinth: A Socio-Historical and Exegetical Study of 1 Corinthians 1–6*. Arbeiten zur Geschichte des antiken Judentums und des Urchristentums 18. Leiden: Brill, 1993.

Cohen, Naomi G. "The Mystery Terminology in Philo." In *Philo und das Neue Testament: Wechselseitige Wahrnehmungen I. Internationales Symposium Zum Corpus Judaeo-Hellenisticum. 1.-4. Mai 2003, Eisenach/Jena*, edited by Roland Deines and Karl-Wilhelm Niebuhr, 173–87. Wissenschaftliche Untersuchungen zum Neuen Testament 172. Tübingen: Mohr (Siebeck), 2004.

Colish, Marcia L. *The Stoic Tradition from Antiquity to the Early Middle Ages: I. Stoicism in Classical Latin Literature*. Studies in the History of Christian Thought 34. Leiden: Brill, 1985.

Collange, J.-F. *Enigmes de la Deuxieme Epitre de Paul aux Corinthiens: Etude Exegetique de 2 Cor 2,14—7,4*. Society for New Testament Studies Monograph Series 18. Cambridge: Cambridge University Press, 1972.

Collins, John J. *Daniel*. Hermeneia: A Critical and Historical Commentary on the Bible. Minneapolis: Fortress, 1993.

Collins, Raymond F. "Constructing a Metaphor. 1 Corinthians 3,9b–17 and Ephesians 2,19–22." In *Paul et L'Unité des Chrétiens*, edited by Jacques Schlosser, 193–216. Colloquium Oecumenicum Paulinum 19. Leuven: Peeters, 2010.

———. *First Corinthians*. Sacra Pagina 7. Collegeville, MN: Liturgical, 1999.

———. *The Power of Images in Paul*. Collegeville, MN: Liturgical, 2008.

Coloe, Mary L. *God Dwells with Us: Temple Symbolism in the Fourth Gospel*. Collegeville, MN: Liturgical, 2001.

Comfort, Philip W. *New Testament Text and Translation Commentary: Commentary on the Variant Readings of the Ancient New Testament Manuscripts and How They Relate to the Major English Translations*. Carol Stream, IL: Tyndale, 2008.

Conzelmann, Hans. *1 Corinthians: A Commentary on the First Epistle to the Corinthians*. Translated by James W. Leitch. Hermeneia: A Critical and Historical Commentary on the Bible. Philadelphia: Fortress, 1975.

Coppens, J. C. "The Spiritual Temple in the Pauline Letters and Its Background." In *Studia evangelica. Vol VI: Papers Presented to the Fourth International Congress on New Testament Studies Held at Oxford, 1969*, edited by Elizabeth A. Livingstone, 53–66. Texte und Untersuchungen zur Geschichte der altchristlichen Literatur 112. Berlin: Akademie Verlag, 1973.

Corbeill, Anthony. "Cicero and the Intellectual Milieu of the Late Republic." In *The Cambridge Companion to Cicero*, edited by Catherine Steel, 9-24. Cambridge: Cambridge University Press, 2013.
Corley, Jeremy. "An Intertextual Study of Proverbs and Ben Sira." In *Intertextual Studies in Ben Sira and Tobit*, edited by Jeremy Corley and Vincent Skemp, 155-82. Catholic Biblical Quarterly Monograph Series 38. Washington, DC: Catholic Biblical Association of America, 2005.
Dahl, N. A. "A Fragment and Its Context: 2 Corinthians 6:14—7:1." In *Studies in Paul: Theology for the Early Christian Mission*, edited by N. A. Dahl, 62-69. Minneapolis: Augsburg, 1977.
Daly, Robert J. *Christian Sacrifice: The Judaeo-Christian Background Before Origen*. Washington, DC: Catholic University of America Press, 1978.
———. *The Origins of the Christian Doctrine of Sacrifice*. Philadelphia: Fortress, 1978.
Daniélou, J. "La Symbolique du Temple de Jerusalem Chez Philon et Josephe." In *Le Symbolisme Cosmique des Monuments Religieux: Actes de la Conférence Internationle qui a eu lieu sous les Auspices de l'Is. M.E.O., à Rome, Avril-Mai 1955*, edited by Raymond Bloch, 83-90. Serie orientale Roma 14. Roma: Is. M.E.O., 1957.
Danker, Frederick W. *II Corinthians*. Minneapolis: Augsburg, 1989.
Davies, G. I. "The Presence of God in the Second Temple and Rabbinic Doctrine." In *Templum Amicitiae: Essays on the Second Temple Presented to Ernst Bammel*, edited by William Horbury, 32-36. Journal for the Study of the New Testament: Supplement Series 48. Sheffield: Sheffield Academic, 1991.
deLacey, D. R. "οἵτινές ἐστε ὑμεῖς: The Function of a Metaphor in Paul." In *Templum Amicitiae: Essays on the Second Temple Presented to Ernst Bammel*, edited by William Horbury, 391-409. Journal for the Study of the New Testament: Supplement Series 48. Sheffield: Sheffield Academic, 1991.
Deming, Will. *Paul on Marriage and Celibacy: The Hellenistic Background of 1 Corinthians 7*. 2nd ed. Grand Rapids: Eerdmans, 2004.
———. "The Unity of 1 Corinthians 5-6." *Journal of Biblical Literature* 115 (1996) 289-312.
Derrett, J. D. M. "2 Cor 6,14ff. a Midrash on Dt 22, 10." *Biblica* 59 (1978) 231-50.
deSilva, David. *4 Maccabees*. Guides to Apocrypha and Pseudepigrapha. London: Continuum, 1998.
———. *The Credentials of an Apostle: Paul's Gospel in 2 Corinthians 1-7*. North Richland Hills, TX: Bibal, 1998.
———. "Meeting the Exigency of a Complex Rhetorical Situation: Paul's Strategy in 2 Corinthians 1 through 7." *Andrews University Seminary Studies* 34.1 (1996) 5-22.
———. "Paul and the Stoa: A Comparison." *Journal of the Evangelical Theological Society* 38.4 (1995) 549-64.
———. "Recasting the Moment of Decision: 2 Corinthians 6:14—7:1 in Its Literary Context." *Andrews University Seminary Studies* 31 (1993) 3-16.
DeWitt, Norman Wentworth. *Epicurus and His Philosophy*. Minneapolis: University of Minnesota Press, 1954.
Dillon, John M. *The Middle Platonists: 80 B.C. to A.D. 220*. Ithaca, NY: Cornell University Press, 1977.
———. "Plutarch and Platonism." In *A Companion to Plutarch*, edited by Mark Beck, 61-72. Malden, MA: Wiley-Blackwell, 2014.

———. "Reclaiming the Heritage of Moses: Philo's Confrontation with Greek Philosophy." *Studia Philonica* 7 (1995) 108–23.

———. "A Response to Runia and Sterling." *Studia Philonica* 5 (1993) 151–55.

Dimant, Devorah. "4Q Florilegium and the Idea of the Community as a Temple." In *Hellenica and Judaica: Hommage à Valentin Nikiprowetzky*, edited by A. Caquot et al., 165–89. Leuven: Peeters, 1986.

Dodson, Derek S. *Reading Dreams: An Audience-Critical Approach to the Dreams in the Gospel of Matthew*. Library of New Testament Studies 397. London: T&T Clark, 2009.

Duff, Paul Brooks. "2 Corinthians 1–7: Sidestepping the Division Hypothesis Dilemma." *Biblical Theology Bulletin* 24 (1994) 16–26.

———. "Apostolic Suffering and the Language of Processions in 2 Corinthians 4:7–10." *Biblical Theology Bulletin* 21.4 (1991) 158–65.

———. "Metaphor, Motif, and Meaning: The Rhetorical Strategy Behind the Image 'Led in Triumph' in 2 Corinthians 2:14." *Catholic Biblical Quarterly* 53 (1991) 79–92.

———. "The Mind of the Redactor: 2 Cor. 6:14—7:1 in Its Secondary Context." *Novum Testamentum* 35 (1993) 160–80.

———. "The Transformation of the Spectator: Power, Perception, and the Day of Salvation." In *Society of Biblical Literature: 1987 Seminar Papers*, edited by Kent Harold Richards, 233–43. Society of Biblical Literature Seminar Papers 26. Atlanta: Scholars Press, 1987.

———. "Transformed 'from Glory to Glory': Paul's Appeal to the Experience of His Readers in 2 Corinthians 3:18." *Journal of Biblical Literature* 127.4 (2008) 759–80.

Dunn, James D. G. "2 Corinthians 3:17: The Lord Is the Spirit." *Journal of Theological Studies* 21.2 (1970) 309–20.

———. *The Theology of Paul the Apostle*. Grand Rapids: Eerdmans, 1998.

Dutch, Robert S. *The Educated Elite in 1 Corinthians: Education and Community Conflict in Graeco-Roman Context*. Journal for the Study of the New Testament: Supplement Series 271. London: T&T Clark, 2005.

Engberg-Pedersen, Troels. *Cosmology and Self in the Apostle Paul: The Material Spirit*. New York: Oxford University Press, 2010.

———. *Paul and the Stoics*. Louisville, KY: Westminster John Knox, 2000.

———. *Paul Beyond the Judaism-Hellenism Divide*. Louisville, KY: Westminster John Knox, 2001.

———, ed. *Paul in His Hellenistic Context*. Studies of the New Testament and Its World. Edinburgh: T&T Clark, 1994.

Enslin, Morton S., and Solomon Zeitlin. *The Book of Judith: Greek Text with an English Translation, Commentary and Critical Notes*. Jewish Apocryphal Literature Series 7. Leiden: Brill, 1972.

Fatehi, Mehrdad. *The Spirit's Relation to the Risen Lord in Paul*. Wissenschaftliche Untersuchungen zum Neuen Testament 128. Tübingen: Mohr Siebeck, 2000.

Fee, Gordon D. "1 Corinthians 7:1 in the NIV." *Journal of the Evangelical Theological Society* 23.4 (1980) 307–14.

———. "1 Corinthians 7:1–7 Revisited." In *Paul and the Corinthians: Studies on a Community in Conflict. Essays in Honour of Margaret Thrall*, edited by Trevor J. Burke and J. Keith Elliott, 197–213. Supplements to Novum Testamentum 109. Leiden: Brill, 2003.

———. "II Corinthians VI.14—VII.1 and Food Offered to Idols." *New Testament Studies* 23 (1977) 140–61.

———. "Christology and Pneumatology in Romans 8:9–11—and Elsewhere: Some Reflections on Paul as a Trinitarian." In *Jesus of Nazareth: Lord and Christ: Essays on the Historical Jesus and New Testament Christology*, edited by Joel B. Green and Max Turner, 312–31. Grand Rapids: Eerdmans, 1994.

———. "Εἰδωλόθυτα Once Again: An Interpretation of 1 Corinthians 8–10." *Biblica* 61.2 (1980) 172–97.

———. *The First Epistle to the Corinthians*. New International Commentary on the New Testament. Grand Rapids: Eerdmans, 1987.

———. *The First Epistle to the Corinthians*. New International Commentary on the New Testament. Revised ed. Grand Rapids: Eerdmans, 2014.

———. *God's Empowering Presence: The Holy Spirit in the Letters of Paul*. Peabody, MA: Hendrickson, 1994.

Ferguson, Everett. *Backgrounds of Early Christianity*. Grand Rapids: Eerdmans, 2003.

———. "Spiritual Sacrifice in Early Christianity and Its Environment." In *ANRW* 23.2:1151–89.

Filson, Floyd Vivian. "The Significance of the Temple in the Ancient Near East. Part IV, Temple, Synagogue, and Church." *Biblical Archaeologist* 7.4 (1944) 77–88.

Finlan, Stephen. *The Background and Content of Paul's Cultic Atonement Metaphors*. Society of Biblical Literature Academic Biblica 19. Atlanta: Society of Biblical Literature, 2004.

Fiore, Benjamin. "Passion in Paul and Plutarch: 1 Corinthians 5–6 and the Polemic Against Epicureans." In *Greeks, Romans, and Christians: Essays in Honor of Abraham J. Malherbe*, edited by David L. Balch et al., 135–43. Minneapolis: Fortress, 1990.

Fisk, Bruce. "Eating Meat Offered to Idols: Corinthian Behavior and Pauline Responses in 1 Corinthians 8–10 (A Response to Gordon Fee)." *Trinity Journal* 10 (1989) 49–70.

———. "Porneuein as Body Violation: The Unique Nature of Sexual Sin in 1 Corinthians 6:18." *New Testament Studies* 42.4 (1996) 540–58.

Fitzgerald, John T. *Cracks in an Earthen Vessel: An Examination of the Catalogues of Hardships in the Corinthian Correspondence*. Society of Biblical Literature Dissertation Series 99. Atlanta: Society of Biblical Literature, 1988.

Fitzmyer, Joseph A. *The Acts of the Apostles: A New Translation with Introduction and Commentary*. Anchor Bible 31. New Haven: Yale University Press, 1998.

———. *First Corinthians: A New Translation with Introduction and Commentary*. Anchor Bible 32. New Haven: Yale University Press, 2008.

———. "Glory Reflected on the Face of Christ (2 Cor 3:7—4:6)." In *According to Paul: Studies in the Theology of the Apostle*, 64–79. Mahwah, NJ: Paulist, 1993.

———. "Qumran and the Interpolated Paragraph in 2 Cor 6,14—7,1." *Catholic Biblical Quarterly* 23 (1961) 271–80.

———. *Tobit*. Commentaries on Early Jewish Literature. Berlin: De Gruyter, 2003.

Flusser, David. "The Dead Sea Sect and Pre-Pauline Christianity." In *Judaism and the Origins of Christianity*, edited by David Flusser, 23–74. Jerusalem: Magnes, 1988.

———. "Two Notes on the Midrash on 2 Sam. vii." *Israel Exploration Journal* 9.2 (1959) 99–109.

Fotopoulos, John. *Food Offered to Idols in Roman Corinth: A Social-Rhetorical Reconsideration of 1 Corinthians 8:1—11:1*. Wissenschaftliche Untersuchungen zum Neuen Testament 2. Reihe 151. Tübingen: Mohr (Siebeck), 2003.

Fraeyman, M. "La spiritualisation de l'Idée du Temple dans les Épîtres Pauliniennes." *Ephemerides theologicae lovanienses* XXIII (1947) 378–412.

Frede, Dorothea. "Stoic Determinism." In *The Cambridge Companion to the Stoics*, edited by Brad Inwood, 179–205. New York: Cambridge University Press, 2003.

Frede, Michael. "On the Stoic Conception of the Good." In *Topics in Stoic Philosophy*, edited by Katerina Ierodiakonou, 71–94. New York: Oxford University Press, 1999.

———. "Stoic Epistemology." In *The Cambridge History of Hellenistic Philosophy*, edited by Keimpe Algra et al., 295–322. Cambridge: Cambridge University Press, 1999.

Friesen, Steven J. "The Wrong Erastus." In *Corinth in Context: Comparative Studies on Religion and Society*, edited by Steven J. Friesen et al., 231–56. Supplements to Novum Testamentum 134. Leiden: Brill, 2010.

———, et al., eds. *Corinth in Context: Comparative Studies on Religion and Society*. Supplements to Novum Testamentum 134. Leiden: Brill, 2010.

Furnish, Victor Paul. *II Corinthians: A New Translation with Introduction and Commentary*. Anchor Bible 32a. New Haven: Yale University Press, 1984.

García Martínez, Florentino. "Priestly Functions in a Community without Temple." In *Gemeinde ohne Tempel: Zur Substituierung und Transformation des Jerusalemer Tempels und seines Kults im Alten Testament, antiken Judentum und frühen Christentum*, edited by Beate Ego et al., 303–19. Wissenschaftliche Untersuchungen zum Neuen Testament 118. Tübingen: Mohr (Siebeck), 1999.

Garcilazo, Albert V. *The Corinthian Dissenters and the Stoics*. Studies in Biblical Literature 106. New York: Peter Lang, 2007.

Gardner, Paul Douglas. *The Gifts of God and the Authentication of a Christian: An Exegetical Study of 1 Corinthians 8—11:1*. Lanham, MD: University Press of America, 1994.

Garland, David E. *1 Corinthians*. Baker Exegetical Commentary on the New Testament. Grand Rapids: Baker Academic, 2003.

Gärtner, Bertil E. *The Temple and the Community in Qumran and the New Testament: A Comparative Study in the Temple Symbolism of the Qumran Texts and the New Testament*. Cambridge: Cambridge University Press, 1965.

Gera, Deborah Levine. *Judith*. Commentaries on Early Jewish Literature. Berlin: De Gruyter, 2014.

Gibson, Richard J. "Paul the Missionary, in Priestly Service of the Servant-Christ (Romans 15.16)." In *Paul as Missionary: Identity, Activity, Theology, and Practice*, edited by Trevor J. Burke and Brian S. Rosner, 51–62. Library of New Testament Studies 420. London: T&T Clark, 2011.

Gill, Christopher. "The School in the Roman Imperial Period." In *The Cambridge Companion to the Stoics*, edited by Brad Inwood, 33–58. New York: Cambridge University Press, 2003.

Gnilka, Joachim. "2 Cor 6:14—7:1 in the Light of Qumran Texts and the Testaments of the Twelve Patriarchs." In *Paul and Qumran: Studies in New Testament Exegesis*, edited by Jerome Murphy-O'Connor, 48–68. London: Geoffrey Chapman, 1968.

Gooch, Peter D. *Dangerous Food: 1 Corinthians 8–10 in Its Context*. Waterloo, ON: Wilfrid Laurier University Press, 1993.

Goodenough, Edwin R. *An Introduction to Philo Judaeus*. 2nd ed. New York: Barnes & Noble, 1963.
———. *By Light, Light: The Mystic Gospel of Hellenistic Judaism*. New Haven: Yale University Press, 1935.
Goodwin, Mark J. *Paul: Apostle of the Living God*. Harrisburg, PA: Trinity Press International, 2001.
Gorman, Michael J. "'You Shall Be Cruciform for I Am Cruciform': Paul's Trinitarian Reconstruction of Holiness." In *Holiness and Ecclesiology in the New Testament*, edited by Kent E. Brower and Andy Johnson, 148–66. Grand Rapids: Eerdmans, 2007.
Goulder, M. D. "2 Cor. 6:14—7:1 as an Integral Part of 2 Corinthians." *Novum Testamentum* 36 (1994) 47–57.
Grant, Robert M. *Paul in the Roman World: The Conflict at Corinth*. Louisville, KY: Westminster John Knox, 2001.
Grässer, Erich. *Der zweite Brief an die Korinther Kapitel 1,1–7,16*. Ökumenischer Taschenbuchkommentar zum Neuen Testament 8/1. Gütersloh: Gütersloher Verlagshaus, 2002.
Gundry, Robert H. *Sōma in Biblical Theology with Emphasis on Pauline Anthropology*. Society for New Testament Studies Monograph Series 29. Cambridge: Cambridge University Press, 1976.
Gupta, Nijay. "The Question of Coherence in Philo's Cultic Imagery: A Socio-Literary Approach." *Journal for the Study of the Pseudepigrapha* 20.4 (2011) 277–97.
———. "Which 'Body' Is a Temple (1 Corinthians 6:19)? Paul Beyond the Individual/Communal Divide." *Catholic Biblical Quarterly* 72.3 (2010) 518–36.
———. *Worship That Makes Sense to Paul: A New Approach to the Theology and Ethics of Paul's Cultic Metaphors*. Beihefte zur Zeitschrift für die neutestamentliche Wissenschaft 175. Berlin: de Gruyter, 2010.
Guthrie, George H. *2 Corinthians*. Baker Exegetical Commentary on the New Testament. Grand Rapids: Baker Academic, 2015.
———. "Paul's Triumphal Procession Imagery (2 Cor 2.14–16a): Neglected Points of Background." *New Testament Studies* 61 (2015) 79–91.
Hadot, Pierre. *The Inner Citadel: The Meditations of Marcus Aurelius*. Translated by Michael Chase. Cambridge: Harvard University Press, 1998.
Hafemann, Scott J. *Paul, Moses, and the History of Israel: The Letter/Spirit Contrast and the Argument from Scripture in 2 Corinthians 3*. Wissenschaftliche Untersuchungen zum Neuen Testament 2. Reihe 81. Tübingen: Mohr (Siebeck), 1995.
———. *Suffering and the Spirit: An Exegetical Study of II Cor 2:14—3:3 within the Context of the Corinthian Correspondence*. Wissenschaftliche Untersuchungen zum Neuen Testament 2. Reihe 19. Tübingen: Mohr (Siebeck), 1986.
Hagner, Donald A. "The Vision of God in Philo and John: A Comparative Study." *Journal of the Evangelical Theological Society* 14.2 (1971) 81–93.
Hall, David R. *The Unity of the Corinthian Correspondence*. Journal for the Study of the New Testament: Supplement Series 251. London: T&T Clark, 2004.
Han, Paul. *Swimming in the Sea of Scripture: Paul's Use of the Old Testament in 2 Corinthians 4:7—13:13*. Library of New Testament Studies 519. London: T&T Clark, 2014.

Hankinson, R. J. "Determinism and Indeterminism." In *The Cambridge History of Hellenistic Philosophy*, edited by Keimpe Algra et al., 513–41. Cambridge: Cambridge University Press, 1999.

———. "Stoic Epistemology." In *The Cambridge Companion to the Stoics*, edited by Brad Inwood, 59–84. New York: Cambridge University Press, 2003.

Harner, Philip B. "Qualitative Anarthrous Predicate Nouns: Mark 15:39 and John 1:1." *Journal of Biblical Literature* 92.1 (1973) 75–87.

Harris, Murray J. *The Second Epistle to the Corinthians: A Commentary on the Greek Text*. New International Greek Testament Commentary. Grand Rapids: Eerdmans, 2005.

Hays, Richard B. *The Conversion of the Imagination: Paul as Interpreter of Israel's Scripture*. Grand Rapids: Eerdmans, 2005.

———. *Echoes of Scripture in the Letters of Paul*. New Haven: Yale University Press, 1993.

———. *First Corinthians*. Interpretation. Louisville, KY: Westminster John Knox, 1997.

Hayward, C. T. R. *The Jewish Temple: A Non-Biblical Sourcebook*. London: Routledge, 1996.

Heil, C. "Die Sprache der Absonderung in 2 Kor 6,17 und bei Paulus." In *The Corinthian Correspondence*, edited by R. Bieringer, 717–29. Bibliotheca ephemeridum theologicarum lovaniensium. Leuven: Leuven University Press, 1996.

Hogeterp, Albert L. A. "Community as a Temple in Paul's Letters: The Case of Cultic Terms in 2 Corinthians 6:14—7:1." In *Anthropology and Biblical Studies: Avenues of Approach*, edited by Louise J. Lawrence and Mario I. Aguilar, 281–95. Leiden: Deo, 2004.

———. *Paul and God's Temple: A Historical Interpretation of Cultic Imagery in the Corinthian Correspondence*. Biblical Tools and Studies 2. Leuven: Peeters, 2006.

Hollander, H. W., and M. de Jonge. *The Testaments of the Twelve Patriarchs: A Commentary*. Studia in Veteris Testamenti pseudepigrapha 8. Leiden: Brill, 1985.

Hooker, Morna D. "'The Sanctuary of His Body': Body and Sanctuary in Paul and John." *Journal for the Study of the New Testament* 39.4 (2017) 347–61.

Hornblower, Simon, Antony Spawforth, and Esther Eidinow, eds. *The Oxford Classical Dictionary*. 4th ed. Oxford: Oxford University Press, 2012.

Horrell, David. Review of *A New Temple for Corinth: Rhetorical and Archaeological Approaches to Pauline Imagery*, by John R. Lanci. *Journal of Theological Studies* 50 (1999) 708–11.

———. *The Social Ethos of the Corinthian Correspondence: Interests and Ideology from 1 Corinthians to 1 Clement*. Edinburgh: T&T Clark, 1996.

Horsley, Richard A. *Wisdom and Spiritual Transcendence at Corinth: Studies in First Corinthians*. Eugene, OR: Wipf & Stock, 2008.

Horst, Pieter W. van der, and Judith H. Newman. *Early Jewish Prayers in Greek*. Commentaries on Early Jewish Literature. Berlin: de Gruyter, 2008.

Howard, J. K. "'Christ Our Passover': A Study of the Passover-Exodus Theme in 1 Corinthians." *Evangelical Quarterly* 41.2 (1969) 97–108.

Hughes, Philip E. *The Second Epistle to the Corinthians*. New International Commentary on the New Testament. Grand Rapids: Eerdmans, 1962.

Hultgren, Stephen J. "2 Cor 6.14—7.1 and Rev 21.3–8: Evidence for the Ephesian Redaction of 2 Corinthians." *New Testament Studies* 49.1 (2003) 39–56.

Hurd, John C. *The Origin of 1 Corinthians*. London: SPCK, 1965.

Ierodiakonou, Katerina, ed. *Topics in Stoic Philosophy*. New York: Oxford University Press, 1999.

Inwood, Brad, ed. *The Cambridge Companion to the Stoics*. New York: Cambridge University Press, 2003.

———. *Ethics and Human Action in Early Stoicism*. New York: Oxford University Press, 1985.

Inwood, Brad, and Pierluigi Donini. "Stoic Ethics." In *The Cambridge History of Hellenistic Philosophy*, edited by Keimpe Algra et al., 675–738. Cambridge: Cambridge University Press, 1999.

Jacobson, Howard. *A Commentary on Pseudo-Philo's Liber Antiquitatum Biblicarum with Latin Text and English Translation*. Vol. 2. Arbeiten zur Geschichte des antiken Judentums und des Urchristentums 31. Leiden: Brill, 1996.

Jewett, Robert. *Paul's Anthropological Terms: A Study of Their Use in Conflict Settings*. Leiden: Brill, 1971.

———. "The Redaction of 1 Corinthians and the Trajectory of the Pauline School." *Journal of the American Academy of Religion: Supplement Series* 46 (1978) 398–444.

Johnson, Luke Timothy. *The Acts of the Apostles*. Sacra Pagina 5. Collegeville, MN: Liturgical, 1992.

———. *Among the Gentiles: Greco-Roman Religion and Christianity*. Anchor Yale Bible Reference Library. New Haven: Yale University Press, 2009.

Jones, C. P. *The Roman World of Dio Chrysostom*. Cambridge: Harvard University Press, 1978.

Kamesar, Adam. "Biblical Interpretation in Philo." In *The Cambridge Companion to Philo*, edited by Adam Kamesar, 65–91. Cambridge: Cambridge University Press, 2009.

———, ed. *The Cambridge Companion to Philo*. Cambridge: Cambridge University Press, 2009.

Keener, Craig S. *1–2 Corinthians*. New Cambridge Bible Commentary. New York: Cambridge University Press, 2005.

———. *Acts: An Exegetical Commentary: 15:1—23:35*. Grand Rapids: Baker Academic, 2014.

———. "Heavenly Mindedness and Earthly Good: Contemplating Matters Above in Colossians 3.1-2." *Journal of Greco-Roman Christianity and Judaism* 6 (2009) 175–90.

———. "The Pillars and the Right Hand of Fellowship in Galatians 2.9." *Journal of Greco-Roman Christianity and Judaism* 7 (2010) 51–58.

———. "Transformation through Divine Vision in 1 John 3:2-6." *Faith & Mission* 23 (2005) 13–22.

———. "We Beheld His Glory! (John 1:14)." In *John, Jesus, and History*. Vol. 2, *Aspects of Historicity in the Fourth Gospel*, edited by Paul N. Anderson et al., 15–25. Leiden: Brill, 2009.

Kempthorne, R. "Incest and the Body of Christ, a Study of 1 Corinthians 6:12-20." *New Testament Studies* 14.4 (1968) 568–74.

Kidd, I. G. "Stoic Intermediaries and the End for Man." In *Problems in Stoicism*, edited by A. A. Long, 150–72. London: Athlone Press, 1971.

Kittel, G., and G. Friedrich, eds. *Theological Dictionary of the New Testament*. Translated by G. W. Bromiley. 10 vols. Grand Rapids: Eerdmans, 1964–76.

Klauck, Hans-Josef. 2. *Korintherbrief*. Neue Echter Bibel 8. Echter: Würzburg, 1986.
———. "Kultische Symbolsprache bei Paulus." In *Freude am Gottesdienst. Aspekte ursprünglicher Liturgie*, edited by J. Schreiner, 107–18. Stuttgart: Verlag Katholisches Bibelwerk, 1983.
Klawans, Jonathan. *Purity, Sacrifice, and the Temple: Symbolism and Supersessionism in the Study of Ancient Judaism*. Oxford: Oxford University Press, 2006.
Klinzing, Georg. *Die Umdeutung des Kultus in der Qumrangemeinde und im Neuen Testament*. Studien zur Umwelt des Neuen Testaments 7. Göttingen: Vandenhoeck & Ruprecht, 1971.
Knibb, Michael A. *The Qumran Community*. Cambridge Commentaries on Writings of the Jewish and Christian World 200 BC to AD 200 2. Cambridge: Cambridge University Press, 1987.
Koester, Craig H. "The Spectrum of Johannine Readers." In *"What is John?" Readers and Readings of the Fourth Gospel*, edited by Fernando Segovia, 5–19. Society of Biblical Literature Symposium Series 3. Atlanta: Scholars Press, 1996.
Konsmo, Erik. *The Pauline Metaphors of the Holy Spirit: The Intangible Spirit's Tangible Presence in the Life of the Christian*. Studies in Biblical Literature 130. New York: Peter Lang, 2011.
Koskenniemi, Erkki. "Philo and Classical Education." In *Reading Philo: A Handbook to Philo of Alexandria*, edited by Torrey Seland, 102–28. Grand Rapids: Eerdmans, 2014.
Kremer, Jacob. *Der Erste Brief an die Korinther*. Regensburger Neues Testament. Regensburg: Friedrich Pustet, 1997.
Kristeller, Paul Oskar. *Greek Philosophers of the Hellenistic Age*. Translated by Gregory Woods. New York: Columbia University Press, 1993.
Kuck, David W. *Judgement and Community Conflict: Paul's Use of Apocalyptic Judgement Language in 1 Corinthians 3:5—4:5*. Supplements to Novum Testamentum 66. Leiden: Brill, 1992.
Kuhn, Heinz-Wolfgang. ""Gemeinde Gottes" in den Qumrantexten und bei Paulus unter Berücksichtigung des Toraverständnisses." In *Das Gesetz im frühen Judentum und im Neuen Testament: Festschrift für Christoph Burchard zum 75. Geburtstag*, edited by Dieter Sanger and Matthias Konradt, 153–69. Novum Testamentum et Orbis Antiquus 57. Göttingen: Vandenhoeck & Ruprecht, 2006.
Lacey, W. K. *Cicero and the End of the Roman Republic*. London: Hodder & Stoughton, 1978.
Lamberton, Robert. *Plutarch*. New Haven: Yale University Press, 2001.
Lambrecht, Jan. "The Fragment 2 Corinthians 6,14–7,1: A Plea for Its Authenticity." In *Studies on 2 Corinthians*, edited by Reimund Bieringer and Jan Lambrecht, 531–49. Bibliotheca ephemeridum theologicarum lovaniensium 112. Leuven: Leuven University Press, 1994.
———. "Paul's Reasoning in 1 Corinthians 6:12–20." *Ephemerides theologicae lovanienses* 85.4 (2009) 479–86.
———. *Second Corinthians*. Sacra Pagina 8. Collegeville, MN: Liturgical, 1999.
———. "Transformation in 2 Cor 3:18." *Biblica* 64 (1983) 243–54.
Lamp, Jeffrey S. *First Corinthians 1–4 in Light of Jewish Wisdom Traditions: Christ, Wisdom and Spirituality*. Studies in Bible and Early Christianity 42. Lewiston, NY: Edwin Mellen Press, 2000.

Lanci, John R. *A New Temple for Corinth: Rhetorical and Archaeological Approaches to Pauline Imagery*. Studies in Biblical Literature 1. New York: Peter Lang, 1997.
Lane, William L. "Covenant: The Key to Paul's Conflict with Corinth." *Tyndale Bulletin* 33 (1982) 3–29.
Lang, Friedrich. *Die Briefe an die Korinther*. Das Neue Testament Deutsch 7G. Göttingen: Vandenhoeck & Ruprecht, 1986.
Lapidge, Michael. "Stoic Cosmology and Roman Literature, First to Third Centuries A.D." *ANRW* 36.3:1379–429.
Laporte, Jean. "The High Priest in Philo of Alexandria." *Studia Philonica* 3 (1991) 71–82.
———. "Sacrifice and Forgiveness in Philo of Alexandria." *Studia Philonica* 1 (1989) 34–42.
Lee, Michelle V. *Paul, the Stoics, and the Body of Christ*. Society for New Testament Studies Monograph Series 137. Cambridge: Cambridge University Press, 2006.
Leonhardt, Jutta. *Jewish Worship in Philo of Alexandria*. Texte und Studien zum antiken Judentum 84. Tübingen: Mohr (Siebeck), 2001.
Leppä, Outi. "Believers and Unbelievers in 2 Corinthians 6:14–15." In *Lux Humana, Lux Aeterna: Essays on Biblical and Related Themes in Honour of Lars Aejmelaeus.*, edited by Antti Mustakallio, 374–90. Helsinki: Finnish Exegetical Society, 2005.
Levinsohn, Stephen H. *Discourse Features of New Testament Greek: A Coursebook on the Information Structure of New Testament Greek*. 2nd ed. Dallas: SIL International, 2000
Levison, John R. "The Spirit and the Temple in Paul's Letters to the Corinthians." In *Paul and His Theology*, edited by Stanley Porter, 189–215. Pauline Studies 3. Leiden: Brill, 2006.
Lévy, Carlos. "Philo's Ethics." In *The Cambridge Companion to Philo*, edited by Adam Kamesar, 146–71. Cambridge: Cambridge University Press, 2009.
Lichtenberger, Hermann. "Atonement and Sacrifice in the Qumran Community." In Vol. 2, *Approaches to Ancient Judaism*, edited by William Scott Green, 159–71. Brown Judaic Studies 9. Chico, CA: Scholars Press, 1980.
Liddell, H. G., R. Scott, and H. S. Jones. *A Greek-English Lexicon*. 9th ed. with revised supplement. Oxford: Clarendon, 1996
Lieber, Andrea. "Between Motherland and Fatherland: Diaspora, Pilgrimage and the Spiritualization of Sacrifice in Philo of Alexandria." In *Heavenly Tablets: Interpretation, Identity and Tradition in Ancient Judaism*, edited by Lynn Lidonnici and Andrea Lieber, 193–210. Supplements to the Journal for the Study of Judaism 119. Leiden: Brill, 2007.
Lightfoot, J. B. *The Epistles of 2 Corinthians and 1 Peter: Newly Discovered Commentaries*. The Lightfoot Legacy Set, vol. 3. Edited by Ben Witherington III and Todd D. Still. Downers Grove, IL: IVP, 2016.
———. *Notes on Epistles of St. Paul*. Edited by J. B. Harmer. Grand Rapids: Baker Book House, 1895.
———. *Saint Paul's Epistle to the Philippians*. Grand Rapids: Zondervan, 1913.
Lim, Kar Yong. "Paul's Use of Temple Imagery in the Corinthian Correspondence: The Creation of Christian Identity." In *Reading Paul in Context: Explorations in Identity Formation. Essays in Honour of William S. Campbell*, edited by Kathy Ehrensperger and Brian J. Tucker, 189–205. Library of New Testament Studies 428. London: T&T Clark, 2010.

Lim, Timothy H. "Studying the Qumran Scrolls and Paul in Their Historical Context." In *The Dead Sea Scrolls as Background to Postbiblical Judaism and Early Christianity: Papers from an International Conference at St. Andrews in 2001*, edited by James R. Davila, 135–56. Studies on the Texts of the Desert of Judah 46. Leiden: Brill, 2003.

Lindemann, Andreas. *Der Erste Korintherbrief.* Handbuch zum Neuen Testament 9.1. Tübingen: Mohr (Siebeck), 2000.

Lindgard, Fredrik. *Paul's Line of Thought in 2 Corinthians 4:16—5:10.* Wissenschaftliche Untersuchungen zum Neuen Testament 2. Reihe 189. Tübingen: Mohr (Siebeck), 2005.

Litfin, A. Duane. *St. Paul's Theology of Proclamation: 1 Corinthians 1–4 and Greco-Roman Rhetoric.* Society for New Testament Studies Monograph Series 79. Cambridge: Cambridge University Press, 1994.

Liu, Yulin. *Temple Purity in 1–2 Corinthians.* Wissenschaftliche Untersuchungen zum Neuen Testament 2. Reihe 343. Tübingen: Mohr (Siebeck), 2013.

Long, A. A. *Epictetus: A Stoic and Socratic Guide to Life.* New York: Oxford University Press, 2002.

———. "Freedom and Determinism in the Stoic Theory of Human Action." In *Problems in Stoicism*, edited by A. A. Long, 173–99. London: Athlone, 1971.

———. *Hellenistic Philosophy: Stoics, Epicureans, Sceptics.* London: Duckworth, 1974.

———. "Roman Philosophy." In *The Cambridge Companion to Greek and Roman Philosophy*, edited by David Sedley, 184–210. Cambridge: Cambridge University Press, 2003.

———. "Stoic Psychology." In *The Cambridge History of Hellenistic Philosophy*, edited by Keimpe Algra et al., 560–84. Cambridge: Cambridge University Press, 1999.

———. *Stoic Studies.* New York: Cambridge University Press, 1996.

———, ed. *Problems in Stoicism.* London: Athlone, 1971.

Long, Fredrick J. *2 Corinthians: A Handbook on the Greek Text.* Baylor Handbook on the Greek New Testament. Waco, TX: Baylor University Press, 2015.

———. *Ancient Rhetoric and Paul's Apology: The Compositional Unity of 2 Corinthians.* Society for New Testament Studies Monograph Series 131. Cambridge: Cambridge University Press, 2004.

———. "'The God of This Age' (2 Cor 4:4) and Paul's Empire-Resisting Gospel." In *The First Urban Churches.* Vol. 2, *Roman Corinth*, edited by James R. Harrison and Laurence L. Welborn, 219–69. Writings from the Greco-Roman World Supplements 7. Atlanta: Society of Biblical Literature, 2016.

———. "Roman Imperial Rule Under the Authority of Jupiter-Zeus: Political-Religious Contexts and the Interpretation of 'The Ruler of the Authority of the Air' in Ephesians 2:2." In *The Language of the New Testament: Context, History, and Development*, edited by Stanley E. Porter and Andrew W. Pitts, 113–54. Linguistic Biblical Studies 6. Leiden: Brill, 2013.

Louw, J. P., and E. A. Nida, eds. *Greek-English Lexicon of the New Testament: Based on Semantic Domains.* 2nd ed. United Bible Societies: New York, 1989.

Mack, Burton L. "Philo Judaeus and Exegetical Traditions in Alexandria." *ANRW* 21.1:227–71.

MacKendrick, Paul. *The Philosophical Books of Cicero.* New York: St. Martin's Press, 1989.

Mackie, Scott D. "Seeing God in Philo of Alexandria: The Logos, the Powers, or the Existent One?" *Studia Philonica* 21 (2009) 25–47.

MacRae, George W. "Heavenly Temple and Eschatology in the Letter to the Hebrews." *Semitica* 12 (1978) 179–99.
Malherbe, Abraham J. "Conversion to Paul's Gospel." In *The Early Church in Its Context: Essays in Honor of Everett Ferguson*, edited by Abraham J. Malherbe et al., 230–44. Supplements to Novum Testamentum. Leiden: Brill, 1998.
———. "Hellenistic Moralists and the New Testament." *ANRW* 26.1:267–333.
———. *Paul and the Popular Philosophers*. Minneapolis: Fortress, 1989.
Mansfeld, Jaap. "Sources." In *The Cambridge History of Hellenistic Philosophy*, edited by Keimpe Algra et al., 3–30. Cambridge: Cambridge University Press, 1999.
———. "Theology." In *The Cambridge History of Hellenistic Philosophy*, edited by Keimpe Algra et al., 452–78. Cambridge: Cambridge University Press, 1999.
Marshall, I. H. "Church and Temple in the New Testament." *Tyndale Bulletin* 40 (1989) 203–22.
Marshall, Peter. "A Metaphor of Social Shame: θριαμβεύειν in 2 Cor 2:14." *Novum Testamentum* 25 (1983) 302–17.
Martin, Dale B. *The Corinthian Body*. New Haven: Yale University Press, 1995.
———. *Slavery as Salvation: The Metaphor of Slavery in Pauline Christianity*. New Haven: Yale University Press, 1990.
Martin, Ralph P. *2 Corinthians*. Word Biblical Commentary 40. 2nd ed. Grand Rapids: Zondervan, 2014.
Matera, Frank J. *II Corinthians: A Commentary*. New Testament Library. Louisville: Westminster John Knox, 2003.
May, Alistair Scott. *The Body for the Lord: Sex and Identity in 1 Corinthians 5–7*. Journal for the Study of the New Testament: Supplement Series 278. London: T&T Clark, 2004.
McDonald, James I. H. "Paul and the Preaching Ministry: A Reconsideration of 2 Cor 2:14–17 in Its Context." *Journal for the Study of the New Testament* 17 (1983) 35–50.
McKelvey, R. J. *The New Temple: The Church in the New Testament*. Oxford: Oxford University Press, 1969.
McNicol, Allan J. "The Eschatological Temple in the Qumran Pesher 4QFlorilegium 1:1–7." *Ohio Journal of Religious Studies* 5.2 (1977) 133–41.
Mendelson, Alan. *Philo's Jewish Identity*. Brown Judaic Studies 161. Scholars Press, 1988.
Merklein, Helmut. *Der erste Brief an die Korinther. Kapitel 1–4*. Ökumenischer Taschenbuch-Kommentar zum Neuen Testament 6/1. Gütersloh: G. Mohn, 1992.
Metzger, Bruce M. *The New Testament: Its Background, Growth, and Content*. New York: Abingdon, 1965.
———. *A Textual Commentary on the Greek New Testament*. 2nd ed. Stuttgart: United Bible Societies, 1994.
Mitchell, Margaret M. "Concerning Περὶ δὲ in 1 Corinthians." *Novum Testamentum* 31.3 (1989) 229–56.
———. *Paul and the Rhetoric of Reconciliation: An Exegetical Investigation of the Language and Composition of 1 Corinthians*. Louisville, KY: Westminster John Knox, 1991.
Mitton, C. L. "New Wine in Old Wineskins: iv, Leaven." *Expository Times* 84 (1973) 339–43.

Moore, Carey A. *Daniel, Esther and Jeremiah: The Additions*. Anchor Bible 44. Garden City, NY: Doubleday, 1977.
———. *Judith: A New Translation with Introduction and Commentary*. Anchor Bible 40A. Garden City, NY: Doubleday, 1985.
———. *Tobit: A New Translation with Introduction and Commentary*. Anchor Bible 40A. Garden City, NY: Doubleday, 1996.
Most, Glenn W. "Philosophy and Religion." In *The Cambridge Companion to Greek and Roman Philosophy*, edited by David Sedley, 300–22. Cambridge: Cambridge University Press, 2003.
Moule, C. F. D. *An Idiom Book of New Testament Greek*. 2nd ed. Cambridge: Cambridge University Press, 1959.
———. "Sanctuary and Sacrifice in the Church of the New Testament." *Journal of Theological Studies* 1.1 (1950) 29–41.
Moulton, J. H., and Nigel Turner. *A Grammar of New Testament Greek*. Vol. 3, *Syntax*. Edinburgh: T&T Clark, 1963.
Murphy-O'Connor, Jerome. "Corinthian Slogans in 1 Corinthians 6:12–20." In *Keys to First Corinthians: Revisiting the Major Issues*, 20–31. Oxford: Oxford University Press, 2009.
———. "Freedom or the Ghetto: (1 Corinthians 8:1–13; 10:23—11:1)." In *Keys to First Corinthians: Revisiting the Major Issues*, 87–128. Oxford: Oxford University Press, 2009.
———. *Keys to First Corinthians: Revisiting the Major Issues*. Oxford: Oxford University Press, 2009.
———. *Keys to Second Corinthians: Revisiting the Major Issues*. Oxford: Oxford University Press, 2010.
Nathan, Emmanuel. "Fragmented Theology in 2 Corinthians: The Unsolved Puzzle of 6:14—7:1." In *Theologizing in the Corinthian Conflict: Studies in the Exegesis and Theology of 2 Corinthians*, edited by Reimund Bieringer et al., 211–28. Biblical Tools and Studies 16. Leuven: Peeters, 2013.
Nestle, Eberhard, et al., eds. *Novum Testamentum Graece*. 27th ed. Stuttgart: Deutsche Bibelgesellschaft, 2013.
Newton, Derek. *Diety and Diet: The Dilemma of Sacrificial Food at Corinth*. Journal for the Study of the New Testament: Supplement Series 169. Sheffield: Sheffield Academic, 1998.
Newton, Michael. *The Concept of Purity at Qumran and in the Letters of Paul*. Society for New Testament Studies Monograph Series 53. Cambridge: Cambridge University Press, 1985.
Nguyen, V. Henry T. *Christian Identity in Corinth: A Comparative Study of 2 Corinthians, Epictetus and Valerius Maximus*. Wissenschaftliche Untersuchungen zum Neuen Testament 2. Reihe 243. Tübingen: Mohr (Siebeck), 2008.
Nickelsburg, George W. E. "Philo among Greeks, Jews and Christians." In *Philo und das Neue Testament: Wechselseitige Wahrnehmungen I. Internationales Symposium Zum Corpus Judaeo-Hellenisticum. 1.–4. Mai 2003, Eisenach/Jena*, edited by Roland Deines and Karl-Wilhelm Niebuhr, 53–72. Wissenschaftliche Untersuchungen zum Neuen Testament 172. Tübingen: Mohr (Siebeck), 2004.
Nikiprowetzky, Valentin. "La spiritualisation des sacrifices et le culte sacrificial au temple de Jérusalem chez Philon d'Alexandrie." *Semitica* 17 (1967) 97–116.

O'Brien, Peter T. *Introductory Thanksgivings in the Letters of Paul*. Supplements to Novum Testamentum 4. Leiden: Brill, 1977.
Oakes, Peter. "Made Holy by the Holy Spirit: Holiness and Ecclesiology in Romans." In *Holiness and Ecclesiology in the New Testament*, edited by Kent E. Brower and Andy Johnson, 167–83. Grand Rapids: Eerdmans, 2007.
Obbink, Dirk. "The Stoic Sage in the Cosmic City." In *Topics in Stoic Philosophy*, edited by Katerina Ierodiakonou, 178–95. New York: Oxford University Press, 1999.
Odell-Scott, David W. *Paul's Critique of Theocracy: A/Theocracy in Corinthians and Galatians*. Journal for the Study of the New Testament: Supplement Series 250. London: T&T Clark, 2003.
Olley, W. "A Precursor of the NRSV? 'Sons and Daughters' in 2 Cor 6:18." *New Testament Studies* 44 (1998) 204–12.
Omanson, Roger L. "Acknowledging Paul's Quotations." *The Bible Translator* 43.2 (1992) 201–13.
Oropeza, B. J. *Exploring Second Corinthians: Death and Life, Hardship and Rivalry*. Rhetoric of Religious Antiquity 3. Atlanta: Society of Biblical Literature, 2016.
———. "Situational Immorality: Paul's 'Vice Lists' at Corinth." *Expository Times* 110.1 (1998) 9–10.
Otzen, Benedikt. *Tobit and Judith*. Guides to Apocrypha and Pseudepigrapha. London: Continuum, 2002.
Paige, Terence. "Philosophy." In *Dictionary of Paul and His Letters*, edited by Gerald F. Hawthorne et al., 713–18. Downers Grove, IL: IVP, 1993.
———. "Stoicism, ἐλευθερία and Community at Corinth." In *Worship, Theology and Ministry in the Early Church: Essays in Honor of Ralph P. Martin*, edited by Michael J. Wilkins and Terence Paige, 180–93. Journal for the Study of the New Testament: Supplement Series 87. Sheffield: Sheffield Academic, 1992.
Parker, Robert. *Miasma: Pollution and Purification in Early Greek Religion*. Oxford: Clarendon, 1996.
Patte, Daniel. "A Structural Exegesis of 2 Corinthians 2:14—7:4 with Special Attention on 2:14—3:6 and 6:11—7:4." In *Society of Biblical Literature 1987 Seminar Papers*, edited by Kent Harold Richards, 23–49. Society of Biblical Literature Seminar Papers 26. Atlanta: Scholars Press, 1987.
Patterson, Jane Lancaster. *Keeping the Feast: Metaphors of Sacrifice in 1 Corinthians and Philippians*. Early Christianity and Its Literature 16. Atlanta: Society of Biblical Literature, 2015.
Pearson, Birger Albert. *The Pneumatikos-Psychikos Terminology in 1 Corinthians: A Study in the Theology of the Corinthian Opponents of Paul and Its Relation to Gnosticism*. Society of Biblical Literature Dissertation Series 12. Missoula, MT: Society of Biblical Literature, 1973.
Perrin, Nicholas. *Jesus the Temple*. Grand Rapids: Baker Academic, 2010.
Phua, Richard Liong-Seng. *Idolatry and Authority: A Study of 1 Corinthians 8:1—11:1 in the Light of the Jewish Diaspora*. Journal for the Study of the New Testament: Supplement Series 299. Edinburgh: T&T Clark, 2005.
Plummer, Alfred. *A Critical and Exegetical Commentary on the Second Epistle of St. Paul to the Corinthians*. International Critical Commentary. Edinburgh: T&T Clark, 1915.

Pogoloff, Stephen M. *Logos and Sophia: The Rhetorical Situation of 1 Corinthians.* Society of Biblical Literature Dissertation Series 134. Atlanta: Society of Biblical Literature, 1992.

Porter, Stanley E. *Idioms of the Greek New Testament.* 2nd ed. Sheffield: Sheffield Academic, 1994.

Powell, J. G. F. "Introduction: Cicero's Philosophical Works and Their Background." In *Cicero the Philosopher: Twelve Papers,* edited by J. G. F. Powell, 1–35. Oxford: Clarendon, 1995.

———, ed. *Cicero the Philosopher: Twelve Papers.* Oxford: Clarendon, 1995.

Price, James L. "Aspects of Paul's Theology and their Bearing on Literary Problems of Second Corinthians." In *Studies in the History and Text of the New Testament in Honor of Kenneth Willis Clark, Ph.D.,* edited by Boyd L. Daniels and M. Jack Suggs, 95–106. Studies and Documents 29. Salt Lake City: University of Utah Press, 1967.

Rabens, Volker. *The Holy Spirit & Ethics in Paul: Transformation & Empowering for Religious-Ethical Life.* Wissenschaftliche Untersuchungen zum Neuen Testament 283. Tübingen: Mohr Siebeck, 2010.

———. "Inclusion of and Demarcation from 'Outsiders': Mission and Ethics in Paul's Second Letter to the Corinthians." In *Sensitivity Towards Outsiders: Exploring the Dynamic Relationship between Mission and Ethics in the New Testament and Early Christianity,* edited by Jacobus Kok et al., 290–323. Wissenschaftliche Untersuchungen zum Neuen Testament 2. Reihe 364. 2014.

———. "Paul's Rhetoric of Demarcation: Separation from 'Unbelievers' (2 Cor 6:14—7:1) in the Corinthian Conflict." In *Theologizing in the Corinthian Conflict: Studies in the Exegesis and Theology of 2 Corinthians,* edited by Reimund Bieringer et al., 229–53. Biblical Tools and Studies 16. Leuven: Peeters, 2013.

Rabinowitz, Peter J. T. "Truth in Fiction: A Reexamination of Audiences." *Critical Enquiry* 4 (1977) 121–42.

———. "Whirl without End: Audience-Orientated Criticism." In *Contemporary Literary Theory,* edited by G.D. Atkins & L. Morrow, 81–100. Amherst, MA: University of Massachusetts, 1989.

Radice, Roberto. "Philo's Theology and Theory of Creation." In *The Cambridge Companion to Philo,* edited by Adam Kamesar, 124–45. Cambridge: Cambridge University Press, 2009.

Reesor, Margaret E. *The Nature of Man in Early Stoic Philosophy.* New York: St. Martin's Press, 1989.

Regev, Eyal. "Abominated Temple and a Holy Community: The Formation of the Notions of Purity and Impurity in Qumran." *Dead Sea Discoveries* 10.2 (2003) 243–78.

Rensberger, D. "2 Corinthians 6:14—7:1—A Fresh Examination." *Studia Biblica et Theologica* 8 (1978) 25–49.

Renwick, David, A. *Paul, the Temple, and the Presence of God.* Atlanta: Scholars Press, 1991.

Reydams-Schils, Gretchen J. *The Roman Stoics: Self, Responsibility, and Affection.* Chicago: University of Chicago Press, 2005.

———. "Stoicized Readings of Timaeus in Philo of Alexandria." *Studia Philonica* 7 (1995) 85–102.

Richardson, Peter. "Judgment in Sexual Matters in 1 Corinthians 6:1–11." *Novum Testamentum* 25.1 (1983) 37–58.

———. "Temples, Altars and Living from the Gospel." In *Gospel in Paul: Studies on Corinthians, Galatians and Romans for Richard N. Longenecker*, edited by L. Ann Jervis and Peter Richardson, 89–110. Journal for the Study of the New Testament: Supplement Series 108. Sheffield: Sheffield Academic, 1994.

Richardson, Philip. "What are the Spiritual Sacrifices of 1 Peter 2:5? Some Light from Philo of Alexandria." *Evangelical Quarterly* 87.1 (2015) 3–17.

Rist, J. M. *Stoic Philosophy*. New York: Cambridge University Press, 1977.

Rives, James B. *Religion in the Roman Empire*. Malden: Wiley-Blackwell, 2007.

Robertson, Archibald, and Alfred Plummer, *A Critical and Exegetical Commentary on the First Epistle of St Paul to the Corinthians*. International Critical Commentary. Edinburgh: T&T Clark, 1911.

Robertson, Paul. "Towards An Understanding of Philo's and Cicero's Treatment of Sacrifice." *Studia Philonica* 23 (2011) 41–67.

Rosner, Brian S. *Paul, Scripture and Ethics: A Study of 1 Corinthians 5–7*. Arbeiten zur Geschichte des antiken Judentums und des Urchristentums 22. Leiden: Brill, 1994.

———. "Temple and Holiness in 1 Corinthians 5." *Tyndale Bulletin* 42 (1991) 137–45.

———. "Temple Prostitution in 1 Corinthians 6:12–20." *Novum Testamentum* 40 (1998) 336–51.

Rowe, Christopher. "Plato." In *The Cambridge Companion to Greek and Roman Philosophy*, edited by David Sedley, 98–124. Cambridge: Cambridge University Press, 2003.

Rowland, Christopher C. "The Second Temple: Focus of Ideological Struggle?" In *Templum Amicitiae: Essays on the Second Temple presented to Ernst Bammel*, edited by William Horbury, 175–98. Journal for the Study of the New Testament: Supplement Series 48. Sheffield: Sheffield Academic, 1991.

Rowland, Christopher C. "The Temple in the New Testament." In *Temple and Worship in Biblical Israel*, edited by John Day, 469–83. London: T&T Clark, 2005.

Runia, David T. *Philo of Alexandria. On the Creation of the Cosmos According to Moses: Introduction, Translation, and Commentary*. Philo of Alexandria Commentary Series 1. Leiden: Brill, 2002.

———. "Response to Runia and Sterling." *Studia Philonica* 5 (1993) 141–46.

———. "Was Philo a Middle Platonist? A Difficult Question Revisited." *Studia Philonica* 5 (1993) 112–40.

Russell, D. A. *Plutarch: Classical Life and Letters*. London: Duckworth, 1973.

Rutherford, R. B. *The Meditations of Marcus Aurelius: A Study*. Oxford Classical Monographs. Oxford: Oxford University Press, 1989.

Sampley, J. Paul., ed. *Paul in the Greco-Roman World: A Handbook*. Harrisburg, PA: Trinity Press International, 2003.

Sandbach, F. H. "Phantasia Katalēptikē." In *Problems in Stoicism*, edited by A. A. Long, 9–21. London: Athlone, 1971.

———. *The Stoics*. London: Chatto and Windus, 1975.

Sandelin, Karl-Gustav. "Philo as a Jew." In *Reading Philo: A Handbook to Philo of Alexandria*, edited by Torrey Seland, 19–46. Grand Rapids: Eerdmans, 2014.

Sandmel, Samuel. *Judaism and Christian Beginnings*. New York: Oxford University Press, 1978.

———. *Philo of Alexandria: An Introduction*. New York: Oxford University Press, 1979.

———. "Philo Judaeus: An Introduction to the Man, His Writings, and His Significance." *ANRW* 21.1:3–46.

Sandnes, Karl Olav. *Belly and Body in the Pauline Epistles*. Society for New Testament Studies Monograph Series 120. Cambridge: Cambridge University Press, 2002.

Savage, Timothy B. *Power through Weakness: Paul's Understanding of the Christian Ministry in 2 Corinthians*. Society for New Testament Studies Monograph Series 86. Cambridge: Cambridge University Press, 2004.

Schenck, Kenneth. *A Brief Guide to Philo*. Louisville: Westminster John Knox, 2005.

Schiffman, Lawrence H. "Community Without Temple: The Qumran Community's Withdrawal from the Jerusalem Temple." In *Gemeinde ohne Tempel: Zur Substituierung und Transformation des Jerusalemer Tempels und seines Kults im Alten Testament, antiken Judentum und frühen Christentum*, edited by Beate Ego et al., 267–84. Wissenschaftliche Untersuchungen zum Neuen Testament 118. Tübingen: Mohr (Siebeck), 1999.

Schmidt, Francis. *How the Temple Thinks: Identity and Social Cohesion in Ancient Judaism*. Translated by J. Edward Crowley. The Biblical Seminar 78. Sheffield: Sheffield Academic, 2001.

Schmithals, Walter. *Gnosticism in Corinth: An Investigation of the Letters to the Corinthians*. Nashville: Abingdon, 1971.

Schnabel, Eckhard J. *Der erste Brief des Paulus an die Korinther*. Wuppertal: R. Brockhaus, 2006.

Schofield, Malcolm. "Stoic Ethics." In *The Cambridge Companion to the Stoics*, edited by Brad Inwood, 233–56. New York: Cambridge University Press, 2003.

———. "Writing Philosophy." In *The Cambridge Companion to Cicero*, edited by Catherine Steel, 73–87. Cambridge: Cambridge University Press, 2013.

Schowalter, Daniel N., and Steven J. Friesen. *Urban Religion in Roman Corinth: Interdisciplinary Approaches*. Harvard Theological Studies 53. Cambridge: Harvard Divinity School, 2005.

Schrage, Wolfgang. *Der erste Brief an die Korinther: 1 Kor 1,1—6,11*. Evangelisch-katholischer Kommentar zum Neuen Testament 7.1. Zürich: Benziger, 1991.

———. *Der erste Brief an die Korinther: 1 Kor 6,12—11,16*. Evangelisch-katholischer Kommentar zum Neuen Testament 7.2. Zürich: Benziger, 1995.

———. *Der erste Brief an die Korinther: 1 Kor 11,17—14,40*. Evangelisch-katholischer Kommentar zum Neuen Testament 7.3. Zürich: Benziger, 1999.

———. *Der erste Brief an die Korinther: 1 Kor 15,1—16,24*. Evangelisch-katholischer Kommentar zum Neuen Testament 7.4. Zürich: Benziger, 2001.

Schreiner, Thomas R. *Paul, Apostle of God's Glory in Christ: A Pauline Theology*. Downer's Grove, IL: IVP Academic, 2006.

Schüssler Fiorenza, E. "Cultic Language in Qumran and in the New Testament." *Catholic Biblical Quarterly* 38 (1976) 159–77.

———. *Rhetoric and Ethic: The Politics of Biblical Studies*. Minneapolis: Fortress, 1999.

Schwartz, Daniel R. "Philo, His Family, and His Times." In *The Cambridge Companion to Philo*. Edited by Adam Kamesar, 9–31. Cambridge: Cambridge University Press, 2009.

———. "The Three Temples of 4Q Florilegium." *Revue de Qumran* 10 (1979) 83–91.

Scott, James M. *Adoption as Sons of God: An Exegetical Investigation Into the Background of υἱοθεσία in the Pauline Corpus*. Wissenschaftliche Untersuchungen zum Neuen Testament 2. Reihe 48. Tübingen: Mohr (Siebeck), 1992.

———. "The Triumph of God in 2 Cor 2.14: Additional Evidence of Merkabah Mysticism in Paul." *New Testament Studies* 42 (1996) 260–81.

———. "The Use of Scripture in 2 Corinthians 6.16c–18 and Paul's Restoration Theology." *Journal for the Study of the New Testament* 56 (1994) 73–99.
Sedley, David. *The Cambridge Companion to Greek and Roman Philosophy*. Cambridge: Cambridge University Press, 2003.
———. "The School, from Zeno to Arius Didymus." In *The Cambridge Companion to the Stoics*, edited by Brad Inwood, 7–32. New York: Cambridge University Press, 2003.
Seifrid, Mark A. *The Second Letter to the Corinthians*. Pillar New Testament Commentary. Grand Rapids: Eerdmans, 2014.
Seland, Torrey. "The 'Common Priesthood' of Philo and 1 Peter: A Philonic Reading of 1 Peter 2.5, 9." *Journal for the Study of the New Testament* 57 (1995) 87–119.
———. "The Moderate Life of the Christian *paroikoi*: A Philonic Reading of 1 Pet 2:11." In *Philo und das Neue Testament: Wechselseitige Wahrnehmungen I. Internationales Symposium Zum Corpus Judaeo-Hellenisticum. 1.–4. Mai 2003, Eisenach/Jena*, edited by Roland Deines and Karl-Wilhelm Niebuhr, 241–64. Wissenschaftliche Untersuchungen zum Neuen Testament 172. Tübingen: Mohr (Siebeck), 2004.
———, ed. *Reading Philo: A Handbook to Philo of Alexandria*. Grand Rapids: Eerdmans, 2014.
Sevenster, J. N. *Paul and Seneca*. Supplements to Novum Testamentum 4. Leiden: Brill, 1961.
Shanor, J. "Paul as Master-Builder: Construction Terms in First Corinthians." *New Testament Studies* 34 (1988) 461–71.
Sharples, R. W. *Stoics, Epicureans and Sceptics: An Introduction to Hellenistic Philosophy*. London: Routledge, 1996.
Shemesh, Aharon. "The Holiness According to the Temple Scroll." *Revue de Qumran* 19 (2000) 369–82.
Shen, Michael Li-Tak. *Canaan to Corinth*. Studies in Biblical Literature 83. New York: Peter Lang, 2010.
Skehan, Patrick W., and Alexander A. Di Lella. *The Wisdom of Ben Sira: A New Translation with Notes, Introduction and Commentary*. Anchor Bible 39. New York: Doubleday, 1987.
Smit, Joop F. *"About the Idol Offerings." Rhetoric, Social Context and Theology of Paul's Discourse in First Corinthians 8:1—11:1*. Contributions to Biblical Exegesis and Theology 27. Leuven: Peeters, 2000.
Smith, Jay E. "The Roots of a 'Libertine' Slogan in I Corinthians 6:18." *Journal of Theological Studies* 59.1 (2008) 63–95.
———. "Slogans in 1 Corinthians." *Bibliotheca sacra* 167 (2010) 68–88.
———. "A Slogan in 1 Corinthians 6:18b: Pressing the Case." In *Studies in the Pauline Epistles: Essays in Honor of Douglas J. Moo*, edited by Matthew Harmon and Jay E. Smith, 74–98. Grand Rapids: Zondervan, 2014.
Snow, Robert S. Review of *The Jerusalem Temple and Early Christian Identity*, by Timothy Wardle. *Bulletin for Biblical Research* 22.2 (2012) 304–5.
Son, Kiwoong. *Zion Symbolism in Hebrews: Hebrews 12:18–24 as a Hermeneutical Key to the Epistle*. Waynesboro, GA: Paternoster, 2005.
Son, Sang-Won (Aaron). *Corporate Elements in Pauline Anthropology: A Study of Selected Terms, Idioms, and Concepts in the Light of Paul's Usage and Background*. Analecta biblica. Roma: Editrice Pontificio Istituto Biblico, 2001.

———. Review of *Temple Purity in 1-2 Corinthians*, by Yulin Liu. *Review of Biblical Literature* 11 (2013). http://www.bookreviews.org/pdf/9192_10133.pdf.

Spicq, Ceslas. *Theological Lexicon of the New Testament*. Translated and edited by James D. Ernest. 3 vols. Peabody, MA: Hendrickson, 1994.

Starling, David. "The ἄπιστοι of 2 Cor 6:14: Beyond the Impasse." *Novum Testamentum* 55 (2013) 45–60.

———. *Not My People: Gentiles as Exiles in Pauline Hermeneutics*. Beihefte zur Zeitschrift für die neutestamentliche Wissenschaft 184. Berlin: de Gruyter, 2011.

Steel, Catherine, ed. *The Cambridge Companion to Cicero*. Cambridge: Cambridge University Press, 2013.

Sterling, Gregory E. "'The Jewish Philosophy': Reading Moses via Hellenistic Philosophy according to Philo." In *Reading Philo: A Handbook to Philo of Alexandria*, edited by Torrey Seland, 129–54. Grand Rapids: Eerdmans, 2014.

———. "The Place of Philo of Alexandria in the Study of Christian Origins." In *Philo und das Neue Testament: Wechselseitige Wahrnehmungen I. Internationales Symposium Zum Corpus Judaeo-Hellenisticum. 1.-4. Mai 2003, Eisenach/Jena*, edited by Roland Deines and Karl-Wilhelm Niebuhr, 21–52. Wissenschaftliche Untersuchungen zum Neuen Testament 172. Tübingen: Mohr (Siebeck), 2004.

———. "Platonizing Moses: Philo and Middle Platonism." *Studia Philonica* 5 (1993) 96–111.

Stevenson, Gregory. *Power and Place: Temple and Identity in the Book of Revelation*. Beihefte zur Zeitschrift für die neutestamentliche Wissenschaft 107. Berlin: De Gruyter, 2001.

Stockhausen, Carol Kern. *Moses' Veil and the Glory of the New Covenant: The Exegetical Substructure of II Cor 3,1—4,6*. Analecta biblica 116. Roma: Pontificio Istituto Biblica, 1989.

Stowers, Stanley K. "Does Pauline Christianity Resemble a Hellenistic Philosphy?" In *Paul Beyond the Judaism-Hellenism Divide*, edited by Troels Engberg-Pedersen, 81–102. Louisville: Westminster John Knox, 2001.

Strack, Wolfram. *Kultische Terminologie in ekklesiologischen Kontexten in den Briefen des Paulus*. Bonner biblische Beiträge 92. Weinheim: Beltz Athenäum, 1994.

Suleiman, Susan R. "Introduction: Varieties of Audience-Oriented Criticism." In *The Reader in the Text: Essays in Audience and Interpretation*, edited by Susan R. Suleiman and Inge Crosman, 3–45. Princeton: Princeton University Press, 1980.

Sweet, J. P. M. "A House Not Made with Hands." In *Templum Amicitiae: Essays on the Second Temple Presented to Ernst Bammel*, edited by William Horbury, 368–90. Journal for the Study of the New Testament: Supplement Series 48. Sheffield: Sheffield Academic, 1991.

Talbert, Charles H. *Reading Luke-Acts in Its Mediterranean Milieu*. Supplements to Novum Testamentum 107. Leiden: Brill, 2003.

Tempest, Kathryn. *Cicero: Politics and Persuasion in Ancient Rome*. London: Bloomsbury Academic, 2011.

Termini, Cristina. "Philo's Thought within the Context of Middle Judaism." In *The Cambridge Companion to Philo*, edited by Adam Kamesar, 95–123. Cambridge: Cambridge University Press, 2009.

Theissen, Gerd. *The Social Setting of Pauline Christianity: Essays on Corinth*. Translated by John H. Schütz. Philadelphia: Fortress, 1982.

Bibliography 269

Thiselton, Anthony C. *The First Epistle to the Corinthians*. New International Greek Testament Commentary. Grand Rapids: Eerdmans, 2000.

———. "Realized Eschatology at Corinth." *New Testament Studies* 24.4 (1978) 510–26.

Thompson, James W. "Paul's Argument from *Pathos* in 2 Corinthians." In *Paul and Pathos*, edited by Thomas H. Olbricht and Jerry L. Sumney, 127–45. Society of Biblical Literature Symposium Series 16. Atlanta: Society of Biblical Literature, 2001.

Thorsteinsson, Runar M. *Roman Christianity and Roman Stoicism: A Comparative Study of Ancient Morality*. New York: Oxford University Press, 2010.

Thrall, Margaret E. "2 Corinthians 1:12: ἁγιότητι or ἁπλότητι?" In *Studies in New Testament Language and Text: Essays in Honour of George D. Kilpatrick on the Occasion of His Sixty-Fifth Birthday*, edited by J. K. Elliott, 366–72. Supplements to Novum Testamentum 44. Leiden: Brill, 1976.

———. *2 Corinthians 1–7: A Critical and Exegetical Commentary on the Second Epistle to the Corinthians*. International Critical Commentary. London: T&T Clark, 1994.

———. *2 Corinthians 8–13: A Critical and Exegetical Commentary on the Second Epistle to the Corinthians*. International Critical Commentary. T&T Clark, 2000.

———. "The Problem of 2 Cor vi.14—vii.1 in Some Recent Discussion." *New Testament Studies* 24 (1977) 132–48.

Tieleman, Teun. Review of *The Stoic Theory of Oikeiosis: Moral Development and Social Interaction in Early Stoic Philosophy*, by Troels Engberg-Pedersen. *Mnemosyne* 48 (1995) 226–32.

Tobin, Thomas H. "Was Philo a Middle Platonist? Some Suggestions." *Studia Philonica* 5 (1993) 147–50.

Tomlin, Graham. "Christians and Epicureans in 1 Corinthians." *Journal for the Study of the New Testament* 68 (1997) 51–72.

Tomson, Peter J. "Christ, Belial, and Women: 2 Cor 6:14—7:1 Compared with Ancient Judaism and with the Pauline Corpus." In *Second Corinthians in the Perspective of Late Second Temple Judaism*, edited by Reimund Bieringer et al., 79–131. Compendia Rerum Iudaicarum ad Novum Testamentum 14. Leiden: Brill, 2014.

———. *Paul and the Jewish Law: Halakha in the Letters of the Apostle to the Gentiles*. Compendia Rerum Iudaicarum ad Novum Testamentum 3.1. Minneapolis: Fortress, 1990.

Toney, Carl N. "Excursus: Resurrection in 2 Corinthians." In *2 Corinthians*, by Ralph P. Martin, 250–56. Word Biblical Commentary 40. 2nd ed. Grand Rapids: Zondervan, 2014.

Trapp, Michael. "The Role of Philosophy and Philosophers in the Imperial Period." In *A Companion to Plutarch*, edited by Mark Beck, 43–57. Malden, MA: Wiley-Blackwell, 2014.

Tucker, Brian J. "The Role of Civic Identity on the Pauline Corinth." *Didaskalia* 72.8 (2008) 71–91.

Tucker, Brian J., and Coleman A. Baker, eds. *T & T Clark Handbook to Social Identity in the New Testament*. London: Bloomsbury, 2016.

Tucker, Paavo. "Reconsidering Βελιάρ: 2 Corinthians 6:15 in Its Anti-Imperial Jewish Apocalyptic Context." *Journal for the Study of Paul and His Letters* 4.2 (2014) 169–85.

Vahrenhorst, Martin. *Kultische Sprache in den Paulusbriefen*. Wissenschaftliche Untersuchungen zum Neuen Testament 230. Tübingen: Mohr (Siebeck), 2008.

van Kooten, George H. *Paul's Anthropology in Context: The Image of God, Assimilation to God, and Tripartite Man in Ancient Judaism, Ancient Philosophy and Early Christianity*. Wissenschaftliche Untersuchungen zum Neuen Testament 232. Tübingen: Mohr (Siebeck), 2008.

van Ruiten, J. T. A. G. M. "Visions of the Temple in the Book of Jubilees." In *Gemeinde ohne Tempel: Zur Substituierung und Transformation des Jerusalemer Tempels und seines Kults im Alten Testament, antiken Judentum und frühen Christentum*, edited by Beate Ego et al., 215–27. Wissenschaftliche Untersuchungen zum Neuen Testament 118. Tübingen: Mohr (Siebeck), 1999.

van Unnik, W. C. "'With Unveiled Face,' an Exegesis of 2 Corinthians iii 12–18." *Novum Testamentum* (1963) 153–69.

Vegge, Ivar. *2 Corinthians—a Letter about Reconciliation: A Psychagogical, Epistolographical and Rhetorical Analysis*. Wissenschaftliche Untersuchungen zum Neuen Testament 2. Reihe 239. Tübingen: Mohr (Siebeck), 2008.

Vermes, G. "The Symbolical Interpretation of Lebanon in the Targums." *Journal of Theological Studies* 9 (1958) 1–12.

Veyne, Paul. *Seneca: The Life of a Stoic*. Translated by David Sullivan. New York: Routledge, 2003.

Vogel, Manuel. "Tempel and Tempelkult in Pseudo-Philos *Lieber Antiquitatum Biblicarum*." In *Gemeinde ohne Tempel: Zur Substituierung und Transformation des Jerusalemer Tempels und seines Kults im Alten Testament, antiken Judentum und frühen Christentum*, edited by Beate Ego et al., 251–63. Wissenschaftliche Untersuchungen zum Neuen Testament 118. Tübingen: Mohr (Siebeck), 1999.

Wagner, J. Ross. "Working Out Salvation: Holiness and Community in Philippians." In *Holiness and Ecclesiology in the New Testament*, edited by Kent E. Brower and Andy Johnson, 257–74. Grand Rapids: Eerdmans, 2007.

Walker, W. O., Jr. "2 Cor 6.14—7.1 and the Chiastic Structure of 6.11–13; 7.2–3." *New Testament Studies* 48.1 (2002) 142–144.

———. "The Burden of Proof in Identifying Interpolations in the Pauline Letters." *New Testament Studies* 33 (1987) 610–18.

Wallace, Daniel B. *Greek Grammar Beyond the Basics: An Exegetical Syntax of the New Testament*. Grand Rapids: Zondervan, 1996.

Wardle, Timothy. *The Jerusalem Temple and Early Christian Identity*. Wissenschaftliche Untersuchungen zum Neuen Testament 2. Reihe 291. Tübingen: Mohr (Siebeck), 2010.

———. "Who Is Sacrificing? Assessing the Early Christian Reticence to Transfer the Idea of the Priesthood to the Community." In *Ritual and Metaphor: Sacrifice in the Bible*, edited by Christian A. Eberhart, 99–114. Society of Biblical Literature Resources for Biblical Study 68. Atlanta: Society of Biblical Literature, 2011.

Ware, James. "Moral Progress and Divine Power in Seneca and Paul." In *Passions and Moral Progress in Greco-Roman Thought*, edited by John T. Fitzgerald, 267–83. New York: Routledge, 2008.

Warren, James, ed. *The Cambridge Companion to Epicureanism*. Cambridge: Cambridge University Press, 2009.

Wassen, Cecilia. "Do You Have to Be Pure in a Metaphorical Temple? Sanctuary Metaphors and Construction of Sacred Space in the Dead Sea Scrolls and Paul's Letters." In *Purity, Holiness, and Identity in Judaism and Christianity: Essays in*

Memory of Susan Haber, edited by Carl S. Ehrlich et al., 55–86. Wissenschaftliche Untersuchungen zum Neuen Testament 305. Tübingen: Mohr (Siebeck), 2013.

Webb, William J. *Returning Home: New Covenant and Second Exodus as the Context for 2 Corinthians 6:14—7:1*. Journal for the Study of the New Testament: Supplement Series 85. Sheffield: Sheffield Academic, 1993.

———. "Unequally Yoked with Unbelievers, Part 1: Who Are the Unbelievers (ἄπιστοι) in 2 Corinthians 6:14?" *Bibliotheca sacra* 149 (1992) 27–44.

———. "Unequally Yoked with Unbelievers, Part 2: What Is the Unequal Yoke (ἑτεροζυγοῦντες) in 2 Corinthians 6:14?" *Bibliotheca sacra* 149 (1992) 162–79.

Weiss, Johannes. *Der erste Korintherbrief*. Göttingen: Vandenhoeck & Ruprecht, 1910.

Wenschkewitz, Hans. *Die Spiritualisierung der Kultusbegriffe: Tempel, Priester und Opfer im Neuen Testament*. Angelos Beihefte 4. Liepzig: Eduard Pfeiffer, 1932.

Wenthe, Dean O. "An Exegetical Study of 1 Corinthians 5:7b." *The Springfielder* 38.2 (1974) 134–40.

Werman, Carl. "God's House: Temple or Universe." In *Philo und das Neue Testament: Wechselseitige Wahrnehmungen, I. Interationales Symposium zum Corpus Judaeo-Hellenisticum, 1.-4. Mai 2003, Eisenach/Jena*, edited by Roland Deines and Karl-Wilhelm Niebuhr, 309–22. Wissenschaftliche Untersuchungen zum Neuen Testament 172. Tübingen: Mohr (Siebeck), 2004.

White, Michael J. "Stoic Natural Philosophy (Physics and Cosmology)." In *The Cambridge Companion to the Stoics*, edited by Brad Inwood, 124–52. New York: Cambridge University Press, 2003.

Wilken, Robert L. "Toward a Social Interpretation of Early Christian Apologetics." *Church History* 39.4 (1970) 437–58.

Williamson, Ronald. *Jews in the Hellenistic World: Philo*. Cambridge Commentaries on Writings of the Jewish and Christian World 200 BC to AD 200 Volume 1, Part 2. Cambridge: Cambridge University Press, 1989.

Willis, Wendell L. *Idol Meat in Corinth: The Pauline Argument in 1 Corinthians 8 and 10*. Society of Biblical Literature Dissertation Series 68. Chico, CA: Scholars Press, 1985.

Wilson, Walter T. *Philo of Alexandria. On Virtues: Introduction, Translation, and Commentary*. Philo of Alexandria Commentary Series 3. Leiden: Brill, 2011.

Windisch, Hans. *Der Zweite Korintherbrief*. Göttingen: Vandenhoeck & Ruprecht, 1924.

Winston, David. *Logos and Mystical Theology in Philo of Alexandria*. Cincinnati, OH: Hebrew Union College Press, 1985.

———. "Philo and the Hellenistic Jewish Encounter." *Studia Philonica* 7 (1995) 124–42.

———. "Response to Runia and Sterling." *Studia Philonica* 5 (1993) 141–46.

Winter, Bruce W. *After Paul Left Corinth: The Influence of Secular Ethics and Social Change*. Grand Rapids: Eerdmans, 2001.

———. "Carnal Conduct and Sanctification in 1 Corinthians: *Simul sanctus et peccator?*" In *Holiness and Ecclesiology in the New Testament*, edited by Kent E. Brower and Andy Johnson, 184–200. Grand Rapids: Eerdmans, 2007.

———. "Gluttony and Immorality at Élitist Banquets: The Background to 1 Corinthians 6:12–20." *Jian Dao* 7 (1997) 77–90.

———. "Identifying the Offering, the Cup and the Table of the 'Demons' in 1 Cor 10:20–21." In *Saint Paul and Corinth: International Scientific Conference Proceedings, Corinth, 23–25 September, 2007*, edited by C. Belezos et al., 847–68. Athens: Psychogios, 2009.

———. *Philo and Paul Among the Sophists: Alexandrian and Corinthian Responses to a Julio-Claudian Movement*. 2nd ed. Grand Rapids: Eerdmans, 2002.
Wise, M. O. "4QFlorilegium and the Temple of Adam." *Revue de Qumran* 15 (1991) 103–32.
Witherington, Ben, III. *The Acts of the Apostles: A Socio-Rhetorical Commentary*. Grand Rapids: Eerdmans, 1997.
———. *Conflict and Community in Corinth: A Socio-Rhetorical Commentary on 1 and 2 Corinthians*. Grand Rapids: Eerdmans, 1995.
———. "Not So Idle Thoughts about Eidolothuton." *Tyndale Bulletin* 44.2 (1993) 237–54
———. *Paul's Narrative Thought World: The Tapestry of Tragedy and Triumph*. Louisville, KY: Westminster John Knox, 1994.
Wolff, Christian. *Der zweite Brief des Paulus an die Korinther*. Theologischer Handkommentar zum Neuen Testament 8. Berlin: Evangelische Verlagsanstalt, 1989.
Wright, Benjamin G., III. "Ben Sira and the *Book of the Watchers* on the Legitimate Priesthood." In *Intertextual Studies in Ben Sira and Tobit*, edited by Jeremy Corley and Vincent Skemp, 241–54. Catholic Biblical Quarterly Monograph Series 38. Washington, DC: Catholic Biblical Association of America, 2005.
———. *Praise Israel for Wisdom and Instruction: Essays on Ben Sira and Wisdom, the Letter of Aristeas and the Septuagint*. Supplements to the Journal for the Study of Judaism 131. Leiden: Brill, 2008.
Wright, M. R. "Cicero on Self-Love and Love of Humanity in De Finibus 3." In *Cicero the Philosopher: Twelve Papers*, edited by J. G. F. Powell, 171–95. Oxford: Clarendon, 1995.
Wright, N. T. *The Climax of the Covenant: Christ and the Law in Pauline Theology*. Edinburgh: T&T Clark, 1991.
———. "Monotheism, Christology and Ethics: 1 Corinthians 8." In *The Climax of the Covenant: Christ and the Law in Pauline Theology*, 120–36. Edinburgh: T&T Clark, 1991.
———. *Paul and the Faithfulness of God*. Minneapolis: Fortress, 2013.
———. *The Resurrection of the Son of God*. Minneapolis: Fortress, 2003.
Yadin, Y. "A Midrash on II Sam. vii and Ps. i–ii (4QFlorilegium)." *Israel Exploration Journal* 9 (1959) 95–98.
Yeo, Khiok-Khng. *Rhetorical Interaction in 1 Corinthians 8 and 10: A Formal Analysis with Preliminary Suggestions for a Chinese, Cross-Cultural Hermeneutic*. Biblical Interpretation 9. Leiden: Brill, 1995.
Yinger, Kent L. *Paul, Judaism, and Judgment According to Deeds*. Society for New Testament Studies Monograph Series 105. Cambridge: Cambridge University Press, 1999.
Young, Frances, and David F. Ford. *Meaning and Truth in 2 Corinthians*. Grand Rapids: Eerdmans, 1987.
Zeilinger, Franz. "Die Echtheit von 2 Cor 6:14—7:1." *Journal of Biblical Literature* 112 (1993) 71–80.
Zeller, Dieter. *Die erste Brief an die Korinther*. Göttingen: Vandenhoeck & Ruprecht, 2010.

Ancient Document Index

OLD TESTAMENT/ HEBREW BIBLE

Genesis

1:1	150
1:26–27	148
2:8	136
2:24 LXX	177
4:4	130
8:20	132
8:21	234
9:6 LXX	165
14:18–20	140
14:20	133
15:9	132, 133
22	37
23:9	147
23:11	147
31	127

Exodus

12:8	125
12:9	135
12:16	157
13:21–22	187
14:22–29	187
16:4	187
17:6	187
19:5–6	157
23:15	138
23:18	135
24:5	136
24:6	131
26:1	150
29:18	234
31:18	223
32:6	187

Leviticus

2:1–2	129
2:14	130
4:1–2	37
4:27	37
4:31	234
5:7	130
5:18	37
6:16	187
6:26	187
7:6	187
7:12	138
8	128
8:21	129
9	128
9:14	129
10:9	125
10:16–20	126
16	38
16:1–4	143
16:4	144
19:6	157
23:2–37	157
23:15	129
26:1	236
26:12	146, 214, 217
26:30	236
27:30	130
27:32	130

Numbers

5:9	187
5:10	187
6	129
6:18	132
11:4	187
11:34	187
14:16	187
14:23	187
14:29–30	187
15:5	234
18:8–20	187
20:11	187
28:25	157

Deuteronomy

4:13	223
5:22	223
6:4	186
7:6	157
8:1	187
17:7 LXX	171
18:10–11	186
24:1 LXX	190
24:6	130
26:19	157
27:6	129
32:17	186
32:21	186

Joshua

3:10	214
8:31	129
9:5	165

1 Samuel

15:22	36
17:36	214

2 Samuel

7:8	214
7:14	214

1 Kings

9:3	2

2 Kings

19:4	214
19:16	214

1 Chronicles

9:23	235
22:14–16	163
29:2	163
29:16	32, 151

2 Chronicles

3:6	163
5:14	2
7:1	2
36:14	32

Job

1:21	80
4:19 LXX	235

Psalms

5:7 LXX	151
5:8	32
26:8	2
40:6	36
43:3	2
49:14 LXX	138
50:17–19 LXX	138
51:16	36
98:6	193
106:22 LXX	138
106:37	186
115:4–8	186
115:8 LXX	138
135:15–18	186
140:2 LXX	132
154:10–11	27

Proverbs

10:2	36
11:6	36
15:8	27
16:7 LXX	36

Isaiah

2:12	193

Ancient Document Index

2:18	236
8:19	186
10:11	236
13:6	193
13:9	193
19:3	186
29:14	160
37:4	214
37:17	214
38:12	235
40:19-20	186
43:6	214, 228
44:9-17	186
49:22	214, 228
52:11 LXX	215
56:7	32, 151
60:4	214, 228
64:10	32, 151
66:20	32, 151

Jeremiah

2:3	157
38:33 LXX	223

Ezekiel

11:19	223
20:34	214
36:26	223
37:27	214
43-48	2

Daniel

4:22	214
5:23	214
7:18-27	157

Joel

2:31	193
3:5 LXX	193

Amos

5:18	193
5:21-24	36

Jonah

2:10 LXX	138

Micah

6:6-8	36

Zephaniah

1:17-18	193

Malachi

3:2	193

APOCRYPHA

Judith

16:16	35
16:18-19	35

1 Maccabees

4:47	129

Prayer of Azariah

15-17	38
15	37

Sirach/Ecclesiasticus

3:3	36
3:30	36
7:29-31	36
24:15	234
35:1-12	36
35:1-2	36
35:4	36
35:5	36
35:8	36
38:9-11	36
40:24	36

Tobit

1:3	36
1:16	36
2:14	36
3:2	36
4:7	36
4:8	36
4:10	36
4:11	36
4:16	36
12:9	36

Tobit (continued)

13:8	36
14:2	36
14:5–6	37
14:10	36
14:11	36

Wisdom of Solomon

3:6	38
9:15	235

PSEUDEPIGRAPHA

2 Baruch (Syriac Apocalypse)

4:1–7	34, 123, 236

1 Enoch (Ethiopic Apocalypse)

14:1–25	34, 236
14:10	151
14:13	151
14:15	151
14:21	151
14:24–26	34, 236
25:5	151
71:5	34, 236

2 Enoch (Slavonic Apocalypse)

44:1–5	36
44:1	36
45:3	36
61:4–5	36
62:1	36
66:2	36

4 Ezra

10:25–28	34, 123, 236

Five Apocryphal Syriac Psalms

2	28

Joseph and Aseneth

8:2	214
8:5	214
11:10	214
19:8	214

Jubilees

2:22	37
6:37	37
15:24–29	37
18:9	28
23:19	37
32:1–15	37

Liber antiquitatum biblicarum (Pseudo-Philo)

18:5	37
32:3	37

Letter of Aristeas

83–99	35
234	35
235	35

4 Maccabees

1:1	35
2:22	35
5:5	35
5:7	35
5:11	35
5:35	35
6:28–29	38
7:7	35
7:9	35
7:21	35
8:15	35
17:21–22	38

Psalms of Solomon

15:3	37
17:26	157

Sibylline Oracles

4:27–30	34
8.56	147–48
8.487	147–48

12.170	147–48	Romans	
		1:7	157
Testament of Levi		1:19–20	59
3:5–6	34	1:21–32	186
19:1	212	1:21	64
		1:29–31	64
Testament of Naphtali		2:22	186
2:6	212	2:29	68
		3:9	59
Testament of Zebulun		3:23	59
9:8	212	3:25	175
		4:19	225
		5:12–21	59
NEW TESTAMENT		6:6	59
Matthew		6:15–23	69
		6:17	59
5:45	58	6:19	211
13:24–30	57	6:20	59
15:18	77	7:7–25	69
15:19	64	8:2	59
16:6	172	8:9–11	173
19:5	177	12:1	1, 236
		13:12	211
Mark		15:16	2, 236
7:14–23	176	16:23	18
7:20–23	64		
7:21–23	77	1 Corinthians	
10:8	177	1:1–9	156
14:58	149, 236	1:1–3	156
		1:1	193
Luke		1:2	156, 162, 168, 182, 184, 193, 195, 233
6:35	81	1:3	162, 192
12:1	172	1:5	193, 195
		1:7–8	193
Acts		1:7	162, 193, 194, 195
2:46	24	1:8	162, 193
3:1	24	1:9	162, 193, 196
7:48	236	1:10—4:21	159, 160, 169
15:20	159	1:10—4:17	155
15:29	159	1:10–17	162
17:23–24	8	1:10	18, 156, 157, 158, 162, 193, 197
17:24	236		
18–19	237	1:11–17	159
18:1–11	2	1:11–12	159
21:25	159	1:11	4, 190
23:6	2	1:12	165
26:5	2	1:13	195

Ancient Document Index 277

1 Corinthians *(continued)*

1:17—2:13	21
1:17	159, 160
1:17–18	195
1:18—2:16	40, 121, 168, 197
1:18—2:13	237, 239
1:18	159, 193, 196, 221
1:19–20	163, 197
1:19	17, 159, 160
1:20	159, 160, 161
1:21	159, 193
1:22–24	21
1:22	159, 160, 161
1:23–24	161
1:23	177, 193, 195
1:24	159, 193, 195
1:25	193
1:26–28	193, 197
1:26	155, 158, 160, 168, 195, 197
1:27	160
1:29	193, 197
1:30	159, 161, 162, 193, 195, 196
1:31	193
2:1	159, 160
2:2	161, 193, 195
2:4	159, 160, 162
2:5	159, 160, 193
2:6	24, 159, 160, 162, 197
2:6–16	196, 197
2:6–8	193
2:7–8	193
2:7	159, 160, 161, 193
2:8	162, 195
2:9–16	193
2:9	17, 161
2:10–16	193
2:10–14	164
2:10–13	182
2:10	160, 161, 162
2:11	162, 177
2:12–15	168
2:12	161, 162, 168, 193, 237, 239
2:13	159, 160, 162
2:14	160, 162
2:15	162, 164
2:16	17
3:1–23	28, 162
3:1–3	168, 197
3:1	39, 161, 162
3:3–4	162
3:3	162
3:5–9	162
3:5–8	162
3:5	162
3:6–9	193
3:6–8	162
3:6–7	162
3:7	162, 193
3:9–15	24
3:9–10	18
3:9	18, 168, 193, 196, 197, 233
3:10–17	150
3:10–15	146, 162, 167, 168, 197
3:10	18
3:11	163, 165, 193, 195, 237
3:12–15	165
3:12	163
3:13–15	193
3:13	163
3:15	163
3:16–18	46
3:16–17	1, 17, 18, 22, 24, 40, 146, 150, 154, 155, 159, 162, 163–68, 171, 178, 179, 182, 183, 196, 230, 233, 238
3:16	1, 4, 9, 24, 41, 42, 43, 55, 149, 159, 164, 168, 173, 178, 189, 193, 195, 210, 213, 214, 236
3:17	18, 164, 165, 168, 178, 193, 197, 233
3:18–20	193
3:18–19	168
3:19–20	17
3:19	159, 237, 239
3:21–23	182
3:21–22	165, 196
3:21	165, 197
3:22–23	193, 194
3:22	165
3:23	159, 165, 168, 172, 186, 195
4:1–4	197
4:4–5	193
4:5	193, 197
4:7–13	208
4:7	193, 194

Ancient Document Index 279

4:8–21	39	6:13	78, 170, 174, 175, 176, 177, 194, 196, 197
4:8–10	197	6:14	174, 177, 194, 195, 196
4:10–13	197	6:15–20	25, 71
4:16	197, 228	6:15–16	196
4:17	197	6:15	163, 170, 172, 175, 177, 196
4:18–19	197	6:16	17, 163, 170, 172, 177
4:20	193	6:17	177
5:1—6:20	169, 170, 174, 192	6:18–20	21
5:1—7:40	170	6:18	170, 173, 174, 175, 176, 178, 197
5:1–13	25, 169, 170, 203, 210	6:19–20	196, 197, 239
5:1–8	165	6:19	1, 4, 11, 14, 24, 25, 40, 41, 42, 43, 149, 154, 155, 163, 169, 170, 172, 173, 174, 177, 178–183, 189, 194, 195, 213, 214, 230, 233, 236, 237, 238, 239
5:1	4, 39, 169, 170, 176		
5:2	170, 171, 197		
5:4–5	197		
5:5	170, 171, 194		
5:6–13	222		
5:6	163	6:20	170, 181, 182, 184, 194, 238
5:6–8	170, 197	7:1—11:1	169
5:6–7	171	7:1–40	25, 169, 170, 183, 192, 203
5:7–8	2, 171	7:1–7	170
5:7	17, 195, 222	7:1	4, 169, 170, 183
5:9–13	169, 170, 197	7:2	170
5:9–11	171	7:3–5	198
5:9–10	176–77, 196	7:4	170, 184, 196
5:9	170	7:7	194
5:10	170, 220, 222	7:8–14	197
5:11	170, 220, 222	7:12–16	170, 222
5:12	220	7:12	212, 221
5:13	194, 222	7:13	212, 221
6:1–20	210	7:14	184, 196, 212, 221, 222
6:1–11	170	7:15	194, 196, 212, 221
6:1–8	158, 170, 172, 197	7:17–40	198
6:1–6	39	7:17	194
6:1	158, 169	7:19	198
6:2	163, 172, 197	7:22–23	194, 196
6:3	163, 172	7:22	194
6:5	160	7:23	179, 184
6:6	212, 221	7:25	169
6:9–20	170, 203	7:34	170, 184
6:9–11	2, 170, 172, 194, 230	7:39	184, 196, 222, 223
6:9–10	197	8:1—11:1	3, 4, 158, 172, 185–189, 187, 192, 210, 220, 230
6:9	163, 172, 176, 220, 221		
6:11	173, 176, 182, 238, 239	8:1—10:22	185
6:12–20	46, 170, 172, 173, 176, 177, 178	8:1–13	188
6:12	169, 172, 173, 176, 186, 187	8:1	18, 169, 185, 186, 198, 220
6:13–14	174, 194	8:3	194, 198

1 Corinthians *(continued)*

8:4–7	218
8:4–6	194, 199
8:4	186, 196, 220
8:5–6	226
8:5	186
8:6	186, 194, 196
8:7–13	187, 198
8:7	2, 186, 187, 196, 198, 215, 220, 230
8:8	194
8:9–13	158
8:9	186
8:10–11	196
8:10	3, 18, 186, 220
8:11	186, 194, 195
8:12	187, 194, 196
9:1—10:22	158
9:1–27	187
9:9	17
9:13	17, 163, 187
9:19–23	197
9:24–27	72, 92, 198
9:24	81, 163
10:1–22	188
10:1–13	2, 187
10:1–10	17
10:4	194
10:5–8	194
10:7–22	198
10:7	187, 220
10:8–11	187
10:9	194
10:12–13	194
10:13	77
10:14–22	158, 187
10:14	3, 187, 220
10:16–17	189
10:16	195
10:18	222
10:19–22	187
10:19	220
10:20	222
10:21–22	194
10:21	221
10:23—11:1	185
10:23–30	198
10:23	18, 173, 186, 198
10:26	17, 194, 196
10:27	212, 221
10:28–29	158
10:31	198
10:32–33	198
11:1–34	192
11:1	197, 228
11:2–16	188, 196
11:2	195
11:3	194, 196
11:7	196
11:11	196
11:12	194
11:13	198
11:17–34	158, 187
11:18	157
11:22	158
11:23–25	195
11:27–29	189
11:27	194
11:29–32	194
11:29	189
11:31–32	198
11:32	197
12:1—14:40	19
12:1–31	189, 192, 197, 198
12:1	169
12:2	2, 188, 220, 230
12:3	182, 188, 198
12:4–6	194, 198
12:4	177, 189
12:6	195
12:7	189, 195
12:8	159, 189
12:9	189
12:10	189
12:11	189
12:12–26	81
12:12–13	195
12:12	189
12:13	189
12:15	189
12:16	189
12:17	189
12:18	195, 198
12:22	195
12:23	190
12:24	190, 195, 198

12:25	157	15:38	195
12:27	195	15:40	190
12:28–30	197	15:41	190
12:31	198	15:42–55	196
13:1–13	196, 198, 199	15:44	190
13:8	195	15:45	17
13:13	195	15:47	190, 196
14:1	198	15:50	197
14:2	195	15:53–54	227
14:3–5	198	15:54–55	17
14:3	18	15:57	195
14:4	18, 186	15:58	199
14:5	18	16:12	169
14:6	198	16:13	199
14:12	18, 198	16:14	199
14:17	18, 186, 198	16:15	190
14:20	198		
14:21	17		
14:22	212, 221		
14:23	212, 221		
14:24	212, 221		
14:25	195		
14:26	18, 198		
14:33–36	198		
14:33	195		
15:1–58	158, 177, 190, 192, 198, 235		
15:3–9	190		
15:3–5	190		
15:3	195		
15:4	195		
15:12	175, 190		
15:14	177		
15:15	195		
15:18	196		
15:19	196, 199		
15:20–24	196		
15:20–23	190		
15:20	190		
15:21–22	196		
15:21	196		
15:22	195, 196		
15:23	195		
15:24–28	195		
15:24	195		
15:26	17		
15:32	17		
15:34	197, 199		
15:35–44	192		

2 Corinthians

1–9	205
1:1	157, 227
1:2–3	226
1:3	219, 226
1:9	226
1:14–15	212
1:19–20	226
1:20	215, 219
1:21	219, 223
1:22	223, 226, 227
1:24	227
2:9	228
2:11	228
2:14—7:4	206
2:14—7:2	234
2:14–16	234, 236
2:14–15	226, 234
2:14	234
2:15	221, 227, 234
2:16	234
2:17	210
3:1–18	17, 225
3:3	223, 226, 227
3:4–18	223
3:4	223
3:6	226
3:14	226
3:17–18	226
3:17	223
3:18	224, 226, 227

2 Corinthians (continued)

4:1	224
4:3-6	208
4:3-4	224
4:3	221, 227
4:4	212, 221, 224, 226, 227, 228
4:5	226
4:6	224, 226, 228
4:7-11	228
4:7-9	228
4:7	224, 235
4:8-9	224
4:10-18	227
4:10-11	226, 228
4:10	225, 228
4:11	225, 227, 228
4:13	17, 225
4:14	226
4:16—5:1	228
4:16	228
4:18	228
5:1-10	226
5:1-7	213
5:1-5	227
5:1-2	235
5:1	149, 227, 235
5:4	235
5:5	225
5:7	225
5:9	228
5:10	226, 227
5:11-21	226
5:11	208, 228
5:12	210
5:15	226, 228
5:17	227
5:18-21	208, 226
5:19	219, 227
5:20	227, 228
6:1-2	226, 227
6:2	17
6:4-10	228
6:4-5	225
6:6-7	225
6:6	225
6:14—7:1	19, 34, 40, 41, 46, 187, 205-229, 230, 234, 239
6:14-16	215
6:14-15	212, 237, 238
6:14	211, 212, 219, 221, 222, 223
6:15	38, 211, 212, 219, 221
6:15-16	212
6:16-18	17, 24, 215
6:16	1, 4, 42, 43, 55, 147, 177, 186, 210, 211, 213, 214, 217, 219, 234
6:17	214, 215, 222
6:18	214, 219, 234
7:1	214, 215, 220, 222
8:15	17
9:9	17
10-13	205, 221
10:17	17
11:2-3	177
11:3	17, 228
11:13	221
11:14	228
12:7	212, 228
12:10	81

Galatians

1:6-9	210
1:10	68
2:9	24
3:22	59
4:8	186
5:9	172
5:19-21	159
5:22-23	72

Ephesians

1:1	157
1:3	237
1:10	237
1:20-22	237
2:1-7	237
2:2	237
2:11-22	237
2:18-22	236, 237
2:19-22	2, 24
2:20	236
2:21	236
2:22	236
3:4-6	237
3:10	237
3:14-21	237

4:6	237
4:13	237
5:2	234
5:5	159
5:8	211
5:31–32	237
5:31	177
6:5–6	68
6:10–20	237

Philippians

1:1	157
2:17	2, 131, 236
3:5	2
3:13–14	81
4:11	81
4:18	2, 234, 236

Colossians

1:1	157
3:1–2	60
3:5	159
3:22–23	68

1 Thessalonians

1:9–10	200
1:9	186
2:4	68
5:5	211
5:23	129

1 Timothy

3:15	237
6:8	81
6:12	92

2 Timothy

1:9	157
2:5	72, 92
4:6	131, 236
4:7	92

Titus

3:3	64

Hebrews

9:11	236
9:24	236
12:1–3	92
12:1	81
12:5–6	60
13:5	81

James

1:12	72
2:8	79
3:2–3	46
3:16	64
4:11	81

1 Peter

2:4–10	24
3:10	81

2 Peter

2:12	164

Jude

3	92
10	164

Revelation

3:12	24
22:15	159

DEAD SEA SCROLLS

1QH

XIV, 15–17	28
XV, 19	28
XVI, 5–7	28
XVI, 5	28
XVI, 6	28
XVI, 9–11	28
XVI, 9	28
XVI, 10	28

1QM

II, 5–6	29

1QpHab

XII, 3, 4	28

1QS

I, 18-19	29
II, 1-2	29
II, 8	27
II, 19-20	29
III, 4	27
III, 6-9	27
III, 9-12	27
V, 2	29
V, 5-6	27
V, 9	29
VI, 3-10	29
VI, 19-20	29
VII, 2-3	29
VIII, 1-10	27
VIII, 1-4	29
VIII, 3-4	27
VIII, 5-9	28
VIII, 5	28
VIII, 10	27
IX, 4-5	27, 31
IX, 6-7	28
X, 6	27
X, 8	27
X, 14	27
XI, 4-5	27
XI, 8-9	28
XI, 8	28

1QSa

I, 2	29
II, 2-3	29

CD

I, 7	28
II, 5	27
III, 12-IV, 4	29
III, 20-IV, 2	32
XI, 17-20	32
XI, 20-21	27
XVI, 13-14	32

4QFlor

I, 6-7	28
I, 6	28, 32

4QSD

7, II, 3	29
7 II, 7-10	27

4QSapWork B

1, 5	29

4QShirShabb^{a}1

I, 3-8	29

4QpIsa

1, 2	29

11Q5 or 11QPsa

154	27
XVIII, 9-12	27

11Q18

20	29

GRECO-ROMAN WRITINGS

Alcinous

Handbook

152.1.2-5	44, 161
153.2.5-8	96
164.10	98
164.10.2.18-26	95
164.10.3.27-29	95
164.10.31-41	95
165.10.3.1-2	95, 151, 167, 216
165.10.4-6	96
165.34—166.14	95
169.14.3—170.4	95
171.1.38—172.2.12	95
171.15.1.15—2.23	95
172.16.2.10-19	96, 180
177.25.33-35	96
177.25.34	96
181.28.1.19-20	96
181.28.3.44-46	96
181.28.22-30	96, 181

182.4.3–8	96, 181	1.30.65	109
		1.32.70	108, 216

Alexander of Aphrodisias

Mixt.

		1.49.110	106, 151, 167, 216
		1.51.115	109
		1.51.117	108
225, 1–2	55	1.52.118	106, 151, 167
		1.53.120	106

Fat.

		1.54.122	106, 166, 180
181,13–182,20	99	1.57.129	109, 180
191,30–192,28	67	1.57.131	109
		2.72.148	105

Apuleius

Metam.

Fin.

		1.5.13—1.21.72	116
3.15	118, 167	1.11.38	115
		2.1.1—35.119	116

Aristotle

De an.

		3.1.2	52
		3.3.10–11	52
1. 411 A	106	3.6.21	52
		3.7.25–26	52
		3.8.28	52

Arius Didymus

Epitome

		3.10.34	52
		3.14.45–48	52
1–3	52	3.15.48–50	52
5b, 5–21 (26)	52, 218	3.20.66	52
5b12, 4–5 (26)	52		
5b12, 10–11 (26)	52	*Leg.*	
5b12, 28–29 (25)	52	1.6.18–19	108
11k, 4–14, (84)	52, 218	1.7.22–23	108
11k, 18–20 (84)	52, 218	1.7.23	107, 108
11k, 26–29 (84)	52, 218	1.7.24	108, 216, 217
11s, 16–19 (98)	52	1.7.25	108, 181
		1.7.26–27	107

Aulus Gellius

Noct. att.

		1.11.32—1.12.33	109
		1.15.43	105
		1.16.45	109
7.1.1–13	75	1.22.58	44, 161
7.2.3–12	75	1.22.59	106, 109, 166, 216
7.2.12–13	113	1.23.60–62	109
		2.2.5	105

Cicero

Amic.

		2.4.8–10	108
		2.4.8	108
4.13	108	2.7.15–16	108, 217
		2.8.19	105

Div.

		2.10.24	105, 218
		2.10.25	105
1.11.17	107	2.10.26	106, 167, 216
1.18.34	108	2.11.26–28	166

Leg. (continued)

2.11.26	106, 167, 216
2.11.27–28	180
2.11.27	106, 216
2.11.28	106, 151

lib. inc. fr.

2	107, 109, 180

Nat. d.

1.15.39	51
1.15.42—17.44	114
1.17.45	114
1.19.51	114
1.20.53	115, 116
2.6.16	51
2.11.30	51
2.14.37—15.39	51
2.28.71	50, 51, 182, 218
2.28.72	51
2.29.73—30.77	51, 216
2.31.78	51
2.32.78	51
2.65.164—66.166	51, 217
3.16.26	115

Parad.

1.14	107, 166

Resp.

1.13.20	108
1.17.28	109
2.10.17	108
2.22.23	108
3.9.14	106
6.15.15	107, 167, 216
6.24.26	107, 167, 179

Tusc.

1.12.27—13.29	109
1.16.36	108
1.22.51	235
1.24.56	107, 166, 180
1.25.62	107, 166, 180
1.26.64	44, 161
1.26.65	107, 166
1.27.66-67	107, 166
1.30.74	107, 166
1.32.76	109
1.49.118	108
3.3.5-6	44, 161
3.6.13	44, 161
3.17.36	45
5.1.1	45
5.2.5	45, 161
5.7.20	46
5.25.70	109
5.26.73-74	116

Cleanthes

Hymn to Zeus

1	69, 75, 217
2–3	75

Dio Chrysostom

Alex.

8	45
12–14	64
15	64
17	64
18	45
20	45

Borysth.

22	64
23	64
29	61
31	65
32	63, 217
36	63

Compot.

7	45

Dei cogn.

22	63, 217
27	64
28	65
36–37	116
60	64
74	63, 217
75	63, 217

Exil.

28	45
35	62, 182
601B	90, 217
607D	92, 143, 180

Fel. sap.

10	63

Gen.

1	65

2 Glor.

1	45
1	161

Hom.

11–12	65
12	64, 217

Invid.

25	64

De lege

2	64
5	64

Nicaeen

8	64

Nicom.

11	64
18	64, 65

De philosophia

7	45
8	45

De philosopho

6	45
10	45

Rec. mag.

3	45, 65

6	65
7	65
12	65
14	65

1 Regn.

16	63, 65, 217
39	63, 217
42	64, 217
56	64, 217

2 Regn.

24	45
26	45, 64, 217
41	235
62–63	64
107	64

3 Regn.

50	64, 217
51	65
52	62
53	65
82	65, 181
115	65

4 Regn.

23	65, 181
76	62
89	63
102	64
118	64
126	64
139	63, 166, 180

Rhod.

15	62
58	65

1 Serv. lib.

17–18	173
17	65

1 Tars.

23	65
28	62, 65

Virt. (Or. 69)

4	65

Diogenes Laertius
Diog. Laert.

1.3.63	44
5.2.36	47
5.2.53	47
6.2.72	176
7.1.54	50
7.1.87	50
7.1.88	50, 181
7.1.89	50, 181
7.1.93–117	50, 181
7.1.119	49, 166, 216
7.1.125	176
7.1.135	49
7.1.137	49
7.1.139	49
7.1.147	49
7.7.179–202	48
8.1.22	110
10.1–11	114
10.77–78	114
10.118–22	115
10.123–25	115
10.123	114
10.139	114
10.31–33	115
10.34	115
10.82	115
10.117	115
10.127–31	115

Epictetus
Diatr.

1.1.4	69
1.1.7	69
1.1.10	68
1.1.23	69
1.1.24	68
1.3.1	69, 217
1.4.1	69
1.4.4	69
1.4.18	70
1.4.19	70
1.6.15	70
1.6.20–21	70
1.9.1–7	69, 217
1.9.4–5	70
1.9.7	69, 217
1.9.22–26	69, 217
1.11.33	70
1.11.37	70
1.12.1–3	114
1.12.16	70
1.12.25	68
1.12.26	72
1.14.6	26, 67, 166, 179
1.14.10	68
1.14.12	67, 166, 180
1.14.14	67, 166, 180, 216
1.14.16–18	70
1.15.5	70
1.17.27	69
1.19.7–8	70
1.19.9	68
1.19.12	68
1.20.5–7	69
1.20.15	70
1.22.15–16	68
1.24.1	72
1.25.1	69, 70
1.25.3	68
1.25.5–6	68
1.25.5	68
1.25.13	68
1.26.1–2	70
1.27.15–19	69
1.28.1–28	69
1.29.2–8	69
1.29.24	69
1.29.60	69
1.30.1	68, 181
1.30.3–4	69
1.30.5	70
2.1.4	69
2.1.5	69
2.1.17	70, 180
2.2.3	69
2.2.7	69
2.2.14	69
2.5.8	70
2.5.13	72

Ancient Document Index

2.6.1	69	3.18.1–5	69
2.6.8	70	3.20.1	181
2.6.9	69	3.21.14	66
2.7.3	71	3.22.21	181
2.7.11	71	3.22.34	181
2.8.2	68	3.22.40–41	181
2.8.10–11	72	3.22.56–59	68
2.8.11–17	216	3.22.82	66
2.8.11–13	39	3.24.16	68
2.8.11	66, 67, 166	3.24.19	68
2.8.12–13	71, 182, 218	3.24.24	69
2.8.12	67, 71, 179	3.24.60	71
2.8.14	67, 166	3.24.84–89	71
2.8.15–17	72	3.24.95–102	70
2.8.15–16	67	3.26.28	68, 217
2.8.17	67	4.1	69
2.8.18–22	71	4.1.1	173
2.18.19	218	4.1.4	173
2.10.1	69	4.1.14	173
2.10.3	70	4.1.18	173
2.11.2–3	69	4.1.60–61	68
2.13.10	69	4.1.66	181
2.14.11	68, 217	4.1.78	181
2.14.13	68, 71, 181	4.1.87	181
2.14.25–26	68, 217	4.1.104	181
2.16.33	67, 68, 166, 217	4.1.112	71, 182, 218
2.16.42	71, 181	4.1.131	68
2.17.22	68, 70, 71	4.1.158	181
2.17.25	68	4.1.172–73	71
2.17.29	70, 71	4.1.175	71, 182
2.8.18–22	182	4.3.9	71
2.18.19	71, 182	4.4.27	71
2.19.26	71, 182	4.4.34	68
2.19.27	71	4.4.47	69
2.20.6–20	72	4.5.23	69
2.22.1–3	69	4.5.34	69
2.23.19	69	4.5.35	70
2.23.42	68	4.7.6–7	72
3.2.1–5	69	4.7.9	70, 71
3.3.10	69	4.7.17	71, 181
3.6	72	4.7.31–32	181
3.7.36	68	4.8.12	69
3.10.18	69	4.8.20	72
3.11.5–6	68	4.8.32	72
3.12.1–12	69	4.8.36	72
3.13.7	68, 217	4.9.17	69
3.15.1–7	72	4.10.2	36
3.15.11–12	72	4.10.12	71

Diatr. (continued)

4.10.14–17	36
4.11.3	68, 217, 218
4.11.5	71, 218
4.12.7	69
4.12.12	70

Ench.

1.1–5	66
1.1	181
2.2	69
2.13	69
2.19	69
2.34	69
8	70
31.1	70
31.5	69
33.1	72
41	72
46	72
48	72
52	72
53	71

Frag.

3	68, 166
4	69, 70, 72
8	68
9	69
26	70, 180

Euripides

Tro.

887–888	89

Homer

Od.

19.40	89
4.392	92, 180

Josephus

Ag. Ap.

2.168	21

Ant.

18.1	33
18.5	33
18.18–22	33

J.W.

2.119–61	33

Lucretius

Rerum nat.

1.44–49	114
1.62–79	114
2.1–1104	114
2.1094–95	114
3.1–15	114
3.18–24	114
3.322	115
3.580–930	115
5.6–12	114
5.73–90	114
5.146–49	114
5.198–99	114
5.1194–1200	115
5.1200–1203	116
6.1–30	114
6.54–67	114
6.75–78	115

Marcus Aurelius

Med.

1.17.6	80
2.1	76, 166, 216
2.3	75, 217
2.4	77
2.12	78
2.13	73, 79, 166, 180, 182, 218
2.17	45, 73, 79, 161, 166, 180, 182, 218
3.3.2	73, 166, 180
3.4.2	73
3.4.3	73
3.5.1	73, 79, 166, 182
3.6.1–3	79
3.6.2	73, 79, 166, 182
3.7	79
3.12	73, 79, 166, 180, 182, 218

3.16	73, 79, 166, 180, 182, 218	7.55.1–2	78, 180
4.1	74, 77, 78, 166	7.55.1	77
4.12	79	7.56	77
4.14	77	7.59	80
4.17	81	7.69	80
4.21.1	77	7.70	77
4.23	75, 77, 78	7.75	75
4.25	81	7.9	166
4.29	78	8.1	80
4.38	76, 77, 166	8.7	77, 80
4.39	78	8.8	81
4.40	75	8.16	80
4.46	76, 77	8.18	77
4.48	78	8.19	80
5.1	75	8.23	75
5.3	77	8.25	80
5.8.1–2	76	8.26	75, 80, 81
5.10	78, 166	8.43	76, 78, 166
5.10.2	74, 180, 216	8.54	75, 78
5.13	76	8.56	81
5.18	77	8.58	77
5.19	76	8.59	81
5.22	81	8.61	76, 81, 166
5.24	76	9.1	75
5.27	73, 74, 80, 166, 180, 182	9.1.1–2	81
5.28	77	9.1.1	81
5.31	81	9.1.3	116
5.33	77	9.1.4	78
6.1	76	9.3.1	77
6.3	80	9.5	77
6.4	77	9.7	76, 77, 79, 166
6.7	80	9.10	76
6.11	80	9.11	81
6.12	45, 80	9.27	76, 217
6.24	77	9.38	77
6.28	77	9.40	76, 80
6.32	78, 180	10.1	75, 78, 217
6.35	76, 166	10.7.2	77
6.36.2	75	10.14	80
6.37–38	76	10.15	78
7.5	76	10.38	74, 166
7.9	73, 75, 216	11.1.2	81
7.10	77	11.12	81
7.13	81	11.16	78
7.16	76, 166	11.18.1	81
7.19	77	11.20	76, 166
7.22	81	12.1	76, 77, 166
7.54	73, 80, 81, 182	12.1.2	74, 77, 166

Med. (continued)

12.1.26	166
12.5	80
12.11	80
12.26	74, 76, 77
12.27	44
12.29	81
12.30	76
12.32	76

Marcus Cornelius Fronto

Epist. Graecae.

8.3, 7	66

Maximus of Tyre

Or.

1.2–3	161
1.2	46
1.3	44
1.8	46
2.1	97, 99, 217
2.2	97
2.3	100
2.10	98
4.8	117
4.9	117
5.4	98
5.8	97, 100
6.1	98
6.4	100
7.2	101
7.5	101, 143, 180
8.7	100
8.8	99, 100
9.2	98, 100
9.6	100, 101, 143, 180
9.6–7	100
10.3–5	101, 180
10.3	101
10.4	101
10.5	101
10.9	101, 143, 180
11.5	98, 99
11.8	98
11.9	98
11.10	101
11.11	98, 180
11.12	98
12	102
13.3–4	99
13.4	99
13.6	100
13.7	99, 217
13.8	99
15.6	102
15.10	102
20.6	46
21.7–8	100
22.6	46, 161
26.1	44, 45, 161
26.9	102, 181
27.8	98, 99
27.9	101
28.2	101
29.6	97
31.4	97, 166
33.7	100
34.3	100
35.2	102, 181
35.6–8	45
37.2	46, 161
38.6	101
39.1	102
39.3	102
40.3	102
40.4	102
40.5	101
41.2	98
41.4	99
41.5	99, 100, 102

Musonius

frag.

8.64.37—66.1	45
16.104.30–32	45
16.104.36–37	45

Origen

Cels.

4.14	75

Ancient Document Index

Philo

Agr.

127	124

Cher.

27	147, 166
85	133
94	126
95–97	126
95	147
98	146, 166, 180, 216
100	146, 166, 180, 216
101	146, 167
127	150

Conf.

137–38	151, 167, 216

Congr.

74–80	123
74–76	121
79	123
96–98	130
98	130
106	133, 172
114–15	132
116–17	152
116	146
168	147

Decal.

133	133

Det.

21	137
90	148, 166, 180
160	152

Deus

7	139, 218
8–9	147, 180
9	147, 218
134	142, 146, 180
135	143

Ebr.

51	123
65	141
66	126
68–76	141
68	140
76	141
79	126
87	132
102–5	141
102	141
103	141
104	141
105	141
125–29	141
128	141
129	125
131	125, 126
134	152
135	147
152–53	131
361–63	145

Fug.

68	123
75	151, 167, 216
80	131
106–12	141
108	141
110	142, 145
114–15	142
115	142
118	142
157–60	126, 127
162	147

Gig.

27	151

Her.

82–85	143
82	147
84	143, 218
85	143
112–13	152, 218
126	127
125–26	132

Ancient Document Index

Her. (continued)

179	127
182–83	131
184	131, 218
185	131
199–200	132

Leg.

1.44	150
1.49–50	136
1.57	123
1.62	147
1.78	149, 151
2.55–56	143, 218
2.56	131, 132
3.4	151, 167, 216
3.46	152, 166, 217
3.72	123
3.82	140
3.94	134
3.123	140
3.125	140
3.126	140
3.141	129
3.165	134
3.193	222
3.239	222

Legat.

188	147
306	147
308	147

Migr.

25	133, 172
67	128, 130
89–93	124
92	124
102	144
103	144
202	130

Mos.

1.21–23	123
1.27	149
1.48	123
2.66	123
2.82	148, 180
2.87	147
2.95	147
2.107	126
2.108	129, 218
2.124–25	144
2.127–30	144
2.133	145
2.135	143, 145
2.137–39	136, 182
2.148–51	136, 182, 218
2.150	136
2.152	147
2.154	147
2.162	126
2.174	147
2.178	147
2.224	134
2.279	126

Mut.

44	144
223	123
240	130, 218
245–47	130
249–51	130

Opif.

8	123
27	150
53	123
55	150
77	123
135	149, 179
137	25, 149, 179

Plant.

33	150
50	149
53	152
61	127
97–99	134
107	126
108	126, 136, 182
126	138, 150
128	139
129	139

Ancient Document Index   295

134	139	2.115	144
162	124, 218	2.116	144
164	127	2.117	144
		2.118	144
Post.		2.120	145
6	151, 167, 216	2.122	144
14	151, 167, 216	2.124	144
30	151, 167, 216		
72	127, 134, 172	*QG* 1, 2, 3, 4	
101	124	1.5	148
102	124	2.4	152
173	147	2.52	133
		3.3	127, 133
Praem.		4.80	147, 166, 180
75	147		
123	147, 166, 180	*Sacr.*	
		53	133
Prob.		63	133, 172
75	33	73	136, 182
		74	130
QE 1, 2		87	130
1.2	125	109–11	136, 182
1.3	134, 172	117	130
1.4	134, 172	136	130
1.7–8	134, 172	139	131
1.10	144, 149, 166		
1.13	125, 134, 172, 218	*Sobr.*	
1.17	135, 182	62	146, 166, 180, 218
2.7	138	68	146, 166
2.14	135		
2.31	136, 182	*Somn.*	
2.33	131	1.122	235
2.50	126, 133	1.148	217
2.51	148, 152, 166	1.149	25, 146, 147, 166, 180, 217
2.71	131, 132	1.212	128
2.83	152	1.215	140, 147, 166
2.85	150	1.218	144
2.98–99	182	1.243	132
2.98	135, 218	2.72	129
2.99	136	2.73–74	182
2.100	127, 148	2.73	137, 218
2.107	144	2.74	137
2.109	145	2.215	180
2.110	144	2.183	131, 142
2.111	144	2.185	142
2.112–14	145	2.187	142
2.112	145	2.188	142

Somn. (continued)

2.189	142
2.230–32	142
2.232	132, 147
2.248	147, 166, 180, 216, 217
2.250–51	166, 180
2.272	130

Spec.

1.66	133, 143, 150, 151
1.67–70	124
1.68	125
1.82	143, 218
1.84	147
1.88–89	145
1.93	145
1.95	143, 145
1.96	143
1.171	132
1.193	138
1.195–96	138
1.201	136, 182
1.203	136, 182
1.215	126
1.217	131
1.224	138
1.231	147
1.252	129
1.253	129
1.254	132
1.257–61	218
1.257–60	135, 182
1.257	135
1.261	127
1.269–71	182
1.269	125, 135, 218
1.270	126, 135, 146, 166
1.271	127, 133
1.272	138
1.274	147
1.275	125, 147
1.279	126
1.283	127, 182
1.286	138
1.287	135, 182
1.288	135
1.290	127
1.297	147
1.336	123
2.35	125
2.145	144
2.147	134, 172
2.163	144
3.1	123
3.185	123
3.186	123
4.69	145

Virt.

188	148, 166, 180

Philostratus

Ep.

26	111, 112
27	111
52	114
58.1–2	112
58.3	112
58.4	113

Vit. Apoll.

1.1.1–3	112, 217
1.1.1–2	113
1.1.1	111
1.1.7	112, 217
1.1.11	112
1.2.3	113, 147
1.10.1–2	111
1.18.1	113, 182
1.24.3	111
1.31.1—32.2.1	111
1.38.1	111
2.5.3	111, 112, 217, 218
2.39.3	112, 113, 182
3.19.1	110, 112, 181
3.42.1–2	111, 113, 182, 218
4.11.1	111
6.11.3	111, 113, 182
6.11.6	111
8.7.20	112, 217
8.7.21–22	113
8.7.22	111
8.7.23	112, 114
8.7.30	111
8.23.1	112

8.31.3 — 112

Pindar

Frag.
206.1 — 89

Plato

[Ax.]
365E — 235
366A — 235

[Epin.]
984A — 88

Leg.
709bc — 99

Phaedr.
81C — 235

Tim.
37c7 — 150
41.BCD — 95
42AB — 96, 180
92C — 88

Plutarch

Adv. Col.
1108C — 46
1123A — 87
1124F — 90, 216, 217
1125A — 117

Alex. fort.
327E — 45
328B — 45
330E — 46

Am. prol.
494F — 91
495C — 91

Amat.
762E — 89

An. corp.
500C — 92
501A — 44, 161

An. procr.
1013ABC — 89
1014BC — 89
1014E — 89
1015E — 89
1016C — 89
1027A — 89

An seni
786B — 91

Comm. not.
1074EF–1075D — 90

Conj. praec.
140D — 91

[Cons. Apoll.]
108CD — 92, 180

Cons. ux.
611EF, 612A

Cupid. divit.
526AB — 94
527F — 93

Def. orac.
413C — 91
413F — 90, 217
420B — 117
423D — 90, 217
426C — 90
436D — 91
437A — 89
437B — 88
437C — 235

E Delph.
393A — 89
393F — 90

Exil.

28	45
35	62, 182
601B	90, 217
607D	92, 143, 180

Frat. amor.

478DEF	91
479CD	91
479D	91
479F	88, 91
480B	91
491DE	93

Garr.

510DE	93

Gen. Socr.

593A	91, 216
593D	92
593DEF	92

Is. Os.

172	89
351D	93
351E	87
352A	87
352C	93
353A	92, 143
355D	87
369D	91
377F	90
378A	93
378CD	93
381–82B	217
381B	89, 217
382AB	93
382B	89
382D	44
382F	44
383A–C	235
383A	89, 92

Lat. viv.

1129F	92

Praec. ger. rei publ.

822B	89
824B	117

Princ. iner.

780E	92
780F	92
781A	92
782A	45

Pyth. orac.

402C–D	235

Quaest. conv.

626B	235
645E	235
720C	89

Quaest. plat.

2, 1001B	88
2, 1001C	89
2, 1002C	89, 180, 216, 217
8	89, 216

Sept. sap. conv.

163E	92, 94, 180, 181

Sera

549F	90
550E–551C	90, 94
550E	94
551D	90
560F	93
561A	93
562D	90

Stoic. rep.

1034B	117
1043B	117

Suav. viv.

1100F–1101C	117
1102A	88
1102B	88
1102D	90
1105C	93

Ancient Document Index

1105D	92

Superst.

164EF	117
167F	90, 217

Tranq. an.

477B	235
477C	88, 216

Virt. prof.

81E	44, 161
86A	89, 167, 216
122E	92, 180

Seneca

Apol.

8	116

Ben.

1.6.2	53
1.6.3	53
2.29.1–6	56
4.2.1	53
4.6.6	57
4.7.1	55, 216
4.7.2	55
7.7.3	54, 88
4.8.2	55
4.8.3	55, 57
4.19.1	116
4.25.1	58, 59, 181, 217
4.26.1–3	58, 217
4.28.1	58, 217
4.28.3	58, 217
5.12.3	59
6.23.5	56
6.23.6	57, 60, 166
7.1.7	60
7.2.3	60
7.2.4	60
7.7.3	88, 167, 216
7.15.4	60

Brev. vit.

4.2	58
4.5	58
14.1	44, 161
14.5	45
15.4	44, 54, 161

Clem.

1.1.2–6	58
1.5.1	58, 200
1.5.7	58
1.6.3	59
1.7.1–2	217
1.7.1	58
1.7.2	58
1.14.2	58
1.19.9	61
2.4.2–3	53

Const.

1.1	60, 61
2.1	60
7.2	61
9.4	54
16.1	114

De otio.

3.2	115
5.8	59, 181

Ep.

5	45
6.5–6	45
6.6	45
7	45
8.1–2	45
8.5	45
10.4–5	61
16.5	45, 161
26.4–7	61
31.2	56, 166, 179, 216
31.8	44, 161
31.9	60, 181
41.1–2	166
41.1	56, 166
41.2	56, 61, 167, 181, 216
41.5	59, 61, 180
41.8	59
44.2	44

Ep. (continued)

44.5	59
48.12	44
53.8	45, 161
53.9	45, 161
57.7–9	59
58.27–28	59
65.10	58
65.17	191
65.23	58
66.12	56, 166, 167, 179
71.16	61
73.12	44
73.16	57, 166, 216
74.17–18	60
74.20	60
79.12	61
83.1	57, 166
87.19	61
89.1–6	44, 161
90.1	44
90.1–3	161
90.2–3	44
90.28	150
90.29	54, 88, 167
90.35	116
92.3	57, 166, 216
92.30	57, 216
95.47–48	54
95.50	54, 60, 181
102.21	59
107.12	60
108.19–22	110
110.2	57, 166, 180, 216
115.5	54
117.6	59
102.21	191
102.28	191
120.14	57, 166, 180, 216
120.18–19	181
124.14	61
124.23	57

Helv.

6.8	216
8.3	55, 57, 181
11.6	61, 180
11.7	57
20.2	57, 61

Ira

2.15.3	59
2.27.1	58, 217
3.6.1	60

Marc.

14.1–2	58
17.6–7	56
21.5–6	60
23.1–2	61, 180
24.5	61
25.3	191

Nat.

Preface.1.13	55
Preface.1.14	55
Preface.12	58
1.3.10	115
2.6.5	55, 181
2.36.1	60
2.37.2	60
2.45.1–2	56
2.45.1	74
2.45.2–3	56
3.9.1	53
3.13.1	53
3.22.1	53
3.29.2	55, 181
3.30.8	60
5.18.5	56
5.18.13–15	56
6.16.1	55, 181
7.19.1	53
7.20.1	53
7.21.1	53
7.22.1	53
7.30.4	58

Polyb.

9.3	61, 180
9.8	61, 180
12.3	58
12.5	58
13.1	58
13.3	58

14.1-2	58	
15.3-4	58	

Prov.

1.5-7	60
1.5	58, 60, 181, 217
2.1-9	60
3.1	60
3.3	60
4.5-12	56
4.7	60
5.1	60
5.8	60
5.9	58

Tranq.

2.3	61
14.9	58

Vit. beat.

3.3	59, 181
7.1	117
8.1	59, 181
8.4	55
10.3	117
13.1	117
15.6	60, 181
16.1-2	60, 181

Sextus Empiricus

Math.

1.75	55
1.128	112

Stobaeus

Anthology

2.9.7	83

Valerius Maximus

V. Max.

4.7 ext. 1	21, 118, 167

Virgil

Aen.

8.352	56

EARLY CHRISTIAN WRITINGS

Eusebius

Praep. ev.

4.13	111

Author Index

Adams, Edward, and David G. Horrell, 159
Adewuya, J. Ayodeji, 19–20, 41, 207, 208, 209, 210, 211, 215, 221, 228, 236
Aernie, Jeffrey W., 209, 214, 221
Algra, Keimpe, 43, 49, 55, 58, 74
Allo, E.-B., 220
Amador, J. D. H., 206, 209
Anderson, R. Dean, 1
Asmis, Elizabeth, 79
Atkinson, Kenneth, 37
Attridge, Harold W., 234
Aune, David E., 17, 156, 201
Aus, Roger David, 234

Bailey, D. R. Shackleton, 105
Balch, David L., 184
Barclay, John M. G., 158
Barker, M., 142
Barnes, Nathan J., 5, 6, 44, 155
Barnett, Paul, 205, 206, 209, 210, 212, 213, 221, 222
Barrett, C. K., 156, 159, 170, 183, 184, 205, 209, 211, 221, 225
Bartchy, S. Scott, 179
Bauckham, Richard, 24
Bauernfeind, Otto, 137
Baumgarten, J. 31, 33
Beale, Gregory K., 15, 28, 150, 162, 208, 209, 214
Beck, Mark, 86
Belleville, Linda L., 156, 223, 224
Best, Ernest, 28
Betz, H. D., 206, 209

Bieringer, Reimund, 209
Birnbaum, Ellen, 124,
Bobzien, Susanne, 48, 69, 99
Borgen, Peder, 40, 121, 122, 124, 128, 142
Böttrich, Christfried, 17
Brenk, Frederick E., 86, 90, 92
Brennan, Tad, 69
Brooke, George J., 28, 30, 31, 32, 33, 207
Brookins, Timothy A., 155, 160, 174, 176, 181, 201
Brunschwig, Jacques, 50
Brunschwig, Jacques, and David Sedley, 43, 48, 115
Brunt, J. C., 185
Bultmann, Rudolf, 206
Burk, Denny, 174, 175, 176
Burton, Ernest De Witt, 177
Byrne, Brendan, 174, 175

Caragounis, C., 183
Carmignac, J., 31
Chester, Andrew, 34
Cheung, A. T., 4, 185, 186, 187, 188
Chow, John K., 158, 159, 170
Ciampa, Roy E., 184
Ciampa, Roy E., and Brian S. Rosner, 156, 157, 158, 161, 162, 163, 169, 170, 173, 174, 176, 183, 184, 188, 189
Clarke, Andrew D., 158, 159, 170
Cohen, Naomi G., 122
Colish, Marcia L., 48, 50
Collange, J.-F., 221, 223, 225, 234, 236

Author Index

Collins, John J., 38
Collins, Raymond F., 156, 157, 159, 161, 162, 163, 164, 169, 170, 171, 173, 175, 183, 184, 189, 198
Coloe, Mary L., 237
Comfort, Philip W., 177, 194, 213, 226
Conzelmann, Hans, 156, 157, 161, 165, 169, 173, 174, 176, 184, 198
Coppens, J. C., 10, 11
Corley, Jeremy, 36

Dahl, N. A., 206, 221
Daly, Robert J., 11–12, 207
Danker, Frederick W., 209
deLacey, D. R., 163
Deming, Will, 6, 170, 176, 184
deSilva, David, 38, 154, 209, 210, 221
DeWitt, Norman Wentworth, 115
Dillon, John M., 86, 89, 91, 92, 94, 120, 122, 142, 146, 150
Dimant, Devorah, 30, 33
Dodson, Derek S., 3
Duff, Paul Brooks, 206, 224, 234
Dunn, James D. G., 192, 198
Dutch, Robert S., 155

Engberg-Pedersen, Troels, 5, 191, 201, 202
Enslin, Morton S., and Solomon Zeitlin, 35

Fee, Gordon D., 4, 154, 156, 157, 159, 161, 162, 164, 165, 169, 170, 171, 173, 174, 175, 176, 177, 182, 183, 184, 185, 188, 191, 198, 207, 208, 210, 213, 220, 221, 223, 224, 225
Ferguson, Everett, 4, 6, 39, 43, 48, 66, 72, 86, 105, 110, 114, 124
Finlan, Stephen, 237
Fiore, Benjamin, 174
Fisk, Bruce, 175, 176, 178, 185
Fitzgerald, John T., 225
Fitzmyer, Joseph A., 2, 5, 36, 156, 157, 159, 161, 162, 171, 173, 174, 183, 184, 187, 188, 206, 207
Flusser, David, 10
Fotopoulos, John, 4, 185, 186
Fraeyman, M., 8–9, 13

Frede, Dorothea, 49, 50, 59, 76, 80
Frede, Michael, 52, 69
Friesen, Steven J., 2, 3, 18, 155
Furnish, Victor Paul, 205, 208, 209, 212, 221, 222, 223, 225, 234

García Martínez, Florentino, 29
Garcilazo, Albert V., 6, 192
Gardner, Paul Douglas, 4
Garland, David E., 156, 159, 161, 165, 169, 173, 175, 178, 198
Gärtner, Bertil E., 9–10, 11, 13, 21, 29, 30, 31, 207
Gera, Deborah Levine, 35
Gibson, Richard J., 236
Gill, Christopher, 53
Gnilka, Joachim, 206, 207
Goodwin, Mark J., 214, 223
Gooch, Peter D., 4, 42, 185, 186, 187
Goodenough, Edwin R., 121, 122, 137, 142
Goulder, M. D., 220, 221, 222
Gundry, Robert H., 174, 175
Gupta, Nijay, 1, 2, 7, 9, 10, 14–15, 17, 19, 22, 41, 42, 132, 144, 151, 173, 178, 209, 221, 234, 236
Guthrie, George H., 205, 206, 209, 213, 215, 223, 225, 234

Hadot, Pierre, 72, 74, 77, 78, 79, 80, 81
Hafemann, Scott J., 223, 234
Hall, David R., 205
Han, Paul, 209, 214, 221, 223
Hankinson, R. J., 48, 69
Harner, Philip B., 164
Harris, Murray J., 41, 205, 206, 208, 209, 212, 213, 214, 215, 220, 221, 222, 223, 224, 225, 226, 227, 234, 236
Hays, Richard B., 14, 157, 158, 161, 171, 173, 174, 175, 189, 198
Hayward, C. T. R., 34, 35, 36, 37
Heil, C., 206–07,
Hogeterp, Albert L. A., 7, 20–22, 28, 41, 162, 163, 178, 180, 209, 210
Hooker, Morna D., 196
Horrell, David, 17, 19, 159, 198

Author Index 305

Horsley, Richard A., 40
Horst, Pieter W. van der, and Judith H. Newman, 37
Howard, J. K., 171
Hultgren, Stephen J., 207
Hurd, John C., 156

Inwood, Brad, 48
Inwood, Brad, and Pierluigi Donini, 61
Jewett, Robert, 156, 162

Johnson, Luke Timothy, 2, 26
Jones, C. P., 61

Kamesar, Adam, 121, 124
Keener, Craig S., 2, 24, 34, 156, 157, 158, 159, 161, 168, 173, 175, 198, 205, 223, 224, 225, 236, 257
Kempthorne, R., 14, 170, 175, 176
Kidd, I. G., 48, 50
Klauck, Hans-Josef, 9, 207, 208
Klawans, Jonathan, 31, 33, 122
Klinzing, Georg, 10–11, 13, 15, 28, 29, 31, 32, 33, 208
Knibb, Michael A., 27
Konsmo, Erik, 1, 14
Koskenniemi, Erkki, 121–22
Kremer, Jacob, 162
Kristeller, Paul Oskar, 48, 75, 104
Kuck, David W., 163

Lacey, W. K., 105
Lamberton, Robert, 86
Lambrecht, Jan, 174, 175, 205, 206, 208, 221
Lamp, Jeffrey S., 160
Lanci, John R., 3, 7, 14, 17–19, 20, 22, 163, 164, 176, 231
Lane, William L., 209
Lang, Friedrich, 156, 161, 183, 198, 207, 212
Lapidge, Michael, 55, 68
Laporte, Jean, 125, 131, 132, 140, 142
Lee, Michelle V., 6, 155, 190, 200, 202
Leonhardt, Jutta, 40, 123, 125, 138
Leppä, Outi, 207
Levinsohn, Stephen H., 164, 211

Levison, John R., 165
Lévy, Carlos, 127
Lichtenberger, Hermann, 31, 32
Lieber, Andrea, 40, 124, 128
Lightfoot, J. B., 184, 193, 225
Lindemann, Andreas, 161
Litfin, A. Duane, 160
Liu, Yulin, 3, 7, 18, 25–26, 42, 164, 170, 171, 209, 221, 231
Long, A. A., 18, 48, 50, 52, 53, 55, 57, 59, 60, 66, 67, 68, 69, 70, 71, 72, 74, 75, 99, 105, 114, 115, 116, 191
Long, Fredrick J., 24, 41, 53, 72, 200, 205, 209, 211, 212, 213, 223, 224, 234

Mack, Burton L., 124
MacKendrick, Paul, 50, 105
Mackie, Scott D., 142
MacRae, George W., 149, 150, 152
Malherbe, Abraham J., 5, 6, 177, 200
Mansfeld, Jaap, 47, 63
Marshall, I. H., 195
Martin, Dale B., 4, 158, 176, 179, 189, 190, 191
Martin, Ralph P., 206, 208, 209, 221, 223
Matera, Frank J., 209, 213, 221
May, Alistair Scott, 4, 175, 183, 223
McDonald, James I. H., 234
McKelvey, R. J., 7, 8, 10, 12–13, 39, 150, 168, 178, 207, 236
McNicol, Allan J., 30, 32
Merklein, Helmut, 159
Metzger, Bruce M., 154, 165, 177, 194, 213
Mitchell, Margaret M., 18, 156, 157, 158, 159, 169, 175, 176, 189
Mitton, C. L., 171
Moore, Carey A., 35, 36, 37
Most, Glenn W., 44
Moule, C. F. D., 16, 174, 175
Moulton, J. H., and Nigel Turner, 178
Murphy-O'Connor, Jerome, 174, 175, 185, 187, 198, 207, 209, 221

Nathan, Emmanuel, 209

Newton, Derek, 4, 185, 188
Newton, Michael, 7, 8, 13–14, 21, 25, 28, 207
Nguyen, V. Henry T., 216
Nickelsburg, George W. E., 121
Nikiprowetzky, Valentin, 40, 128

Obbink, Dirk, 78
Omanson, Roger L., 175
Oropeza, B. J., 172, 205, 209, 215, 221
Otzen, Benedikt, 36

Paige, Terence, 176
Parker, Robert, 26
Patte, Daniel, 221
Patterson, Jane Lancaster, 237
Pearson, Birger Albert, 40
Perrin, Nicholas, 237
Phua, Richard Liong-Seng, 4, 186
Plummer, Alfred, 221, 222, 224, 225, 234, 235
Pogoloff, Stephen M., 160, 161
Porter, Stanley E., 211
Powell, J. G. F., 50, 105
Price, James L., 205

Rabens, Volker, 221, 222, 224
Rabinowitz, Peter J. T., 2, 3
Radice, Roberto, 142
Reesor, Margaret E., 48, 49, 50, 69
Regev, Eyal, 27
Rensberger, D., 208, 220, 221
Renwick, David, A., 235
Reydams-Schils, Gretchen J., 48, 122
Richardson, Peter, 170, 187
Richardson, Philip, 127
Rist, J. M., 48, 50, 52, 60, 63, 99
Rives, James B., 4
Robertson, Paul, 124
Robertson, Archibald, and Alfred Plummer, 156, 161, 162, 165, 184
Rosner, Brian S., 171, 173, 174, 175, 176, 183, 184, 188, 189
Rowland, Christopher C., 34
Runia, David T., 122, 149, 150
Russell, D. A., 86
Rutherford, R. B., 72, 77, 78, 79, 80

Sampley, J. Paul, 6
Sandbach, F. H., 44, 48, 49, 51, 53, 58, 59, 66, 69, 72, 82
Sandelin, Karl-Gustav, 122, 124
Sandmel, Samuel, 121, 122, 124, 137, 142
Sandnes, Karl Olav, 174
Savage, Timothy B., 224
Schenck, Kenneth, 121, 122, 124, 142
Schiffman, Lawrence H., 30, 31, 33
Schmidt, Francis, 30, 31, 33
Schmithals, Walter, 156
Schnabel, Eckhard J., 156, 157, 161, 173, 183
Schofield, Malcolm, 48, 61, 105
Schowalter, Daniel N., and Steven J. Friesen, 3
Schrage, Wolfgang, 156, 157, 158, 159, 161, 162, 171, 173, 174, 183, 184, 190, 198
Schreiner, Thomas R., 192
Schüssler Fiorenza, E., 7, 10, 13, 15–16, 21, 32, 207
Schwartz, Daniel R., 30
Scott, James M., 209
Sedley, David, 48, 50, 58
Seifrid, Mark A., 205, 209,
Seland, Torrey, 121, 128, 140, 149
Sevenster, J. N., 193
Shanor, J., 163, 164
Sharples, R. W., 43, 48, 69, 114, 115
Shen, Michael Li-Tak, 4
Skehan, Patrick W., and Alexander A. Di Lella, 36
Smit, Joop F., 4, 185, 186, 187, 188
Smith, Jay E., 174, 175, 176
Snow, Robert S., 24
Son, Kiwoong, 237
Son, Sang-Won (Aaron), 26, 168, 207
Spicq, Ceslas, 222
Starling, David, 209, 221, 226
Sterling, Gregory E., 122
Stevenson, Gregory, 3, 25
Stockhausen, Carol Kern, 223
Stowers, Stanley K., 200
Strack, Wolfram, 10, 16, 22, 163
Suleiman, Susan R., 3

Talbert, Charles H., 2, 3
Tempest, Kathryn, 105
Theissen, Gerd, 158, 159, 185
Thiselton, Anthony C., 2, 156, 157, 158, 159, 160, 161, 162, 163, 165, 169, 171, 173, 174, 175, 177, 179, 183, 184, 185, 187, 188, 189, 190, 191, 198
Thompson, James W., 210
Thorsteinsson, Runar M., 48, 53, 61, 66, 72
Thrall, Margaret E., 41, 205, 206, 207, 208, 209, 211, 212, 213, 214, 220, 221, 223, 224, 225, 226, 234, 235, 236
Tieleman, Teun, 191
Tobin, Thomas H., 122
Tomlin, Graham, 174
Tomson, Peter J., 186, 207
Toney, Carl N., 235
Trapp, Michael, 44, 97, 98, 99
Tucker, Brian J., 158
Tucker, Brian J., and Coleman A. Baker, 3
Tucker, Paavo, 212

Vahrenhorst, Martin, 7, 22–23
van Kooten, George H., 160
van Ruiten, J. T. A. G. M., 37
van Unnik, W. C., 224
Vegge, Ivar, 216
Vermes, G., 28
Veyne, Paul, 53
Vogel, Manuel, 37

Walker, W. O., Jr., 206, 209
Wallace, Daniel B., 33, 74, 164, 177
Wardle, Timothy, 7, 8, 16, 23–25, 29, 30, 32, 33, 42, 209
Ware, James, 168

Warren, James, 115
Wassen, Cecilia, 28, 30, 162, 178
Watson, Francis, 15
Webb, William J., 207, 208, 209, 212, 213, 220, 221, 222
Weiss, Johannes, 164
Wenschkewitz, Hans, 5, 7–9, 10, 11, 12, 15, 21
Wenthe, Dean O., 171
Werman, Carl, 40, 150
White, Michael J., 49
Wilken, Robert L., 4
Williamson, Ronald, 121, 124, 141, 142
Willis, Wendell L., 4, 42, 185
Wilson, Walter T., 148
Windisch, Hans, 205, 212, 221, 222, 226
Winston, David, 122, 142
Winter, Bruce W., 2, 3, 16, 155, 158, 159, 160, 176, 187, 188
Wise, M. O., 29, 30
Witherington, Ben, III., 2, 156, 157, 161, 164, 165, 169, 173, 174, 185, 191, 198, 205, 209, 210, 221, 223
Wolff, Christian, 208, 212, 221
Wright, Benjamin G., III., 36
Wright, M. R., 52
Wright, N. T., 5–6, 48, 53, 66, 72, 157, 158, 168, 186, 189, 191, 192, 202, 224, 235

Yadin, Y., 29, 30
Yeo, Khiok-Khng, 4, 188
Yinger, Kent L., 165
Young and Ford, 205, 209, 221, 226

Zeilinger, Franz, 221
Zeller, Dieter, 156, 157, 161

www.ingramcontent.com/pod-product-compliance
Lightning Source LLC
Chambersburg PA
CBHW050618300426
44112CB00012B/1564